FOR THE LOVE OF MUSIC:
A HISTORY OF WIND BANDS IN CANADA
AND THE CANADIAN MUSIC THEY PLAYED

by

CHARLES E. CHARLES

Tellwell Talent
www.tellwell.ca

ISBN
978-1-7794-1308-6 (Paperback)

To Kathleen

Your love, strength, wisdom and patience made this possible.

CONTENTS

PART TWO: AND THE CANADIAN MUSIC THEY PLAYED

ACKNOWLEDGEMENTS

This book has been years in the making. It began in the early 1990s as a personally funded project to create a supplemental library of low-cost sight-reading materials for a militia band. Using a network of contacts established after many years as a reserve summer instructor at the Canadian Forces School of Music, first at CFB Esquimalt and then at CFB Borden, the search involved the collection of older, public domain adult band scores. Many of these turned out to be by late nineteenth and early twentieth century Canadian composers whose names were totally new to me. I am indebted to the hundreds of Canadian Forces musician branch personnel, serving and now retired, regular force and reserve, who gave me unlimited access to their libraries, some of which were already well over a hundred years old at the time. There is insufficient space to name them all but the enthusiastic support in particular of Rita Arrendz, Jacques Destrempes, Jean-François Dubois, Richard Emond, François Ferland, Jim Goodfellow, Marlene Holmes, Dave Jackson, Jack Kopstein, Sheila McPherson, Mike Lawson, Mike Malloy, Paul McKay, Jim Milne, Jill Pensa, Christian Thibault, Brian Thorlacius, Jim Underwood and Richard Van Slyke deserve special mention. Similarly, many community bands opened their libraries to me including those of the Waterloo Musical Society Band, the Kitchener Musical Society Band, the Perth Citizens Band, the St. Mary's Band and the Galt Kilties Band. One particularly valuable source was the Chatfield Brass Band Lending Library of Chatfield, Minnesota, whose collections include a treasure trove of early Canadian wind band music. Early support was also freely given by Dr. S. Timothy Maloney, then head of the Music Division at the National Library of Canada in Ottawa, whose own wind band expertise nurtured the growing focus on historical Canadian band music. Equally helpful was access granted to me by staff at Québec City's Musée du Grand Seminaire du Québec and Montréal's Bibliothèque nationale du Québec. Carl Ehrke of Belleville was also a rich source of information on both the Belleville Kilties Band and early winds bands in North America.

I was fortunate to have received encouragement in my early research from a number of outstanding Canadian composers of music for wind band now deceased: Ben Bogisch, Howard Cable, James Gayfer, Alfred Kunz, Ron Milne and Michael Purves-Smith. More recently I would like to recognize the contributions of Jean Philippe Côté Angers, Chris DeRosenroll, Richard Dooley, David Dunnet, Robert Eklund, Anne Fleming-Read, Mark Fisher, Lori Fox-Rossi, Dr. Steve Harris, Bernard Hébert, Brent Johnson, Karen MacKay, Marilyn Mann, Bob Mossing, Harry Pinchen, John Ramsay, Elizabeth Raum, John Reid,

Vincent Roy and Elmer Riegal. Special thanks go to Drs. Mark Hopkins, Fraser Linklater and Gillian McKay for their kind input on the state of university wind ensembles in Canada. A special nod also to my fellow musicians in Calgary's Sherwood Community Band whose joy in making music together further reinforced my belief in the importance of adult community bands in contemporary Canadian musical culture.

To Dr. Jeremy Brown of the University of Calgary and Jim Forde, Past President of the Canadian Band Association, a special thank you for taking the time to review the completed manuscript and for your thoughtful insights and suggestions for making it better. Once again, I owe my wife Kathleen an enormous debt of gratitude for her patience, time and attention as my editor. Her passion for accuracy, clarity and concision guided me every step of my way.

Finally, I would like to apologize to the hundreds of military, cadet, community, school and university bands as well as the marching showbands whose stories I could not include because of a lack of time and resources. I can only hope that the accounts of bands that have found a place in the narrative mirror your own experience. If so, then I have at least succeeded in painting a relatively accurate portrait of Canadian wind bands, past and present. There may still be factual errors and for these I am fully and solely responsible.

INTRODUCTION

Wind bands and wind band musicians have made an enormous contribution to the development of musical culture in Canada. From the earliest reports of performances by organized groups of wind musicians in both Halifax and Montréal in 1770 and 1771 respectively, wind bands, known also as military bands, concert bands, community bands, wind ensembles or just simply bands, became the primary mode of large instrumental artistic expression in communities across the country until the mid-twentieth century. The musicians who performed in and conducted these bands also served as our first music "infrastructure" in the cities, towns and villages they called home. They became music teachers, instrument importers, sheet music distributors and concert promoters. It was through their efforts that the foundations were laid for our present-day symphony orchestras, operatic societies, conservatories and music schools. These musical pioneers also supported a growing musical literacy in what was a rugged frontier society, and helped create a small but important body of wind ensemble repertoire, written in and about Canada for their own ensembles. The first known compositions for wind band written in Canada, *Royal Fusiliers Arrival at Québec, 1791* and *Marche de Normandie*, were followed by over two centuries of wind band literature, written in all genres, by prominent bandmasters of their respective generations including the names of Vézina, Laurendeau, Thiele, Gagnier, O'Neill, Gayfer and Cable.

The popularity of Canadian wind bands and the extent to which they dominated the field of large instrumental performance practice in this country until after the Second World War can best be measured by consulting a progress report on the state of music in Canada published in 1955. Edited by Sir Ernest MacMillan, *Music in Canada* (Toronto: University of Toronto Press, 1955) was intended to highlight the achievements of the musical arts in Canada. The single volume covered every conceivable means of musical expression save one: bands. Although Sir Ernest conceded that a chapter on bands had been planned, he then went on to say that it had to be "regretfully" abandoned. In doing so he acknowledged that there were at least a thousand or more bands in Canada at the time and that they had a very wide audience.

Music in Canada contained only one chapter on large instrumental ensembles, the symphony orchestras. Authored by the eminent French-Canadian conductor Wilfred Pelletier, it painted a glowing picture (for 1955) of the thirty orchestras then in existence across the entire country. Six were listed as being professional ensembles and of those, only two were fully professional in the sense of full-time employment (Montréal and

Toronto). A further seven were listed as being semi-professional and another twelve were identified as being amateur groups. The remaining five consisted of three student and two youth orchestras.

By way of comparison, the following year (1956), the Department of National Defence maintained eighteen regular force bands [full-time] with an average strength of forty to fifty-five professional musicians each in addition to fifty or so semi-professional reserve/militia bands. Community bands continued to perform, from Vancouver Island to the Maritimes and many of these same groups also sponsored youth bands. Yet the 1950s were also a time of transition. The community band movement was already in decline and was directing its efforts towards the emerging school band programs. In Ontario alone, by 1955, there were seventy-five or more high school band programs in existence.

Unlike the orchestras that Sir Ernest chose to include in his report, which were largely homogenous in instrumentation and size, the thousand or more bands he dismissed were much more varied. Ranging from the navy's twelve piece "Ship's Bands" to the 150 plus Burlington Boys and Girls Band, bands came in all shapes and sizes and they flourished in large and small communities across the dominion. What they all had in common was that they were a genuine expression of popular musical culture.

The fact that the band continues to evolve to the present day is a testament to both its vitality and relevance. Beginning in the late eighteenth century as an organized group of six to eight wind instrumentalists, through its growth in the nineteenth century, the wind band continues to explore new forms. Since the mid-twentieth century, new combinations of wind instruments and percussion, known as "Showbands", have been formed to fill the void left by the abandonment of the marching band component once considered obligatory for any proficient community band. The instrumentation of these new groups, with their ranks of percussion and specially designed bells front marching brass bear little resemblance to the smaller, leaner but no less expressive ensembles of earlier generations. Similarly, our finest university wind ensembles have also evolved. Although their woodwind and brass sections have changed little from those of early twentieth century bands, the percussion sections have added an enormous range of new melodic instruments and tone colour effects, all of which require the services of a significantly larger number of skilled percussionists. Ultimately, they are all wind bands; some combination of woodwinds (including flutes and clarinets), brass and percussion.

Over sixty years have passed since the publication of *Music in Canada*. It is now time to acknowledge the thousand or more bands that were once considered to be unimportant in the Canadian musical landscape. They and the Canadian music they performed are indeed worthy of study. This is their story.

PART ONE: A HISTORY OF WIND BANDS IN CANADA

CHAPTER ONE

NEW SOUNDS FROM DISTANT SHORES

Setting the Stage

The history of wind instruments and concerted wind music in Canada is almost as old as the history of European settlement on the North American continent. In 1535, during his second voyage to the New World, the French explorer Jacques Cartier sailed up the St. Lawrence River and landed at the native village of Hochelaga, on the site of present-day Montréal. After a presentation of gifts "…the captain [Cartier] next ordered trumpets and other musical instruments to be sounded, whereat the Indians were much delighted."[1] The reception must have been warm since Cartier and his men eventually wintered over in Hochelaga before returning to France the following spring. The discovery of an abundant source of furs, as well as promises of gold and other precious metals, had whetted the appetite of the French crown for its share of the spoils of the New World and several more expeditions back to the Americas were financed during the remainder of the sixteenth century. These all ended in failure as France itself was convulsed by a vicious series of religious wars. It was not until 1608 that Samuel de Champlain managed to establish a permanent French settlement in what is now Québec City.

This fragile toehold was under constant threat from disease, starvation, a harsh climate and hostile First Nations. For the first fifty years of its existence, its survival was in doubt. Champlain's enterprise relied on three factors to sustain it, the crown, commerce and the Church. The commitment of the first two was half hearted at best "…Crown and commerce were only perfunctorily concerned with the life of the colonists. The former as feeble protector, the later as powerful exploiter in the name of mercantilism. Neither was capable of building a politically and economically strong and lasting colony."[2] It was the Roman Catholic Church that became the foundation, both spiritual and secular, of the struggling French enclave in North America. The missionary orders who came including the Jesuits, the Recollets and the Ursuline Sisters built the first permanent institutions

---

[1] H.P. Bigger, ed. *The Voyages of Cartier* (Publications of the Public Archives of Canada, no. 11) (Ottawa:1924) 166, as cited in Helmut Kallmann, *A History of Music in Canada 1524-1914* (Toronto: University of Toronto Press, 1960) 9.
[2] Willy Antmann, *Music in Canada 1600-1800* (Montréal: Habitex Books, 1975) 59.

dedicated to the provision of schools for its young, orphanages for its abandoned children and hospitals for its sick and dying. The measure of their commitment was such that after the treaty of Paris in 1763, it was the Catholic Church that became the "de facto" guarantor of the religion, language and laws of New France, an authority it was to maintain until the "Quiet Revolution" of the 1960s.

The early missionaries however, were primarily interested in the business of saving souls, both French and native, and not just ministering to the physical needs of the colony's inhabitants. Their approach to music was similarly focused as they devoted their considerable musical knowledge to the encouragement of sacred and liturgical music. In doing so, they actively discouraged the expression of most types of secular music. The same secular music that had blossomed in Europe since the late Middle Ages to entertain and recreate. Music that by the mid-seventeenth century had reached parity with the sacred masterpieces of the Renaissance. The Reformation and subsequent Counter-Reformation had further impassioned French priests, brothers and nuns with a religious zeal that led them to supress any musical activity of a non-religious nature. Amongst the first "habitants," any expression of popular music, whether in song or dance, was considered an invitation to moral decay. Across those territories claimed by France, including the little enclave known as "Acadie" in the Annapolis Basin of Nova Scotia, the clergy were warned "...not to condone dancing on Sundays or Feasts after sundown and never if lascivious chansons are sung."[3]

Even instruments associated with the small garrison were not welcome: "When Pierre de Voyer d'Argenson, governor of New France from 1658 to 1661, announced the "intra-missam" on the main holy days, he had the fifes and tambours play, much to the annoyance of Bishop Laval."[4] By 1665, as competition for the lucrative fur trade with England intensified, France sent the Carignan-Salières regiment, the first regular troops in Canada, to bolster the colony's defenses. Included with each company were two drummers and a fifer. This was the musical support allowed to each infantry regiment of the French Army at the time and was to remain that way until the fall of New France "...jusque vers le milieu du dix-huitième siècle, la musique des troupes de France consistait généralement dans le fifre et le tambour de l'infanterie..."[5] [up until the middle of the eighteenth century, music for French troops consisted generally of the fife and field drum]. Yet in France, the

[3] Antmann, *Music in Canada*, 22.
[4] Auguste Gosselin, *Vie de Monseigneur de Laval*, Vol. 1 (Québec, 1890) 220, as cited in Kallmann, Potvin and Winters, eds., "Bands," *Encyclopedia of Music in Canada* (Toronto: University of Toronto Press, 1981) 13.
[5] Georges Kastner, *Manuel Général de Musique Militaire : A L'Usage des Armées Françaises* (1848) (Genève : Minkoff Reprint, 1973) 116.

seventeenth century also witnessed a dramatic increase in the use of wind instruments in the concerted music of Lully and Charpentier. Louis XIV (1638-1715), France's "Sun King", surrounded himself with pageantry and lavish spectacle, not just in his palace at Versailles and its ornate manicured gardens, but also with the musical resources that attended his daily activities. For the more intimate indoor occasions he was accompanied by the virtuoso string ensemble known as "les vingt-quatre violons du roi". For large outdoor gatherings, both military and equestrian, "La Grande Ecurie" of oboes, bassoons, trumpets and timpani was often used.[6] The problem of course, was that the artistry and skill necessary to perform works such as Lully's *Carrousel de Monsieur* (1686) [Fig. 1.1] were directly proportional to their proximity to the king and his treasury. This music required full-time musicians who could not possibly have been supported by the meagre resources of a vulnerable young colony.[7] Thousands of kilometers away in New France, the Baroque splendour of Versailles' wind virtuosi was but a faint whisper.

The one secular music form that was not only tolerated but encouraged was the folksong tradition from France's westernmost provinces, Brittany and Normandy, the point of origin for the majority of New France's earliest settlers. Ironically, it was the very isolation of the Breton and Normand folksong repertoire in its new home, imposed at first by geography and after the Treaty of Paris in 1763, by language, religion and culture, that sustained it. Cut off and protected from external influences as well as enriched by the life experiences of its practitioners, the literature grew ever more vibrant and robust. With the publication of Ernest Gagnon's *Chansons Populaires du Canada* in 1865[8], a European tradition had evolved through isolation and practice to become a French-Canadian birthright. It was the discovery of this literature in the late nineteenth century that provided subsequent generations of Canadian [and American] composers with a rich source of inspiration for a genuinely Canadian band repertoire.

European Contact with First Nations Peoples

European contact had a catastrophic effect on the lives and culture of indigenous peoples. Diseases, primarily smallpox, for which they had no natural immunity, reduced their populations by almost half within fifty years.[9] Across the entire expanse of New

---

[6] Kastner, *Manuel Général*, 116.

[7] Antmann, *Music in Canada*, 154.

[8] See Ernest Gagnon, *Chansons Populaires du Canada*, 10th ed. (Montréal: Éditions Beauchemin, 1955)

[9] Conrad Black, *Rise to Greatness: The History of Canada from the Vikings to the Present* (Toronto: McClelland and Stewart, 2014) 59. For one of the most plausible explanations as to why indigenous

France's territorial claims, from the Mi'kmaq and the Maliseet in the east to the Algonquin of the north, none were spared. But of all, it was the eastern sedentary peoples, the Haudenosaunee [Iroquois] and the Wendat [Huron] who suffered most. They had developed sophisticated cultures based on agriculture supplemented by hunting and fishing.[10] Their large palisaded communities characterized by multi-family longhouse structures were particularly susceptible to the unknown infectious agents from Europe. The destabilization of those cultures by disease combined with the increased competition in the fur trade led to open warfare between the two peoples. A situation made all the worse with the active encouragement of British, French and Dutch fur traders. The French alliance with the Wendat was to prove disastrous as the powerful Haudenosaunee Confederacy, allied with the British, would ultimately prevail.

The music of the native peoples however, proved to be enormously resilient. The first French missionaries who chronicled the role of music in indigenous life did so from a European perspective. Music was a thing that could be compartmentalized, secular or sacred, vocal or instrumental, dramatic or dance. Yet to most native peoples these were concepts that were totally foreign "…there are no words in most Native North American languages for "music". In other words, "music" is a noun that fails to convey the processes and relationships that singing and drumming embody in many North American contexts."[11] It was an integral part of daily life. Songs and the drum, augmented by shakers, rattles and other percussive instruments were a manifestation of the spirit in all things. Feasts and celebrations, which coincided with the agricultural calendar, were accompanied by music, performed in praise and in supplication. Both the community and individuals sought the intercession of the spirit world in planting and harvest, sickness and health, war and peace, life and death.

As such, the early French observers saw it only through their own lenses, as ritual music, or more particularly, as music intended for worship, a worship of pagan gods that the Catholic missionaries did their very best to suppress. They found that the native peoples they sought to convert to Catholicism, with its willing embrace of the role of music in liturgical celebration were gifted and talented students. Although contemporary accounts of the musical progress of native converts refer specifically to the performance of music in a church setting, their own traditions were not lost. They just went underground.

---

peoples worldwide were so vulnerable to European diseases, especially smallpox, see Jared Diamond, *Guns, Germs and Steel* (New York: W.W. Norton, 1997)

[10] Elaine Keillor, *Music in Canada: Capturing Landscape and Diversity* (Montréal and Kingston: McGill-Queen's University Press, 2006) 34.

[11] Beverly Diamond, *Native American Music in Eastern North America* (New York: Oxford University Press, 2008) 25.

In 1968, the National Museums of Canada published a scholarly report by Gertrude Prokosch Kurath entitled *Bulletin 220: Dance and Song Rituals of the Six Nations Reserve, Ontario* (Ottawa: National Museum of Canada, 1968). The report was the culmination of sixteen years of intensive study from 1948 to 1964, and it meticulously recorded the song and dance traditions of four longhouses on the Six Nations Reserve, near Brantford, Ontario. The participants were all descendants of the Haudenosaunee nations who were in conflict with the French in the seventeenth century. It is probably safe to infer that the music and customs observed reflect closely the rituals first documented by the early French religious in their encounters with the Wendat, whose own language and culture were similar to those of the Haudenosaunee.

Ms. Kurath's research details an annual cycle of eight seasonal ceremonies during the year starting with Midwinter celebrations in January or February and ending with a harvest festival in October.[12] Included in each are songs and dances related to the Food Spirits, and in particular, to the gifts of the "Three Sisters": corn, beans and squash. Even after three hundred years, the vitality of these First Nations musical traditions has persisted. A later study, Beverly Diamond's *Native American Music in Eastern North America*, published in 2008, serves as a follow-up to Kurath's original work and reveals that the Six Nations longhouse tradition is thriving.

By 1755, the population of New France had grown to over 60,000 souls. It was finally a politically stable and economically viable colony largely unaware of the demographic time-bomb on its southern border; Britain's American colonies had achieved a population in excess of 1.5 million.[13] Since the arrival of the Pilgrim Fathers, the Thirteen Colonies had grown to the point that they represented almost twenty-five percent of the total population of England and Scotland combined. The opportunities afforded by the New World had attracted some of Great Britain's most energetic and entrepreneurial human capital, a process that effectively reduced the mother country's growth rate to zero. England's colonies in North America, however, were facing some serious challenges. The British settlers' voracious appetite for land was severely limited by French territorial claims. These were enforced by a string of defensive forts that ran across their northern border and extended from the western edge of Lake Erie southwards through the Ohio valley and down the Mississippi to New Orleans. Repeated appeals to the crown to rid North America of the French presence grew ever and ever louder. In July 1756, the spark that ignited the Seven Years War (1756-1763) was provided by the Prussian warrior king

---

[12] Gertrude Prokosch Kurath, *Bulletin 220: Dance and Song Rituals of Six Nations Reserve, Ontario* (Ottawa: National Museum of Canada, 1968) 4.
[13] Black, *Rise to Greatness*, 116.

Frederick II.   Although England had already declared war on France two months earlier over a series of provocations in North America, it was Frederick's invasion of Saxony that drew Austria, France and Russia into the conflict.   England, by default, found itself allied with Prussia in a war that saw forces engaged in Europe, North America, the Caribbean and India.   It was this full mobilization of all of Europe's armies and navies that initiated the chain of events that led to the emergence of the country we now call Canada.   With the signing of the Treaty of Paris in 1763, the map of North America was redrawn; France agreed to give up its North American colonies in exchange for two islands in the Gulf of St. Lawrence, St. Pierre and Miquelon, and several sugar producing possessions in the Caribbean.   It was also the year that new sounds were heard from the other side of the Atlantic.

The First Bands

In 1763 European armies began to include organized groups of wind instrumentalists in the ranks of their infantry regiments.   It began with Frederick II of Prussia [Fig. 1.2], the continent's warrior king whose actions had precipitated the Seven Years War.   Although best known for his considerable military achievements which earned him the title of "Der Grosse" [the Great], he was also an accomplished musician.   A talented flautist, he wrote over 100 sonatas for the instrument and his court composers included both C.P.E. Bach and J.J. Quantz.   In 1747, still early in his lengthy reign (1740-1786), he welcomed Johann Sebastien Bach to his court at Potsdam and presented the composer with a theme that Bach worked into the masterpiece known as the *Musical Offering*.[14]   By 1763, recognizing the importance of music to the efficiency of his armies, Frederick ordered that regiments of Prussian infantry be assigned bands which were "…to consist of two oboes, two clarinets, two horns and two bassoons, a combination that was known as "harmoniemuzik"[15] Neither had the positive influence of music on eighteenth century soldiers gone unnoticed in England.   The previous year (1762), the Royal Artillery had recruited its first band in the German states with an instrumentation of "…two trumpets, two French horns, two bassoons and four hautbois or clarinetts [sic]."[16]   The Prussian model soon gained popularity throughout the British army, predisposed as the country itself was with all things Germanic with the Hanoverian kings on the throne.   Shortly thereafter, the bands began to cross the Atlantic.

---

[14] Manfred Bukofzer, *Music in the Baroque* (New York: W.W. Norton, 1947) 300.

[15] Henry George Farmer, *The Rise and Development of Military Music* (London: William Reeves, 1912) 56.

[16] George Henry Farmer, *History of the Royal Artillery Band* (London: Royal Artillery Institution, 1954) 9.

Halifax, established in 1749, had been quickly recognized by the Royal Navy as a port of strategic importance on the east coast of North America. With its large year-round ice-free harbour, proximity to Europe and easily defensible location, it rapidly became home to a British naval base and the garrison needed for its defence. By 1770, those garrison troops were bringing their bands with them. A report in the Nova Scotia *Chronicle* of August 7, 1770, states "...two bands of music travelled to St. Paul's Church...for the celebration of St. John the Baptist [June 24]"[17] A year later, 1771, the earliest reference to a British regimental band in Montréal appears as an advertisement in *Le Gazette de Québec* dated November 28, 1771. It refers to an upcoming public concert and ball and states that tickets can be purchased "...chez M. Prenties, au caffé, ou par aucun de la Troupe de Musiciens du dixiéme Régiment."[18] [at Mr. Prenties' home, at the café, or from any musician in the 10th Regiment]. As long as British troops were garrisoned in Montréal, Québec and Halifax, they were increasingly bringing their "harmoniemuzik" formations with them. As luck would have it, the slow trickle of the early 1770s would soon become a torrent thanks to the Thirteen Colonies to the south.

The American colonists who took up arms against the British at the start of the American Revolutionary War (1775-1783) have often been portrayed as poor, simple, peaceful and freedom loving gentlemen farmers who stood together against a tyrannical oppressor. It is, however, a narrative that only tells one side of the story. "By 1770, the American colonies had more than 25 percent of the British Isles population and a substantially larger share of wealth and income, far greater resources and a fraction of the indigenous debt."[19] It was the British government that carried the debt, incurred largely as a result of the Seven Years War, most of which was related to campaigns in North America to dislodge the French from the New World. To the British government it seemed entirely reasonable to expect the Thirteen Colonies, who were the prime beneficiaries of those campaigns, to help pay for them. The Americans saw it quite differently. To them, the British Army was no longer needed, so why should they be expected to pay for it? The fact that American representatives sent to London to present their case, arguing with equal validity that there should be "No taxation without representation", were treated by British colonial officials with appalling arrogance and colossal insensitivity only made things worse. The Québec Act of 1774 was just one more in a series of "final straws" for the Americans as the

---

[17] As cited in Timothy J. McGee, *The Music of Canada* (New York: W.W. Norton, 1985) 29.

[18] *Le Gazette de Québec*, 360 (November 28, 1771) as cited in Dominique Bourassa, "La Contribution des bandes militaires Britanniques au dévéloppement de la musique au Québec de la conquête à 1836" (M. Mus diss., Université Laval, 1993) 24.

[19] Black, *Rise to Greatness*, 134

inhabitants of the former New France were given the protection under English law to retain their language, religion and civil code. Most vexing though was the provision that those territories that had been formerly claimed by France were to be allocated solely to the French speaking populace. It was sure to infuriate the Americans and it did.

When war was finally declared in April of 1775, the small French speaking enclave in North America found itself far more comfortable with its British military governors than it did with its American cousins to the south. The feeling was entirely mutual as British administrators and officials in Canada found the francophone "habitants" to be quiet, self-reliant, hardworking and accommodating. They were not at all like the Americans, whom Britain's colonial rulers with their own aristocratic prejudices considered to be brash, arrogant and only interested in plundering the extensive commercial networks of the former New France. The Americans invaded Canada in late 1775 with an invitation to its inhabitants to join the new republic. The French refused, knowing full well that to accept would mean complete assimilation. Although Montréal fell to invading forces, Québec successfully resisted the assault and remained in British hands. Once more, troopships crossed the Atlantic to strengthen French Canada's defences but this time they brought more than just fighting forces, they also brought their bands, "…of the seventy regiments of foot that were on the British establishment in 1775, forty-nine or 70 percent, had bands of music."[20] This figure refers just to the British Army. Great Britain had also hired almost 30,000 mercenary troops from the German states, including Hesse and Brunswick, to fight in North America. Some of these regiments were eventually stationed in both Montréal and Québec and they too had their own bands.

The American Revolutionary War ended on September 23, 1783 with the signing of another Treaty of Paris. The United States of America may have failed in its first attempt to invade Canada in 1775 but it was obvious to the British government that "Yankee" expansionist ambitions were still very much alive. It was clear that its remaining North American territories would have to be robustly defended as well as a population which had more than doubled in size "…approximately fifty thousand [United Empire] Loyalists had fled the American colonies and settled in Québec or on the north shore of Lake Ontario and in Nova Scotia…the combined population in the colonies north of the new American country was about 150,000 people, almost 60 percent of them French."[21] New Brunswick was also a refuge with St. John earning the title of "The Loyalist City".

---

[20] Raoul F. Camus, *Military Music of the American Revolution* (Westerville, Ohio: Integrity Press, 1975) 68.
[21] Black, *Rise to Greatness*, 156

The new settlements north of Lake Ontario required defensive installations and garrison communities sprang up in Kingston, York (Toronto) and Newark (Niagara on the Lake). The return of peace also brought the boredom of peacetime garrison duty and it was here that bands quickly came to be recognized as an effective means of relieving that tedium. As one visitor to Québec in 1785 remarked "…we went at 7 o'clock to the Parade, a spacious opening made for Place d'Armes. Here we saw the 53rd regiment and the 65th, which are in garrison here… [the 65th] have an elegant band of music. The 53rd have one also, but not equal to the other. (11 August)[22] Two days later he continued "…in the evening we took a walk upon the ramparts and parade…the music of the two bands and the company of so many officers must be a very great inducement for preferring this place to any other. (13 August)[23] In the garrison communities of Québec and Montréal the increased availability of public open-air concerts by large instrumental groups was enthusiastically received by the citizens of the former New France who would have rarely, if ever, had the opportunity to enjoy them under the "ancient régime". The British in return, could curry favour with the local population with little or no direct cost to the crown.

Unlike military bands of today, whose costs including salaries are provided for by the state, bands in the British Army in the late eighteenth century were completely supported by their officers. Commissioned ranks [officers] were required to subscribe to a band fund, out of their own pockets, that paid the band's expenses.[24] There was rarely any reluctance to support the band since every young officer was well aware of its benefits. The satirical treatise entitled *Advice to Officers of the British Army* by Francis Grose, published anonymously in 1782, was quite emphatic when it came to the subject of bands.

> If your regiment should not be provided with a Band of Music you should
> immediately persuade the captains to raise one. This, you know, is kept at their
> expense while you reap the principal benefit; for besides keeping them with your
> own company and treating them as your private Band, they will, if properly
> managed, as by lending them to private parties, assemblies, etc., serve to raise you
> a considerable interest among the gentlemen of the country, and, what is more,
> among the ladies.[25]

---

[22] Joseph A. Hadfield, *An Englishman in America* 1785, ed. Douglas S. Robertson (Toronto: Hunter-Rose, 1933) as cited in McGee, *Music in Canada*, 31.
[23] Ibid., 31.
[24] George Henry Farmer, *Military Music* (London: Max Parrish & Co., Ltd., 1950) 30
[25] As cited in P.L. Binns, *A Hundred Years of Military Music* (Gillingham, Dorset: The Blackmore Press, 1959) 22.

Although the last line of the above quote was an "inhouse" joke for generations of British and Canadian military bandmasters, it is the middle section that is most relevant to our story. Because officers were encouraged to treat the band as their own private property, musicians were called upon to perform at a wide variety of functions that had nothing to do with their military duties. Dinners, balls, and soirées, in fact any social event at which young, single and wealthy gentlemen might be expected to attend were legitimate performance venues. In late eighteenth-century Canada, where there was little or no formal music making other than that of the Church in Québec, the regimental bands became a critical element in the development of a secular musical culture, a growing movement that began to demand resources of its own that included teachers, instrument importers and sheet music dealers. It was the military musicians who were the first to identify this new market and respond to it.

Friedrick Heinrich Glackmeyer (1751-1836) was born in Hanover, Germany, and came to Canada in 1777 as bandmaster of a Brunswick mercenary regiment hired by the British during the American Revolutionary War. He took his discharge from the army in 1783 and decided to remain in Québec. As with most military musicians of the time he played several instruments "...the violincello, the organ, the clarinet and most likely some other instruments."[26] Upon his release he set himself up as a teacher but soon realized that revenue was limited by the lack of instruments available in the city at the time. Seeing an opportunity he "...embarked on the importation of musical instruments and the firm of F.H. Glackmeyer was inaugurated."[27] By 1788 he was also able to offer a wide range of musical supplies from pianofortes to music for harpsichord, bound song collections, a few operas, divine music, music for military band as well as bassoon and oboe reeds, fiddle pegs, bridges and strings for harpsichord, pianoforte, guitar and violin."[28] In 1820 Glackmeyer was appointed first director of the Québec Harmonic Society and was a highly respected figure in the early musical life of Canada.[29] During his years in Québec he had been both military musician and bandmaster, then drawing on the skills acquired in wind bands, he shared them with the larger community as teacher, music dealer, instrument importer, repairman and impresario. He set a precedent that military band musicians in Canada have and continue to follow to the present day.

---

[26] Willy Amtmann, *Music in Canada 1600-1800* (Montréal: Habitex Books, 1975) 210.
[27] Ibid., 211
[28] Ibid., 211
[29] Helmut Kallmann, *A History of Music in Canada 1534-1914* (Toronto: University of Toronto Press, 1960) 52.

The Band of the Royal Fusiliers

The last decade of the eighteenth century in Canada was a particularly good one for bands. Not only were the regimental bands that came larger and more accomplished but they were more numerous as the garrison communities to which they were stationed extended further west as far as the Niagara peninsula. The most prestigious of these wind groups was the band of the Royal Fusiliers [7th Regiment of Foot]. Prince Edward Augustus, Duke of Kent and future father of Queen Victoria [Fig. 1.3] assumed command of the 7th Regiment, the Royal Fusiliers in 1790 while it was still in Gibraltar.[30] The following year he accompanied his regiment to its new home in Québec. As with many of his royal contemporaries, he was used to having musical entertainment on hand and was determined to ensure that he could maintain this luxury while in Canada. Even though the War Office had granted authority in 1783 for the recruitment of up to eight musicians per infantry regiment, limits were strictly monitored.[31] Any additional expenses such as uniforms, music, instruments and the cost of hiring a bandmaster were still the responsibility of the officers. Not content with the limits imposed by the War Office, the Prince engaged sufficient additional musicians to form a band of at least sixteen performers "…quatre clarinettistes, quatre cornistes et quatre bassonistes. A ce noyau s'ajoutent probablement des musiciens jouant de la flûte, du piccolo, du serpent, de la trompette, et des instruments de percussion. "[32] [four clarinetists, four hornists and four bassoonists. To this core are probably added musicians playing flute, piccolo, the serpent, trumpet (natural) and percussion]

With this ensemble of trained European musicians at his disposal, the prince and his regiment sailed for Québec. Shortly after arriving, their contribution to the musical life of the city was noted by Mrs. Elizabeth Simcoe, wife of John Graves Simcoe, the newly appointed Lieutenant Governor of Upper Canada [Ontario] who at the time was residing in the city. She was an avid chronicler of life in Canada and her diary entry for November 21, 1791, reads "…I went to a subscription concert, Prince Edward's band of the 7th Fusiliers played and some of the officers of the Fusiliers. The music was thought excellent.

---

[30] Dominique Bourassa, "Régards sur la formation et la composition de la bande des Fusiliers royaux en garnison à Québec de 1791-1794" , *Cahiers de la société québecoise de recherche en musique* 2/2 (nov 1998) 73.

[31] The original approval extended only to the regiments of guards, but the outcry that followed resulted in its eventual extension to all regular establishment infantry regiments.

[32] Bourassa, "Régards", *Cahiers*, 75

The band costs the Prince eight hundred a year." [33]   One week later, on Sunday, November 27, she wrote "…I went to church…Prince Edward always goes to church, and his band plays during the service."[34]   In addition to concerts and church services, the band was also a constant presence at many of the balls that were held in Québec during the long dark winter months.   Mrs. Simcoe's entry for Friday, March 2, 1792, explains why officers of British regiments were rarely reluctant to support the bands with their own money:

> The Fusiliers are the best dancers, well dressed and the best-looking figures in a ballroom that I ever saw.   They are all musical and like dancing and bestow as much money, as other regiments usually spend in wine, in giving balls and concerts which makes them very popular in this place.[35]

The music performed on these many occasions was a reflection of European popular taste at the time.   The formats were often varied because it was not unusual for officers of the regiment, many of whom were skilled amateur musicians, to perform alongside the enlisted bandsmen.   A program published in the *Quebec Gazette* of February 23, 1792, gives some idea of the range of music, both vocal and instrumental that was presented. Although there are a number of performers listed as well as several small ensemble pieces on the program, there is little doubt the entire band would have been present for those selections requiring a large instrumental ensemble.   The program is reproduced below in its entirety because of the names Jouve, bandmaster of the Royal Fusiliers and Glackmeyer, the former army bandmaster who by this time was an active freelance musician in Québec. Both appear as performers and, in the case of the former, as composer.

---

[33] Mrs. John Graves Simcoe, *The Diary of Mrs. John Graves Simcoe, Wife of the First Lieutenant Governor of the Province of Upper Canada, 1792-1796*, compiled with notes and a bibliography by J. Ross Robertson, 1911 (Reprint) (Toronto: Prospero Books, 2001) 55.   According to the historical currency converter on the website www. Historicalstatistics.org, accessed 26 March 2018, £800 in 1791 is the equivalent of CAD $228,296 in 2015, a princely sum indeed.

[34] Ibid., 55.

[35] Ibid., 79.

CONCERT[36]

vocal et instrumental

Au Bénefice du Sieur JOUVE, Musicien de Son Altesse Royale,
Demain (Mardi 21 février) dans la nouvelle Salle des Spectacles

---

PREMIER ACTE

1. Ouverture d'Iphigenie, Musique de Gluck
2. Second Quatuor, de Jouve
3. Ariettes Boufonnes d'Opéras Comiques, avec accompagnement de Guitare Française.
4. Pièce d'Harmonie, pour Clarinet et Basson obligé.
5. Duo de Blaise et Babet, par Glackmeyer et Jouve [by Dézède, 1783]
6. Carillon des Cloches de France, à grande orchestra [sic], Musique de Jouve.

SECOND ACTE

1. Ouverture de Panurge, Musique de Grétry [1785].
2. Ariette du Soldat lassé des alarmes de la Guerre, qui a été redemandée, chantée par Madame Allen.
3. Ariette, de la Melouranie, avec tous les instrumens [sic] et le canon obligé, redemandée au concert, et chanté par Jouve.
4. Concerto de Cor de Chasse par Rhen.
5. Une Scène et Ariette d'Atis [Atys by Piccini, 1780?], avec accompagnement de Harpe.
6. Le Sommeil d'Atis avec Harpe, chanté par Messieurs Bentley, Glackmeyer et Jouve.
7. Le Concert sera terminé par la Grande Chacoune de Cephale et Procris, musique de Grétry [1775].

Le Concert commencera à sept heures.   On trouvera des Billets à la porte; depuis Quatre Heures à trois Chelins [shillings?] les premiers et un chelin et demi les seconds.

---

[36] Kallmann, *History of Music*, 59-60.

The Band of the Royal Fusiliers continued to play an active part in the city's musical life until 1794 when the regiment was transferred to Halifax. As in Québec, Prince Edward's musicians were equally engaged in the community. His band played a regular series of Saturday morning promenade concerts and the prince had a special bandstand built that is preserved to this day.[37]

There were many British regimental bands stationed both in Québec and elsewhere between 1775 and 1871 but the Royal Fusiliers deserve special mention. Because of the prestige of their colonel Prince Edward Augustus and the depth of his purse, the band was larger and more musically proficient than those of most other regiments of the time. These other regimental bands generally numbered eight to ten players, consisting of some variation of the "harmoniemuzik" combination with the possible addition of a natural trumpet, serpent or possibly flute. In addition, the Fusiliers band's arrival provided the "…spark for the composition of the first [Canadian] marches, among which was the *March* [sic] *de Normandie,* written in 1791 by a civilian notary, Charles Voyer de Poligny d'Argenson."[38]

The influx of United Empire Loyalists after 1783 led to the creation of the Province of Upper Canada in 1791. The newly appointed Lieutenant Governor, John Graves Simcoe, after wintering over in Québec 1791-1792, took up his duties at the provincial capital of what is now Niagara on the Lake after a gruelling voyage by boat. His wife, the tireless observer of their time in Québec, continued to record, with her same attention to detail, both the journey and the conditions she found in her new home. Her descriptions of life in what was then a remote outpost of the empire, were softened by the soothing impact of music performed by the bands. On Wednesday, April 3, 1793, she wrote:

> Immediately after I have dined I rise from the Table, one of the officers attends me home, and the band plays on the parade before the house until six o'clock. The music adds cheerfulness to this retired spot and we feel much indebted to the Marquis of Buckingham for the number of instruments he presented to the regiment.[39]

---

[37] Jack Kopstein and Ian Pearson, *The Heritage of Canadian Military Music* (St. Catharines, Ont,: Vanwell Publishing, 2002) 18.

[38] S. Timothy Maloney, "Canadian Wind Ensemble Literature" (D.M.A. diss., University of Rochester, 1986) 6.

[39] Simcoe, *The Diary*, 158.

Lieutenant Governor Simcoe's duties involved extensive travel throughout the province overseeing the defence of its isolated communities. One of these was the village of York on the site of present-day Toronto. It too had a garrison band which Lady Simcoe refers to in an entry dated February 19, 1796, "…a band of music stationed near."[40] Despite the hardships of their location, the officers of the regiments in the York garrison used their bands to replicate, as much as possible, the privileged lifestyles of their families in England. With obvious echoes of Handel and his *Water Music* in mind, Mrs. Simcoe, much enchanted, writes of an excursion on the Don River on July 1, 1796 "…a large party from the garrison to dinner. A boat with music accompanied them, we heard it in the evening until they passed the town. It sounds delightfully."[41]

Later that month, John Graves Simcoe and his family left for England, where he died ten years later in 1806. Elizabeth Simcoe lived until her eighty-fourth year, dying on January 17, 1850. During her years in Canada, Lady Simcoe's keen powers of observation, both in her many drawings as well as in the text of her diaries, shed a warm light on Canadian life during the last decade of the eighteenth century.

---

[40] Ibid., 307
[41] Simcoe, *The Diary*, 332.

CHAPTER ONE GALLERY

Figure 1.1. "Prelude" to *Carrousel de Monsieur* by Jean Baptiste Lully, 1686. From an arrangement for band by Robert Clérisse, published by Alphonse Leduc in 1954. The three-line condensed score in the key of B flat is a transcription of the composer's original work for hautboys [oboes], trumpets [natural], bassoons and kettledrums. The upper stave contains the oboe parts, the middle [after measure 10] the trumpet parts and the bottom the bassoon and percussion parts. It is a work of elegance and sophistication requiring the skills of technically advanced performers who could not have been supported by the young colony at Québec. Source: Author's collection.

Figure 1.2. Frederick II of Prussia. Portrait by Johann Georg Ziesenis (1763). Frederick's decision to assign organized groups of wind musicians, consisting of two oboes, two clarinets two bassoons and two horns to infantry regiments of the Prussian Army set in motion the growth of the modern wind band. He was an accomplished flautist and composer of more than 100 sonatas for the instrument. Source: Wikimedia Commons.

Figure 1.3. Edward Augustus, Duke of Kent and future father to Queen Victoria. Portrait by George Dawe. Edward's patronage of the Regimental Band of the Royal Fusiliers while it was in Canada was the impetus for the composition of the first two known works for wind band by a Canadian; Charles Voyer de Poligny d'Argenson's *Royal Fusiliers Arrival at Quebec, 1791* and *Marche de Normandie*. Source: Wikimedia Commons.

CHAPTER TWO

THE EARLY NINETEENTH CENTURY: PEACE AND WAR

The Military Bands

British regimental bands continued to dominate the field of wind band music in Canada during the first half of the nineteenth century. As long as the Imperial Government in London felt that its remaining North American colonies were threatened by the new republic to the south, British regiments and their bands stayed in place. It didn't take long for those fears to be realized. By 1812, the Royal Navy was routinely stopping and searching American ships on the high seas.[1] It was a situation no sovereign state could tolerate and on June 18, 1812, the United States declared war on Great Britain. Although the Americans could claim with some justification that they had been provoked by the high-handed tactics of the British fleet, they had other ulterior motives. These included the widespread belief amongst "hawks" in the U.S. Congress that the entire continent was destined to be gathered under the eagle's wings. Others were more opportunistic. They were convinced that Britain, which had been at war with Napoleon's armies in Europe since 1803, would have neither the resources nor the stomach for a renewed conflict in North America. In fact, they were so confident of victory that former president and author of the Declaration of Independence Thomas Jefferson observed, shortly after the war was declared that "…the conquest of Canada was a mere matter of marching."[2] Of course it didn't quite turn out that way. Under the leadership of General Issac Brock, a skilled soldier and astute statesman, Canada's defenders, British regulars, English and French speaking local militias and First Nations warriors under the leadership of the Shawnee chief Tecumseh managed to stem the American tide. Even though Brock was killed early on in the war at the Battle of Queenston Heights, his example and sacrifice served to further strengthen Canadian resolve. After two years of skirmishes back and forth, peace was signed at the Treaty of Ghent on December 24, 1814.

The experience however impressed once more upon the British the need for constant vigilance against American territorial ambitions. Throughout much of the remaining first half of the nineteenth century Great Britain invested large sums of money on the construction of defensive fortifications: the Halifax Citadel, La Citadelle de Québec, the

---

[1] Conrad Black, *Rise to Greatness: The History of Canada from the Vikings to the Present* (Toronto: McClelland and Stewart, 2014) 175.

[2] Ibid., 175.

strategically important Rideau Canal and Fort Henry in Kingston. All of which were garrisoned by British regiments and their bands.

The presence of bands in the garrison communities had given local populations a taste for musical diversion and the bands in turn had come to be considered an integral part of everyday musical life. Montréal, which remained home to a British garrison of more than 2,500 troops until the late 1840s was perhaps the best example.[3] Once again, in addition to their military duties, the regimental bands often performed outdoor evening concerts during the summer months. The "Champ de Mars" was a favourite location and the French-Canadian press was eager to solicit the support of each new Commanding Officer, who had the final say on the use of his band, especially when it came to providing free public concerts for the local population. An appeal published on June 11, 1834, made that very clear :

> A cette occasion, plusieurs journaux de cette ville ont rappelé qu'a une époque peu éloignée de nous, la musique du régiment en garnison à Montréal avait l'habitude de jouer de temps en temps les soirs sur le champ de Mars. Nous joignons nos vœux aux leurs pour souhaiter que le colonel du Régiment actuel veuillent [sic] bien condescendre à accorder cette satisfaction au public.[4]
> [At this time, several newspapers in the city have recalled that not that long ago, the regimental band in the Montréal garrison would from time-to-time play in the evening on the "Champ de Mars". We add our wishes to theirs in the hope that the present colonel of the regiment will agree to granting the public this favour]

Ten years later, in May of 1844, *The Gazette,* reporting on the arrival of the 93rd Sutherland Highlanders stated enthusiastically that the "…band of the 93rd is one of the finest we have heard in a long time and will be a great acquisition to the evening amusements of our good city."[5] Another military band that had a significant effect on the musical life of the city was that of the 71st Regiment. As well as performing for the usual activities, both military and civil, the ensemble was also lent to a number of local Roman

---

[3] Elinor Kyte Senior, *British Regulars in Montreal: An Imperial Garrison 1832-1854* (Montréal: McGill-Queens University Press, 1981) 163.

[4] *L'Ami du people, de l'ordre et des lois*, 2, 94 (June 11, 1834) 375 as cited in Dominique Bourassa, "La Contribution des bandes militaires Britanniques au développement de la musique au Québec de la conquête à 1836" (M.Mus diss.; Université Laval, 1993) 53.

[5] As cited in Senior, *British Regulars*, 164.

Catholic institutions to provide music for their festivals including a solemn high mass on the feast day of St. Jean Baptiste.[6]

One of the strengths of the British Empire was its policy of raising militias to assist regular troops in defence of the colonies. These part-time soldiers, drawn from the local population, were called upon in wartime or in times of civil unrest to maintain law and order. In the case of the War of 1812 they were critical to the defence of Canada. Wherever possible, they modelled themselves on British patterns and were a fixture in early Canadian population centres. The militias were well established by 1814 and as the nineteenth century progressed, their colonels, who were often wealthy local business or professional men, began to make provision for their own bands.

The earliest record of a Canadian militia band is that of the Canadian Artillery formed in Québec in 1831 under the direction of John Chrysostomus Brauneis (1785-1832). Born in Germany, Brauneis had arrived in Canada with the band of the 70th Regiment but left military service in 1818 "…to become a music teacher and instrument dealer in Québec."[7] Although he died of cholera in 1832, there is evidence to suggest that the band continued to perform until 1836 when it was revived under the name of "La Musique Canadienne."[8] Under its new director Charles Savageau, who had been a member of the original Artillery band, the ensemble of fifteen players "…took part in the first celebration of St. Jean Baptiste Day [the patron saint of Québec] on June 24, 1842."[9] The band was also involved in subsequent parades and ceremonies until Savageau's death in 1849. In communities served by the British regimental bands there appears to have been little incentive for local militia bands to be formed. In less populated areas of the colonies however, especially in those with well-established Loyalist militia traditions, there would have been significant pressure brought to bear for the formation of a local militia band. A report from the *Chatham Gleaner* [N.B.] of August 3, 1846, describes the presence of a band at a Presentation of Colours ceremony for the second battalion Northumberland Militia. Although the name of the band is never given, the description of the parade manoeuvres and the various "martial airs" performed suggests the band, like the battalion itself, was comprised of militiamen.[10]

---

[6] Ibid., 165

[7] S. Timothy Maloney, "Canadian Wind Ensemble Literature" (D.M.A. diss., University of Rochester, 1986) 11.

[8] Bourassa, "La Contribution", 33.

[9] Maloney, "Canadian", 11.

[10] Will R. Bird, *North Shore (New Brunswick) Regiment* (Fredericton, N.B.: Brunswick Press, 1963) 37.

The Civilian Bands

Most of the earliest homegrown wind bands in Canada were associated with militia units. It is therefore somewhat poetic that our first documented civilian band belonged to a community known as the "Children of Peace". They were a religious sect established under the leadership of David Willson (1778-1866) whose home was in the community of Sharon, not far from the present-day city of Newmarket, Ontario. The sect actively promoted the use of music in its worship services and by 1820 a small band had been organized under the direction of Richard Coates, an ex-military musician and "…a veteran bandmaster of the Battle of Waterloo and the Peninsular War."[11] [Fig. 2.1]. Although the instrumentation of the group during the first decade of its existence consisted of both strings and winds, by 1833 it was a wind band of ten: 1 octave flute [probably recorder], 3 clarinets, 1 bassoon, 1 keyed bugle, 2 French horns, 1 trombone and 1 drum.[12] Performing in a temple built expressly for its prayer gatherings [Fig. 2.2], the musicians at Sharon, both vocal and instrumental, managed to impress even their religious detractors "…a British clergyman of the Anglican church…had to admit that he was pleased with the music."[13] Coates resigned in 1848 and by the 1860s the band's emphasis had shifted to the performance of secular rather than sacred music. During the same period, in what was definitely a Canadian first, the band included female performers on flute, cornet and ophicleide.[14] [Fig. 2.3] A set of silver instruments was purchased in 1860 and thereafter the group became known as the "Sharon Silver Band." Under this name it performed at local towns including Uxbridge and Newmarket and during the summer months entertained passengers on nearby Lake Simcoe steamers. With the death of David Willson, the community's leader in 1866, the movement began to decline and the last meeting of the Children of Peace took place in August of 1886. For over fifty years the Children of Peace supported a musical society in almost complete isolation and according to William Lyon MacKenzie, the first mayor of Toronto was "…unequalled in any part of the Upper and scarcely surpassed even by the Catholics in the Lower Province.[15]

---

[11] Helmut Kallmann, *A History of Music in Canada 1534-1914* (Toronto: University of Toronto Press, 1960) 73. The Peninsular War is the name given to the series of conflicts between British forces and Napoleon's armies on the Spanish Peninsula 1804-1812.
[12] Elaine Keillor, *Music in Canada: Capturing Landscape and Diversity* (Montréal: McGill -Queens University Press, 2006) 97.
[13] Kallmann, *A History of Music*, 75.
[14] Keillor, *Music in Canada*, 97.
[15] W.L. MacKenzie, *Sketches of Canada and the United States* (London: 1833) 122-3, as cited in Kallmann, *A History of Music*, 75.

By the 1840s the number of town bands had begun to grow. Military musicians, like Glackmeyer, Brauneis and Coates who had taken their discharges in Canada, continued in their new civilian lives as teachers and bandleaders. Wind groups were to be found in the Maritimes in Fredericton and in Antigonish. In Upper Canada bands appeared in Guelph, Cobourg and Niagara on the Lake. Hamilton was already the province's second largest city with a population of almost 10,000 when its "Sons of Temperance" band was established in 1851. That same year in the small Niagara community of Thorold, a town band was established that would remain active to the present day. Another long serving band was created the following year (1852) in the military settlement of Perth, southwest of Ottawa. The local Temperance society was eager to provide music to accompany its meetings so the "...sons procured brass instruments for any amateur willing to be trained."[16] In Bytown, the growing community to the northeast that would soon become Ottawa, the Bytown Amateur Band "...was active in 1842 and a brass band had been formed by Paul Favreau in 1844."[17]

Montréal in the 1840s continued to be served by the garrison bands but there is evidence that suggests there may have been one or more local community groups active at the same time. A petition dated 1843 to Sir Richard Jackson, requesting that he restrict the British regimental bands from performing at "...balls, quadrille parties, public assemblies and at private residences...in many cases, free of charge..."[18], suggests that the military bands were denying local musicians their source of income. Ironically, the primary author of the petition, Joseph Maffré, was a Montréal "Professor of Music" who had previously been employed as bandmaster of the 71st Regiment while it was in garrison in the city.[19] It is likely he may have engaged in the same practices that he then found himself denouncing. This early complaint about the activities of military bands coming into direct competition with their local community counterparts was just the first in a long history of such tensions which persisted well into the twentieth century.

Ever since its arrival in the New World, the Roman Catholic Church had encouraged and supported the use of music in its liturgical celebrations. Its role, however, extended well beyond the religious sphere. Education in French Canada remained almost

---

[16] Daphne Overhill, *Sound the Trumpet: The Story of the Bands of Perth 1852-2002* (Privately published: A. Rosenthal, 2002) 14.

[17] Elaine Keillor, "Musical Activity in Canada's New Capital City in the 1870s" in *Musical Canada: Words and Music Honouring Helmut Kallmann*, John Beckwith and Frederick A. Hall, eds. (Toronto: University of Toronto Press, 1988) 118.

[18] Senior, *British Regulars*, 166.

[19] How a local French-Canadian music professor ended up as bandmaster of a British regimental band is explained in Chapter Three.

exclusively the domain of the Church throughout the nineteenth century. It was inevitable that the ceremonial possibilities inherent in wind music, so often the preserve of the military bands, would be applied to the elaborate rituals of the Roman rite. As early as 1823, the popular press in Québec had noted the presence of a British military band in a procession honouring the feast of "Fête-Dieu."[20] It didn't take long for that association to be noticed in the nearby seminary. In 1833, students at the Petit Séminaire of Québec formed a student orchestra under the direction of Adam Schott, bandmaster of the 79th Regiment, which was in garrison at the time. Three years later "…Schott was replaced by James Ziegler Jr., commander of the 66th Regiment, who transformed the orchestra into a military band 1836-1838."[21] There followed a succession of bandmasters including Charles Savageau, founder of "La Musique Canadienne", but most were British Army bandmasters rotated through every three or four years. The official name of the band was "La Société Sainte Cécile", named after Saint Cecilia, the patron saint of music. It was a wind ensemble that continued to exist, without interruption, until 1967. Not only was La Société Ste Cécile Canada's first school band but it also retains the distinction of being the longest continually active school band in Canadian history [Fig. 2.4].

Wars can effect changes in national policy on a very large scale in a very short time. It was a combination of two wars, one in North America and the other on the far side of the globe that brought the era of the British regimental bands to an end. The Mexican-American War (1846-1848) was an incredibly one-sided affair that resulted in the United States acquiring "…nearly 1.2 million square miles [of territory] which provided the future states of Texas, Oklahoma, Utah, Colorado, New Mexico, Arizona, Nevada and California."[22] This sudden addition of vast stretches of new land to the republic, plus the growing rot of slavery that would soon tear the union apart, drained away much of the expansionist zeal that had been focused on the Canadian border since the end of the War of 1812-1814. It soon became apparent to the War Office in London that the American threat to its North American colonies had largely disappeared. Britain was free to turn its attention elsewhere and six years later increased Russian aggression in the Crimean Peninsula led to the unlikely alliance of England, France, the Italian states and the Ottoman Empire against the Russian Empire.[23] The Crimean War (1854-1856) represented the first

---

[20] Bourassa, "La Contribution", 61.

[21] Hélène Plouffe, "Seminaire de Québec", *Encyclopedia of Music in Canada*, Kallmann, Potvin and Winters, eds. (Toronto: University of Toronto Press, 1981) 861.

[22] Black, *Rise to Greatness*, 263.

[23] Vladimir Putin's annexation of the Crimea in 2014 and his invasion of Ukraine in 2022 are only the latest chapters in a very long story. It even has a Canadian footnote. Fort Rodd Hill National Historic Site near Victoria, B.C., is a series of artillery emplacements built by the British and Canadian governments in the

test of arms for the British Army against a continental rival since the end of the Napoleonic Wars (1815).   At that time, Great Britain maintained an all-volunteer army.   In order to find enough troops for the impending conflict it withdrew most of its North American garrisons.   Although some did return after the war in 1856, their stay was short-lived.   By 1871, British regulars were recalled to England for the last time.   With the final departure of the regiments and their bands the first chapter of Canada's wind band story came to an end.

The Legacy of the British Military Bands

For almost 100 years the British regimental bands nurtured the growth of a secular musical culture in a way that would have been impossible in the colonies had they been left to their own devices.   Canada was a land whose settlement was hardly conducive to leisurely pursuits such as concerted music.   As Helmut Kallmann observed "…the officers' patronage of the bands is the closest parallel to be found in Canada to the aristocratic sponsorship of music in European countries."[24]   Yet just as those European aristocrats helped support the creation of some of the greatest masterpieces of Renaissance, Baroque and Classical art music, so too the British regimental bands helped create the conditions that allowed not just Canadian wind bands but Canadian music in general to flourish as the century progressed.

These contributions were multilayered.   Initially the regimental bands, through their many public performances found audiences in the local populace and created an appetite for concerted music as a leisure activity.   More substantively, as army musicians and bandmasters trained in Europe chose to stay in Canada at the end of their military service, they "…became instrumental teachers and musical entrepreneurs, training the first Canadian bands and ensembles, importing sheet music, instructional materials and instruments and organizing and performing in public concerts."[25]   Beginning with Glackmeyer and Brauneis in Québec, Coates at Sharon, Grossman in Hamilton and Kastner in Antigonish, N.S., their efforts and those of many others helped establish our own musical "infrastructure".   Their contribution didn't stop there.   There was an even greater influence at the socio-cultural level that helped attract ever larger audiences and turn them into active participants in the enterprise of making music.

---

early 1890s to defend the nearby naval base at Esquimalt.   The threat that prompted their construction? The fear of a surprise attack by the Imperial Russian Navy.
[24] Kallmann, *A History of Music*, 48.
[25] Maloney, "Canadian", 7.

The Royal Fusiliers Band in 1791 Québec performed at a number of venues but its audiences would have been drawn from a very select few: wealthy merchants, the professions and the governing class. Over the next two generations, especially in the growing cities of the east, open air concerts would have begun to reach a far wider audience. As the nineteenth century progressed the country witnessed the emergence of a new urban working class. Although the relationship of the regimental bands to this growing segment of the population in Canada has not been studied closely, it has in Britain. Since Britain was also the home and parent to our first bands, it is worth examining the results of these studies. In Trevor Herbert and Helen Barlow's *Music and the British Military in the Long Nineteenth Century* (Oxford: Oxford University Press, 2013), the role of the military in the evolution of British musical culture has been studied exhaustively. The new urban working class was critical to that growth:

> From about the mid-point of the nineteenth century there was a sudden and
> massive expansion in all aspects of the commercial infrastructure of the music
> industry…fuelled by the creation of a relatively new, urban working-class
> community that had acquired a taste and a modest capacity for leisure.[26]

It was the British Army bands that first reached this "…far wider public many, if not most, of whom were unaccustomed to listening to music of this scale and quality as a leisure activity."[27] In addition to the free open-air concerts that first attracted this wider public, two other factors were at play. Since 1783, when the War Office approved the payment of salaries to military musicians, members of the band were considered to be common soldiers rather than hired professional musicians. This represented a significant downward shift in their social status as military bandsmen were now relegated to the "lower classes". It was natural then that the emerging working-class music market would be more receptive to wind bands and wind band music simply because they saw in its practitioners members of their own class. In Britain, the final piece of the puzzle that led to the exponential expansion of the amateur musical movement in the mid-nineteenth century was the "perfection" of piston valve brass instruments following the designs of the Belgian instrument maker Adolphe Sax.[28] A large working-class population eager for musical diversion, inspired by the achievements of and taught by members of their own class in the

---

[26] Trevor Herbert and Helen Barlow, *Music and the British Military in the Long Nineteenth Century* (Oxford: Oxford University Press, 2013) 155.
[27] Ibid., 157.
[28] Ibid., 161.

military bands, embraced the newest brass instrument technologies. The result was the British Brass Band movement. Encouraged by the Victorian governing class, who saw music making as a "morally noble" activity, the new working classes were so enthusiastic in their adoption of the brass band that it became necessary to distinguish between the new all brass ensembles, "brass bands" and the earlier military ones with their mixture of woodwinds and brass, "military bands".

There was an unintended consequence of the working class embrace of both brass and military bands. A fault line had been drawn:

> The type of people who became wind musicians at this time and the didactic traditions to which they were subject, were radically different from those that had been inherited from the art music tradition and that were being enshrined throughout Europe in the practices of the recently founded conservatories.[29]

These differences were to follow the bands to the New World and although frontier Canada was a far more egalitarian society than Victorian England, they would persist well into the twentieth century. The newly emerging Canadian wind bands and wind band musicians were generally more likely to be drawn from the working population than the upper middle classes and more interested in appealing to the common people than wealthy elites. They showed a preference for amateur rather than professional status and they favoured close associations with those institutions that had the most direct impact on their lives: their communities, their employers, their fraternal lodges and their churches.

Britain's military bands defined the parameters that helped direct the growth of Canada's nineteenth century bands. They attracted audiences in the largely English and French speaking garrison communities of Eastern Canada and then encouraged and supported those audiences to become music makers themselves. Most of all, the British regimental bands set the example for those that would follow. It started with the instruments they played.

---

[29] Herbert and Barlow, *British Military*, 155.

CHAPTER TWO GALLERY

Figure 2.1. Richard Coates, 1865, at the age of 86. A former British Army bandmaster during the Peninsular War, he led the band of the "Children of Peace" from the 1820s until his retirement in 1848. Initially a mixed ensemble of strings and winds, by the early 1830s it performed exclusively as a wind band. Under his direction the group won accolades not only from the clergy of other denominations but from Toronto's first mayor, William Lyon MacKenzie. Source: Sharon Temple Museum Society. Image no. 932.4.1. Used by permission.

Figure 2.2. Sharon Temple. Now a national historic site, it was built as the religious home of the "Children of Peace". Included in its design were spaces for instrumental performers who formed Canada's first civilian wind band. Source: Wikimedia Commons.

Figure 2.3. Ophicleide. A keyed brass instrument invented in 1817 and patented in 1821. It remained popular through much of the early nineteenth century and was eventually replaced by the modern tuba, euphonium and bass trombone. Fitted with a brass mouthpiece but keyed like a saxophone it was a transitional design intended to provide a chromatic brass voice in the bass baritone registers. Source: Wikimedia Commons.

Figure 2.4. La Société Ste. Cécile, Petit Séminaire du Québec, 1867. Canada's oldest and longest continually active school band, 1838-1967. Originally led by British Army bandmasters, it was directed by Joseph Vézina from 1884 until 1924. Note the ophicleide, front row, fifth from right. Source: Archives du Séminaire du Québec.

CHAPTER THREE

THE GROWING NINETEENTH CENTURY BAND

The British regimental band that serenaded Mrs. Simcoe on Toronto's Don River that July summer's day in 1796 probably numbered no more than ten to twelve players (Chap. 1). It would have consisted of some variation of the "harmoniemuzik" combination with the possible addition of a flute, a trumpet or serpent. Just over a hundred years later, a Canadian military band appears in a 1901 photograph taken in front of Hamilton's Dundurn Castle. It is the band of the 13th Regiment and what is immediately clear is that the number of musicians has grown dramatically. The portrait shows an ensemble of thirty-eight pieces whose instrumentation is indistinguishable from that of the modern wind band. [Fig. 3.1] How is it that in the space of a century, the wind band in Canada had evolved from being essentially a large chamber group to become the performing ensemble with which most modern readers are familiar?

One of the published sources consulted in the preparation of this history was Alwyn and Gordon Turner's three volume set entitled *The History of British Military Bands* (Staplehurst, Kent: Spellmount Limited, 1994). In addition to providing exhaustive notes on bands in the British Army over a period of three centuries or more it also contains hundreds of historical photographs. Six of these date from the 1860s and 1870s. These six, although somewhat grainy and indistinct are nevertheless clear enough to accurately document the instrumentations of groups ranging in size from twenty-four to thirty-eight musicians. We can safely infer from this photographic record that by the late 1860s, the evolutionary changes in instrumentation in British military bands, with the exception of saxophones, were more or less complete. From previous chapters we have also seen that it was those same British bands that were the dominant large instrumental performing groups in early nineteenth century Canada. Even as the number of Canadian bands began to grow by 1850, the regimental band presence still acted in a kind of "elder sibling" role, providing both an example and setting standards until 1871. If we wish to answer our question as to how the band's instrumentation could evolve so dramatically during the first half of the century, we must look to England for our answer.

The sequence of events that precipitated these changes in band instrumentation may seem improbable to the modern reader but the evidence is compelling. Rather like a good recipe our story has a handful of essential ingredients: a musical fashion craze that swept Europe, an aristocratic officer class intent on maintaining its privileges, an epic sea battle and systemic financial fraud that would land a modern band director behind bars in a heartbeat.   Add just a pinch of human folly, a dash of greed then bring to a boil with perhaps the most disastrous massed military band concert in the mid-nineteenth century and, *voilà*, the modern wind band is born.

Turkish Music

The first ingredient, certainly the most colourful, was originally known as "Janissary" music.   The Janissaries were elite army units of the Ottoman Empire [modern day Turkey] whose advance across Europe was finally checked at the gates of Vienna in 1683.   When in battle their bands would be stationed near the tent of the pasha commanding and play continuously to encourage their combatant fellows [Fig. 3.2].   Melody instruments consisted of three or more shrill sounding double reed instruments "…called "zarnas", two or more instruments of the same kind but pitched an octave lower, and one or more fifes."[1] Then there was percussion:

> …one large kettledrum, two small ones, three or more drums (similar to our tenor
> drums), one big bass drum (one side of which was beaten with a heavy felt headed
> drumstick, whilst the other side of which was beaten with a kind of broom
> sounding the unaccented beats of the time).   One pair of very large cymbals, two
> pairs of small ones, and several triangles[2].

By the 1720s, Europe's princes were so taken with these groups that the Sultan, as a sign of peaceful intent, presented a complete Janissary Band to August II, King of Poland and Elector of Saxony.   Frederick II of Prussia, who ordered the first wind bands for his army, was also the proud owner of a complete Janissary Band.[3]   As the original players died out, Ottoman melodic instruments were replaced by their European equivalents: oboes and bassoons.   Horns and trumpets soon followed.

> But those characteristic percussion instruments of the Turks, previously unknown
> in the military band of the western powers, namely the bass drum, cymbals,

---

[1] Jacob Kappey, *A Short History of Military Music* (London: Boosey and Co., 1896) 82.
[2] Ibid., 82.
[3] Which begs the question: did he obtain the band before 1763 or after? If it was before then it is possible that the modern wind band can trace its lineage back to the Ottoman Turks.   The sources consulted provide no dates.

triangles and the crescent, kept their place as necessary ingredients of military music.[4]

It didn't take long for the craze to spread across Europe. In doing so the combination of percussion instruments listed above became known as "Turkish Music". The only change was the addition of small bells to the crescent which was carried high on a pole, earning it the name of "Jingling Johnnie". This Turkish influence extended well beyond the wind bands. Mozart's opera, *The Abduction from the Seraglio* (1781) and Haydn's *Military Symphony* (1794) both employed elements of Turkish music. It was with Beethoven's "Turkish March", from the incidental music to *The Ruins of Athens* (1812) and the sublime "Turkish March" interlude from the final movement of his *Ninth Symphony* (1824), that the instruments of the Turkish music craze became permanent fixtures of the symphony orchestra.

British military bands were a bit slower than their continental counterparts in adopting the fashion but by the 1770s the Turkish Music trend had spread. "In the British Army, we see cymbals in the 24th Foot (1777), with bass drum and tambourine added in the Royal Artillery (1782), and a Jingling Johnnie and 2 tambourines in the Coldstream Guards (1785)."[5] The addition of these new exotic percussive effects however created a problem: an imbalance in the delicate "harmoniemuzik" ensemble effectively drowning out the melodic voices. The situation was made worse by late eighteenth-century Europe's fascination with not just the sound of Turkish Music but with their appearance as well. Regimental bands across the British Army vied with each other to engage three or more black musicians as percussionists and then dressed them up in outlandish costumes meant to simulate the warlike Turk [Fig. 3.3]. Adorned with oversized turbans, feathers and plumes, these men were encouraged to play in an exaggerated way, integrating athleticism and the odd contortion into their theatrical performance routines [Fig. 3.4].[6] The net result was even more banging and clanging. Because the fashion persisted until the 1840s, an immediate solution was needed and it was obvious to all: increase the size of the band. For guidance as to which direction to follow, the British only had to look across the English Channel.

---

[4] Kappey, *Short History*, 82.

[5] Henry G. Farmer, *Military Music* (London: Max Parrish & Co. Ltd., 1950) 35.

[6] Elements of the "Turkish Music" fashion persisted well into the twentieth century. High stepping drum majors making breathtaking mace tosses and baton twirlers are all echoes of the practice. Bass drummers in Royal Canadian Navy bands prior to unification (1968) wore a real leopard skin as an apron when on parade.

The French Revolution of 1789 represented a fundamental shift in European governance. The slogan "Liberté, Egalité et Fraternité" sought to draw all of France's citizens to the new republic and in order to reach them, grand national "Fêtes" were held "…in furtherance of political and philosophical doctrines as in the "Fête de la Fédération" and the "Fête de la Raison" …for the most part in the open air."[7] These were ideal venues for wind bands and the French were quick to employ them in the service of the revolution. One of the first, the band of the National Guard, was established in 1789 "…with forty-five performers, who, in the following year, were taken over by the Paris municipality."[8] Although the band only survived until 1792, when it was abandoned for economic reasons, it was the basis for "L'Ecole Gratuite de Musique de la Garde Nationale Parisienne." In 1795, "L'Ecole Gratuite" was merged with the ancien régime's "Ecole Royale de Chant" to form the "Conservatoire de Musique".[9]

Even before the newly formed Paris Conservatory could release its recommendation for the instrumentation of French military bands in 1795, one trend was clear: the emergence of the clarinet as the dominant soprano woodwind voice. The instrument's range, tonal characteristics and reliability, especially in outdoor settings, gave it the role of melodic leader in the evolving wind band; a fact duly noted by the Paris Conservatory "…as planned by the Conservatoire, the military band of 1795 consisted of 1 flute, 6 clarinets, 3 bassoons, 1 trumpet, 2 horns, 1 serpent with bass drum and cymbals."[10] This balance was maintained even for the massed bands employed at the "Grand Fêtes" "…10 flutes, 30 clarinets, 18 bassoons, 4 trumpets, 2 "tubae curvae", 2 buccins, 12 horns, 3 trombones, 8 serpents with 10 side, bass and kettledrummers, cymbalists and triangle beaters."[11] From the conservatory's modest fourteen piece ensembles to the monster bands of 100 or more, the realignment of the woodwind section managed to accommodate the problem of the growing percussion section. The British had been paying attention and by 1794, the Grenadier Guards Band included "…1 flute, 6 clarinets, 3 bassoons, 1 trumpet, 3 horns, 2 serpents and Turkish Music."[12] This, however, was an isolated case. The bands of the French Republic were free to grow for the simple reason that the state paid for that growth.

---

[7] Farmer, *Military Music*, 37.

[8] Ibid., 37.

[9] Ibid., 37. It is one of the delicious ironies in our wind band story that one of the great bastions of the European art music tradition, the Paris Conservatory, was originally established for military (read wind band) musicians.

[10] Farmer, *Military Music*, 37,

[11] Ibid., 37.

[12] Ibid., 39.

In England, the War Office had no intention of doing so. The Grenadier Guards were able to balance their band because their officers could and would pay for it.

The Purchase System

As previously noted in Chapter One, British military bands were entirely supported by their officers until 1783. That year the War Office begrudgingly authorized the Guards regiments one musician per company of infantry [the average British infantry regiment in the late eighteenth century consisted of eight to ten companies of approximately 50 men each]. Enormous pressure was brought to bear and within a short period of time the provision was extended to all regular army infantry regiments. The War Office limit of eight to ten per regiment was to remain in place until 1823 but it didn't really matter to officers across the army. They continued to pay the band's expenses, including the salaries of additional musicians if necessary, for the simple reason that money was no object. Most were independently wealthy. This wealth was largely a result of the British Army's curious practice of obtaining its officers through the purchase of commissions.[13] It was this practice that provides the second ingredient in our recipe.

The purchase of commissions was a holdover from previous centuries when aristocrats would raise their own fighting forces. By the late seventeenth century, Europe's monarchies began establishing and paying their own standing armies. The leadership of those armies, however, remained exclusively in the hands of the wealthy, land owning classes. The purchase system set a price for each officer's rank which varied depending on the branch of service; infantry, cavalry or artillery and the prestige of the regiment. As an example, in 1773, the price of a lieutenancy in a troop of Horse Guards [a very prestigious London based regiment] was 1500 pounds.[14] The initial cost of the commission, plus ongoing regimental fees for uniforms, wine and the band, were usually well in excess of a junior officer's annual salary. The only way to survive was to be provided with an independent source of income: usually family money. Access to that kind of wealth was limited to the landed gentry and beginning in the early nineteenth century, a small, upwardly mobile and increasingly affluent middle class. This requirement to pay vast sums of money, in advance, should a regimental vacancy occur

---

[13] An officer's commission is a warrant from the Sovereign granting the holder the authority to lead the nation's military forces. An officer in the Canadian Armed Forces is still referred to as a "Commissioned" rank.

[14] Trevor Herbert and Helen Barlow, *Music and the British Military in the Long Nineteenth Century* (Oxford: Oxford University Press, 2013) 39.

practically ensured that the only people who could apply were the sons of the privileged few. Aptitude, experience and training meant next to nothing. It was assumed that if an individual possessed wealth, then he also possessed the leadership skills necessary to be an officer. The practice of purchasing commissions was not abolished in England until 1871, long after it had been abandoned by Europe's continental armies. The irony is that the system provided the ideal conditions for the nurture and growth of Britain's military bands.

Military bands on the continent were supported much more directly by their national governments than in Britain. As today however, this made them vulnerable to the inevitable economic cycles of growth and recession. When times were good, the bands did well, when conditions changed for the worse, the bands suffered. The early nineteenth century was an especially tumultuous time in European history so continental military bands often faced extended periods of instability that restricted their growth, and more importantly, their exposure to wider civilian audiences. The opposite was true in England. An independently wealthy officer corps, still largely responsible for the costs of the band, with minimal government bureaucracy to oversee their activities, gave Britain's military bands the financial stability and freedom to experiment with and expand their instrumentations as well as cultivate an ever-growing pool of appreciative listeners and imitators.

Although the War Office regulations of 1783 limiting regiments to eight to ten musicians were still in effect in the early nineteenth century, they were systematically ignored. The band of the Royal Fusiliers was a perfect example, consisting of sixteen musicians in 1791, not including percussion. There were several ways additional musicians could be added to regimental strengths: by direct hire as Prince Edward Augustus had done, by listing musicians as "acting bandsmen" and paying them from the regular establishment or by dipping into a regimental "non-effective" fund. The fact that general officers of districts in England were required to submit half-yearly reports on the status of their bands suggests that individual commanding officers often broke the rules.[15] Such was certainly the case with the Scots Guards Band of 1805. Its instrumentation included 1 small flute, 3 hautboys [oboes], 1 small clarinett [sic], 6 "grand" clarinetts [sic], 2 bassoons, 3 trombones, 2 trumpets, 2 French horns, 1 serpent, 1 bass horn, drums, tambourine and cymbals.[16] The county regiments also actively flaunted the rules. The

---

[15] Henry G. Farmer, *The Rise and Development of Military Music* (London: Wm. Reeves, 1912) 93.

[16] Herbert and Barlow, *Music and the British Military*, 304. The reader is again reminded that this was one of the prestigious London regiments whose officers had very deep pockets indeed.

band of the 24th Regiment of Foot in 1812 could boast a complement of 1 flute, 5 clarinets, 3 bassoons, 3 horns, 1 trumpet, 1 bass horn, tambourine, bass drum and cymbals.[17]

The growth was equally apparent in those bands stationed in Canada. On April 13, 1813, an advertisement appeared in the *Quebec Mercury* for an auction of "Instruments for a Field Band". These consisted of 6 fifes, 9 clarinets, 2 bassoons, 1 trumpet, 3 bugles, 3 horns, 2 tambourines, 1 timpani and 2 triangles. The following month, on May 28, a set of instruments belonging to the band of the 49th Regiment of Foot was lost in a fire at Fort George in the Niagara Peninsula. The loss was well documented: 10 flutes, 14 clarinets, 2 bassoons, 1 trumpet, 2 horns, 1 serpent, and 2 triangles.[18] [The second list is somewhat problematic. It is unlikely that there were 10 flautists and 14 clarinettists in the band; in all probability there may have been several types of each instrument available that were employed as required but never all at the same time.]. The pattern of growth however is evident and by 1820 the Band of the Royal Artillery, based at Woolwich just outside of London, boasted an instrumentation not unlike that of the modern wind band:

2 Flutes	3 Key Bugles	1 Ophicleide
3 Oboes	2 French horns	2 Serpents
11 Clarinets	1 Alto Trombone	2 Bass horns
3 Bassoons	1 Tenor Trombone	5 Percussion
2 Trumpets	1 Bass Trombone	Total: 39[19]

This instrumentation represented the very top end of the scale for the British Army as the Royal Artillery's funding source was entirely separate from that of the other branches. Even though the War Office increased the allowance for musicians in infantry regiments to fifteen in 1823, officially recognizing what had been going on for years, it would take another forty years for the remainder of the army bands to catch up. This was a process that was largely facilitated by one of history's most famous sea battles and the third ingredient in our evolving instrumentation "recipe".

---

[17] Turner and Turner, *History of British Military Bands*, Vol 3, 113.

[18] Dominique Bourassa,"La Contribution des bandes militaires Britanniques au développement de la musique au Québec de la conquête à 1836" (M.Mus diss., Université Laval, 1993) 42.

[19] Farmer, *Rise and Development*, 98.

Trafalgar

In 1805, Napoleon's "Grande Armée" was unstoppable. His forces advanced unchecked across Europe and although he had abandoned plans for an invasion of England in August of that year, his presence across the narrow English Channel was a potent reminder to the British Army of its vulnerability. It was clear to most in England that should the two armies meet in battle, British Redcoats stood little chance against the French Goliath. All of that changed on October 21, 1805. The Royal Navy, under the command of Rear Admiral Horatio Nelson, engaged a numerically superior combined Spanish-French fleet off of Spain's Cape Trafalgar. Thanks in large part to Nelson's tactical genius as well as the discipline and affection that the fleet's crews had for their admiral, the outcome was a decisive victory for the British. So complete was that victory, it established the Royal Navy as the undisputed master of the world's oceans for over a century up to the start of the Great War in 1914.[20] The impact on the British Army was equally far reaching. The Royal Navy's maritime supremacy effectively meant that the army never had to plan for the possibility of fighting a defensive land war on home soil. Consequently, pressures towards centralisation and standardisation that were transforming standing armies on the European continent after the end of the Napoleonic Wars [1815] were largely ignored in England. As a result, the British Army "...was more inclined to cling to the past and to develop its own peculiarities."[21] One of those peculiarities was the management of its bands.

The British Army's heavy lifting in the nineteenth century was done largely by the infantry regiments. They maintained exceptional discipline and "esprit de corps" through adherence to customs and traditions that were unique to each unit and that had been born and nurtured through years of service and sacrifice. After 1815, the increasingly singular traditions that identified each regiment were further magnified and intensified by the freedom granted the army by the Royal Navy's "de facto" responsibility for home defence. Although the regiments would travel to the far corners of the globe to build an empire, they were fiercely independent and resisted any attempt by higher authority to dictate policy when it came to what was considered purely internal matters, including the regimental band. This was a position that was entirely understandable considering that it was the

---

[20] Nelson died in the battle, victim of a French sniper's musket ball and his body was returned to England. A grateful nation recognized the debt it owed him and erected a series of monuments to his memory, the most famous of which is his column in London's "Trafalgar Square". That gratitude extended all the way to Canada. There is a Nelson column in Old Montréal's "Place Jacques-Cartier" erected in 1809.
[21] Byron Farwell, *Mr. Kipling's Army* (New York: W.W. Norton, 1984) 13.

regiment's officers who were still paying the lion's share of the band's expenses. One of these, and the final ingredient in our recipe, was the ever more burdensome cost of a civilian bandmaster.

The Civilian Bandmasters

There was intense rivalry between regiments as to who had the best bands and at the time it was felt that civilian bandmasters were more qualified to achieve superior results. Not just any civilian would do. There was a rare form of reverse snobbery in the army that believed foreign bandmasters were infinitely better than domestic ones. Italians were acceptable but candidates from the German speaking states were preferred. England's love affair with all things Germanic continued unabated, especially after the marriage of the young Queen Victoria to her first cousin Prince Albert of Saxe Cobourg and Gotha in 1840. The only problem was that many of these German bandmasters couldn't speak a word of English so they needed agents to act on their behalf. English instrument makers were more than happy to be of assistance. Whenever a regiment found itself with a vacancy for a civilian bandmaster, its officers would approach the manufacturers to act as "recruiters" to find a suitable candidate. Money never changed hands, but what began as a temporary arrangement soon became standard practice, "…when a new bandmaster took over his appointment, his first action was to condemn all the instruments in use…rewarding the instrument maker to whom he owed his appointment, by ordering a new set of instruments."[22] As the system became more and more entrenched, a new problem arose. Many civilian bandmasters became increasingly reluctant to accompany the regiment overseas when it was ordered to deploy. As Britain's empire grew so too did the demands on the army to police it. By 1846 the British Army had 112 infantry regiments, of these over 77 were posted to India and elsewhere.[23]

Unwilling to face the privations of life in the colonies, many civilian bandmasters, some showing barely concealed contempt for their military paymasters, would promptly resign when the regiment was posted. They would then seek to fill a vacancy with a returning regiment and the cycle, including a complete replacement of the band's instruments, would start all over again. This is why regimental bands arriving in colonial postings often found themselves obliged to hire local musicians as bandmasters, such as Montréal's Joseph Maffré, while away from England. The army high command was certainly aware of the

---

[22] Farmer, *Rise and Development*, 96.
[23] Herbert and Barlow, *Music and the British Military*, 241.

problem but was powerless to do anything about it because of the reluctance of the regiments to surrender any control of their bands.

There was, however, a small "silver lining" to hiring foreign bandmasters, especially those from the German states. They would probably have been familiar with the military band reforms sweeping France and Prussia in the 1840s. The invention of piston valve brass instruments in the 1820s, and their introduction to the orchestral idiom, "…the "cornet à pistons" was used at Paris in Rossini's *Guillaume Tell* in 1829"[24], soon led to their widespread adoption by Prussian infantry bands. In 1843, Adolph Sax's designs for homogenous groups of valved brass instruments called saxhorns were recommended for use by French Army bands. Two years later, their use was made obligatory.[25] By 1848, these new instrumental designs had been adopted in England. The instrumentation of the Grenadier Guards Band, one of the elite London regiments, stood at "…2 flutes, 1 piccolo, 3 Eb clarinets, 8 Bb clarinets, 3 bassoons, 4 French horns, a family of trumpets, 1 althorn, 3 ophicleides, 3 tambourines and drums."[26] Line regiments slowly followed and by 1860, even the lowest on the order of precedence could boast of bands of thirty-five pieces or more. One such example that year was the band of the 106th Regiment of Foot which consisted of 3 flutes and piccolo, 1 oboe, 2 Eb clarinets, 9 Bb clarinets, 2 bassoons, 4 cornets, 2 trumpets, 1 althorn, 2 euphoniums, 3 trombones, 3 bombardons [tubas] and 3 drums.[27] A photograph of the band of the 43rd Light Infantry Regiment taken in 1866, while in New Zealand, clearly illustrates a similar balance [Fig. 3.5].[28]

Over a period of some eighty years, Britain's regimental bands had quadrupled in size through a random process of trial and error with little to no centralized control. This exponential growth was a response to musical fashion, changing tastes and technological innovation all of which were made possible by the enthusiastic financial support of the country's military elites. This growth however had come at a price and the entire way of "doing business" in British Army bands in the 1850s had to change and it did. The spark that finally brought the pot to a boil occurred at the start of the Crimean War [1854] in an obscure Turkish town called Scutari [suburb of present-day Istanbul].

---

[24] Farmer, *Military Music*, 45

[25] Georges Kastner, *Manuel Général de Musique Militaire à l'Usage des Armées Françaises 1848* (Genève : Minkoff Reprint, 1973) 292

[26] Turner and Turner, *History of British Military Bands*, Vol 2, 16.

[27] Farmer, *Rise and Development*, 127-128.

[28] Turner and Turner, *History of British Military Bands*, Vol. 3, 196.

It was in Scutari on May 24, 1854, that a grand military review was held to honour Queen Victoria's birthday.[29]   16,000 British and allied troops were on parade that day. The highlight was supposed to be a rousing three cheers by all followed by a performance of *God Save the Queen* by the massed bands.   Because of the lack of any centralized control or coordination of the British Army bands present, not only were they playing from different arrangements, in different keys, but it is also probable that they were playing on instruments pitched to different "A's" [the international standard of A=440 had not yet been adopted].   They were certainly under rehearsed and were performing together for the first time.   As one observer noted, in a classic case of British understatement, "…the bands playing *God Save the Queen* in different keys spoilt the effect."[30]   Although no lives were lost that day, the British High Command certainly lost face.   In the normal course of events there may have been some recriminations, even a public inquiry, but after sufficient time had elapsed, the incident may have been forgotten.   This didn't happen because of one man, who in all probability was there that fateful day to witness the discordant disaster. Two years later he was appointed Commander in Chief of the British Army at the tender age of thirty-seven.

The Royal Military School of Music - Kneller Hall

George William Frederick Charles, the Duke of Cambridge, was a grandson of George III and cousin to Queen Victoria.   He had a distinguished career as a soldier and more importantly for our wind band story, was an able administrator.   He recognized immediately that the root causes of the fiasco at Scutari were the lack of any centralized control of the bands, in part due to regimental resistance and the complete disrespect most civilian bandmasters displayed towards Britain's military ethos.   He also knew how to fix the problem; establish a training school for military musicians that would provide serving members of the army bands with the necessary skills to be competent bandmasters.   Such an institution would, over time, eliminate the need for civilian bandmasters altogether and provide uniform standards for all army bands.   Guided by the principle that when dealing with large inertia prone bureaucracies it is easier to ask for forgiveness than for permission,

---

[29] Throughout the British Empire during Victoria's long reign, May 24 was an occasion for patriotic festivals, open air celebrations and community gatherings. These were ideal venues for wind band participation.   The reader will note that this date appears often in our narrative especially during the second half of the nineteenth century.

[30] Somerset John Gough-Calthorpe, *Letters from Headquarters or Realities of the War in the Crimea*, Vol 1, 2nd ed. (London: Murray, 1857) as cited in Herbert and Barlow, *Music and the British Military*, 141.

the duke identified a site for the school, arranged for funding by the regiments and began a search for the most qualified faculty, all before receiving War Office approval.

The location chosen for the new military school of music was Kneller Hall, the former country home of Sir Godfrey Kneller, court painter to English monarchs from Charles II to George I [Fig. 3.6]. By the 1850s it had been abandoned as a residence and was being used as a teacher training institute so the acquisition of the facility came at no cost to the army. It was simply a matter of transferring the property from one government department to another. The problem of funding the school's operations met with some resistance but the experiences of most regimental colonels with civilian bandmasters was enough to overcome their initial objections and they agreed to pay the school a fixed sum from their own regimental funds. Lastly, the Duke was of the opinion that in order to establish its credibility as soon as possible, it would be necessary to hire the best teachers. He insisted that London's finest orchestral musicians be engaged as civilian staff. Two of the first faculty members were Henry Lazarus and Apollon Barret, instructors on clarinet and oboe respectively, whose published methods for their instruments are still commercially available today.[31] As the Duke had anticipated, the Royal Military School of Music at Kneller Hall, henceforth simply referred to as Kneller Hall in this history, gradually expanded its role from training musicians and potential bandmasters to setting standards for all army bands. This included their instrumentation. In 1869, the school's director, Charles Mandel recommended the following for a band of 32 performers "...1 flute/piccolo, 1 oboe, 1 bassoon, 1 Eb clarinet, 7 Bb clarinets, 1 alto clarinet, 1 bass clarinet, 1 saxophone [no indication as to which] 1 sarrusophone, 4 French horns, 2 Bb cornets, 4 Bb trumpets, 1 Eb tenor horn, 1 Bb baritone, 3 trombones, 1 string bass 1 drum."[32] Ultimately, by the time the last British regimental bands left Canada in 1871, their appearance differed little from that of a band today. It was this instrumentation to which the growing list of Canadian wind bands aspired.

The Canadian Variant

Most Canadian bands however achieved full instrumentation through a slightly different route than their British mentors. The core voices of the British regimental bands in the late eighteenth century were the melodic woodwinds: oboes, clarinets and to a lesser degree, bassoons. This was because they were the only available fully chromatic

---

[31] P.L.Binns (Gillingham, Dorset: The Blackmore Press, 1959) 60.

[32] Herbert and Barlow, *M, A Hundred Years of Military Music usic and the British Military*, 310.

instruments. Canada's earliest bands, those that were in existence prior to 1840, followed much the same pattern. In 1831, William Lyon MacKenzie described a meeting in Hope [Sharon] where he observed musicians performing on "…three or four clarionets [sic], two French horns, two bassoons, besides German and octave flutes, flageolets, etc.,"[33] Five years later, Québec's "La Musique Canadienne", directed by Charles Savageau, consisted of fifteen pieces including "…a piccolo, three clarinets, a bassoon, three horns, two trombones, a tuba, timpani and percussion."[34]

The vast majority of Canada's early wind bands however, whether militia based or in the community, didn't begin to appear until mid-century, by which time families of fully chromatic piston valve brass instruments were becoming widely available. Eminently more suitable for outdoor performance, robust and easier to maintain, these instruments became the core voices of the country's emerging band movement. As in England, one of the most valuable sources of information about the evolving instrumentation of these bands is the photographic record. One of the earliest is of the first Waterloo, Ontario band taken in 1867 which shows a group of nine brass players and two percussionists. [Fig. 3.7] With the exception of one cornet, all other brass instruments are of the "over the shoulder, bell to the rear variety".[35] In those communities garrisoned by British troops, woodwinds begin to appear but the brass choir still predominated. Canada's first school band, La Société Ste. Cécile in Québec appears in a photograph also dated 1867. [Fig. 2.4] Of the 24 musicians in the photo "…on compte seulement cinq bois, soit quatre clarinettes et une flûte."[36] [we count only five woodwinds, four clarinets and a flute.] Ottawa's Governor General's Foot Guards Band of 1873 is remarkably similar: 21 musicians consisting of 1 flute, 4 clarinets, 4 trumpets/cornets, 3 horns, 3 trombones, 2 euphoniums, 2 tubas and 2 percussion.[37] It seems that the introduction of woodwinds in any significant way came originally in those communities with large population bases. Toronto was one such centre by 1878. A photograph of the Queen's Own Rifles Band taken that year clearly illustrates the growth of the woodwind section. Of forty-three musicians, there are 2 Eb clarinets, 6

[33] W.L. MacKenzie as cited in Kallmann, *A History of Music*, 74.
[34] S. Timothy Maloney, "Canadian Wind Ensemble Literature", (D.M.A. thesis: University of Rochester, 1986) 11.
[35] John Mellor, *Music in the Park: C.F. Thiele Father of Canadian Band Music* (Waterloo, Ont.: Melco History Series, 1988) 14.
[36] Jean Philippe Côté-Angers, "Joseph Vézina et l'orchestre à vent : l'expression d'un nationalisme musical canadien" (M. Mus diss. : Université Laval, 2010) 55.
[37] Jack Kopstein and Ian Pearson, *The Heritage of Canadian Military Music (St. Catharines, Ont.: Vanwell Publishing Limited, 2002) 261.*

Bb clarinets and 1 flute. The remaining brass choir includes over 8 cornets, as well as Eb alto horns, baritones, trombones and basses.[38] [Fig. 3.8]

The increasing diversity of the woodwind section was not just restricted to the militia bands. An undated photo of a later Waterloo Musical Society Band, most certainly taken during the closing decades of the nineteenth century, includes 1 piccolo, 1 oboe, 7 Bb clarinets and 1 bass clarinet as well as brass choir. Of particular interest is that the three Eb alto horns are of the circular mellophone variety rather than the older upright pattern suggesting a gradual shift towards the "brass-reed" or "military" band model.[39] As the country's population grew and expanded westward, so too did the "woodwindification" of previously brass only bands. By the 1890s, from Manitoba to British Columbia, well established brass bands found themselves with increasing numbers of woodwinds, beginning invariably with clarinets.

One family of woodwind instruments conspicuously absent from this evolution in the late nineteenth century was the saxophones. It seems that when they do appear, more often than not it starts with community bands. The Belleville, Ontario, Oddfellows band, under the direction of W. B. Riggs, purchased a quartet of saxophones from France in 1888 "… which aroused great curiosity, as they were the first used by any band in Canada."[40] Whether this is in fact accurate is impossible to say but the existing photographic record doesn't disprove it either. It is not until the first decade of the twentieth century that band photos begin to document the presence of saxophones in any consistent way.[41]

Although the growth of wind bands across the country was not uniform, lagging behind in smaller communities and newly settled areas of the west, it was relentless. By the end of the nineteenth century wind bands were Canada's pre-eminent large instrumental performance ensemble. Any city, town or village that considered itself worthy of the name, could boast at least one and in many cases, more than one band, bands that looked very much like those that we listen to today.

---

[38] Ibid., 30.

[39] Mellor, *Music in the Park*, 15.

[40] Nick and Helena Mika, *Belleville: Portrait of a* City (Belleville, Ont.: Mika Pub. Co., 1983) as cited in Benzie Sangma, "A Musical Legacy Which Continues Today", *Belleville Intelligencer*, May 28, 2007.

[41] One of the first was George Robinson's 13th Battalion Band referred to in the beginning of this chapter. The reticence to use saxophones, especially in militia bands may be as a result of the British influence. The Turner Brothers' *History of British Military Bands* contains many fine photographs of British Army bands taken in the 1880s and 1890s and nowhere are saxophones to be seen. They only begin to appear in the first decade of the twentieth century. When they do it is often as a substitute for bassoons.

CHAPTER THREE GALLERY

Figure 3.1. The 13th Battalion Band of Hamilton, Ontario, 1901. The bandmaster, George Robinson, is the white bearded individual seated in the front row. Source: Courtesy of the XIIIth Regimental Foundation, Hamilton.

Figure 3.2. Mehterhane [Turkish], Military Band, 1836. Painted by Arif Pasha. The importance of percussion in Janissary bands is clearly evident. Source: National Museum, Ankara, Wikimedia Commons.

Figure 3.4. Tambourinist of the Coldstream Guards, c. 1790. Mezzotint engraving by Mrs. Ross. The extravagant nature of the headdress was a feature of "Turkish" music performers. Some, such as the individual portrayed in this engraving were celebrities in their own right. It was the dramatic increase in the dynamic levels of the percussion section caused by the addition of these highly valued black musicians that necessitated the rapid growth of the wind band during the early nineteenth century. Source: Henry G. Farmer, *Military Music,* 1950.

Figure 3.3.   Changing the Guard at St. James, London, engraving c. 1790.   A Band leads the parade followed by three black percussionists (with turbans) and several ranks of boy drummers.   Source: Henry George Farmer, *The Rise and Development of Military Music,* 1912.

Figure 3.5.   43rd Light Infantry Band, New Plymouth, New Zealand, 1866.   Clearly evident in this image are two of the defining characteristics of British Army bands in the mid-nineteenth century: a full woodwind section, less saxophones and the presence of boys as members of the ensemble.   Source: Puke Ariki Heritage Collection at www.collection.pukeariki.com.

Figure 3.6.   Kneller Hall Training School, Postcard, 1850. Source: Wikimedia Commons

Figure 3.7.   Waterloo Band, 1867.   The group appears in its original brass band configuration. Most mid-nineteenth century Canadian community bands began as brass ensembles.   Source: Waterloo Public Library.

Figure 3.8.   Queen's Own Rifles of Canada Band, Toronto, 1878.   The bandmaster is William Carey, seated centre in civilian clothes.   Although the brass choir still predominates, the growth of the woodwind section is apparent: one flute, two Eb clarinets and six Bb clarinets.   Source: Queen's Own Rifles of Canada Museum and Archive.

CHAPTER FOUR

CANADIAN MILITARY BANDS IN THE NINETEENTH CENTURY

For almost eighty years British military bands and their music were heard in small isolated garrison communities along the border with the United States. Without the support of the regimental officers, who paid for most expenses including bandmasters' salaries, music, uniforms, instruments and their maintenance, the level of musical activity they provided would have been impossible for local populations whose primary focus was on merely surviving. By the time Britain withdrew the bulk of its troops at the start of the Crimean War, the map of Canada had changed both geographically and demographically. The populations of both Upper and Lower Canada, soon to become the provinces of Ontario and Québec respectively, had each reached almost one million. The three oldest Maritime provinces together counted for a further half million. Similarly, the small garrison towns of eighty years earlier had grown into mature urban centres and with them growing audiences eager to continue enjoying the simple pleasures of wind band music. More importantly their citizens now had both the leisure time and the money to support it. Thanks to several generations of ex-military musicians, starting with Glackmeyer in Québec in 1783, there were music teachers, music dealers and instrument importers ready to supply the needs of a rapidly growing domestic market. This process had already begun several decades earlier with the appearance of our first militia bands, a natural result of the example set by the British regimental bands.

Militia Bands in Eastern Canada

In the mid 1850s a new incentive was introduced that further encouraged the growth of those militia bands. As Canada moved slowly towards limited self-government, it became obvious, especially with the outbreak of hostilities in the Crimea, that the young country would have to take greater responsibility for its own defence. The Militia Act of 1855 established a paid volunteer militia of up to 5,000 men. By 1869, this number had grown to 43,500.[1] It is probably safe to assume that a percentage of these funds were also

---

[1] Canada, Department of National Defence, *Traditions and Customs of the Canadian Forces: Part 3 – Bands and Music* (Ottawa: National Defence headquarters, 1990) 38. This militia was similar to reserve forces maintained by the Canadian Forces today. Members were part-time soldiers paid by the crown only for the actual time spent participating in military training exercises on evenings, weekends and during summer concentrations.

allocated to the employment of musicians. This would certainly explain the rapid increase in the number of bands. In Hamilton, the Independent Artillery Company Band was formed in 1856 under the direction of Peter Grossman, a German bandmaster, and in 1866 it was reformed as the band of the 13th Battalion. The Queen's Own Rifles Band of Toronto was formed in 1862 under the direction of clarinettist Adam Maul. The following year, the Band of the Royal Regiment of Canada was established, also in Toronto.[2] To the southwest in St. Catharines, the Lincoln and Welland Band could trace its origins back to the formation of the Lincoln Militia in 1863.[3] In Ottawa there were two militia bands in existence in the 1860s, one of which, the Ottawa Field Battery Band had been formed in 1855.[4] On the other side of the continent in New Westminster, William Haynes, bandmaster of the Royal Engineers Band (which had been on the West Coast during the construction of the Cariboo Road), retired from the British Army in 1863 when his unit was recalled to England. He moved to Victoria and assumed leadership of the Victoria Volunteer Rifles Band in 1865.[5] The following year one of Canada's most prestigious militia bands, La Musique des Voltigeurs (9e bataillon) was formed in Québec City.[6] [Fig. 4.1] In 1869, inspection reports of the Department of Militia and Defence catalogued the existence of forty-nine bands and included comments about their size and musical proficiency:

29th Bn [battalion]	-	A fair band of 11 musicians
45th Bn	-	One of the best bands in the district, 21 performers
65th Bn	-	Brass band, 15 musicians, just organized[7]

By 1851, Montréal was Canada's largest city with a population of 57,715 inhabitants. It was followed in turn by Québec City, population 42,052, and Toronto with a population

---

[2] D.J. Goodspeed, *A History of the Royal Regiment of Canada: 1862-1979* (Toronto: Royal Regiment of Canada Association, 1979) 626.

[3] Jack Kopstein and Ian Pearson, *The Heritage of Canadian Military Music* (St. Catharines, Ont.: Vanwell Publishing Limited, 2002) 72.

[4] Elaine Keillor, "Musical Activity in Canada's New Capital City in the 1870s" in *Musical Canada: Words and Music Honouring Helmut Kallmann*, John Beckwith and Frederick A. Hall, eds. (Toronto: University of Toronto Press, 1980) 118.

[5] Dale McIntosh, *History of Music in British Columbia 1850-1950* (Victoria, B.C.: Sono Nis Press, 1989) 22.

[6] Jacques Castonguay, *Les Voltigeurs de Québec: Premier régiment canadien-français* (Québec, QC : Les Voltigeurs de Québec, 1987) 477.

[7] Canada, Department of National Defence, *The History of Bands in the Canadian Army* (Ottawa: National Defence headquarters, 1952) 4.

of 30,775. As a growing metropolitan centre Montréal had already achieved a form of musical "critical mass". It had enthusiastically embraced the open-air concerts of its British regimental bands and when they were first withdrawn in 1854, local musicians Joseph Maffré, Guillaume Hardy, Jean Baptiste Labelle and Henry Prince were quick to fill the void. With the end of the war the regiments returned but in much reduced numbers. Their bands had been missed, especially in Montréal despite the best efforts of Henry Prince and his contemporaries, "…the entry of the 39th Regiment was met with a thunderous ovation. The long winters without the music of the bands were over for the time being."[8] It was not to last. By 1871 the British were gone.

After the departure of imperial troops, citizens of Montréal had to once again look to their own to provide the musical services that had made the British regimental bands so popular. By 1870, the band of the Brigade of Fusiliers was playing weekly concerts at "Les Jardins Viger" on Rue St. Denis.[9] Throughout the remainder of the 1870s several Montréal based militia bands featured prominently in the amusements of the rapidly growing city but their military associations were somewhat fluid at best. Two civilian bands in particular, Edmond Hardy's "Harmonie de Montréal" and Ernest Lavigne's "Bande de la Cité" were the actual performers on behalf of a number of the city's militia units: the 65th Regiment, the Carabiniers Mont Royal, the 3rd Battalion Victoria Rifles, the 85th Infantry Battalion, the Fusiliers and the Garrison Artillery. Unlike many Canadian cities of the time in which the local militia band was the focus of civic musical pride, Montrealers chose to invest their enthusiasm primarily on these two community bands. In doing so, they nurtured a tradition that in less than two decades would usher in a golden age of wind bands in Canada's largest city; a tradition that featured bands, directed by native sons, attracting appreciative audiences as the city's pre-eminent form of large instrumental performance practice.

In Québec City the band of the Voltigeurs was described in several militia reports for 1879 and 1884 as "…a fine band of 24 musicians" and "…a very efficient band, composed of brass and reed instruments"[10] Although militia bands across the country were employed on a part-time basis, there was one also in Québec City that was not. The "B" Battery Band, Royal Canadian Artillery was part of what was known as the permanent militia and as such was essentially a full-time military band. [Fig. 4.2].

---

[8] Kopstein and Pearson, *Heritage*, 19.

[9] Yvan Lamonde and Raymond Monpetit, *Le Parc Sohmer de Montréal : Un lieu populaire de culture urbaine* (Québec QC : Institut Québécois de recherche sur la culture, 1986) 34.

[10] Castonguay, *Voltigeurs*, 477.

English Canada experienced a similar growth in both the quantity and quality of its bands. Smaller centres in the Maritime provinces could boast of their own bands: the 62nd Saint John Battalion of Infantry Band of Charlottetown, P.E.I. (1875), the Infantry Corps School Band of Fredericton, N.B. (1884) and the 75th Battalion Band of Lunenburg, N.S. (1884). In Ontario militia units in towns throughout the Loyalist heartland, Whitby, Peterborough, Oakville, Cobourg and Oshawa all supported bands of various sizes, instrumentations and abilities. London, Ontario's, 7th Fusiliers Band was formed in the 1860s and in nearby Berlin (renamed Kitchener in 1916), the 29th Battalion Band was raised in 1878 from two previously existing community bands. Ottawa, the national capital of the new dominion had been home to many bands since the 1840s. In 1872 a new militia unit was authorized for the express purpose of participating in "ceremonies of state" befitting the new seat of government. Designated "The Governor General's Foot Guards" [GGFG], this new formation included a band of twenty-two musicians that by 1900 had grown to a strength of thirty-five.[11] During the first decades of its existence the GGFG Band went through a succession of bandmasters, two of whom would later emigrate to the United States and once there would make significant contributions to the profile and development of the wind band.

The first of these GGFG bandmasters was Alessandro Liberati, a gifted cornetist and natural showman, born in Italy in 1847 but a resident of Ottawa from 1873 to 1874. In addition to his responsibilities with the newly formed militia band, there is evidence that he also conducted the nearby Perth Town Band for "…its town hall concerts in 1873 and 1874."[12] By 1876 he had left for the United States and was soon performing as soloist with Patrick Gilmore's Band. Within fifteen years he was touring America with his own eighty piece "Liberati's Band". The second GGFG bandmaster to head south was Arthur A. Clappé. He was born in 1850 and graduated from both Trinity College, Cambridge and Kneller Hall where he subsequently taught oboe, harmony and solfeggio.[13] In 1877 he accepted the position of bandmaster of the Governor General's Foot Guards Band where he remained until 1884, when he relocated to New York. In 1888 on the recommendation of Patrick Gilmore, he "…was appointed teacher of music and bandmaster at the United States Military Academy at West Point, New York."[14] Although he left West Point and

---

[11] James Milne, *A History of the Governor General's Foot Guards Band* (Ottawa: Unpublished history, 1988) 5.

[12] Daphne Overhill, *Sound the Trumpet: The Story of the Bands of Perth 1852-2002* (Perth: A. Rosenthal, 2002) 37.

[13] William Carter White, *A History of Military Music in America* (New York: The Exposition Press, 1944) 142.

[14] Ibid., 144.

active service in 1895, he remained committed to the U.S. Army's bands and was the driving force behind the establishment of the United States Army Music School.

Toronto by 1880 had a population approaching 85,000 and was Ontario's largest city. The Queen's Own Rifles Band, formed eighteen years earlier, had grown to a strength of forty-two musicians and was recognized as one of the community's finest performing ensembles. [Fig. 3.8]   The regiment took great pride in its band and could boast that by 1879, of the twenty-five that had joined the band since 1875, "…all but a few subsequently earned their living as professional musicians."[15]   During the 1880s the band further solidified its reputation by undertaking a series of tours across Canada and the United States.[16]   The Queen's Own Rifles Band however was an anomaly.   There was an upper limit to the size of militia bands since musicians' salaries were paid by the crown.   Even though the Officers Mess Band Committees were still responsible for almost every other facet of the band's expenses, the Department of Militia and Defence insisted that the limit on the size of the band, known as "authorized strength", was not to be exceeded without prior approval.   It seems that the generally accepted authorized strength for militia bands in the 1880s was twenty-four musicians.

The *Canada Gazette* is the official newspaper of the Government of Canada and has been in publication since 1841.[17]   It contains regulations, statutes and amendments primarily of interest to elected officials [and lawyers] at all levels of government.   In the nineteenth century it also contained information of an administrative nature from Militia Headquarters in Ottawa, some of which dealt with bands.   The *Canada Gazette* of June 2, 1883 contained the following directions:

> In order to secure uniformity on occasions when the bands of several corps require to be brigaded [play together as massed bands] each regimental band will be supplied, for ordinary use, with a set of marches arranged for 24 parts.   On the cards: (1.) The National Anthem [God Save the Queen]: (2.) Slow march for salute; (3 and 4) Quick Step for marching in Column and Quarter Columns; (5.) Trot Past; also a tuning fork…Commanding Officers will be so good as to return any of these cards not required for their bands, in order that they may be distributed amongst bands having more than 24 performers.[18]

[15] W.T. Barnard, *The Queen's Own Rifles of Canada 1860-1960: One Hundred Years of Canada* (Don Mils, Ont.: The Ontario Publishing Company, 1960) 363.
[16] Kopstein and Pearson, *Heritage*, 32.
[17] *Canada Gazette,* at http: gazette.gc.ca accessed 07 September 2018.
[18] "Militia General Orders", *Canada Gazette*, Saturday, 02 June 1883.   The author is indebted to Jim Milne of Ottawa for making copies available for research.

We can infer from this source that most bands had an authorized strength of twenty-four but that some were permitted to exceed it. Unfortunately, the *Canada Gazette* gives no indication as to what instruments the twenty-four parts were for. The directive quoted above also makes one other thing clear. References to the use of a tuning fork and standardized arrangements of the national anthem clearly suggest the memory of Scutari was still fresh in the minds of staff officers at militia headquarters.

The key to the success of the militia bands appears to have been the drive and energy of each individual bandmaster. The musical proficiency of the bands varied greatly and even the size of the local populace was not always a determining factor. By the end of the nineteenth century, one of the best militia bands in Canada was that of the 13th Battalion in Hamilton, first raised in 1856 as the Independent Artillery Band. [Fig. 3.1] Hamilton was an industrial centre. It could boast none of the conservatories or music schools that were emerging in Toronto and Montréal. What it did have was George Robinson. He had served with the band of the Rifle Brigade while it was garrisoned in Canada, took his release from regular British service in 1866 and settled in Hamilton. Becoming bandmaster in 1869 of what by then had been renamed the 13th Battalion Band, he held that position until his retirement in 1917. For almost half a century, by virtue of his own high standards, he created an ensemble that included "…clarinets, oboes, the double bass and slide trombone, bassoon, French horns and even saxophones."[19] Loyalty to the band was such that members gladly practiced two hours a day or more and attended two practices a week. Despite the demands of their civilian jobs and families, the band performed weekly concerts during the winter and during the summer months played "…five and six engagements a week…garden parties, park concerts, out of town engagements and moonlight excursions on the paddle steamers that plied Lake Ontario." [20] George Robinson's extraordinary contribution to the musical life of the city was recognized by his contemporaries and can still be found today on the bandshell in Hamilton's Gage Park that bears his name.

---

[19] Kingsley Brown Sr., Kingsley Brown Jr. and Brereton Greenhouse, *Semper Paratus: The History of the Royal Hamilton Light Infantry (Wentworth Regiment) 1862-1977* (Hamilton, Ont.: The RHLI Historical Association, 1977) 86.
[20] Ibid., 88.

Militia Bands in Western Canada

As Canada's population grew and moved westward, so too did the militia bands. The 90th Winnipeg Battalion of Rifles was formed on November 9, 1883 and within two years was on active duty during the Northwest Rebellion. The battalion's officers wished to also form a band and by the time of the outbreak of hostilities with Louis Riel's Métis forces, a seventeen-piece brass band accompanied the battalion into the field.

> According to the first regimental history published in 1906, the band was the pride and joy of the force. It was said that the playing of the band improved wonderfully during the campaign and that even the enemy- the local Métis- would sneak around the camp at night to listen to it play.[21]

Initially a brass band, by the end of the century it had added a sizeable complement of woodwinds. A photograph of the band taken in 1901, known by then as the Royal Winnipeg Rifles Band, reveals a thirty-piece ensemble consisting of brass choir plus at least seven clarinets, two saxophones, alto and tenor, and a bassoon.

In British Columbia the Victoria Volunteer Rifles Band, originally formed in 1865 by William Haynes, was renamed the 5th Royal Canadian Artillery Regiment Band in 1896. It is an ensemble that remains active in Victoria to the present day. Elsewhere in B.C. militia bands appeared in New Westminster in 1885 and later in 1901 in Vancouver itself. This comparative scarcity of militia bands in nineteenth century British Columbia was the result of slower population growth and the absence of any significant armed conflict with America's Oregon Territories. The European settlement of Canada's Pacific Coast didn't really begin until almost a century after the arrival in Canada of the first British regimental bands. Although British Columbia entered Confederation in 1871, it did so on the explicit guarantee of an intercontinental railroad which wasn't completed until 1885. There was no easy way to go west except by sea or through the United States after the completion of their own intercontinental railway. In addition to a smaller population which made the establishment of a local militia difficult, there also appeared to be little need since the British and Oregon Territories had never known significant conflict. The western border between Canada and the United States had been negotiated in 1846 and so there was no requirement for defensive fortifications and the troops to garrison them. Equally

---

[21] Captain Danielle Gaudry, "Pork, Beans and Hard Tack: The Regimental Band of the Royal Winnipeg Rifles", *Canadian Winds* 6, no. 2 (Spring 2008): 58.

important, the two largest urban centres in British Columbia during the late nineteenth century were Vancouver and Victoria, both port cities. Maritime defence remained a British responsibility until the creation of the Royal Canadian Navy in 1910. It is possible that the proximity of the Royal Navy's base at Esquimalt, a significant establishment by the late 1800s, may have convinced many in those two communities that large militia forces were unnecessary. Ironically, even though there were comparatively few militia bands in British Columbia during the last decades of the nineteenth century, the explosion of wind bands in the province that followed as the twentieth century dawned more than compensated for the slow start.

NWMP (North West Mounted Police) Bands

Sir John A. MacDonald, Canada's first prime minister was a visionary leader. He recognized early in his political career the need for Confederation as the only way to stop the piecemeal assimilation of British North America by the United States. That threat was the single most potent argument for the union of the disparate British North American colonies.[22] It was a measure of his genius for negotiation, compromise and tenacity that he, along with his fellow French speaking visionary, Georges Etienne Cartier, managed to convince the fractious four colonies of Ontario, Québec, Nova Scotia and New Brunswick to join Confederation despite their regional, economic, religious and linguistic differences. MacDonald further understood that once created, the new country needed to extend from the Atlantic to the Pacific in order to prevent American incursions up the centre that would divide the two flanks. In 1869, he achieved this in part by negotiating the transfer to Canada, by the British, of the vast territories deeded by charter to the Hudson's Bay Company. These lands, known at the time as the Northwest Territories, would eventually become the provinces of Manitoba, Saskatchewan and Alberta. Like British Columbia, the population base of these newly acquired territories was so sparse that it precluded the formation of effective local militia forces. It rapidly became clear that the territories would require an external policing authority to uphold the right [law]. "Maintiens le Droit" would become the motto of that force, the North West Mounted Police [NWMP], established in

---

[22] The threat was real. By the end of the U.S. Civil War in 1865, the Union Army numbered over one million battle hardened men led by some very capable generals. The British Army was one fifth the size with almost half of its regiments stationed in India. Had the Americans been so inclined, the takeover of Canada would have been assured. Two things that may have stopped them were their own profound war weariness and the fragile promise of a new unified nation to the north championed by MacDonald and Cartier. For a more detailed account of the threat of assimilation see Richard Gwyn's *John A: the man who made us; the life and times of John A. MacDonald*, Vol. 1 1815-1867 (Random House Canada, 2007).

1873. It was through this organization, the parent of today's Royal Canadian Mounted Police, that wind bands were first introduced to the prairie provinces of Saskatchewan and Alberta in any systematic way.

Within two years of the establishment of the force, NWMP Commissioner French '…made an official request for the formation of a band in October, 1875…In a letter addressed to the Deputy Minister of Justice, French suggested an ensemble form at the newly established NWMP Headquarters in Swan River, Manitoba (also known as Fort Dufferin)."[23] Even though French's request was denied, a volunteer group of musicians formed a band at a meeting on February 23, 1876. They "…purchased their own instruments from a retailer in Winnipeg, who dispatched the shipment to Swan River by dogsled in April 1876."[24] Within months the band started to perform and in August of that year it travelled to Fort Carleton to participate in the Treaty 6 signing ceremonies with the Cree First Nation.

As the Force moved west, so too did the bands. These were volunteer ensembles in the sense that rehearsals and practice were done in off duty hours, all members being obliged to fulfill their primary responsibilities as police officers first. Yet there was no shortage of potential musicians. In 1876, the Force's headquarters moved from Swan River to Fort McLeod, Alberta. Renamed "H" Division, its band "…was not only a strong presence in the region performing for several police and community events, but it was also beginning to expand its performance ability and instrumentation."[25] By 1878, "F" Division at Fort Walsh, Saskatchewan (now a national historic site) could also boast of a band. It "…participated in public events at the local dancehall, which included concerts plus accompanying theatrical performances and minstrel shows. The band also staged concerts for important figures such as Sitting Bull [Sioux leader of the Battle of the Little Bighorn fame, 1876].[26] Although the Fort Walsh band was the first NWMP musical ensemble to receive instruments paid for by the federal government, it is best known for the circumstances surrounding its demise. A contemporary account contained in the diary of Staff Sergeant Issac Forbes explains:

> In celebration of the news of Lord Robert's smashing victory over the Afghans
> [September 1, 1880, Second Afghan War] and his extraordinary march from

---

[23] Darren Wayne Oehlerking, "The History of Instrumental Wind Music within the Royal Canadian Mounted Police Band" (D.M.A. thesis, University of Iowa, 2008) 12.
[24] Ibid., 13.
[25] Ibid., 14.
[26] Ibid., 16.

Kabul to Kandahar, Commissioner Irvine authorized a special issue of grog [rum] to the men who were giving a concert in front of the Officers Mess. Stimulated by this liquid refreshment, the Band, in high spirits decided to turn out on the parade ground that evening and give vent to patriotic British airs. Apparently, they had obtained some liquor in addition to the official issue for when they took their places they were in no condition to produce harmonious music. Whether the first trombone player objected to having a clarinet wailing in his face or they couldn't decide what piece to play, is not known. But the fact remains that they began to quarrel amongst themselves. Shortly a free-for-all ensued. The music making instruments became weapons in the fight and most were destroyed. As a result the band was disorganized. This was the tragic end of the first and only band at Fort Walsh.[27]

Of particular interest in this account, beyond the all too human dimension, is the reference to a clarinet. As such it offers evidence that some of the first NWMP bands included woodwinds as well as brass and percussion instruments.

As other posts appeared, "B" Division in Fort Qu'Appelle, "C" Division in Battleford and "G" Division in Fort Saskatchewan, volunteer bands also emerged. The effectiveness and efficiency of these groups however, depended on their members, who were regularly transferred from one posting to another as conditions and policy dictated. It was primarily at "Depot" Division in Regina and "E" Division in Calgary where the contributions of the NWMP bands were most pronounced, largely through the efforts of bandmasters Harry L. Walker in Regina and Fred Bagley in Calgary.

The NWMP established its permanent headquarters in Regina in 1883. The positive impact of music, both on members of the force and the local community was recognized early on and the Regina band quickly became the focus of efforts by senior leadership to keep good musicians at Depot by circumventing or totally ignoring their own regulations with respect to regular personnel transfers. The Regina band was the largest and most permanent ensemble within the NWMP "… the ensemble would not only perform for Officer Force functions, but also for government affairs, including dedication ceremonies, visits by officials and dignitaries, and local celebratory events [Fig. 4.3]."[28] The band's most productive years came with the arrival of Sergeant Harry L. Walker as bandmaster in 1891. Under his direction, which lasted almost ten years, regular weekly performances

---

[27] As cited in Oehlerking, "The History of Wind Instrumental Music", 17.
[28] William Beahan and Stan Horall, *Red Coats on the Prairies: The Northwest Mounted Police 1886-1900* (Regina: Centax Books, 1998) 292 as cited in Oehlerking, The History of Wind Instrumental Music", 20.

became a vibrant part of Regina's cultural life [Fig. 4.4]. "The Force invited the citizens of Regina to make their way to the Depot grounds (on the outskirts of town) by bicycle, foot or other modes of transportation on Friday evenings for a night of music, beginning in 1897..."[29]

As with the Depot band, the success of the "E" Division band in Calgary was largely a function of the efforts of its bandmaster, Fred Bagley. [Fig. 4.5] Although members of this band first purchased their instruments in 1886, it was with Bagley's arrival the following year that their reputation began to grow "...Bagley's ensemble received requests for numerous performances as representatives of the NWMP and thus gave concerts for important heads of state and other dignitaries"[30] [Fig. 4.6] One of these was the Governor General of Canada, Lord Stanley of Preston [of Stanley Cup fame] on the occasion of the opening of the Banff Springs Hotel in 1889. The highlight of Bagley's time as bandmaster was the Calgary band's participation in Queen Victoria's Diamond Jubilee celebrations in London in 1897.[31]

Much like militia bands in eastern Canada, the activities of the NWMP bands in the growing communities of the Prairies had a profound influence on the local populations they served. This was not just as performers and teachers. Of equal importance they were inspirational role models to those in the towns and cities that heard them play.

---

[29] Oehlerking, "The History of Wind Instrumental Music", 23.
[30] Ibid., 26.
[31] Ibid., 27.

CHAPTER FOUR GALLERY

Figure 4.1. La Musique des Voltigeurs, 1869.   Image taken during summer training camp.   The bearded baritone player seated at the far left is the twenty year old Joseph Vézina who would go on to become one of the giants in Canadian band history.   Source: Jean-Philippe Côté Angers.

Figure 4.2. "B" Battery Band, Royal Canadian Artillery, Québec, 1892.   Joseph Vézina is now bandmaster, seated in the front row, middle with sergeant's stripes. Source: Royal Canadian Horse Artillery Association, Kingston.

Figure 4.3. N.W.M.P. Foot Drill Parade, Regina, 1890. Seventeen musicians including one clarinet. Source: RCMP Historical Collections Unit/Groupe des collections historiques de la GRC at Regina SK.

Figure 4.4. Sgt. Henry "Harry" L. Walker and his Family, Regina, c. 1892-1899. Source: RCMP Historical Collections Unit/Groupe des collections historiques de la GRC at Regina SK.

Figure 4.5. "Sergeant Frederick Augustus Bagley, NWMP", 1884, [NA993-1] Bagley joined the force as a bugler at the age of 16 and was part of the original march west in 1874. He was one of the NWMP's most successful bandmasters but in 1899 joined the Canadian Army to serve in the Boer war. On his return to Calgary, he established the Calgary Citizens Band which he directed until 1920. In 1924 he relocated to Banff where he led the Banff Citizens Band. He died there in 1945. Courtesy the Glenbow Library and Archives. Modifications to this image include cropping.

Figure 4.6. "North West Mounted Police Band, Banff, Alberta", 1887. [NA 2328-8] Bandmaster Frederick Bagley. Courtesy Glenbow Library and Archives. Modifications to this image include cropping.

CHAPTER FIVE

THE TOWN BANDS AND OUR FIRST YOUTH BANDS

One of the works consulted in the preparation of this book was Daphne Overhill's delightful and exhaustively researched *Sound the Trumpet: The Story of the Bands of Perth [Ontario] 1852-2002* (Perth, Ont.: A. Rosenthal, 2002). In her introduction the author makes an observation about the role bands played in community life in the late nineteenth and early twentieth centuries. Because it applies not just to Perth but to the entire country, it is worth quoting in its entirety:

> …they [bands] once occupied every corner of civic life: greeting guests, serenading notable citizens, providing music to frolic to, traveling abroad to collect prizes and awards for their talent, presenting to many their only opportunity to hear good music at all. Civic leaders on a regular basis honoured them with tributes and banquets and opened up the public purse to support their cause. In our own age of TV, computer games, CDs and movies, we have largely forgotten the bands inestimable contribution to making an early town an interesting and decent place to live, and a source of envy to its neighbours![1]

As before in our story, sponsorship was the key. The British regimental bands relied on their officers for the cost of almost everything save their salaries. Similarly, Canadian militia bands, following the British example were sponsored by their own officers in the form of Officers' Mess Band Committees. By the end of the 1850s, as towns and cities in eastern Canada and the Maritimes grew and prospered, so too did their appetite for wind band music. As in England the relationship was no longer just a passive one with the community acting solely as receptive audience. Civilian populations [albeit the male half only] eagerly embraced the opportunity to actively engage as performers in the enterprise of music making. Although it was generally only the bandmaster who received some form of remuneration for his efforts, the prestige of performing and representing one's town, employer, fraternal lodge or association was more than enough to supply a steady stream of potential recruits to the movement. In return cities, towns and villages, local religious groups, commercial enterprises, service organizations and benevolent societies were ready

---

[1] Daphne Overhill, *Sound the Trumpet: The Story of the Bands of Perth 1852-2002* (Perth, Ont.: A. Rosenthal, 2002) III

to provide the necessary funds and facilities that enabled the wind bands to perform on a regular basis for audiences in their respective communities. In many cases these groups were civilian reflections of the militia bands. The music they played was for the same popular audiences.

The Community Bands

Unfortunately, the tradition of unpaid service plus the limited resources of local sponsors left many community bands without any effective form of documentation. This was in contrast to the military where the payment of salaries by the crown required the involvement of a large administrative bureaucracy; one that demanded annual reports and manifests of personnel on strength, which together have left us with a relatively clear picture of the activities of most militia bands. The vast majority of community bands however, operated without the benefit of this support system and have subsequently left us with little or no record of their existence. The study of community bands in Canada in the second half of the nineteenth century is therefore destined to be somewhat speculative and incomplete.

It was not uncommon for community bands to have been established first as militia bands prior to reorganization as civilian groups. One of the earliest was "Le Cercle Philharmonique de St. Jean sur Richelieu", founded initially as the St. John's Band in 1852. It was a collaboration between British soldiers in the nearby St. Jean garrison and several civilians in the region. Directed at first by an officer of the garrison, the band evolved into an entirely civilian organization after the departure of British troops. In 1887 the ensemble made a formal request to civic authorities to recognize its existence; a request that was finally approved in 1899.[2] Similarly the Forest Excelsior Band of Forest, Ontario [community close to Sarnia], was originally established in 1864 as the 7th Militia Battalion Band but by 1884 had completed the transition to civilian status. [Fig. 5.1] These two examples were but the first in a long tradition that persisted throughout the remainder of the nineteenth century and well into the twentieth. The distinction between military and community bands was often blurred and sometimes disappeared altogether [Montréal being a case in point].

Communities that were fortunate enough to have had wind bands prior to the outbreak of the Crimean War experienced a significant increase in the number of their bands as the

---

[2] "Histoire*", Le Cercle Philharmonique de St. Jean sur Richelieu*, at www.cercle-philharmonique-de-st-jean.org accessed 16 July 2018.

1850s came to a close. Berlin, Ontario [renamed Kitchener in 1916], had sponsored an earlier brass band but by 1859 could boast of two town bands.[3] By the 1860s Ottawa's two town bands, established in the 1840s had grown to at least five. Two were military, the Ottawa Field Battery Band (organized in 1855) and the band of the 100th Regiment. The remaining three were all civilian groups: the St. Patrick's Brass Band, the Victoria Band and the Canadian Band.[4] The small town of Perth, southwest of Ottawa on the Rideau waterway, was home to its own St. Patrick's Band from 1856 to approximately 1870.[5]

The decade that followed Confederation in 1867 witnessed an exponential growth in the number of community bands. Montréal's love affair with wind bands continued through the 1860s and early 1870s with a succession of military and civilian ensembles until the emergence of two community bands that were to dominate the city's musical life for almost half a century. In 1874 Edmond Hardy created L'Harmonie de Montréal which was followed two years later by Ernest Lavigne's Bande de la Cité. Hardy's group began with a modest fifteen musicians but within six years had grown to over fifty-five. In 1883 the band performed at the Foreign Exhibition in Boston establishing a reputation for excellence that was to continue under Hardy's baton until his retirement in 1934.[6] Hardy wasn't content to just conduct. He, like so many band directors before him was also a music dealer, instrument importer, publisher and organizer. It was in this last capacity that in 1886 he assembled "...representatives of all the bands in Québec, and the meeting led to the founding in 1887 of the "Association des corps de musique de la province de Québec.""[7] By that time French Canada's community bands were to be found in most of the province's urban centres.

In Québec City Joseph Vézina had organized several community bands. These included L'Union Musicale de Québec in 1870, the concert band of St. Gregoire de Montmorency in 1872 and L'Harmonie de Notre Dame de Beauport in 1876. Across the province bands sprang up in larger communities: L'Union Musicale de Trois-Rivières in 1878, L'Harmonie de Sherbrooke in 1884 and La Société Philharmonique de St. Hyacinthe

---

[3] June Countryman, "Kitchener and Waterloo", *Encyclopedia of Music in Canada* (Toronto: University of Toronto Press, 1981) 497

[4] Elaine Keillor, "Musical Activity in Canada's New Capital City in the 1870s" in *Musical Canada: Words and Music Honouring Helmut Kallmann*, John Beckwith and Frederick A. Hall, eds. (Toronto: University of Toronto Press, 1988) 118.

[5] Daphne Overhill, *Sound the Trumpet: The Story of the Bands of Perth 1852-2002* (Perth, Ont.: A. Rosenthal, 2002) 22.

[6] Gilles Potvin, "Edmond Hardy", *Encyclopedia*, 412.

[7] Ibid., 412.

in 1879.   A photograph of this last ensemble taken in 1895 is not only instructive but somewhat whimsical. [Fig. 5.2]   The image clearly shows the presence of both alto and tenor saxophones, unusual for the period; the fact that the musicians are also all standing knee deep in snow is a delightfully Canadian touch.[8]   Some smaller centres started even earlier.   L'Union Musical de Joliette had been in existence since at least 1866 and the town of Coaticook in the Eastern Townships could also boast of its own band.   A report in the *Stanstead Journal* of 28 January 1869 stated that the "…Coaticook Cornet Band had performed a concert during a Wesleyian missionary meeting exactly a week before."[9]

In the Maritimes the growth was equally widespread but the lack of supporting documentation makes specific identification difficult.   It is only in those communities where a civilian band has operated continuously since the nineteenth century that we find concrete examples.   One such group was the Parrsboro, N.S., Citizens Band which along with the neighbouring Springhill Band was active from 1877.   Along the province's South Shore the Bridgewater Brass Band was formed in 1868.   It was subsequently renamed the Bridgewater Citizens Band and by 1885 woodwind instruments had become part of the ensemble.[10]

Ontario's existing bands were joined by the Newmarket Citizens Band in 1872, the Belleville Oddfellows Band in 1881 and in 1876 the Berlin Musical Society was formed by the merger of two previously existing groups.   Within two years this ensemble would be designated as the Band of the 29th Infantry Regiment.   Berlin's sister city of Waterloo established its own Waterloo Musical Society in 1882, creating a band tradition that was to make Waterloo a household name in Canadian band circles until the mid-twentieth century.[11]   It was also in the late nineteenth century that the first industrial bands begin to appear.   Based on the British brass band model these groups relied on their employers for financial support.   The Brampton Mechanics band was formed in 1884 and was so named because a number of its members were employees of a local foundry.   In Toronto the Taylor Safe Works Band (1888) and the Heintzman Band (1890) were both directed by the young cornetist Herbert L. Clarke.

---

[8] "Historique", *Orchestre Philharmonique de Saint-Hyacinthe*, at www.spsh.wordpress.com accessed 02 April 2020.   Once again, wind bands set the stage: think of Gilles Vigneault's *Mon Pays* (ce n'est pas un pays, c'est l'hiver).

[9] Michael Dougherty, "The Coaticook Band: 140 Years of History", *Canadian Winds* 9 no. 2 (Spring 2011) 88.

[10] Kay Greene, "Bridgewater Fire Department Band", *Canadian Winds* 10 no. 2 (Spring 2012) 31.

[11] John Mellor, *Music in the Park: C.F. Thiele Father of Canadian Band Music* (Waterloo, Ont.: Melco History Series, 1988) 15.

The explosive growth in the number of bands wasn't just restricted to larger communities. In Eastern Ontario from Pembroke in the north to Westport on the St. Lawrence there is evidence of no fewer than twenty-two bands in existence between 1868 and 1887. This number includes only those bands in towns and villages like Pakenham, Almonte, Smith Falls, Carleton Place and Merrickville.[12] In all probability there were many more.

Community bands followed the western movement of the country's population. The Winnipeg City Band (1874) was one of several led by Harry L. Walker. He was later to establish himself as a much sought after band leader in Saskatchewan as well as eventually becoming bandmaster of the NWMP Depot Band in Regina.[13] Saskatchewan and Alberta didn't begin to benefit from eastern migration until the last two decades of the nineteenth century. Consequently, most community bands in what was then known as the Northwest Territories [Manitoba joined Confederation 1870] followed the Canadian variant in the evolution of the wind band; they were initially formed as brass bands. "[Saskatchewan's] first civilian band appears to have been the Prince Albert Cornet band, organized in 1883."[14] Although the instruments were ordered in April of 1883 they didn't arrive until November. The fact that the band's first concert took place on February 20, 1884 and included some thirteen selections, is a testament to the enthusiasm of its first members.[15] The militia regiments that were rushed out west during the North-West Rebellion of 1885 were accompanied by two bands, the 90th Battalion Band of Winnipeg and the Montreal Garrison Artillery Band. It appears that they may have "…whetted the appetites of Reginans for band music and in fact led to the formation of the Regina Brass Band in June of the next year, 1886."[16] Although the NWMP Depot Band was already active in the community there were apparently many opportunities for the city's newly formed Brass Band to play "…a farmers' picnic at Long Lake, an ice carnival, a Promenade concert: an annual Calico Ball …various open-air concerts."[17]

Elsewhere in the province brass bands formed the nuclei for future brass and reed bands that were established in Qu'Appelle (1886), Moose Jaw (1889) and Grenfell (1891). Of

---

[12] Overhill, *Sound the Trumpet*, 153.

[13] Elaine Keillor, *Music in Canada: Capturing Landscape and Diversity* (Montreal and Kingston: McGill-Queen's University Press, 2006) 134.

[14] Ed Wasiak, "Saskatchewan's First Bands: 1873-1913, Pt. 1" *Canadian Band Journal* 13, no. 1 (Fall 1997) 22.

[15] Ibid., 22.

[16] Ibid., 23.

[17] H. Bruce Lobaugh, "Bands During the Riel Rebellion", *Slur-Official Newsletter of the Saskatchewan Band Association* (Summer 1993) 8 as cited in Wasiak, "Saskatchewan's First Bands Pt. 1)" 23.

particular interest, the bandmaster of both the Qu'Appelle Band, from 1887 and the Moose Jaw Band, was Harry L. Walker, later to rejoin the NWMP in Regina.

In Alberta, as in Saskatchewan, the earliest civilian bands were initially created as brass bands. The International Order of Oddfellows (I.O.O.F.) sponsored Calgary's first community band in 1885. A report in the *Calgary Herald* dated July 22, 1885, stating "...that two new cornets and a piccolo plus music had arrived in town,"[18] suggests the presence of at least one woodwind.[19] By 1890 however, the band had ceased operations and "...a set of band instruments was purchased from the Oddfellows Lodge by D.W. March and presented to the Fire brigade together with uniforms and music."[20] The Fire Brigade Band grew during the 1890s and on May 24, 1901:

> ...when the Lieutenant-Governor, premier and members of the Territorial Legislature were invited by the Board of Trade to convince them that Calgary was the logical site for the Territorial or permanent capital, a parade was held down Stephen Avenue and back on Atlantic Avenue led by the Fire Brigade Band and four others bands from Medicine Hat, Edmonton, and Canmore.[21]

Even though the Calgary band won a band competition later that day it failed to sway the invited guests and Edmonton was eventually chosen as the provincial capital.

It was the Fire Brigade that first provided the necessary conditions for Edmonton's earliest wind band "...established in 1891, it was formed by the Fire Chief 'as a way to keep the men occupied while remaining on hand at the Fire Hall.' "[22] This first band was limited to firefighters and their sons but by 1893 pressure was mounting for the Fire brigade to change its bylaws so non-firefighters could participate.[23] In 1894 a second band, the Edmonton Band or the Citizens' Band was formed and like so many others went through several name changes between 1894 and 1907.[24]

One would think that British Columbia's first community bands would appear on the lower mainland or on the southern tip of Vancouver Island. This however, was not the

---

[18] Norman Draper, *Bands by the Bow: A History of Band Music in Calgary* (Calgary: Century Calgary Publications, 1975) 7.
[19] It is conceivable that the reference may have also been to an Eb cornet – piccolo trumpet.
[20] Draper, *Bands by the Bow*, 9.
[21] Ibid., 11.
[22] Taina Lorenz, "The First Wind Bands in Edmonton", *Canadian Winds* 15, no. 1 (Fall 2016) 42.
[23] The question of non-members or "associates", performing with uniformed bands (firefighters, militia) was to prove a major challenge throughout the twentieth century.
[24] Ibid., 42.

case. The province's earliest recorded community band performance took place "...on 4 February 1869 as part of a variety entertainment at the Theatre Royal in Barkerville."[25] This rough and tumble mining town was situated in the province's central interior and had grown rapidly during the Cariboo Gold Rush.   Once again, as with the militia bands, the success of any civilian band in Canadian history is largely a function of the energy, drive and vision of the person or persons leading it.   The spark for the Barkerville band was the Reverend James Reynard, Church of England.   He had arrived in 1866 and was posted to the remote community two years later.   For three gruelling years he served his parishioners both spiritually and educationally.   He tutored a wide range of academic subjects as well as giving music lessons but his health failed and in 1871, he relocated to Nanaimo on Vancouver Island.   Once there he immediately lobbied several prominent citizens to establish the Nanaimo Brass Band which gave its first performance on May 24, 1873.   The band's reputation grew locally and in 1889 it was renamed the Nanaimo Silver Cornet Band.   By the end of the century, it was travelling regularly to Comox, New Westminster, Vancouver and Seattle.[26]

On the lower mainland, New Westminster was the first community to sponsor a number of brass bands starting with the Royal City Brass Band in 1880 and the Excelsior Brass Band in 1882.   In 1888 the Royal City Brass Band was renamed the Royal City Band and a photograph of the group taken in 1892 shows the reason: there are at least three clarinet players in the back row.[27] [Fig. 5.3].   The city of Vancouver doesn't appear to have had a community band, initially brass, until 1886.

One particularly active late nineteenth century band community in British Columbia was Kamloops in the province's interior.   The Kamloops Pioneer Band was formed in 1886 and in 1891 was amalgamated with a second town band, the Independent Band.   The "Inland Cigar Company" in one of the first examples of industrial sponsorship in the province, formed its own band in 1895.   By the end of the century there were no fewer than twenty-nine documented community bands in British Columbia.   These were to be found in towns and cities from Nelson and Revelstoke in the east, through Kelowna and Vernon in the Okanagan to Nanaimo and Comox on Vancouver Island.[28]   As elsewhere throughout Canada, most of the community bands that flourished during this period,

---

[25] Dale McIntosh, *History of Music in British Columbia 1850-1950* (Victoria, B.C.: Sono Nis Press, 1989) 25.
[26] Ibid., 26.
[27] McIntosh, *History of Music in British Columbia*, photo plate iv.
[28] Ibid., 50-61.

whether English or French, were descended from a European cultural tradition as were most of their members. There were exceptions.

First Nations Bands in British Columbia

The First Nations peoples of British Columbia's Pacific Northwest coast embraced the brass band with an enthusiasm that was totally unexpected. So much so that "…no less than thirty-three of these native bands existed in British Columbia between 1864 and the first decades of the twentieth century."[29] Originally begun as an outgrowth of missionary efforts, the first was established in the community of Metlakatla near Prince Rupert. By 1875 the band numbered twenty-one pieces and performed on instruments that were gifts from a London silk manufacturer. The influence of this group was soon felt throughout the area and shortly thereafter bands were formed in the communities of Kincoleth and Fort Simpson. By 1900 the [now] Port Simpson Band was renamed Nelson's Cornet Band after its leader Job Nelson, a Tsimshian native. [Fig. 5.4]. These bands competed informally amongst themselves until they were noticed by the department of Indian Affairs and invited to compete at the Dominion Exhibition of 1905 in New Westminster. "A total of seven bands, from Nass River, Sechelt, Port Simpson, Bella Coola, Aiyanish, Squamish and Bute Inlet duly arrived…"[30] and when they were not performing in competition, they provided public concerts on the streets and in the parks of the city. The scoring was based on British Brass band contests and eventually the overall winner was the Port Simpson Band under the direction of Job Nelson. The results of the competition were so striking that Prince Rupert "…decided to institute a series of similar contests there, which began in 1908 and lasted until about 1914."[31]

The British Army, the Catholic Church and the First Youth Bands

The second half of the nineteenth century also witnessed a slow but steady increase in the number of youth bands associated with educational institutions. Canada's first school band, La Société Ste. Cécile at Québec City's Petit Séminaire was formed in 1838 and until the withdrawal of British troops in 1871 was directed largely by bandmasters from the Québec garrison [Fig. 2.4]. It was a collaboration between two organizations with diametrically opposed purposes and world views: the British Army and the Roman

---

[29] Ibid., 44.
[30] Ibid., 46.
[31] Ibid., 46.

Catholic Church. Both, however, were in agreement, for their own very practical reasons on the benefits of instrumental music education for the young. It was these two institutions who were primarily responsible for nurturing the growth of youth bands in Canada for the remainder of the nineteenth century and into the first decades of the twentieth. The influence of the British Army, although an indirect one, was to persist long after its departure by virtue of the attitudes, experiences and training that successive generations of British and later, Canadian military musicians were exposed to during their periods of service.

During the nineteenth century it would have been an entirely natural expectation for British Army bandmasters to instruct the young men of La Société Ste. Cécile during their time in Québec. Teaching boys to play an instrument was an accepted part of every bandmaster's duties in both the British Army and the Royal Navy. As early as 1812, the Royal Artillery Band had enlisted boys as singers with the provision that when they were of age a vacancy would be found for them in the regiment.[32] Within thirty years boys were regularly being accepted into the band at the age of thirteen. By 1856, the same band's authorized strength of eighty musicians included fourteen boys.[33] In the Royal Navy the situation was similar "…training ships for boys were established between 1860 and 1862 at Devonport, Portsmouth and Portland. In 1863, the first class of sixteen boys was entered as training for bandsmen."[34] By 1883 the total number of musicians in the Royal Navy's band service stood at 567 of whom 104 were boys. Within the space of fifteen years the number of boy bandsmen had grown to 220.[35] Although the exact age at which these boys joined the service is not clear, a photograph of the boys band aboard the training ship H.M.S. *Caledonia,* taken in 1903, would suggest the equivalent of today's grade seven or eight students.[36] The curriculum for bandmasters at the army's Kneller Hall included courses not only for conducting and orchestration but also an introduction to the problems associated with providing instruction to young beginners. H.E. Adkins' *Treatise on the Military Band* (London: Boosey & Co., 1931) was a standard text for British Army bandmasters for years and it contained a chapter entitled "Training of a Young Band." This was a pedagogical guide as it included suggestions on how to assign instruments to beginning players on the basis of physical characteristics, education and musical aptitude.

---

[32] Henry George Farmer, *History of the Royal Artillery Band* (London: Royal Artillery Institution, 1954) 103.

[33] Ibid., 185.

[34] John Trendall, *A Life on the Ocean Wave: The Royal Marines Band Story* (Dover, Kent: Blue band Magazine, 1990) 29.

[35] Ibid., 31.

[36] Ibid., 33.

The recruitment of boys into both the army and the navy was done not only for the practical reason of ensuring a steady supply of trained musicians ready to fill the ranks of the adult bands when older members left or retired.   There was also an unwritten social contract in place where the sons of common soldiers in the parent regiment and boys from the workhouses, foundling homes [orphanages] and pauper schools were given an opportunity to learn a skill and get an education.   By the mid-nineteenth century some of these institutions, especially in London had begun to include instrumental music instruction for youth in their care.   For boys, musical training made them ideal candidates for service in the military bands.   In 1863, Charles Dickens reported on the success of the pauper schools of London's Stepney Parish Union:

> Is there any proof in these boys being in greater demand for the Regimental Bands than the Union can meet?   Or, in ninety-eight of them having gone into Regimental Bands in three years?   Or, in twelve of them being in the band of one regiment?   Or, in the colonel of that regiment writing, "We want six more boys, they are excellent lads."   Or, in one of the boys having risen to be band corporal in the same regiment?"[37]

This concern for the welfare of boys from the lowest classes of Victorian society extended well beyond the ranks of the army.   The wife of Prime Minister William Gladstone took orphaned boys off the streets of London and placed them in an industrial school she founded where they were taught to read and write.   Those who demonstrated an aptitude for music were given lessons by the bandmaster of the Scots Fusilier Guards and placed in regimental bands… "by the end of the [nineteenth] century, it was said that every regimental band in the army contained at least one bandsman who had been recovered from the streets of London by Mrs. Gladstone."[38]

Canada had no official full-time military bands prior to 1899 and consequently no tradition of band boy service before or since.   The practice of educating boys to play in wind bands however, was deeply ingrained in the many former British Army musicians who assumed leadership roles in Canadian militia and community bands throughout the second half of the nineteenth and early twentieth centuries.   Their openness to the benefits

---

[37] Michael Slater and John Drew, eds., *The Uncommercial Traveller and Other Papers 1859-70*, The Dent Uniform Edition of Dicken's Journalism, vol. 4 (London: J.M. Dent, 2000) 245-46. As cited in Trevor Herbert and Helen Barlow, *Music and the British Military in the Long Nineteenth Century* (Oxford: Oxford University Press, 2013) 138.

[38] Byron Farwell, *Mr. Kipling's Army* (New York: W.W. Norton, 1981) 130.

of music education for boys was to grow through the first decades of the new century and blossom during the period between the wars as former British military musicians started our first community-based boys' bands.

The Roman Catholic Church, especially in French Canada had a significant effect on the development of youth bands. Education in Québec remained almost exclusively the domain of the Church throughout most of the nineteenth century. After 1871, la Société Ste. Cécile at Québec City's Petit Séminaire went through a succession of local bandmasters until 1884 when Joseph Vézina, himself a former student, assumed direction of the band. It was a position he would hold until his death in 1924. Although less is known of the musical activities in the religious colleges of Montréal, the presence of such established bandmasters as Edmond Hardy, who accepted the leadership of the Collège Mont St. Louis band in 1904, suggests that group itself was active well before then. To the north in the Laurentians, the Collège de Joliette could boast of a brass band as of 1872. By 1887 it numbered over twenty-five students including performers on clarinet and piccolo. Under the direction of Brother Louis Vadeboncoeur, the band played regularly for religious processions, consecrations, student picnics and theatrical presentations.[39] Ottawa in the 1870s was a city with large French speaking and Irish populations. There were two college bands, the St. Joseph College band and the band of the Christian Brothers School.[40]

Elsewhere in Canada, Catholic teaching orders were equally involved with bands. Père Belcourt established a high school for boys at the Rustico Parish house in Rustico, PEI, in the 1860s and engaged the services of J.D. Landry of Montréal to teach music. Landry organized a band which in 1865 was a participant in the closing exercises of St. Dunstan's College in Charlottetown. The *Charlottetown Examiner* noted:

> The Rustico Band under the direction of Mr. Landry was present and added largely to the entertainment by playing lively French airs wherever there was a pause in the examination closing exercises. The members of the band, all dressed in white, presented a most creditable appearance. Although many of them were

---

[39] Raymond Locat, *La Tradition Musicale à Joliette, 150 ans d'histoire* (Joliette, QC : Librairie Martin, 1993) 67.

[40] Elaine Keillor, "Musical Activity in Canada's New Capital City in the 1870s", in *Musical Canada: Words and Music Honouring Helmut Kallmann*, John Beckwith and Frederick A. Hall, eds. (Toronto: University of Toronto Press, 1988) 123.

the merest youngsters, they performed their parts with an ease and skill worthy of practised artists.[41]

Memramcook, N.B., was home to its own Collège St. Joseph and it supported a St. Cecilia Society which "...included a choir, orchestra and band."[42]   Across the Bay of Fundy at Church Point, N.S., Collège Ste. Anne was established in 1890.   Within three years it could also boast of a band active in the school's religious celebrations.[43]

The Industrial School Bands

As the country expanded westward from Ontario so did the Church eager to establish missions amongst First Nations peoples.   The Qu'Appelle Industrial School, a Catholic residential school in Lebret, Saskatchewan, organized a brass band in 1891 under the leadership of Father Dorias.   It gave its first concert the following year.   "Throughout the 1890s, the Qu'Appelle Industrial School Brass Band quickly assumed a prominent role within the school and the surrounding district...at sports days, picnics, and "entertainments and receptions" in the area."[44]   In 1895 and again in 1897 it won first prize at band competitions held at the Territorial Exhibition in Regina.

Alberta's first school band was also associated with the Catholic Church's native residential schools.   The St. Joseph's Industrial School or the Dunbow School, so named because of its proximity to the settlement of Dunbow at the confluence of the Highwood and Bow rivers south of Calgary, was established in 1884.   In 1891 the new principal, Father Albert Naessens applied for and received permission from the Indian Commissioner to start a brass band.   One of the two academic teachers at the school was William Scollen, who had emigrated from England in 1877 and where, prior to his departure, he had played euphonium in British brass bands.   In November of 1891 the school received its first ten instruments and the band began to practise.[45]   Progress was steady and by 1895 the band was competing at the Territorial Exhibition in Regina.   Assistant Indian Commissioner

---

[41] As cited in J. Paul Green and Nancy F. Vogan, *Music Education in Canada: A Historical Account* (Toronto: University of Toronto Press, 1991) 40.

[42] Ibid., 21.

[43] Ibid., 27.

[44] Ed Wasiak, "Saskatchewan's First Bands: 1878-1913, Pt. 2" *Canadian Band Journal* 22, no. 2 (Winter 1997) 11.

[45] Tom Dust and George Buck, "Dunbow School Brass Band and William Scollen: Two Alberta "Firsts", *Canadian Winds* 7, no. 1 (Fall 2008) 3.

A.E. Forget, in his report of September 1895 specifically mentions four industrial school brass bands:

> The brass bands belonging to Qu'Appelle, St. Joseph's (High River) [Dunbow], Regina and St. Albert supplied nearly all the music at the fair, and won universal praise for the excellence of their playing, their time and attack being admirable, especially considering the fact that they were only Indian lads from ten to eighteen years of age.[46]

By 1896 the band had grown from the original ten to twenty students and it had also evolved. Clearly evident in a photograph taken that year are Eb and Bb clarinets as well as a full complement of brass and percussion instruments.[47] William Scollen moved the following year to Kamloops B.C. where he accepted a teaching position at the Kamloops Industrial School. Within a year, it too had a brass band.

British Columbia had already had a long history of mission school brass bands. The first was the St. Mary's Mission Brass Band, a group in existence since 1864 and the second, the Okanagan Mission Band, established in 1870. The St. Mary's boys ranged in age from six to twelve and remained active until 1940. No other religious denomination in Canada had the combination of musical tradition, financial resources and access to trained educators as did the Roman Catholic Church. Prior to the First World War it was the only institution in the country that sponsored wind instrumental education for young people in any systematic way.

By the end of the nineteenth century, Canada's wind band movement had progressed from struggling infancy in the 1850s to strapping adolescence in 1899. Every Canadian city and town of any stature had its militia band, community bands, industrial bands and for those with large enough Catholic populations, religious college bands. Nowhere however, did the wind band and its conductors achieve the same levels of prestige, admiration and respect than they did in French Canada's two largest cities, Montréal and Québec.

---

[46] Dust and Buck, *Dunbow School*, 4. Of particular interest in Forget's comments are his reference to "attack", a term which in French refers to articulation.
[47] Ibid., 5.

CHAPTER FIVE GALLERY

Figure 5.1.   The Forest Excelsior Band, 1884.   Conductor is R.A. Hill.   By the 1880s most town bands were beginning to add woodwinds.   Source: Forest Museum.

Figure 5.2.   Société Philharmonique de Saint-Hyacinthe, 1895.   Note the presence of saxophones.   Town bands were generally quicker in adopting the new family of instruments. Source: www.sphs.wordpress.com

Figure 5.3. Royal City Band, New Westminster, B.C., 1892. Source: Truman and Caple Photo, Vancouver, B.C., New Westminster Museum and Archives, Photo no. IHP 0015.

Figure 5.4. Job Nelson's Cornet Band, Port Simpson, B.C., 1910. The West Coast First Nations brass bands were enormously popular at the end of the nineteenth century and at one point there were over thirty-three in existence. Source: Vancouver City Archives

CHAPTER SIX

UN CONTE DE DEUX HOMMES

Halifax, Montréal and Québec City were the beneficiaries of British regimental bands longer than any other Canadian city. For almost a century these bands helped create and nurture the growth of enthusiastic audiences as well as the vital infrastructure of music teachers, sheet music dealers, instrument suppliers and publishers that sustained the colonies after the departure of imperial troops. In English Canada, when the time came to find band directors it was only natural to look to England and the United States for qualified candidates. In Ontario with its Loyalist roots, former British Army graduates from Kneller Hall were preferred for the province's militia bands. The most notable examples were to be found in Hamilton (George Robinson of the 13th Battalion), Toronto (John Waldron of the Royal Regiment of Canada and John Bayley of the Queen's Own Rifles) and Ottawa (Arthur Clappé of the Governor General's Foot Guards). In Québec with its distinct character as a French speaking Catholic enclave in North America, English speaking foreign imports were not an option. Québec had to look to its own native sons to find bandmasters who could lead and inspire wind band musicians in the final decades of the nineteenth century. In Montréal and Québec City two bandmasters would emerge as significant figures in the history of bands in Canada.

These two Québec bandmasters were conductors, performers, arrangers and composers. Both were francophone Quebecers and Roman Catholics. They had little formal musical training but were blessed with abundant talent and were tireless organizers, innovators and advocates for the wind band. In every other respect it is hard to imagine two men more dissimilar than Ernest Lavigne and Joseph Vézina.

Ernest Lavigne

Ernest Lavigne (1851-1909) was born in Montréal [Fig. 6.1]. He came from a musical family and had two brothers, Arthur (1845-1925) and Emery (1859-1902) who were equally renowned as musicians in the province at the time. Ernest's chosen instrument was the cornet on which he developed rapidly as a skilled performer. On January 27, 1868, at the age of sixteen, he turned his back on a promising musical career and comfortable, sheltered lifestyle to enlist in the Papal Zouaves as a cornetist.   Three weeks later he landed in Rome with the 4th Detachment.[1]

The original Zouaves were native North African light infantry troops raised by the French, in the 1830s, in what are now Morocco and Algeria.   Led by French Army officers they earned a fearsome reputation during the Crimean War for courage and bravery under fire.   So impressed were their colonial masters that the French Army continued to maintain Zouave units until 1962 and the end of the Algerian War.   It wasn't just the French who admired them.   Both sides in the U.S. Civil War also raised Zouave units as light infantry forces.   Nineteenth century Zouave forces are best remembered today, not for their fighting prowess but rather for their colourful and exotic uniforms: baggy trousers gathered at mid-calf by leather gaiters, tight fitting jackets, colourful sashes and often a fez or turban as headgear.[2]   The Papal Zouaves that Lavigne joined were an international force of young, unmarried catholic men that by May of 1868 numbered over 4,500.   Made up of volunteers from catholic countries from around the globe, including almost 500 from Québec, they enlisted in an attempt to prevent the loss of the Papal States during Garibaldi's unification of Italy.[3]

As soon as Lavigne arrived in the Eternal City, he became a member of the Zouaves band and was promoted to the position of first cornet in 1869.   Rome fell to Garibaldi's forces in September of 1870 and the Papal Zouaves were disbanded to become a colourful footnote in history.   For Ernest Lavigne it was the start of the European phase of his musical education.   For three years he would remain in Europe absorbing as much as he could:

> …Lavigne vit alors de son talent musical, séjourne près d'un an à Naples et voyage en Italie, en France, en Allemagne en Belgique.   Il s'y familiarise avec la musique préferée des foules, avec les jardins, les concerts promenades, les conservatoires de musique, les musiciens, belges en particulier.[4]
> [Lavigne lived by his musical talent, spent almost a year in Naples and travelled in Italy, in France, in Germany in Belgium.   He familiarized himself with the preferred music of the crowds, with the gardens, the promenade concerts, the music conservatories, musicians, Belgians in particular.]

---

[1] Yvan Lamonde et Raymond Monpetit, *Le Parc Sohmer de Montréal 1889-1919 : Un lieu populaire de culture urbaine* (Québec, QC : Institut Québécois de recherche sur la culture, 1986) 44.

[2] "Zouave", *Wikipedia* at www.en.m.wikipedia.org accessed 18 September 2018.

[3] "Papal Zouaves," *Wikipedia* at www.en.m.wikipedia.org accessed 18 September 2018.

[4] Lamonde et Monpetit, *Parc Sohmer*, 44.

Lavigne returned to North America by way of the United States, spending 1873 and 1874 in New York, Philadelphia and Boston. While there he performed as cornetist, may have conducted bands and certainly observed the growing influence of public band concerts. These included those presented by "Gilmore's Grand Boston Band" and Theodore Thomas' "Central Park Garden" concerts in New York.[5]

Returning to his native province at the end of 1874, he worked briefly at his brother Arthur's music store in Québec City but in 1876 went home to Montréal where he quickly established his credentials as a dynamic musical personality.[6] Once there he assumed the leadership of "La Bande de la Cité", known also as "La Musique de la Cité" or "Fanfare de la Cité" and took the group to Philadelphia where it won a grand prize in a competition celebrating the centenary of U.S. Independence.[7] Two years later on May 24, 1878, the group took two first prizes at the Montreal Musical Jubilee, a competition at the Victoria Skating Rink "…in which some 20 Canadian, U.S. and English civilian and military bands participated."[8] Not content with just conducting, he opened his own music store in 1877. It offered instruments, supplies and sheet music for sale as well as publishing piano arrangements of works composed for band and performed by his own "Bande de la Cité". Ernest Lavigne managed all of this before reaching his 27th birthday.

The early years of the 1880s saw the consolidation of both his musical and business interests. "La Bande de la Cité" gave regular open-air concerts at the Jardins Viger during the summer months and Lavigne entered into a commercial partnership with the accountant Louis-Joseph Lajoie forming "Lavigne et Lajoie". It was an enterprise that was soon to become one of the city's most successful music retailers. At the same time his civilian band was also functioning effectively as the regimental band of the 65th Regiment, also known as Les Carabiniers Mont-Royal [parent unit of today's Fusiliers Mont Royal]. He was appointed the regiment's first official director of music and was granted the rank of Lieutenant in the militia. These achievements however impressive, were all just a prelude to his most ambitious project in which he and his wind ensemble were to become Montréal's musical superstars.

His years of travel in Europe and the United States had planted the seeds that were to come to fruition on June 1, 1889. Lavigne had seen first-hand, especially in France the

---

[5] Ibid., 22.
[6] Ibid., 44.
[7] Gilles Potvin, "Bande de la Cité," *Encyclopedia of Music in Canada* (University of Toronto Press, 1981) 52.
[8] Ibid., 52.

powerful appeal of the "café-concerts" with their potent mix of " …le plein air, la musique, le spectacle, l'ombre et la lumière, l'alcool [et] les coloris des vêtements à la mode…"[9] [fresh air, music, live entertainment, shadow and light, alcohol and brightly coloured fashionable clothing].   He and his business associate Lajoie recognized that Montréal was ready for its own version of an urban oasis similar to those he had seen overseas.   By 1889 the city had a population of over 200,000 souls and was already Canada's commercial heart as well as a vibrant cosmopolitan centre.   The timing was right for Lavigne's bold experiment.

The two partners acquired by lease and then purchase a four-acre parcel of parkland at the corner of Panet and Notre-Dame Streets bordering the St. Lawrence River to the south, across from Ile Ste. Hélène.   It was enlarged by a further two acres in 1891.   The site chosen was to be called "Le Parc Sohmer" [Sohmer Park] after a New York piano manufacturer whose instruments were only available through the firm of "Lavigne et Lajoie".   Inspired by the "café-concerts" of France, Sohmer Park was a commercial enterprise.   It was a walled enclosure that charged a modest admission fee but once inside the visitor was transported into an impressionist painting.   There were mature trees and greenery throughout with night turned into day by Mr. Edison's recently invented electric lighting.   The result was an almost fairy world effect.   Inside there was a restaurant and concessions celling cigars, lemonade and soda.   At the "terrasse promenade" by the river, guests could order French style "petits gâteaux" served by white aproned waiters.[10]   For thirsty patrons there was also beer but the main attraction was the music.

With the opening of the park, Lavigne's "Bande de la Cité', which ranged in size from forty to fifty musicians, became the "house band" [Fig. 6.2].   For its first two seasons in 1889 and 1890, the ensemble performed on an outdoor stage twice a day, seven days a week from May until late September or early October.   These concerts were varied affairs with vaudeville acts including comedians, jugglers, acrobats and puppeteers amongst others interspersed between musical selections.   On May 3, 1891, a new indoor pavilion was opened with seating capacity for over 6000 people that permitted performances "rain or shine".

Always on the lookout to broaden the park's appeal, Lavigne made significant changes to the group's instrumentation in preparation for its third season.   Endeavouring to raise the "serious" nature of regular season performances he engaged twenty musicians from the Conservatoire de Liège in Belgium.   Most of these were string players so the wind band

---

[9] Lemonde et Monpetit, *Parc Sohmer*, 26.
[10] Ibid., 66.

that had helped establish the park's popularity became almost overnight a forty-four piece chamber orchestra. The orchestral experiment however proved to be a failure blamed in part on the acoustics of the newly built indoor pavilion. After one season it was abandoned. The Sohmer Park band, thereafter known as "La Bande du Parc" or "La Musique du Parc", returned and would remain a wind band numbering between thirty to forty musicians until the final closure of the park in 1919.[11]

The key to the band's success was Lavigne himself. A born entertainer, he was urbane, sophisticated and flamboyant much like the city he called home. His larger-than life persona drew the crowds through the gates and filled the seats in front of the bandstand. There the podium was his stage. As one observer noted…

> On apercevait monsieur Lavigne…on entendait plus rien que les applaudissements, Lavigne saluait la foule…il nous regardait rien qu'une minute avant de se revirer…Tout le monde retenait son souffle…on restait là, les yeux rivés sur les deux mains de Lavigne qui battaient comme deux ailes blanches. Puis, quand le troisième numéro était fini, c'était une explosion d'applaudissements. Lavigne, la figure toute transfigurée, se retournait pour nous saluer.[12]
>
> [We saw Mister Lavigne…we heard nothing but applause, Lavigne bowed to the crowd…he looked at us for less than a minute before turning around…Everyone held their breath…we stayed there, eyes glued on Lavigne's two hands that beat like two white wings. Then, when the third number was finished, there was an explosion of applause. Lavigne, his face transfigured, turned about to bow.]

Even though the park gradually introduced other attractions, including a Merry-Go-Round and a small zoo, it was always the music that was the primary draw. Ernest Lavigne was finally forced to relinquish his baton in 1907 due to ill health. He returned to the podium briefly in 1908 but passed away the following year at the age of fifty-eight.

His contribution to the growing acceptance of the wind band as a serious medium of musical expression was far reaching. During the nineteenth century the brass reed band was largely associated with the military, outdoor events and community celebrations. Bandmasters held a position somewhat akin to that of a "journeyman musician: necessary and appreciated but not part of the upper social hierarchy. In Montréal, Lavigne and his

---

[11] Lamonde et Monpetit, *Parc Sohmer*, 115a

[12] Jean Narrache, "Le Parc Sohmer*" Reveries de Jean Narrache à Radio-Canada* (Editions du Pauvre Yabe (n.d.) 1, no. 2) 11-12 as cited in Lamonde et Monpetit, *Parc Sohmer*, 50.

"Bande de a Cité" changed that. For twenty years he was the star of Sohmer Park and his musicians were referred to "Les artistes" in the local press.[13] The prestige that he brought to his wind band put it on an equal footing with similar groups in the United States led by such luminaries as Patrick Gilmore and John Philip Sousa. Like them, he engaged his audiences in a way that had not been done widely in Canada before. Prior to Sohmer Park, open air concerts in the nation's public places were unfocused performances. There was little expectation that audiences would actually sit and listen attentively to an entire program. More often than not they would be strolling in and out of earshot and visiting amongst friends. The music was merely part of the ambient soundscape.

Lavigne's approach required patrons to purchase admission to the venue and then through a combination of shrewd marketing and brand loyalty (Lavigne himself), listen to the music attentively. This represented a profound shift in the relationship between audiences and the performers. Of course, this kind of listener had existed for well over a century in the concert halls of Europe and increasingly, the United States. There were even venues in Montréal at the time that catered to this clientele but the cost of admission was well beyond the reach of most of Sohmer Park's regulars. Lavigne's genius was that he made good music accessible to all classes of Montréal society. Almost anyone could afford the 10 cents admission fee and once seated in front of the band, Lavigne's presence alone was enough to ensure that listeners truly became active participants in the performance. After the final number the park's other attractions beckoned…including the beer.

There was another unintended though highly beneficial consequence of Lavigne's initiatives at Sohmer Park. Those twenty Belgian string players engaged for the ill-fated 1891 season "…remained in Montréal, it was they who formed the nucleus of the first MSO [Montréal Symphony Orchestra], set up as a cooperative by its concertmaster, J.J. [Jean-Joseph] Goulet."[14] Under the direction of Guillaume Couture this first MSO was active for two seasons before internal disputes forced its closure in 1896. Two years later it was revived under the direction of its concertmaster J.J. Goulet as conductor until 1919. After remaining dormant for another eight years a new artistic director was found in the person of J.J [Jean-Josephat] Gagnier who conducted the orchestra from 1927-1929.[15]

In one of those historical ironies that occur from time to time in our Canadian wind band story, both J.J.'s were also conductors of the "Bande du Parc Sohmer" after Lavigne's

---

[13] Ibid., 41.

[14] Cécile Huot and Gilles Potvin, "Montreal Symphony Orchestra", *Encyclopedia*, 639.

[15] Ibid., 640.

death: Goulet from 1911 to 1914 and Gagnier from 1917 to 1919.[16] Their band associations went well beyond that. Goulet, the MSO's first concertmaster taught band at Montréal's Collège Mont St. Louis, was Director of Music of the regimental band of Les Fusiliers Mont Royal and served as president of the Canadian Bandmasters Association [parent of the Canadian Band Association] from 1933 to 1934.[17] Gagnier's achievements set him on the international stage. He was Director of Music of the Canadian Grenadier Guards Band from 1913 to 1947 and his reputation as both conductor and composer was such that he was not only a member of the Canadian Bandmasters Association but also a founding member of the American Bandmasters Association in 1929.

By the time of Lavigne's death Sohmer Park was already in decline. It had fallen victim to new technologies including silent films and the automobile as well as increased competition from newer parks with their greater range of Coney Island style amusements. Sohmer Park's nineteenth century "café-concerts" theme now seemed quaint and passé. The music however remained a favourite pastime for many "Montréalais" until fire destroyed the indoor pavilion on March 24, 1919, at which point Sohmer Park ceased operations permanently. In one final tribute to Lavigne's vision which embraced all levels of society, the land on which the park sat became the site of a Molson's brewery.

Joseph Vézina

Joseph Vézina was the second towering figure in Québec's "belle époque" of bands that lasted through the late nineteenth and into the early twentieth century. The most important source of information on Vézina consulted for this history was Jean-Philippe Côté-Angers' Master's thesis submitted to L'Université Laval in 2010. This exhaustive study, entitled "Joseph Vézina et l'Orchestre à Vent: l'expression d'un nationalisme musical canadien" [Joseph Vézina and the wind orchestra: the expression of a Canadian musical nationalism] is a document that richly details Vézina's musical life and the influences that shaped it.[18]

At the centre of that life was the wind band, an idiom with which he performed, conducted, arranged and composed as well as taught for almost sixty years. Notwithstanding his contributions to both symphonic music and music education at the

---

[16] Lamonde et Monpetit, *Parc Sohmer*, 115-116.
[17] Marie-Claire Lefebvre, "Goulet", *Encyclopedia*, 388.
[18] Jean Philippe Côté-Angers, "Joseph Vézina et L'Orchestre à Vent : l'expression d'un nationalisme musical canadien" (M.Mus diss. Université Laval), 2010. The author is indebted to M. Côté-Angers for his support.

post-secondary level, it was his involvement with wind bands that helped establish the status of that ensemble as an equal participant in the musical life of Québec. [Fig. 6.3]

Joseph Vézina (1849-1924) was born in Québec City and was surrounded by band music from the very beginning. His father, François Vézina was a house painter by trade but an amateur clarinettist who performed with Charles Savageau's "Musique Canadienne". After Savageau died in 1849 it was the elder Vézina who led the ensemble from 1850 to 1860. The family's passion for music also extended well beyond the young Joseph. Like Ernest Lavigne in Montréal, Joseph Vézina also had two brothers, Alfred and Ulrich who both followed careers in music. The twelve-year old Joseph entered the Petit Séminaire de Québec in 1861 and initially did very well but after two years his grades began to slip. Although he became a member of the Société Ste. Cécile in 1863 it wasn't enough to maintain his interest in his schooling and later that year he abandoned his studies altogether. His life-long association with the military began the following year when he enrolled in the Quebec Military School. In 1867 he joined "La Musique du 9e bataillon (Voltigeurs de Québec) as a baritone saxhorn player [similar to a modern baritone horn] and within a further two years was officially appointed its bandmaster, a position he would hold until 1879.[19] [See Fig. 5.1]

The Voltigeurs however were a militia unit; the work was part-time and the pay minimal. In 1871 he joined his brother Alfred and opened a music store, "A and J Vézina". It was an enterprise that would soon be in direct competition with a similar retail establishment operated by Arthur Lavigne, Ernest's brother. As the 1870s progressed he formed several wind bands which he also led: the Notre-Dame de Beauport Band in November of 1874 and the Montmorency and Charlesbourg Bands the following year.[20] There were others: La Musique de L'Asile de Beauport, the Total Abstinence Band and the Hibernian Band. When one considers that the total population of Québec City in 1871 was approximately 60,000 and that by 1881 it had only grown to 62,446, then the number of community bands in the region is impressive. That Vézina conducted so many while still in his 20s is even more so.

Military bands, then as now were often called upon to perform at large public events of national significance. One such event took place on June 24, 1880.[21] It was an international gathering of French Canadians known as "La Convention nationale des Canadiens français". The highlight was to be a High Mass [sung] followed by a concert

---

[19] Juliette Bourassa-Trépannier, "Vézina, Joseph" ,*Encyclopedia*, 974.

[20] Jean-Philippe Côté-Angers, "Joseph Vézina", 17.

[21] The reader will recognize the date of June 24 as the feast day of St John the Baptist, the patron saint of Québec. The date has gradually been secularized and is now known in Québec as "La fête nationale".

that evening at the Québec Skaters Pavilion. Vézina was chosen by the organizing committee chaired by Ernest Gagnon to be musical director. He assembled a massed band of over 100 performers with participants coming from his own "B" Battery Band, whose leadership he had assumed the previous year, as well as musicians from bands in Beauport and from as far away as Fall River, Massachusetts.[22] In addition to conducting the massed bands, Vézina also arranged two works specifically for the convention. The first was Henri Dumont's *Messe Royale* which was performed during the liturgical celebration and for the final concert that evening he prepared an arrangement of a newly composed patriotic song written by his friend Calixa Lavallée. Entitled *O Canada*, it was a "chant national" intended to celebrate the strength, resilience and vitality of French Canada. Vézina incorporated Lavallée's new theme into the triumphant finale of a larger medley of French-Canadian folksongs entitled *Mosaique sur les Airs Canadiens* [a work which will be analysed at length in the second half of this book]. The success of the "convention nationale" helped solidify Vézina's reputation and for the next three decades he and the "B" Battery Band were actively involved musically accompanying renowned "artistes" and performing for visiting church leaders as well as foreign dignitaries.[23]

In the autumn of 1884, while still serving on a full-time basis with the permanent militia, Vézina was approached by the board of the Petit Séminaire with an offer to assume direction of its Société Ste. Cécile. This was the same school band that he had been a member of over twenty years earlier. He accepted and remained in the post until the year of his death in 1924. The ensemble he inherited had been operating as a brass band but under his leadership it flourished and in 1900 after years of intense lobbying, woodwinds were reintroduced.[24] Not content with musical activities that spanned both professional military and school bands, Vézina also took on the responsibilities of organist at the Irish community's St. Patrick's Church.[25]

In 1899 Major-General Edward Hutton, Commanding Officer of the Canadian militia was able to report:

> A permanent band for the Royal Canadian Artillery has been organized at Quebec under a competent bandmaster…the band in question will shortly be available for purposes of state and public occasions of importance.[26]

---

[22]Bourassa-Trépannier, "Vézina, Joseph", *Encyclopedia,* 973.

[23] J-P. Côté-Angers, "Joseph Vézina", 19.

[24] Ibid., 20.

[25] Ibid., 21.

[26] Militia reports, 1899, Article 15 as cited in Canada, Department of National Defence, *History of Bands in the Canadian Army* (Ottawa: National Defence Headquarters, 1952) 4.

The "competent bandmaster" of course was Joseph Vézina.   Even though the "B" Battery Band had been functioning as a quasi-professional ensemble for almost two decades, General Hutton's directive was significant.   It is likely that the decision to employ the band on a full-time basis prior to 1899 had been made at the district level.   Canada was divided into militia districts for administrative purposes that often corresponded to its geographical regions.   Then, as now, these districts were granted a certain degree of autonomy when it came to the disbursement of training funds.   The presence of a full-time band in the Québec Military District decades before any other region in the country may have been one example of this local discretionary spending.   With the realignment of 1899, the "B" Battery Band became a nationally constituted unit with the support of and under the direction of Militia Headquarters in Ottawa.   Although the shuffle in the command structure may have had little real impact on the day to day operations of the band, it set a precedent for permanent, later to be known as regular force, professional brass-reed bands fully supported by the Department of National Defence.   As such the "B" Battery Band became the first of many in the twentieth century that would make huge contributions to the growth of the wind band movement not just in the military but in communities and schools across the country. [Fig. 6.4]

The fact that Vézina was chosen bandmaster speaks volumes to the respect and admiration in which he was held by his English-speaking superiors. He was also the ideal candidate for the position, one that he would hold until his retirement from the army effective January 1, 1912.   By 1902, already busy with a full-time career as military bandmaster, teaching duties at Le Petit Séminaire and performance obligations at St. Patrick's, Joseph Vézina was ready for a new chapter in his professional life.   That same year, after directing a successful performance of Theodore Dubois' oratorio *Le Paradis perdu,* he was offered the post of conductor of the newly established Quebec Symphony Orchestra, renamed La Société symphonique de Québec the following year.[27]   With their newly installed director in place the young orchestra began modestly enough offering two concerts a season.   In 1907 the orchestra "…won the Earl Grey Trophy in Ottawa and performed at the Monument national in Montréal."[28]   Obviously pleased with his leadership, the orchestra retained Vézina as conductor until the year of his death.

After his retirement from the army in 1912 Vézina also abandoned his responsibilities as organist at St. Patrick's Church in order to assume the duties of choirmaster at Québec's

---

[27] Marc Samson, "Quebec Symphony Orchestra", *Encyclopedia,* 787.
[28] Ibid., 787.

Notre-Dame Cathedral.   In this capacity he was only responsible for directing the choir since the position of organist was filled by Gustave Gagnon.[29]   Leaving the army however didn't mean abandoning the wind band.   He took over the leadership of an ensemble called "Les Cadets de Saint Jean-Baptiste", a group which despite its name had no military affiliation whatsoever.

Ever the organizer, Joseph Vézina was a driving force behind the creation of the Université Laval School of Music in 1922 where he was promptly engaged as professor of orchestration, harmony and solfège.[30]   That same year on October 5, no doubt in recognition of his extraordinary service to the musical life of his native city, he was awarded an honorary doctorate by Laval.

On July 27, 1924, the venerable bandmaster Joseph Vèzina conducted his "Cadets de Saint Jean-Baptiste" at an outdoor concert near Cap Santé.   Bare headed under a bright summer sun he suffered a sunstroke from which he never fully recovered and he died at Québec in October of that year at the age of seventy-five.[31]   Composer, arranger, bandmaster, choir director, symphony conductor, church organist, secondary school music teacher and university professor, he was by any standard a musical titan.   When one considers that with the exception of six months of harmony lessons with his friend Calixa Lavallée in 1878, he was entirely self-taught, his achievements become even more extraordinary.   The thousands that attended his funeral service only give a small measure of the esteem and love he knew from both the musical community and the general population of his native city.   The foundational experiences of this musical life were rooted in the wind band, an ensemble with which he was associated his entire life; an ensemble that he and his fellow Quebecer Ernest Lavigne set on an equal footing both technically and artistically with every other instrumental performance idiom in early twentieth century Québec.   In doing so they both provided an example to future generations of band directors, emerging not only in French Canada but across the country; leaders whose influence would extend well beyond the bands they conducted to every facet of Canadian musical life.

---

[29] Côté-Angers, "Joseph Vézina", 21.
[30] Ibid., 23.
[31] Ibid., 23.

CHAPTER SIX GALLERY

Figure 6.1. Ernest Lavigne (1851-1909) Montréal, undated. Lavigne was a consummate showman whose bands at Sohmer Park helped establish the city as the home of Canada's first "Golden Age" of band music. His "artistes" drew in large audiences from all levels of society and set new standards for performances by wind musicians. It was with these resources at his disposal that he greatly increased the wind band's acceptance as an ensemble worthy of "serious" music. Cornetist, conductor, composer, arranger, entrepreneur, businessman and military bandmaster, his activities spanned all areas of bands and their music. Source: Wikimedia Commons.

Figure 6.2. La Musique du Parc Sohmer, Montréal, 1890. Lavigne, with top hat, is standing in front of his ensemble. Although a cello appears in the photograph, his experiment with strings was quickly abandoned. Source: Wikimedia Commons.

Figure 6.3. Joseph Vézina, Québec, 1924. Photo by Paul Audet. Performer, bandmaster, composer, arranger, symphony conductor, organist, choirmaster, teacher and co-founder of Université Laval's School of Music. With the exception of six months private lessons in harmony from his friend Calixa Lavallée in 1878, he was entirely self- taught. A tireless organizer and man of extraordinary energy, he is one of the giants in the history of wind bands in Canada. Source: Musée de la civilisation.

Figure 6.4. "B" Battery Band, Québec, 1901. Bandmaster Vézina appears in centre in civilian dress. In all probability because he was not a Kneller Hall graduate. Note the full instrumentation including saxophones. Leaning against the back wall is a "Jingling Johnnie", a holdover from the nineteenth century "Turkish Music" craze. Source: Royal Canadian Horse Artillery Association, Kingston.

CHAPTER SEVEN

CANADA'S CENTURY: THE GOLDEN AGE OF COMMUNITY BANDS 1900-1939

Canada's first French speaking prime minister, Sir Wilfred Laurier, confidently predicted in 1904 that "...the 20th century shall be the century of Canada and Canadian development."[1] His observation, when applied to the country's growing band movement in the first half of the twentieth century, was remarkably prophetic. It started almost at once in the Ontario community of Belleville, where in 1900, Canada's first full-time civilian band was established. The Belleville "Kilties" were the project of local businessman and hotel owner T.P.J. Power who was prepared to invest the necessary funds to provide Belleville with one of the finest bands in the country. Whether he was inspired by the success of Toronto's 48th Highlanders Band, formed in 1892, or as some have suggested was simply endeavouring to relieve some of the pressure on the Toronto militia group is unclear but the net result was the same.[2] The Belleville Kilties were named after their dress uniform which was patterned on that of Britain's 92nd Gordon Highlanders, complete with bonnets, spats, sporrans, tunics and kilts. The appeal to Highland tradition in the choice of uniform and repertoire was no accident. It was a brilliant marketing strategy aimed at the many Canadians of Scottish descent who made up an increasingly influential segment of the Canadian population.

After the disaster at Culloden in 1746 and the even more calamitous Highland clearances of the late eighteenth and early nineteenth centuries, almost three million Scots left their homes to find better lives elsewhere. They sought out English-speaking enclaves across the globe and with their native industry and thrift soon built prosperous communities and successful enterprises. Canada, with its familiar northern climate and rugged landscapes was a destination of choice ["Nova Scotia" means "New Scotland" in Latin]. Scots were massively involved in the fur trade so much so that "...by the turn of the eighteenth century four out of five employees [of the Hudson's Bay Company] were Scots."[3] After the 1821 merger with its fiercest competitor, the Northwest Company, the Hudson's Bay Company became "...the largest corporate land holder in the world."[4] Its

---

[1] Anthony Wilson-Smith, "Canada's Century: Sir Wilfred Laurier's Bold Prediction", *The Canadian Encyclopedia* at www.thecanadianencyclopedia.ca accessed 22 December 2018.

[2] Helmut Kallmann, Jack Kopstein and Patricia Wardrop, "Bands", *Encyclopedia of Music in Canada* (Toronto: University of Toronto Press, 1981) 59.

[3] Arthur Herman, *How the Scots Invented the Modern World* (New York: Broadway Books, 2001) 363.

[4] Ibid., 364.

president George Simpson, a West Highlander, would travel to the farthest reaches of this territory often by canoe, accompanied by his own bagpiper. The political landscape was no different. Canada's first two prime ministers, Sir John A. MacDonald and Alexander Mackenzie, were both native born Scots as were eight of ten participants at the 1866 Confederation Conference in Québec.

> By the turn of the [20th] century, Scots and persons of Scottish descent were virtually running the country. One third of Canada's business elite was of Scottish origin and Scots single-handedly ran entire industries, such as papermaking…iron and steel, oil and gas and the fur trade.[5]

Members of this Scottish community also made enormous contributions to the country's system of higher education founding amongst others Dalhousie University (1818), McGill University (1821) and the University of Toronto (1827).[6]

With each passing generation bitter memories of misery and hardship gave way to nostalgia for a romanticized way of life made especially poignant by the Scottish Revival and the resulting boom in the Scottish tourist trade. This was a growing industry given an enormous boost by Queen Victoria's discovery of the Highlands and the purchase of her new summer home at Balmoral. Equally bewitched as the monarch herself by rugged landscapes and empty spaces [created in large part by almost a hundred years of forced evictions of which the young Queen herself was almost entirely oblivious], England's leisure classes flocked north to embrace a mythical version of Scottish history. In a world yet without electricity and thus no radio, film, television or internet, this reconnection with one's roots was impossible for the millions in the Scottish diaspora including those in Canada. The only practical way to do so locally was through a synthesis of music, dance and costume which was exactly what the Belleville Kilties provided.

The Belleville Kilties

It was a touring ensemble with its owner T.P.J. Power acting as manager. Immediately after its formation the band began a short tour of the United States that proved to be so successful that for the 1902-03 season "…the Kilties travelled 32,000 miles in 48 weeks,

---

[5] Herman, *How the Scots*, 368.
[6] Ibid., 368.

covering the Atlantic to the Pacific and going as far south as Mexico."[7]   The band began 1904 by traveling once again to the United States with one of the stops on its American tour being Philadelphia's Willow Grove Park, a performance venue made famous for its annual Sousa Band concerts from 1901 to 1926.   In August of that year "…the band played a two-week engagement at the World's Fair, St. Louis, Mo., U.S.A, the only Canadian band honoured with such an engagement.   Here the Kilties established themselves as great favourites."[8] [Fig. 7.1]   The group returned briefly to Belleville and on September 9, 1904, it performed a farewell concert at the city's opera house prior to leaving for its first European tour.   One of the highlights of the trip in England was a command performance for King Edward VII at Balmoral Castle.   On completion of the performance "…the King decorated W.F. Robinson, the bandmaster, with the Victorian Order.   The King was delighted with the concert."[9]   Following their return to London the band "…met with an ovation, and their tour of Great Britain began with a series of triumphs, the Band being dubbed by the newspapers 'The Conquering Kilties.'"[10]   They were honoured with a second command performance on Wednesday, November 9 at Sandringham on the occasion of the King's 63rd birthday.   At the second appearance the King presented "…the bandmaster with an elegant baton, surmounted by a miniature crown with 'E.R.' set in rubies and diamonds."[11]

As the band's fame grew so did the scope and scale of its touring commitments which culminated in the world tour of 1908.   It was a tour de force of both organization and stamina.

> The tour started at Belleville, Canada on May 24, 1908 and closed at New York on August 7, 1910.   During the two years and three months of the remarkable tour, the Kilties travelled over 86,000 miles, visited 20 different countries and spent 110 days at sea.   The countries visited are as follows: Canada, France, Australia, England, Scotland, Ireland, Wales, New Zealand, Italy, Egypt, India,

---

[7] Bill Hunt, "The Best Band in the World," *The* [Belleville*] Intelligencer*, 31 December 1999, 17.   Copy courtesy Mr. Carl V. Ehrke, Belleville, Ont.
[8] Melissa Wakeling, "Belleville Kilties Souvenir Album," *Glanmore National Historic Site* at www.glanmore.ca accessed 19 January 2019.
[9] "King Was Delighted with Belleville Kilties," *The Daily Intelligencer*, 28 September 1904, 7.
[10] Wakeling, *Kilties Souvenir Album*, 2.
[11] Ibid., 2.

Ceylon [Sri Lanka], Sicily, Spain, Burmah [sic], Tasmania, Fiji, Arabia, Hawaii, Mexico."[12]

In 1911 the band ceased its operations. It was revived again from 1918 to 1920 and one last time from 1923 until its final dissolution in the early 1930s. By this time its star had been eclipsed by Canadian bands even more accomplished and renowned on the world stage.

From its creation until at least the end of its first overseas tour of 1904, the Kilties were led by William F. Robinson, son of George Robinson, bandmaster of Hamilton's 13th Battalion Band. The younger Robinson must have paid close attention to his father's techniques especially with respect to instrumentation. A photo of the 13th Battalion Band taken in 1901 [Fig. 4.1] and an undated one of Kilties taken during one of their early tours [Fig. 7.2] are very similar. Both show instrumentally balanced ensembles of approximately 35-40 musicians. Of particular significance is the presence of double reeds, a fact duly noted in a review of the Kilties farewell concert at Belleville on September 9, 1904 "…the bassoons, oboes and other rare instruments add a mellowness to the tone that blaring brass can never give: the reeds are more in number and superior in quality."[13]

Like British regimental bands early in the previous century with their black percussionists dressed in opulent "Turkish" costumes, the Kilties also had a visual "hook" to help then stand out in a field that included many fine bands. In addition to their distinctive highland dress they also had a secret weapon in the person of their drum major Mr. Roderick Bain MacKenzie.[14] Mr. MacKenzie stood over seven feet tall and when wearing the highland bearskin almost surpassed the eight-foot mark. His presence in front of the band as it marched in parades at its many tour stops would certainly have contributed to the band's celebrity status. The appeal to the "Highland" memory required more than just the band. Within its ranks there were sixteen who formed a male choir and the touring ensemble also included pipers and dancers, four of whom were female. The dance troupe

[12] Alfred Edward Zealley and J. Ord Hume, *Famous Bands of the British Empire* (London: J.P. Hull, 1926) 55.

[13] "Farewell to the Kilties*", The* [Belleville] *Daily Intelligencer*, Saturday, 10 September 1904.

[14] For readers with no marching band experience the Drum Major (DM) is the individual who leads the band on parade. In the British military band tradition, the DM carries a ceremonial mace, a wooden rod approximately four feet/120 cm in length surmounted by a grapefruit sized metal sphere. It is used to give directions to the band while it is playing. These can be musical in nature, stopping and starting to play or marching instructions such as stepping off, halting and changing direction.

was led by Albert Johnstone, director of Johnstone's Academy in Belleville who at the age of sixteen "…won the World Championship Piper and Dancer Contest in Paris."[15]

It was inevitable that the success of the Belleville Kilties would inspire similar groups elsewhere. Four of these bands continue to the present day: the Galt Kiltie Band [now part of Cambridge, Ont.] formed in 1902, the Chatham Kiltie Band established in 1927 [Fig. 7.3], the Orillia Kiltie Band which was renamed from the earlier Orillia Citizens Band by 1923 and the Cobourg Kiltie Band. Although all these groups have abandoned the highland dress that was once so popular, they continue to bear witness to the community pride that took the Belleville Kilties around the world. One final footnote to the Belleville story is that in 1902 the Belleville Kilties were the first Canadian instrumental ensemble to make a sound recording. It was Alexander Muir's *The Maple Leaf Forever*.

The number of community bands grew steadily as Canada entered the twentieth century but in English Canada the surge in patriotic pride that followed the end of the Boer War [1902] was the impetus for a marked increase in the number of militia bands. In some cases, this growth came at the expense of local civilian bands who simply exchanged names, uniforms and little else in order to be affiliated with nearby militia units. In Perth, Ontario, two previously existing community bands were reformed as the Band of the 42nd Regiment of Lanark and Renfrew.[16] The Bridgewater, Nova Scotia, town band became the Band of the 68th Regiment of Kings County in 1908.[17] Starting in 1903, the Rocky Mountain Rangers Band of Kamloops, B.C., quickly absorbed musicians from the city's three previously existing community bands. In most larger communities however, civilian bands continued to operate alongside their militia brethren often sharing the same musicians and bandmasters.

It was only in Québec where the number of militia bands did not grow significantly in the period preceding the Great War. It appears that the opposite occurred. "Les Unions Musicales" as many community bands in French Canada were known, increasingly assumed the duties of militia bands. Even the prestigious Band of the Voltigeurs, whose leader had once been Joseph Vézina, was replaced by the civilian "L'Union Lambilotte" in 1900.[18] The contractual arrangement whereby a civilian band provided musical support

[15] Hunt, "Best Band".
[16] Daphne Overhill, *Sound the Trumpet: The Story of the Bands of Perth 1852-2002* (Perth: A. Rosenthal, 2002) 88.
[17] Kay Greene, "Bridgewater Fire Department Band," *Canadian Winds* 10, no. 2 (Spring 2012) 30.
[18] Jacques Castonguay, *Les Voltigeurs de Québec : Premier régiment canadien-français* (Québec, QC : Les Voltigeurs de Québec, 1987) 479.

to a militia unit was commonplace throughout the province so much so that it was noted with some concern by higher authorities.[19]

These "Unions Musicales" however, were just as popular as their community band counterparts outside Québec and were to be found in most populated areas from the "Union Musicale de Joliette" in the Laurentians north of Montréal to similar organizations in Shawinigan, The Saguenay region, Trois-Rivières [Fig. 7.4], Cap de la Madeline, St. Jean sur Richelieu and the Eastern Townships. A provincial festival of municipal bands, held in Joliette on August 24, 1907, attracted over 500 musicians from the following bands: "…L'Alliance de Montréal (J.J. Goulet), La Philharmonie de St. Hyacinthe (Leon Ringuet), La Philharmonie de St. Jean (Napol. Boisvert), L'Union Musicale de Joliette, L'Harmonie de Sherbrooke, celle de Trois-Rivières, la Fanfare du 65eme bataillon de Montréal, celles de St. Jerome de Terrebonne."[20] In addition to the performance venues that these groups had in common with community bands elsewhere in the country, there is every reason to believe they were also involved in Roman Catholic religious festivals, especially those associated with the feast of St. Jean Baptiste.

The art and science of photography had improved dramatically by the end of the nineteenth century and community band pride was increasingly reflected in the photographic record. By the first decade of the new century greater clarity and resolution in these band images offer important clues as to the size, instrumentation and demographic composition of Canada's wind bands, both military and civilian. Two of the Country's oldest community bands, the Thorold town band established in 1851 and Le Cercle Philharmonique de St. Jean, 1852, both appear in photos from the early 1900s. The Thorold Band [Fig. 7.5] numbers thirty-six musicians consisting of full brass choir as well as one flute, six clarinets and tenor and baritone saxophones.[21] The St. Jean group [Fig. 7.6] consists of thirty-five performers distributed as follows: four cornets, two trumpets, four trombones, three Eb alto horns, 1 Eb mellophone, two tubas, 2 baritones, five saxophones (1 soprano, 2 altos, 1 tenor and 1 baritone) and seven clarinets. There are a further five individuals at the rear of the band but it is difficult to make a positive identification as to what instruments they play.[22] Period photographs are equally helpful in tracing the "woodwindification" of previously existing brass bands across the Prairies.

---

[19] Jean-Yves Gravel, *L'Armée au Québec : un portrait social 1868-1900* (Montréal : Boreal Express, 1974) 105.

[20] Raymond Locat, *La Tradition Musicale à Joliette : 150 ans d'histoire* (Joliette, QC : Raymond Locat, 1993) 267.

[21] Photo courtesy Mr. Brian Williams

[22] "1900-1910 Histoire", Le Cercle Philharmonique de Saint Jean sur Richelieu at www.cercle-philharmonique-de-st-jean.org accessed 20 January 2019.

By 1905 the Regina Citizens band could boast an instrumentation of one piccolo, one oboe, one Eb clarinet, three Bb clarinets, one tenor saxophone, four cornets, four alto horns, two tenor horns, two trombones, one euphonium, three Bb basses, three Eb basses, bass drum, snare drum and cymbals.[23]   Seven years later and one province to the west the Calgary Citizens Band appears with over fifty members including a piccolo, two flutes, twelve clarinets, one bassoon and three saxophones (alto, tenor and baritone) as well as full brass choir.   Even the Native brass bands of British Columbia's First Nations were not immune. A photo of "Nelson's Cornet Band" of Port Simpson taken in 1910 [Fig. 5.4] clearly shows the presence of a piccolo, one Eb clarinet, two Bb clarinets and an alto saxophone.

By 1914 the evolution of the wind band in Canada was almost complete.   The Berlin [Kitchener] Musical Society Band and its conductor, J.Harry Stockton, posed that year for a photograph that illustrates this growth [Fig. 7.7].   The ensemble consists of one flute, one oboe, one bassoon, eleven Bb clarinets, one alto and one tenor saxophone, five cornets, four alto horns, five trombones, two baritones, two tubas and percussionists.   It is also worth noting the inclusion of melodic percussion instruments in the picture, orchestra bells and chimes.   Although many of the band's engagements would still have involved outdoor performances, the presence of these particular instruments suggests an increasing emphasis on the performance of concert repertoire.   Kitchener was a large, prosperous city with a rich European musical heritage.   Smaller centres would not have had its resources and so their own bands in all probability would not have been as large nor as well balanced.

In early August of that same year, Sir Edward Gray, the British Foreign Secretary noticed a London lamplighter lighting the city's streetlamps as evening fell.   Deeply troubled by recent events he made a poignant observation as impending disaster was about to engulf the world: "…the lights are going out all over Europe, we shall not see it again in our lifetime."[24]   On August 4, 1914, Great Britain, honouring an 1830 treaty guaranteeing the independence of Belgium, declared war on Germany.   Canada, as the oldest dominion in the empire rallied to the cause.   There was consequently a drastic reduction in community band activity until the end of the war.   In some cases, local bandsmen simply joined a nearby militia unit "en masse" and served out the war as a military band.   Others just ceased their activities as a result of losses suffered as men volunteered for active service.   Bands were not silent during the Great War, they continued to perform as much as ever except they did it in the army.

---

[23] Ed Wasiak, "Saskatchewan's First Bands: 1878-1913, Part 2" *Canadian Band Journal* 22, no. 2 (Winter 1997) 10.
[24] As cited in Conrad Black, *Rise to Greatness: The History of Canada from the Vikings to the Present* (Toronto: McClelland and Stewart, 2014) 466.

The Anglo-Canadian Leather Company Band

The year 1918 marked not only the end of "The War to End All Wars" but also the start of one of the most extraordinary chapters in the history of community wind bands in Canada. This was the story of the Anglo-Canadian Leather Company [ACLC] Band of Huntsville, Ontario. It all started in the 1890s with the arrival in Huntsville (population 2000) of American businessman Charles Orlando Shaw. He was owner of the Anglo-Canadian Leather Company, an enterprise that at one point became the largest shoe leather producer in the British Empire.[25] The company had recruited a number of experienced tannery workers from Italy. One of these, Vincenzo Grosso started an employees' band that rehearsed on Sunday afternoons. Shaw, an amateur cornet player, was so impressed with their enthusiasm and progress that he joined them and by 1914 "...the ensemble, known as the "Little Italian Band" was active and Shaw was supporting it financially in addition to providing rehearsal space and other resources."[26] The rehearsal space was a vacant schoolhouse that had been purchased and renovated expressly for that purpose with seating for up to seventy-five musicians as well as spectators. "Other resources" included uniforms and instruments for the men who couldn't afford them. Eager to improve the group's performance skills, Shaw hired Bracebridge, Ontario bandmaster George R. Simmons in 1915 and gave him considerable control in the selection and training of the band's personnel. Under Simmons' leadership the ensemble developed musically and grew from 33 to 50 musicians.

Shaw was prepared to invest whatever was needed to build the best band he could and so in order to move to the next level musically...

> [He] decided that a change in leadership was also in order. His first significant move was hiring Edmund A. Wall, who had recently retired as the solo clarinetist of the John Philip Sousa band, to train and rehearse the woodwinds and to perform with the ACLC Band.[27]

In early 1918, while in Chicago taking lessons from Herbert L. Clarke, who for years had been Sousa's solo cornetist and assistant conductor, Shaw convinced Clarke to accept

---

[25] Ed Terziano, ed. *The Little Town Band that Grew and Grew* (Huntsville, Ont.: Forester Press Ltd., 1986) 12.

[26] Joseph Resendes, "Herbert L. Clarke and the Anglo-Canadian Leather Company Band," *Canadian Winds* (Fall/Automne 2017) 37.

[27] Ibid.," 37.

the leadership of his band offering him a five-year contract paying an annual salary of $15,000.[28] [Fig. 7.8]   In addition to his own salary, Clarke was essentially given a blank cheque to further improve the band… "In his memoirs, H.L. Clarke records that he had literally 'Carte Blanche' from Mr. Shaw to get 'who you need and who you want'"[29] Musicians were employed by the tannery doing a wide range of jobs but were allocated two hours a day for individual practice as well as being given rent-free housing and access to a company store that sold the daily necessities at cost.[30]   In addition to personal practice time and weekly sectionals on company time the full band rehearsed twice weekly in the evenings.   Renamed the Anglo-Canadian Leather Company Band, their first performance under Clarke's baton took place "…on May 16, 1918 at the Susan Street bandstand in Huntsville, one month after his arrival."[31][Fig. 7.9]   By September of that year the band was invited to perform at the Canadian National Exhibition [CNE] in Toronto on the same stage as the famous Creatore Band of New York City.   Their debut was a resounding success and as a result "…the ACLC Band received more invitations to perform at the CNE between 1918 and 1926 than any other band.   By 1922, its CNE concerts were regularly broadcast over radio station CFCA in Toronto"[32]

Herbert L. Clarke left Huntsville and the ACLC Band at the end of his contract in 1923. By that time it had grown into a formidable concert ensemble of 69 pieces: 4 flutes/piccolos, 4 oboes, 1 English horn, 2 bassoons, 1 Eb clarinet, 15 Bb clarinets, 1 alto clarinet, 1 bass clarinet, 3 alto saxes, 2 tenor saxes, 1 baritone sax, 1 bass sax, 6 cornets, 4 trumpets, 6 alto horns, 5 trombones, 1 baritone, 1 euphonium, 5 tubas and percussion.[33] The leadership passed to Toronto musician Frank Welsman for two years and then to renowned cornetist Ernest Pechin for a year.   In 1926 C.O. Shaw decided to discontinue the band's operations citing the lack of time and other pressing business concerns.   In doing so he closed the door on what was recognized at the time as "…the finest industrial plant band in the world."[34]   The truth is the band had nowhere to go in a small remote community and there was increased pressure on its personnel as more and more musicians were being poached by lucrative performance opportunities in larger cities to the south.

---

[28] According to the website "Historicalstatistics.org," fifteen thousand Canadian dollars in 1918 were worth over CAD $137,000 in 2015. *Historical Statistics. Org* at www.historicalstatistics.org accessed 26 January 2019.
[29] Terziano, *Little Town Band*, 3.
[30] Resendes, "Herbert L. Clarke," 38.
[31] Ibid., 38.
[32] Ibid., 38.
[33] Ord Hume and Zealley, *Famous Bands*, 52.
[34] Alfred Zealley as cited in "Anglo-Canadian Leather Company Band," *Encyclopedia of Music in Canada* (Toronto: University of Toronto press, 1981) 21.

Despite its closure, the legacy of the ACLC band continued for many years. Former members such as clarinetist Joe Lomas, first Canadian member of Sousa's Band, moved to Brockville as bandmaster and then to the northern Ontario mining town of Timmins to conduct the McIntyre Mine Concert band. Others led bands in Windsor, Owen Sound, Oshawa, Woodstock and St. Catharines. A number of bandsmen including Clifford Guise, Bert Jones and Barrow Reg Sr. filled positions with the Toronto Symphony Orchestra. Many of the Americans hired by Clarke returned home, some to Sousa's touring band or to chairs with the Chicago Symphony, The Metropolitan Opera and the New York City Ballet.[35] As for Herbert L. Clarke, he wrote a march dedicated to the citizens of Long Beach, California entitled *Long Beach is Calling* (Carl Fischer, 1925) and it was there that he died on January 30, 1945.

If the period before the Great War was one of growth and standardization for community bands in Canada, especially in terms of instrumentation, the period between the wars (1918-1939) was one of consolidation and organization. Charles Frederick Thiele (1884-1954) arrived in Waterloo, Ontario, in 1919 to take up the position of conductor of the Waterloo Musical Society Band. He was an experienced musician and had previously held a similar post in Rumford, Maine, leading not only the town's adult senior band but separate boys' and girls' bands. Once established in Waterloo, he set a standard of excellence for himself and his musicians that by the 1930s demanded that members of the adult band rehearse twice weekly in the evenings and devote Sundays to sectional practices.[36] By 1929 the Waterloo Musical Society Band was presenting a series of radio broadcasts every Tuesday evening at 9 PM on CKCR radio Waterloo. The membership of the band was drawn from the finest musicians in the community which, like its sister city Kitchener, had a strong German heritage. In a photo taken in the 1932, on the occasion of the Society's fiftieth anniversary [Fig. 7.10], the band consisted of one flute, two bassoons, eleven clarinets, one bass clarinet, one alto and one tenor saxophone, four cornets, one alto horn, three French horns, five trombones, one baritone, two euphoniums, three tubas, one string bass and two percussionists. The highlight of the band's appearance at the 1949 Canadian Bandmasters Conference in Waterloo was a performance of Thiele's own arrangement of Beethoven's *Symphony No. 5* conducted by Sir Ernest MacMillan, the then music director of the Toronto Symphony Orchestra. By 1951 Thiele's health was failing and he left the podium to his handpicked successor Fred Roy. Over the thirty-two years of his tenure Thiele's perseverance and dedication to the Waterloo Musical Society

---

[35] Terziano, *Little Town Band*, 20.

[36] John Mellor, *C.F. Thiele: Father of Canadian Band Music* (Waterloo, Ont.: Melco History Series, 1988) 78.

Band had earned him the nickname of "The Professor" and more importantly had guaranteed the band a place in Ontario's community band "Triple Crown" along with the Belleville Kilties and the Anglo-Canadian Leather Company Band.

Thiele was much more than a fine conductor and inspired teacher. He was a tireless organizer and an entrepreneur with a keen eye for business opportunities. [Fig. 7.11] In 1921 he established the Waterloo Music Company and with its success he was able to sponsor a number of initiatives that had a profound effect on the growth of the Canadian band movement. Five years after his arrival in Canada "…he formed the Ontario Amateur Bands Association in 1924, was elected the first president by his peers, and continued to reign as president for the next twenty years."[37]   With Thiele's support the association agreed to conduct annual band competitions at the CNE in Toronto.

The Band Competitions

The CNE had introduced its "Music Day" in 1904 as a venue to introduce fairgoers to the finest wind bands in the world. From its inauguration until 1918 there was a succession of British military bands that included the Grenadier, Coldstream, Irish and Scots Guards Bands as well as two famous American groups, Creatore's Band and Pat Conway's Band. In 1918 the ACLC Band was invited to join the roster. The competitions themselves had only begun in 1921 and were limited to just '…military bands [who] played set pieces for adjudicators and were awarded prizes."[38]   As the reputation of the competitions spread it was later opened up to non-military entries. The CNE was a nationally respected venue that gave bandmasters and audiences alike an opportunity to hear, in addition to guest ensembles like the ACLC, some of the country's finest civilian and military bands.

Similar initiatives were taking place in Québec. In 1927 a band festival took place in the municipality of Grand'Mère [now part of Shawinigan] to celebrate the 50th anniversary of "L'Union Musicale de Trois-Rivières". The success of the event provided the momentum that led to the formation of "L'Association des fanfares amateurs de la province de Québec". The new group's first formal festival gathering was held in 1929 with six bands taking part "…celles de Trois-Rivières, Joliette, St. Jean, St. Hyacinthe, Drummondville et Sherbrooke."[39]   By 1931, bands from Granby, Valleyfield, and Shawinigan had joined and with the addition of "L'Union Musicale de Grand'Mère" in

---

[37] *The Canadian Bandmaster* (March 1954) as cited in Mellor, *C.F. Thiele*, 20.
[38] Jack Kopstein and Patricia Wardrop, "Band Festivals," *Encyclopedia*, 52.
[39] "Historique," *Fedération des Harmonies et Orchestres Symphoniques du Québec*, at www.fhosq.org accessed 27 January 2019.

1936, the association's membership had grown to ten. It has remained active since then and in 1978 was renamed La Fedération des Harmonies du Québec.[40] As with its Ontario counterpart, one of the core activities of its mandate was the support and promotion of band festivals.

Band festivals were not new. The first recorded one in Canada took place in Berlin [Kitchener] in 1877 and the following year one was held in Montréal with nineteen competitors. The Waterloo Musical Society sponsored a "...16 band tournament in 1885 and other Ontario cities held festivals in later years...it was not until 1921 that an organized band competition on a national level was begun."[41] This was at the CNE, which from 1921 to 1939, provided a competitive stage that exposed participants to the highest performance standards. In conjunction with adjudication at the competitions by some of the most respected figures in the field of wind band music, Toronto's annual fair served to significantly improve the levels of band performance throughout Central Canada.

As previously mentioned, Thiele had established the Waterloo Music Company in 1921 and it had proven to be enormously lucrative. He used the proceeds from his company to support many of his activities related to the promotion of bands and their music. In 1931 the Canadian Bandmasters Association [precursor of the Canadian Band Association] was formed with his financial and moral support. The following year on the occasion of the fiftieth anniversary of the formation of the Waterloo Musical Society Thiele established the Waterloo Music Festival.

> Twenty-three bands from all across the province of Ontario accepted Thiele's invitation to attend the Festival and compete in band contests in various categories. Captain Charles O'Neill, D. Mus., Bandmaster of the Royal 22nd regiment, Quebec, and the senior Bandmaster of the Canadian Permanent Forces, who had been the adjudicator of the Ontario Amateur Bands Association Concerts at the CNE Toronto, agreed to be the chief adjudicator.[42]

The Waterloo Music Festival was to continue with the exception of the war years until 1958. In 1949 it attracted thirty-two brass and reed bands as well as twenty-eight trumpet and bugle bands and eight Accordian bands. Over 20,000 spectators came to watch and hear the various performances. The following year highlights of the event were broadcast

---

[40] Ibid.
[41] Kopstein and Wardrop, "Band Festivals," 52.
[42] Mellor, *C.F. Thiele*, 47.

live, coast to coast, on the CBC's "Saturday Magazine."[43]   With Thiele's death in 1954, support for the Festival waned and it was finally abandoned by the Waterloo Music Company four years later.   Perhaps the best measure of Thiele's contribution to the growth of community bands was the support he was able to rally for an amendment to the Ontario Municipal Act of 1936 that allowed communities to levy a tax in order to finance the local band or musical society.   Known as the "Band Tax Law" and passed in 1937, this ensured that Ontario municipalities could use taxpayer dollars "…for the support and aid of a town's civilian band organization."[44]

Ontario and Québec may have been the epicenters of community band activity during the interwar years because they had the population bases but the rest of the country certainly wasn't idle.   As in Ontario, community bands elsewhere resumed their activities with even greater enthusiasm after the First World War.   One such example was to be found in Yorkton, Saskatchewan, where by December of 1919 there were already two community bands in operation.[45]   Many of the established bands returned to their prewar levels of activity and some types that had existed before the war with modest success suddenly flourished.   This latter scenario applied to bands sponsored by community-based businesses such as C.O. Shaw's Anglo-Canadian Leather Company.   Public utilities as well as private companies supported bands with two examples being the Toronto Transit Commission Band and the Vancouver Parks Board Band in the 1920s.[46]

Community band activity in western Canada's larger centres was equally intense.   In 1930, Calgary had a population of only 85,000 yet it was home to at least four civilian bands.   The Calgary Elks Concert Band was formed in 1921 by Fred Bagley, former NWMP bandmaster at Fort Calgary while a second band, the Temple Concert Band wore three different uniforms and performed under three different names one of which was the "Cowboy Band".   The field was completed with the Maple Leaf Band and the Calgary Premier Band.[47]   To the west Vancouver could also claim a minimum of four active community bands.   By 1932 these included the Fire Department Band, the Greater Vancouver Concert Band, the Home Gas Band and the Musicians Union Band.[48]

---

[43] Ibid., 113.

[44] Government of Ontario, "Section 405, Sub-section 65, The Municipal Act, Chap. 266, R.S.O. 1937" as cited in Mellor, *C.F. Thiele*, 60.

[45] Kerry Linsley, "Yorkton and District Band Programme," *Canadian Winds* 4, no. 1 (Fall/Automne 2005) 6.

[46] Kallman, Kopstein and Wardrop, "Bands," *Encyclopedia* 58.

[47] Norman Draper, *Bands by the Bow: A History of Band Music in Calgary* (Calgary: Century Calgary Publications, 1975) 45-47.

[48] McIntosh, *History of Music in British Columbia*, 59.

Industrial bands continued to perform across the country but thanks to Dale McIntosh's *History of Music in British Columbia* 1850-1950 (Victoria, B.C.: Sono Nis Press, 1989) their activities are perhaps best documented in British Columbia. It was in the province's mining sector where town and industrial bands were most popular. From Ladysmith and Nanaimo on Vancouver Island to Fernie, Michel and Natal in the Crowsnest Pass region near the Alberta border, miners' bands were the predominant form of large instrumental music making in their respective communities. The first band in the town of Trail, near the United States border, was formed in 1897 and it continued as a community supported group until 1920 when sponsorship passed to the local Elks Lodge. In 1928 the newly appointed conductor William Donnelly "...convinced the Consolidated Mining and Smelting Company [now Teck Cominco] that it would be of benefit both to the company and the community if, when hiring new staff, preference would be given to musicians who could play with the band."[49] For eight years Donnelly worked with the band until his resignation in 1936. Its reputation was such that "...an advertisement for a new director brought forth 214 applications."[50] Not only did the mine support its own band, the town's Italian community had also formed a band known as the Italian Band or the Colombo Band after its association with the Cristoforo Colombo Lodge. By 1917 this group had renamed itself the "Trail Maple Leaf Band" and as it grew so did its popularity. In the 1930s it regularly accepted out of town engagements in Spokane and Kelowna as well as Vancouver in 1936.[51]

The two small mining communities of Michel and Natal [near the present-day community of Sparwood] formed a co-operative band in the early 1920s that in 1925 took first prize at the Calgary Stampede. A photograph of the band taken after the win shows an ensemble of five clarinets, two alto saxophones, five cornets, four alto horns, two trombones, three baritones, basses and percussion.[52] The communities that were home to these ensembles were not large yet the pride evident in belonging to the local band was tangible and universal. Across the country, mining centres like Thetford Mines, Asbestos and Arvida in Québec, Timmons and Sudbury in Ontario and many others across the west could all lay claim to their own wind bands.

The vast majority of community bands studied in previous pages were amateur ensembles. Some were not. One of the best known of these professional groups was the

---

[49] Ibid., 37.
[50] Ibid., 37.
[51] Steve Guidone, *Trail Maple Leaf Band 90th Anniversary Photo Album 1917-2007* (Salmon Arm, B.C.: Steve Guidone, 2007) 6.
[52] McIntosh, *History of Music in British Columbia*, 43.

Toronto Symphony Band. It was formed in 1915 for the express purpose of providing summer employment for members of the Toronto Symphony Orchestra and local theatre orchestras. The band was a regular performer "…at the CNE, Hanlan's Point Park, and Scarborough Beach Park and each Spring at the Toronto Skating Club carnivals."[53] After the TSO became a full time orchestra the group lost many of its original members but still managed to perform "… in the Toronto area, and during the early years of World War II made over a 100 broadcasts for the CBC."[54] The ensemble continued to play through the 1950s but with the death of its founder and co-president R.L. Jose, it was forced to cease operations.

The Ladies' Bands

The First World War set in motion profound changes in Canadian society, especially with respect to the participation of women in the workforce. During the war, with so many men overseas, there was a desperate need to fill working positions, particularly in the munitions and defence industries. Women filled these roles and started the wheels moving on movements that would eventually lead to the vote, equal property rights and much later, the lifting on all restrictions on their employment in the Canadian workplace. Much the same held true for the nation's bands. As noted earlier the membership of most community and all militia bands prior to August of 1914 was exclusively male. With the start of the Great War that too began to change.

Rouleau, Saskatchewan is a prairie community not far from Regina. It was there in 1916 that Andrew King, a successful local printer and businessman, formed the Rouleau Ladies Band. King had apprenticed in Winnipeg and while there played slide trombone in a local band. He moved to Rouleau in 1909 and the following year started the Rouleau Citizens Band.[55] Like so many community bands across the country, the onset of hostilities in 1914 forced it to end its activities. Undeterred, King sought out women in the town to form a band and they began practicing together in 1916. [Fig. 7.12] The group made its debut concert appearance the following year and within five years was winning awards in the Military Band Class "B" competitions at the Saskatchewan Music Festival in Regina. The Rouleau Ladies Band had the distinction of being one of the first ladies' bands in Western Canada and it travelled extensively throughout the south of the province performing at both Regina and Moose Jaw fairs. They had the use of a Pullman rail car,

---

[53] Nancy McGregor, "Toronto Symphony Band," Encyclopedia, 927.
[54] Ibid., 927
[55] Jessie King McBain, daughter of Andrew King, interview by author, Calgary, AB, 11 October 2006.

donated by the Canadian Pacific Railway, which was attached to passenger or freight trains as they passed through the small agricultural town of 1100 people.[56]   When at home the band rehearsed in the town hall and would perform on Saturdays at the indoor rink.   Its membership was drawn primarily from married women in the community, both housewives and those who worked outside the home, ranging in age from their 20s to middle age.   By the early 1920s, the men had returned, life was back to normal and the Rouleau Ladies Band ceased to exist.   Its legacy lived on however in the many friendships formed and its ground-breaking contribution to the expansion of the Canadian wind band movement.[57]

In 1925, George Ziegler (1889-1981), conductor of the Kitchener Musical Society Band, the Scots Fusiliers Band of Canada and director of the Kitchener Conservatory of Music "…conceived the idea of forming a ladies' band, most of whose early members had learned their instrumental skills at the Conservatory."[58]   The ensemble eventually became the world's largest ladies' band at the time with a membership at its peak of ninety-four musicians.   A photograph of the group in its first year shows an instrumentation of one flute, thirteen clarinets, two alto and two tenor saxophones, eight cornets, four alto horns, two trombones, two baritones, two tubas and percussion.   The Kitchener Ladies Band appeared in both Canada and the United States and won great acclaim for its performances. It was forced to abandon its activities during the depression years but "…during its existence had received no less than 100 invitations to play."[59]

From Nova Scotia to Vancouver Island, community bands flourished during the first half of the twentieth century.   This chapter has focused largely on the superstars and the trailblazers of the period for the simple reason that their activities were so well documented. Without photographs or contemporary newspaper accounts there is little record of the existence of town bands and the place of honour they held in the communities they once called home.   Further compounding the problem is the passage of time as many of the local newspapers that witnessed the events of the day have ceased to exist as have, in some cases, the communities they served.

---

[56] Ernest Deane Charles, telephone interview by author, 29 March 2003.   "Deane", the author's uncle, was born in Rouleau in 1922 and lived there until he joined the Navy in WWII.

[57] Jessie King McBain, Interview.   In Fig. 7.12, the cornet player in the front row, second from the right is the author's paternal grandmother.

[58] Sybil Carol Crawford, "George Henry Ziegler (1889-1981)," *Waterloo Historical Society Journal* 76 (1988)72.   Although the term "ladies" generally refers to adults, there is no specific reference in the works reviewed as to the actual ages of the participants.   It is entirely possible the "Ladies' Bands" may have been girls' bands or some combination of adults and young people.

[59] Ibid., 73.

CHAPTER SEVEN GALLERY

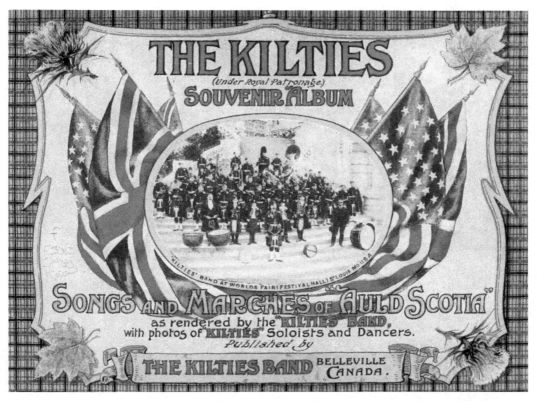

Figure 7.1. Front Cover of Belleville Kilties Souvenir Album, Belleville, c.1910.   Source: Glanmore House National Historic Site, Belleville, Ontario.

Figure 7.2.   The Belleville Kilties, undated photograph. Source: Carl V. Ehrke, Belleville.

Figure 7.3. The Chatham (Ontario) Kilties Band, 1930s. Formed in 1927, it was one of the more successful "Kiltie" Bands inspired by the renowned Belleville Kiltie Band. Bandmaster Sidney Chamberlain. Source: Waterloo Music Company.

Figure 7.4. L'Union Musicale de Trois-Rivières, 1908. Many community bands in Québec were known as "Unions Musicales", they were widespread throughout the province and equally popular as their counterparts in English Canada. Source: Wikimedia Commons.

Figure 7.5. The Thorold Town Band c. 1900.   Source: Brian Williamson

Figure 7.6. Le Cercle Philharmonique de Saint-Jean-sur-Richelieu, c.1910.   This group, along with the Thorold Town Band [Fig. 7.5] and the Perth Citizens Band are amongst the oldest continually active community bands in Canada, tracing their origins back to the early 1850s. Source: "Histoire 1900-1910", at www.cercle-philharmonique-de-st-jean.org

Figure 7.7. The Berlin Musical Society Band, 1914. Conductor J. Harry Stockton. The city changed its name to Kitchener in 1916 in response to growing anti-German sentiment during World War One. Source: Kitchener Musical Society.

Figure 7.8. Charles Orlando Shaw (Right) and Herbert L. Clarke, 1918-1923. Clarke, Sousa's former assistant director of music was considered to be the finest North American cornet virtuoso of his generation. In 1918, while taking lessons in Chicago, Shaw lured Clarke north to Huntsville to conduct his company band for five years. It was Shaw's financial sponsorship, which essentially included giving Clarke a blank cheque to hire whoever he wanted, that helped make the Anglo-Canadian Leather Company Band one of the finest industrial plant bands in the world. Shaw continued to support the group for three years after Clarke's departure in 1923, but in 1926, citing business concerns, he terminated the band's operations. Source: Huntsville Public Library.

Figure 7.9. The Anglo-Canadian Leather Company Band at the Susan Street bandstand, Huntsville, Ontario, c. 1918. Herbert L. Clarke, conductor. By 1923 the band had a membership of sixty-nine carefully selected musicians. Source: Huntsville Public Library.

Figure 7.10. The Waterloo Musical Society Band, 1932. Charles F. Thiele, conductor, seated in front row centre. This photo was taken on the occasion of the Society's fiftieth anniversary. Source: Waterloo Public Library.

Figure 7.11 Charles Frederick Thiele (1884-1954). Conductor, composer, arranger, astute businessman and tireless advocate on behalf of the Canadian band movement. He used his considerable fortune from the operations of the Waterloo Music Company to support the creation of the Canadian Bandmasters Association in 1931 (parent of today's CBA) and lobbied extensively for both regional festivals and the CNE's annual music days competitions. Affectionately known as the "Professor", he had an enormous influence on the subsequent generation of Canadian band directors who led this country into the immediate postwar period. Source: Waterloo Public Library

Figure 7.12. The Rouleau (Sask.) Ladies Band, 1917. Conductor Andrew King. King started the band in 1916 and by 1917 it was travelling to regional fairs and exhibitions in Moose Jaw and Regina using a Pullman rail car donated by the Canadian Pacific Railway. At the time, Rouleau was a small town of less than 1,100 people yet the group was one of the first Ladies' Bands in western Canada. The author's paternal grandmother is seated in the cornet section, second from the right, front row. Image courtesy of Peel's Prairie Provinces, a digital initiative of the University of Alberta Libraries.

CHAPTER EIGHT

THE MILITARY BANDS: BUILDING THE FUTURE

The 1899 decision to authorize Joseph Vézina's "B" Battery Band as a permanent [regular] force unit was assurance of stable funding from National Militia headquarters. The band was certainly a beneficiary as a comparison of two photos of the group, one taken in 1892 [Fig. 4.2] and a second taken in 1901, [Fig. 6.4] clearly shows. Total band strength in the earlier image is twenty-three. In the second photograph it has grown to thirty-three consisting of one piccolo, one bassoon, one Eb clarinet, eight Bb clarinets, one alto clarinet, one bass clarinet, one alto saxophone, two French horns, either two alto horns or flugelhorns, four cornets, three trombones, one baritone, one euphonium, two tubas and three percussion. The army must have considered the experiment a success because in 1905 two more permanent force bands were created, the "A" Battery Band in Kingston and the Royal Canadian Regiment Band in Halifax. Unlike the Québec model however, where leadership was given to the veteran French-Canadian Joseph Vézina, the positions of bandmaster for both newly formed groups in English Canada were granted to former British Army bandmasters.

Although there were militia bands elsewhere in the country that were equal to and in some cases much better than the first full time military bands, the permanent force bands provided the environment necessary for the development of a succession of outstanding Canadian band composers and directors that lasted for over a century. Whereas the size, skill and proficiency of the militia bands depended largely on the enthusiasm and talent of their respective directors, as well as the support and financial largesse of their militia unit's officers, permanent force bands were limited by the authorized number of paid positions. Kingston's Royal Canadian Horse Artillery Band in 1910 [formerly the "A" Battery Band], was modelled on the British regimental "line" band of the period consisting of twenty-four musicians and a bandmaster. It included full brass choir plus one flute/piccolo, an oboe, bassoon, Eb and Bb clarinets, two saxophones and percussion.[1] [Fig. 8.1]

The effect of the Boer [South African] War (1899-1902) on the growth of military bands was profound and far reaching. For the first time Canada supported one of the Empire's colonial wars as a quasi-independent ally. Over eight thousand Canadians eventually

---

[1] "R.C.H.A. Band 1905-1968" *The Canadian Gunner* (Shilo, MB: The Royal Canadian School of Artillery, 1968) 45. A "line" band refers to a band attached to a regiment of the line. Infantry regiments in the British Army were ranked in order of precedence with the oldest and most prestigious (and wealthiest) at the head of the line. Regiments further down the list were known as "line" regiments.

served in the conflict and distinguished themselves not just as subjects of the crown but as Canadians. This was a tremendous source of national pride and in conjunction with concerns over Theodore Roosevelt's aggressive continentalism to the south, found:

> …a popular expression in the rapid spread of the Canadian Clubs and the beginning of the use of "O Canada" as a national anthem in English Canada [an unofficial anthem since *God Save the Queen* was our official anthem until July 1, 1980]. Here was the beginning of a national sentiment, not exclusively French, nor exclusively British, but indigenous to the land and history of Canada.[2]

One of the immediate effects of this patriotic fervour was an increase in authorized militia strengths and the formation of new units across the country. Included with the expansion was an increase in the number of authorized bands. In addition to the already large numbers of militia bands in the major urban centres of Eastern Canada, new bands were formed across the West. One example of these, formed in 1907, was the Band of the Lake Superior Scottish Regiment of Port Arthur [renamed Thunder Bay in 1970].[3]

Perhaps the most interesting example of the importance attached to the role of militia bands as an instrument of government policy was the establishment of the Band of the 103rd Rifles Regiment in Calgary in 1910. The militia, especially in Western Canada, was seen as a cost-effective way of reinforcing the dominant role of Anglo-Saxon culture in a region that was experiencing heavy immigration from both Eastern Europe and the United States. Four days after the regiment's authorization was confirmed, the Band of the 103rd Rifles, under the direction of A.L. Augade, performed its first concert, complete with instruments, music, uniforms and fully rehearsed musicians.[4] In British Columbia, by 1912, there were at least eight militia bands in existence in communities as diverse as Victoria and Nelson.[5]

The instrumentation of early twentieth century militia bands had been more or less standardized by the beginning of the century. The British line band of twenty-four that had been the basis for the first permanent force Canadian bands was the general rule. There was certainly some flexibility and the photographic record supports the contention that

---

[2] W.L. Morton, *The Kingdom of Canada: A General History from Earliest Times*, 2nd ed. (Toronto: McClelland and Stewart Limited, 1969) 399.

[3] Philip M. Wults, Jean Brittal and Glen B. Carruthers, "Music in Thunder Bay", the *Canadian Encyclopedia* at www.thecanadianencyclopedia.ca accessed 03 February 2019.

[4] A. Judsen, curator KOCR [successor unit to the 103rd] Museum, interview by the author, Calgary, AB, 01 February 2003.

[5] Dale McIntosh, *A History of Music in British Columbia 1850-1950* (Victoria: Sono Nis Press, 1989) 50-61.

local conditions as well as the stature of the bandmaster affected the final result. Well established bands such as George Robinson's 13th Battalion Band of Hamilton had an effective strength in 1901 of thirty-seven musicians including double reeds and saxophones. [Fig. 3.1] In Berlin, Ontario, where the local German speaking community possessed a strong musical tradition, the 29th Regiment Band of 1903 could boast a similar instrumentation [Fig. 8.2]. Even on the sparsely populated prairies, Calgary's 15th Light Horse Band in 1905 consisted of twenty-two members including a string bass. Two years later the same band had grown to over thirty-five in preparation for its upcoming tour of the British Isles.[6]

World War I (1914-1918)

With the declaration of war on August 4, 1914, young Canadian men flocked to the army's recruitment centres. The growth of the Canadian Army during the first four months of the "Great War" was matched by the growth in the number of bands. "Although the war establishment had no provision for regimental bands, many of the units formed their own bands."[7] By November, three months after the start of the war, the minister of militia and defence, Sam Hughes, granted the option to each CEF [Canadian Expeditionary Force] battalion to enlist one bandmaster and twenty-four musicians for overseas service. It appears that the option was exercised by many units. The importance of the bands to the war effort was probably best reflected in a letter from the Commanding Officer of Military District No. 3 in Kingston to Captain Light, bandmaster of the permanent force Royal Canadian Horse Artillery Band. Captain Light had written his superior to inform him that several of the musicians in the band had applied to serve overseas on the firing lines. The response was an emphatic "no" on the grounds that their service as musicians was much too valuable:

> You will kindly point out to these men that their patriotism in volunteering for active service has been noted and is much appreciated. The authorities, however, consider their services are of more value in their present appointments. It has

---

[6] Norman Draper, *Bands by the Bow: A History of Band Music in Calgary* (Calgary: Century Calgary Publications, 1975) 10-11.
[7] Jac Kopstein and Ian Pearson, *The Heritage of Canadian Military* Music (St. Catharines, ON: Vanwell Publishing Limited, 2002) 43.

been estimated that one hundred men have been enlisted for, and through the music of, each bandsman retained at home.[8]

The total number of bands serving with the Canadian Army during the First World War is difficult to determine with any accuracy because of the existence of unofficial bands alongside those recognized by the Department of Militia and Defence. The issue is further complicated by the many types of bands that were in operation. Contemporary records often fail to identify what kind of band was attached to each unit. The wind band familiar to most readers was just one of many. There were also bugle bands, pipe bands and brass bands. The exact number is therefore the subject of some speculation but by examining the records of just one training camp we can get some idea of the importance attached to the role of bands.

In the Spring of 1916, the Dominion government purchased a large tract of land near Barrie, Ontario, and named it Camp Borden after the prime minister of the day, Sir Robert Borden. Within months there were over forty thousand soldiers under training in the area. On August 16, 1916, a local newspaper, the *Orillia Packet* described the first tattoo [military ceremony often associated with sunset] held at the camp. Of particular interest was the description of the individual entries of twenty-eight regimental bands. The article goes on to describe the massed performances of *O Canada*, *We'll Never Let the Old Flag Fall* and *Keep the Home Fires Burning*. At the conclusion of the ceremony the massed bands accompanied the troops on parade with the evening hymn *Abide with Me*.[9] Those same massed bands would appear one more time later that month at the CNE [Fig. 8.3]. The musical director at Camp Borden during the war years was Captain John Slatter who, prior to the start of hostilities, been the director of Toronto's 48th Highlanders Band. By 1918 he had helped train sixty-three bands at the Camp and was awarded the Order of the British Empire for his service. Considering that Camp Borden was just one of several such facilities across the country, the scale of the commitment to the maintenance of military bands becomes apparent.

The many surviving photographs of CEF battalion bands show that the total number of bands grew as well as the number of musicians in each band. Of the fifteen World War One battalion brass-reed bands pictured in Kopstein and Pearson's *The Heritage of Canadian Military Music* (St. Catharines, ON: Vanwell Publishing Limited, 2002), over half exceed the regimental standard of twenty-four musicians, in some cases by as much

---

[8] Ibid., 43.
[9] Ibid., 47.

as fifteen men.   When the bands finally did arrive overseas, they confined their music making to places behind the front lines [Fig. 8.4].   The number of concerts and parades must have still been considerable in view of the fact that almost every one of the 260 or more CEF battalions had some kind of band [Fig. 8.5].   These performances consisted primarily of playing troops in and out of the trenches, giving concerts and occasionally going on tour.   In the trenches they fulfilled secondary roles as stretcher bearers.[10]

The Interwar Years (1919-1939)

With the end of hostilities on November 11, 1918, the Canadian Army gradually reverted to its peacetime status.   There were massive cuts in defence spending and for the next twenty years, military bands, both regular and reserve, existed on shoestring budgets. By 1922 there were only four full time regular force bands left.   These were the RCHA [Royal Canadian Horse Artillery] Band in Kingston, the RCR [Royal Canadian Regiment] Band, formed in Halifax but relocated to London, Ontario, the PPCLI [Princess Patricia's Canadian Light Infantry] Band in Winnipeg and the R22eR [Royal 22nd Regiment] Band, formerly known as the "B" Battery Band, in Québec City.   In the climate of financial restraint of the time, the success of each ensemble was largely determined, as in the militia, by its director of music.   The PPCLI and R22eR Bands were fortunate in having, in their respective leaders, Captains Tommy James and Charles O'Neill, men with exceptional musical and leadership skills.   As a result, the two bands flourished.   The PPCLI Band performed at the British Empire Games in 1924 at Wembley Stadium and "…gave a series of sold out concerts at various theatres and a broadcast from Savoy Hill Radio Station."[11] Back home, the band maintained a busy schedule of concerts and tours through the Prairie provinces and the American Midwest until the effects of the Great Depression prompted locals of the American Federation of Musicians to complain to Army Headquarters in Ottawa.   In 1932, members of the Saskatoon Musicians Association claimed that free concerts by regular force bands constituted an unfair denial of employment to professional civilian musicians.   Army Headquarters agreed and regulations were drafted that limited the numbers and types of engagements that could be performed by full time army bands.[12]

---

[10] Canada, Department of National Defence, *Report No. 47 History of Bands in the Canadian Army* (Ottawa: National Defence Headquarters, 1952) 9.

[11] Kopstein and Pearson*, Heritage*, 62.

[12] Ibid., 62.   The claim that military bands deny local civilian musicians employment has persisted to the present day and has often been a source of friction between AFM [American Federation of Musicians] locals and both regular force and reserve military bands.   It usually occurs when bands are requested to

Despite these restrictions the PPCLI Band continued to be active through the 1930s. In 1933, it performed sixty-four concerts and three parades in and around Winnipeg. Of these, only six involved any type of remuneration.[13] Not included in that number were engagements of a military nature such as regimental parades and mess dinners.

[Author's note: for readers with no military experience, mess dinners, also known as regimental dinners, are a military tradition whose origins date back to the late eighteenth and early nineteenth centuries. As previously noted in Chapter Three, officers in the British Army were drawn almost exclusively from the wealthy leisure classes. When posted overseas they sought to replicate their privileged lifestyles in the farthest corners of the Empire. This included lavish formal dinners in their living quarters which were called "messes". The presence of the regimental band playing live background music further contributed to an atmosphere of refined gentility. Times have changed and so have mess dinners. They are now generally held only on special occasions such as regimental birthdays, in recognition of promotions, postings or retirements and mess members pay the full cost of the meal. Through the years the tradition has persisted because it fosters "esprit de corps" and group cohesion. These are qualities that though intangible in nature have proven time and time again to dramatically improve military effectiveness. The presence of a military band further permits the continuation of another custom associated with the mess dinner; the playing of regimental and branch marches. At the conclusion of the dinner, after the toast to the Sovereign, the band plays the regimental/branch marches of the diners present. There is a great deal of unit pride attached to these marches and members of that unit are expected to stand while it is being played. Some regimental marches, such as those of the PPCLI and RCR also have lyrics and it is not uncommon for officers of those units to sing along. In Canadian Army mess dinners, both regular and reserve, where guests may come from many regiments and sub-units, each with its own regimental march, there can sometimes be a succession of twenty or more marches. In cases like this, the band will often play only one phrase of each march.]

Towards the end of the decade however, the PPCLI Band found itself in a position of being unable to recruit suitable musician candidates. Low pay and the prohibition on payment from private engagements were often cited as the primary causes.[14] The other two full time bands in English Canada were facing similar problems. The RCHA Band in Kingston and the RCR Band, which had been relocated to London, Ontario, after the First

---

play in support of or on the property of commercial ventures, city parks, malls, etc., where, as the argument goes, the sponsor could pay a civilian band.

[13] Canada, Department of National Defence, *Report No. 47*, Appendix "C".

[14] Canada, Department of National Defence, *Report No. 47*, Appendix "B".

World War, were both operating below strength. A "…1938 RCR Band photograph taken in Wolseley Barracks [London] shows a band of eighteen on parade."[15]

The "B" Battery Band in Québec City had been under the direction of Captain Charles O'Neill since Joseph Vézina's retirement on January 1, 1912. O'Neill, the first Canadian Army musician to be sent to and graduate from the Kneller Hall bandmasters' course was a superb musician and skilled composer who completed a Doctorate in Music from McGill University in 1924 while still on active service [Fig. 8.6]. After the band had been renamed the Band of the Royal 22nd Regiment in 1922, he managed to persuade his superiors to maintain its paid establishment at thirty-five musicians despite budgetary cutbacks nationally. This left him with an instrumentation of one flute, one oboe, one bassoon, one Eb clarinet, ten Bb clarinets, two saxophones, three horns, three cornets, two trumpets, three trombones, two euphoniums, two tubas, one string bass and two percussionists.[16] With this ensemble he attained a popularity in the province that was the envy of military bands across the country "…it appeared frequently in Québec City and Montréal…at the CNE in Toronto in 1927 and in a tattoo with the RCR and RCHA in 1930."[17] The pinnacle of Charles O'Neill's military career and the high point for the Canadian Army's full time bands during the Depression years came in 1937 when he was selected to lead a composite group of thirty-five musicians to represent Canada at the coronation ceremonies for King George VI in London [Fig. 8.7]. Just prior to its departure for England, this specially chosen ensemble performed a charity concert at Québec City's Capitol Theatre on April 21, 1937. The programme was significant in that it included two of O'Neill's own compositions for band: his folk medley *Souvenir de Québec* and the overture *Builders of Youth*.[18]

The militia, like the permanent force, suffered severe shortages between the wars due to lack of funding. Militia bands however, especially those with well-established community bases managed to thrive. Because militia bands were part-time organizations, restrictions on the total number of musicians in each group could and were regularly circumvented. The fact that these groups often performed as civilian bands was a further

---

[15] Kopstein and Pearson, *Heritage*, 76.
[16] Ibid., 66.
[17] Ibid., 66.
[18] Jack Kopstein, *When the Band Begins to Play: A History of Military Music in Canada* (Kingston: Apple jack Publishers, 1992) 117. It is interesting to speculate whether O'Neill was trying to make a musical statement or not. After his retirement from the army in 1937 he began a second career as professor of composition at the State Teachers College in Potsdam, N.Y. *Souvenir de Québec* may have been a fond look back at his long association with the Québec based R22eR Band whereas *Builders of Youth* was a glance forward to his future in academia.

incentive to professional musicians from the local area to join the militia. Consequently, some militia bands were much larger and better equipped than their permanent force counterparts. By 1928, there were 125 authorized bands in the Non-Permanent Active Militia [part-time militia], mostly in the infantry battalions.[19] Although they were active in every province, the best known were to be found in the major urban centres of Toronto and Montréal. As before the war, the key to their success was often their respective directors of music, whose reputations attracted the finest musicians in the community.

Toronto was home to at least three outstanding militia bands during the twenties and thirties: The Royal Regiment of Canada Band, The Queen's Own Rifles Band and the Band of the 48th Highlanders. The first of these, the "Royals" as they were affectionately known, was under the direction of Walter M. Murdoch.

> Under his outstanding leadership the strength of the band increased to sixty men, and their musical proficiency was such that the unit won the Dominion Championship for Class A Bands in the annual challenge competition at the Canadian National Exhibition. The 1926 triumph was duplicated in 27, 28, 29, 30 and 31, until at last the contest was abandoned for want of competitors.[20]

For the remainder of the 1930s the band performed for a wide variety of civic functions including the opening of Maple Leaf Gardens in 1933 and the centenary celebrations of the incorporation of the City of Toronto. In 1939 it was asked to provide the music for the official reception of King George VI and Queen Elizabeth in Toronto.

The Band of the Queen's Own Rifles, which like the "Royals" was one of Canada's oldest militia bands, enjoyed critical success through much of the 1920s thanks to the efforts of its director Captain R. B. Hayward. Like so many of his contemporaries, he had had a successful career as a bandmaster in the British Army prior to emigrating to Canada. After settling in Toronto, he accepted the position of supervisor of wind instrument instruction at the Toronto Conservatory of Music in addition to his responsibilities with the militia [Fig. 8.8]. A photograph of the band published by Boosey and Company in 1924 showed an instrumentation of one flute, ten clarinets, two saxophones, one bass clarinet, four horns, four cornets, four trombones, two euphoniums, four tubas and three percussionists. R.B. Hayward retired from the militia in 1928 and was succeeded by

---

[19] Canada, Department of National Defence, *Report No. 47*, 9
[20] D.J. Goodspeed, *A History of the Royal Regiment of Canada: 1862-1979*. 2nd ed. (Toronto: Royal Regiment of Canada Association, 1979) 627.

another former British Army bandmaster, James J. Buckle.[21]   Leaving the army gave Hayward the freedom to concentrate on his new role as conductor of the Toronto Concert Band until 1939 as well as support the creation of organizations devoted to advocating for the wind band movement.

Perhaps the best known and certainly the most widely traveled of the Toronto militia bands in the period between the wars was the Band of the 48th Highlanders under the baton of Captain John Slatter.   Framed by performances for royal visits in 1919 and 1939, the band toured extensively in both Canada and the United States.   Slatter had been Director of Music since 1896 and was the dean of Canadian militia bandmasters after the retirement of Hamilton's George Robinson in 1917.   He had been supervisor of Canadian Army bands in World War I and was, along with C.F. Thiele, one of the driving forces behind the creation of the Canadian Bandmasters Association [parent to the Canadian Band Association] in 1931 [Fig. 8.9].   A tireless promoter of not just military bands, he was honoured by being elected the first president of the association he helped create.   His support for the establishment of the Toronto Cadet Band, one of the country's earliest non-religious school band programs made him one of the most influential band directors of his generation.[22]   With Slatter at its head, the 48th was a magnet for many of Toronto's best musicians.   A photograph of the ensemble taken in 1924 shows a group of forty-six musicians including four tubas, three euphoniums, six trombones, four horns, seven cornets, two trumpets, woodwinds and percussion [Fig. 8.10].

Militia bands in Montréal were in some ways even more successful.   Since the days of the British regimental bands in the previous century, Montrealers had acquired a taste for bands and their music.   The late nineteenth century community bands had been closely affiliated with the city's militia units and as noted previously, were often the "de facto" regimental band.   By the 1920s that had begun to change and the distinction between civilian and military ensembles was being more clearly drawn.   Units such as the Royal Highlanders of Canada, originally formed in 1862 as the 5th Battalion Volunteer Militia Rifles had acquired their own bands.   By the 1930s the unit had been renamed the Royal Highland Regiment of Canada (The Black Watch).   Its band was one of several in the city and in the late 1940s, the first trumpet chair was held by a young prodigy from Verdun by the name of Maynard Ferguson.[23]   Ferguson would go on to become one of North

---

[21] Kopstein and Pearson, *Heritage*, 70.
[22] Jack Kopstein, "Slatter, John," *Encyclopedia of Music in Canada* (Toronto: University of Toronto Press, 1981) 874.
[23] The Black Watch Band (Militia) ceased operations in the 1950s after the regiment was put on active service.   Its music library eventually found its way to the HMCS York Band library in Toronto.   It was

America's jazz greats.   Another successful militia band was that of the Fusiliers Mont Royal under the direction of J.J. Goulet, one-time concertmaster and conductor of the MSO [Montreal Symphony Orchestra].   Proficient as these and other groups were however, they were completely overshadowed by the Band of the Canadian Grenadier Guards.

In 1913, General F.S. Meighan, a wealthy railroad businessman and music lover, offered Jean Josephat Gagnier the position of Director of Music of the Canadian Grenadier Guards Band.   At the age of twenty-eight, when he accepted the commission, Gagnier had already established himself as one of Montréal's brightest musical stars.   He had played clarinet in silent movie theatres, bassoon in both the MSO and the Montreal Opera Orchestra as well as conducting local choirs and bands [Fig. 8.11].   The association between Gagnier and the Canadian Grenadier Guards Band lasted from 1913 until 1947 and during his tenure as leader, the ensemble became the "crown jewel" of Canadian militia bands.[24]   Originally intended to provide music of a martial nature for the regiment, under Gagnier's baton the group rapidly established itself as one of the country's premier concert organizations.   With the continued financial support of F.S. Meighan, the band performed regularly with acclaimed Canadian and foreign solo artists.   Radio broadcasts "…were relayed nationally…and several of those made in 1931 were heard in the U.S. as well, on the CBS and NBC networks."[25]   Like the Band of the 48th Highlanders in Toronto, the Canadian Grenadier Guards Band was comprised of some of Montréal's finest musicians. At any given time, over half of its membership earned their livelihoods in the practice of music.   A photo of the band taken between the wars [Fig. 8.12] affirms its concert nature. The ensemble numbers forty-two musicians: two flutes, one oboe, one bassoon, ten clarinets, one alto and one bass clarinet, three saxophones, six trumpets, four horns, four trombones, two euphoniums, three tubas, one string bass and three percussion.   Manuscript copies of compositions for the band written by Gagnier himself and now held at the "Bibliothèque nationale du Québec" in Montréal clearly indicate that he had at his disposal a wind ensemble of exceptionally skilled musicians.

In Ottawa, military music was provided by the Band of the Governor General's Foot Guards.   By 1922, the band had begun to return to its prewar strength and had resumed many of its former activities.   The untimely death of its long serving Director of Music, Captain Joseph Brown in 1923, led to the appointment of his son, Joseph Thomas Brown

---

here that the author discovered a medley entitled *Pleasant Recollections* (New York: Carl Fischer, 1935). Handwritten on a copy of the Solo/1st Cornet part were the words "property of Maynard Ferguson".

[24] Gabrielle Bourbonnais, "Notes Biographiques", *Inventaire Sommaire du Fonds J.J. Gagnier* (Montréal : Bibliothèque nationale du Québec, 1989) 11.

[25] Hélène Plouffe, "Canadian Grenadier Guards Band," *Encyclopedia of Music in Canada* (Toronto: University of Toronto Press, 1981) 145.

as bandmaster the following year. Under his leadership the band appeared in the United States on several occasions and performed regularly in ceremonies of state held at Rideau Hall [official residence of the Governor General]. In 1925 the band was invited to participate at the opening of Madison Square Gardens in New York City. While there, its forty-five musicians also paraded up Broadway to City Hall and played a joint concert with the United States Military Academy [West Point] Band at the New York Neurological Institute.[26] Other U.S. visits included annual performances at the Ogdensburg Fair in Ogdensburg, New York. In addition to military parades, state functions and charity concerts in the Ottawa area, the band also began to play for radio broadcasts starting in 1928. The Director of Music, Captain Joseph Brown retired from the militia in 1938 to accept the position of Director of Music of the newly formed Royal Canadian Mounted Police Band in Regina. During his tenure the Governor General's Foot Guards Band had grown to over fifty musicians and had performed through much of eastern Canada and the United States.

Within the geographical boundaries of Southern Ontario there were militia bands in almost every community with a resident militia unit. These ranged from Kingston, Brockville and Ottawa in the east to St. Catharines in the Niagara peninsula and Windsor and London in the province's southwest corner. The event that best puts their numbers in perspective was the Canadian Corps Reunion which took place at the height of the Great Depression:

> In August 1934, over ten thousand First World War veterans gathered for the Canadian Corps Reunion in Toronto. Twenty-five bands appeared in a drum-head service [an outdoor military religious service] and a tattoo during the weekend of 4-6 August organized by Captain John Slatter. The grand tattoo occurred on the sloping hills of Riverdale Park, which is known today as the Don Valley. It brought together one of the greatest number of people ever assembled to watch a single event in Canada; three hundred thousand saw the performance.[27]

Although the names of all twenty-five participating bands are not yet known, it is probably safe to assume that units from across southern Ontario were present. These

---

[26] James Milne, "History of the Governor General's Foot Guards Band," (Ottawa. ON: Unpublished History, 1990) 11. The relationship between the Ottawa based militia band and the band of the US Military Academy was a function of their shared association with Arthur Clappé.

[27] Canada, Department of National Defence, Directorate of Ceremonial, *Traditions and Customs of the Canadian Forces, Part 3: Bands and Music* (Ottawa: National Defence Headquarters, 1990) 81.

would have included the Lincoln and Welland Band of St. Catharines, the Scots Fusiliers Band of Kitchener, the Elgin Regiment Band of St. Thomas, the Royal Hamilton Light Infantry Band, the Ontario Regiment Band of Oshawa and the Brockville Rifles Band. Each one of these and the many others that were in attendance that day reflected, as much as the Toronto bands did, the highest musical standards of their respective communities. Ontario's militia bands were also active well beyond the Lake Ontario and Lake Erie corridor. To the northwest there were bands attached to both the Sault Ste. Marie Regiment and the Lake Superior Scottish Regiment in what was known then as Port Arthur.

Elsewhere in Canada, especially in the smaller communities, the documentary evidence for the existence and activities of militia bands is not readily available.[28] The trail is further muddied by militia reorganizations that occurred immediately after the First World War and again in 1936. The battalion numbering system that had been in use since the Militia Act of 1855 was abandoned and many local units were either amalgamated or disbanded altogether leading to changes in or loss of regimental affiliations. One of the more obscure but useful sources from the interwar period are the annual "Militia Lists" published by the Department of National Defence. These were essentially nominal rolls of actively serving militia personnel in command or leadership positions which included a member's name, rank, unit and seniority in rank. These lists included two categories for those responsible for bands; directors of music [commissioned officers] and bandmasters [non-commissioned ranks]. The Militia List for 1933 contains the names of fifteen directors of music, almost all of whom were from Montréal, Ottawa, Toronto and Hamilton and thirty-eight bandmasters.[29] Considering that the Militia Lists did not include civilian bandmasters nor bandmasters below the rank of warrant officer, it is not inconceivable that the number of militia bands for the year 1933 was in excess of the fifty-three band leaders identified in the yearly report. Of equal importance was the geographical distribution of those bands.

In the Maritimes, bands were attached to the Princess Louise's Fusiliers in Halifax, the St. John and North Shore Regiments of New Brunswick as well as the New Brunswick Rangers Band of Sackville, a group which also continued to operate as the Sackville Citizens Band.[30] On the prairies, the strength of the Winnipeg Rifles Band dropped to between twenty and twenty-five during the interwar period, a trend that was reflected

[28] By readily available, the author is referring to online sources, periodicals, books or academic papers.
[29] Canada, Department of National Defence, *Militia List, 1933* Courtesy of Dr. Steve Harris, Directorate of History and Heritage, Department of National Defence, Ottawa. E-mail correspondence with the author 23 April 2019.
[30] Paul Jenson, "History," *Sackville [NB] Citizens Band* at www.sackvillecitizensband.wordpress.com accessed 19 February 2019.

through much of the region.[31]   Increasingly, militia bands responded to the challenge of attracting trained musicians by recruiting former members of local boys' bands.   In the 1930s the Battleford Light Infantry Band of North Battleford Saskatchewan drew on former members of that city's Rotary Boys' Band to increase its numbers.[32]   In Calgary, a pre-existing cadet band became the nucleus of the Canadian Army Service Corps Band which presented its first concert on March 12, 1933.   In the years leading up to the Second World War "…the band appeared in Stampede parades, Armistice [Remembrance] Day ceremonies throughout the southern part of the province, concerts at Bowness Pavilion and hockey games in the Calgary Arena."[33]   Other militia bands in the region included those of the Yorkton Regiment, the Regina Rifles and the Loyal Edmonton Regiment.

In British Columbia, the interwar militia bands were equally widespread.   Vancouver, like Toronto and Montréal, had a large enough population to support at least two militia bands, the British Columbia Regiment Band and the Westminster [later Royal Westminster] Regiment Band, formed after the First World War by Harry Moss.   This second group appeared frequently at openings of the legislature in Victoria, gave summer concerts in the Queen's Park Bandshell and in 1939 performed for a visit by King George VI and Queen Elizabeth.[34]   On Vancouver Island, Victoria's 5th Field Battery Band, Royal Canadian Artillery also continued to play an active part in the capital's musical life.   One of the most successful smaller community militia bands in Western Canada was the Rocky Mountain Rangers Band of Kamloops, B.C.   This success was due in large part to the efforts of John T. Parle who brought the group up from a strength of sixteen in 1922, when he arrived, to forty-three in 1926.   As soon as he assumed the leadership of the band, he established a junior group for the express purpose of feeding the adult ensemble.   It was a visionary innovation that would quickly become the norm across the country.[35]

---

[31] Danielle Gaudry, "Pork, Beans and Hard tack: The Regimental Band of the Royal Winnipeg Rifles," *Canadian Winds* 6, no. 2 (Spring 2008) 58.

[32] Katelyn Hannotte, "North Battleford City Kinsmen Band at 65," *Canadian Winds* 13, no. 2 (Spring 2015) 29-30.

[33] Norman Draper, *Bands by the Bow,* 47.

[34] Jack Kopstein, Barclay McMillan, Helmut Kallmann and Patricia Wardrop, "Music Bands," *The Canadian Encyclopedia*, last edited 16 December 2013 at www.thecanadianencyclopedia.ca accessed 17 February, 2019.

[35] Dale McIntosh, *History of Music in British Columbia*, 38.

NWMP - RCMP Bands

While Canada's participation in the Boer War provided an enormous boost to the growth of the country's military bands, it had the opposite effect on the volunteer bands of the Northwest Mounted Police. The continued existence of some of the NWMP divisional bands was already in question as a result of the Klondike Gold Rush of 1896. The rapid influx of upwards of one hundred thousand prospectors to the Yukon required that the Force redirect manpower, including some of its musicians, from "B" and "H" Divisions north to the goldfields. This diversion was essential to the establishment and maintenance of law and order in the region but it also negatively impacted some of the bands. With the onset of the Boer War in 1899, there was a further drain on the already strained resources of the NWMP as over 245 members volunteered for active service with the Canadian Army.[36] Skilled horsemen and trained in the use of small arms, these men were ideal candidates for service as cavalry soldiers. One of them was Calgary's bandmaster Sergeant Fred Bagley. Their contribution to the war effort must have been significant because at some point prior to 1907, King Edward VII granted the prefix "Royal" to the NWMP making it the RNWMP. It was in that year that Toronto's Whaley-Royce Company published a march for band entitled *Ride of the R.N.W.M.P.* by the Calgarian A. Glen Broder. The work is significant because the "A" in the composer's name stands for Annie. The march represents the first example in Canada of a published composition specifically for wind band by a female composer.

One silver lining to the NWMP's struggles at the end of the nineteenth century was the brief appearance of the Dawson City Volunteer Band from 1902 to 1905 when its presence "…played a necessary and important role in maintaining the Force's authority in the region, due to the extremely large American population in Dawson City."[37] By 1905 the goldrush was over, the City's population was rapidly declining and there was far less need for an enhanced police presence in the North. As members were reassigned the band ceased its operations as did other NWMP bands across the west. The official support that had characterized the first quarter century of their existence was waning and it would be another three decades before it would re-emerge. Smaller ensembles and dance orchestras however, were still active during this period, especially in the larger detachments situated

---

[36] Darren Oehlerking, "The History of Instrumental Wind Music within the Royal Canadian Mounted Police Band (D.M.A. Thesis: University of Iowa, 2008) 29.
[37] Ibid., 29.

in Winnipeg, Ottawa, Regina and Edmonton. On special occasions a band would be formed on an "ad hoc" basis.[38]

The Canadian government restructured dominion police forces in 1920 and in doing so gave the RNWMP a new name, the one that it retains to this day, the Royal Canadian Mounted Police. Its bands may have been temporarily ignored but they weren't forgotten. In 1934, Assistant Commissioner S.T. Wood heard a performance of the London Metropolitan Police Band while on a visit to England. On his return to Ottawa, he began to petition for the creation of a RCMP Band similar to the permanent bands of the Canadian Army. It took him four years, but when he became Commissioner of the Force in March of 1938, he finally secured approval from his federal paymasters for the establishment of the Royal Canadian Mounted Police Band. Captain J.T. Brown, formerly Director of Music of Ottawa's Governor General's Foot Guards Band was engaged as bandmaster and thirty-six musicians, mostly new recruits, were auditioned and assembled in Regina. Although they were selected to perform as musicians, they were also expected to work full-time as policemen with rehearsals and private practice occurring during off-duty hours.[39] The band's first performance took place on May 25, 1939 in Regina during the visit of His Majesty, King George VI and one week later the entire ensemble was transferred to Ottawa. The Royal Canadian Mounted Police Band, despite its part-time status, would begin to grow in both popularity and stature in the months to come largely as a result of the storm clouds gathering across the Atlantic.

The Legacy of Canadian Military Bands (1900-1939)

The period spanning the first half of the twentieth century stretches from 1900 to 1939 and during this time the country's military bands, especially the militia bands, enjoyed enormous popularity. They were the longest lived, reached the widest audiences and attracted the most skilled players and dynamic leaders in their respective communities. Militia pay for rehearsals and performances were certainly incentives, but band directors were lured with other enticements. The British Army tradition of officer patronage persisted well into the twentieth century. In the militia, private regimental funds channeled through the Officers' Mess Band Committees were used to attract quality candidates to the position of Director of Music. Paid as honoraria, these funds enabled militia units in Toronto, Ottawa, Montréal and elsewhere to seek out highly qualified musicians to lead

---

[38] Ibid., 30.
[39] Oehlerking, "History of Wind Instrumental Music", 38.

their bands. Once a band achieved a certain measure of success, regimental pride, often in the form of a regimental association, did its best to ensure that the band continued to thrive. Ultimately, unit loyalty helped maintain the continuity that permitted some bands to function successfully for generations.

It wasn't just the militia bands that benefitted from the activities of their leaders. In their civilian lives, directors of music were often teachers, administrators and musical entrepreneurs. Montréal's J.J. Gagnier [Canadian Grenadier Guards Band] taught at the Conservatoire Nationale and the McGill Conservatorium of Music.[40] In Toronto, R.B. Hayward [Queen's Own Rifles Band] was director of wind instrument instruction at the Toronto Conservatory and conducted the Toronto Concert Band until 1939. Collectively men such as these and many others like them also contributed to the creation and training of boys' bands: the Toronto Cadet Band (Slatter), the Ottawa Lions Boys' Band (Brown) and at Montréal's Collège Mont St. Louis (J.J. Goulet) when instrumental music was virtually non-existent in most schools. Their activities were also of an organizational nature, not only in Canada but in the United States as well. In 1929, Edwin Franko Goldman, leader of the famed Goldman band, gathered together in New York City with eight of his professional colleagues. They were all celebrated band leaders of the day and the purpose of their meeting was to form an organization to lobby composers and music publishers for more and higher quality music for wind band. Three of the founding members of the American Bandmasters Association, as it came to be known, were Canadians: Captain Charles O'Neill, Captain J.J. Gagnier and Captain (recently retired) R.B. Hayward.[41] [Fig. 8.13] Two years later, in 1931, the Canadian Bandmasters Association was formed. Of the seventeen founding members, five were militia bandmasters.[42][See Fig. 8.9] The leadership skills they exercised over their militia bands were sometimes also transferred to adult community bands. Lt. George Ziegler, Director of Music of Kitchener's Scots Fusiliers Band also conducted the Kitchener Musical Society, just as Joseph Vézina had conducted the Beauport Concert Band and the "B" Battery Band in Québec half a century earlier. In many cases the membership lists and libraries of local militia and community bands were often closely integrated. Only the rehearsal space and the uniforms changed.

---

[40] Bourbonnais, *Inventaire Sommaire*, 12.

[41] Jennifer Scott, "History," 1995, revised 2006, *American Bandmasters Association* at www.americanbandmasters.org accessed 08 April 2019.

[42] John Mellor, *Music in the Park: C.F. Thiele- Father of Canadian Band Music* (Waterloo, ON: Melco History Series, 1988) 45.

CHAPTER EIGHT GALLERY

Figure 8.1.   Royal Canadian Horse Artillery Band, Camp Petawawa, 1910.   Director of Music Captain A.L. Light.   The "line" band instrumentation of twenty-four musicians plus bandmaster is clearly evident.   Source: *The Canadian Gunner*, 1968 (Shilo, Manitoba)

Figure 8.2.   Berlin 29th Battalion Band, Ontario.   Director of Music Noah Zeller. 1903.   Early twentieth century militia bands, especially in the larger urban centres, were generally well-balanced ensembles.   Source: Kitchener Musical Society.

134

Figure 8.3. Massed Bands from Camp Borden, Canadian National Exhibition, Toronto, 1916. Seated in front of the bands are their twenty-eight respective directors and bandmasters. Source: George Metcalf Archival Collection, Canadian War Museum.

Figure 8.5. Band of the 202nd Battalion, CEF, Sarcee camp, Calgary, 1916. Note the distinctive "bandsman" badge on each musicians' right sleeve just above the elbow. The stylised lyre was the commonly accepted way of identifying military musicians. Source: Wikimedia Commons.

Figure 8.4. Band of the Royal Canadian Regiment, France, 1917. Director of Music, Lt. H.G. Jones. [NA 3596-164] Many WWI Canadian Army bands exceeded the authorized limit of twenty-four musicians plus bandmaster. Source: Glenbow Archives, Calgary.

Figure 8.6. Captain Charles O'Neill, Director of Music R22eR Band, Québec, undated photograph. O'Neill held a doctorate from McGill, was a founding member of the American Bandmasters Association and served as its president from 1933 to 1934. After his retirement from the Canadian Army, he began a second career as professor of music at the State Teachers College in Potsdam, New York. A tireless advocate of wind bands he was a highly respected composer, arranger, adjudicator and clinician. He died in Québec City in 1964. Source: La Musique du R 22e R, Québec.

Figure 8.7. Coronation Band, 1937. Director of Music Charles O'Neill. This was an ensemble of specially selected musicians from Canada's four permanent force bands. Source: La Musique du R 22e R, Québec.

Figure 8.8. Captain Richard Benjamin Hayward, Director of Music Queen's Own Rifles of Canada, Toronto, undated photograph. A former British Army bandmaster he was also director of wind instrument instruction at the Toronto Conservatory. After his retirement from the militia, he led the Toronto Concert Band until 1939 and also served as president of the American Bandmasters Association from 1940 to 1941. Source: *Famous Bands of the British Empire*, 1926.

Figure 8.9. Inaugural meeting of the Canadian Bandmasters Association, 1931. C.F. Thiele (with baton) is seated fourth from right, front row. To his right is Captain John Slatter. The association was renamed the Canadian Band Association in 1986. Source: Music Division, National Library of Canada.

Figure 8.10. The Band of the 48th Highlanders, Toronto, 1924. Director of Music Captain John Slatter, seated front row centre.   The 48th were one of Canada's most popular and accomplished interwar militia bands.   Source: Waterloo Music Company.

Figure 8.11. Captain Jean-Josephat Gagnier, Director of Music, the Canadian Grenadier Guards Band, Montréal, undated photograph. In addition to his conducting duties, Gagnier was also a regional director for the CBC, composer and arranger. He held a doctorate from the University of Montréal and taught at several of the city's post-secondary music schools. He authored the first *Catalogue of Canadian Composers* in 1947 and along with Charles O'Neill and R.B. Hayward was a founding member of the American Bandmasters Association. [See Fig. 8.13]   Source: Music Division, National Library of Canada.

Figure 8.12.   The Canadian Grenadier Guards Band, Director of Music Captain J.J. Gagnier, Montréal, undated photograph.   Source: Bibliothèque nationale de Québec.

Figure 8.13.   Inaugural meeting of the American Bandmasters Association, July 5, 1929. Founding members included Canadians J.J. Gagnier, second row left, R.B. Hayward, second row right and Charles O'Neill, front row right. Source: Archives of the American Bandmasters Association, Special Collections in Performing Arts, University of Maryland Libraries.

CHAPTER NINE

THE YOUTH BANDS (1900-1939)

At the beginning of the twentieth century, band programs that specifically focused on young players were still found primarily in religious colleges, especially in Québec, private schools and in the native industrial schools of the west. The establishment of the St. Mary's Boys Band in St. John, New Brunswick, in 1903 is one of the earlier examples of sponsorship outside of an educational institution. Originally known as "The St. Mary's Boys Brigade" it was a mission outreach program supported by the St. Mary's (Anglican) Church parish in what was then a blue-collar east-side neighbourhood of the city.[1] [Fig. 9.1]. In Loyalist Ontario it is highly probable that Orange Lodges and fraternities also supported boys' bands. A series of marches published by Toronto's Whaley-Royce Company entitled *12th July March* (1890), *Orange March* (1890), *Protestant Boys* (undated) and *No Surrender* (undated) all suggest some affiliation with the Protestant Order.[2] Instrumentations that include parts for piccolo and clarinets as well as brass choir further confirm a wind band model although there is no firm documentary evidence yet to definitely prove performance by a youth band. One other youth organization that sponsored bands was the Boy Scouts with one of their first being the Victoria (B.C.) Boy Scouts Band, established in 1910.

The rapid expansion of community and militia bands in the aftermath of the Boer War certainly required that there be musicians to fill them. The photographic record shows that in some communities the training of younger players took place within the adult community band. An image of the Parrsboro (N.S.) Citizens Band of 1910 shows at least one younger player [Fig. 9.2] as does a 1913 photograph of L'Union Musicale de Joliette, which reveals at least two musicians who are definitely underage [Fig. 9.3].[3] Trail B.C.'s Italian Band of 1913 is unique in that the group's standing front row consists of boys holding a variety of brass and reed instruments but seated directly in front of them are eight girls – all holding mandolins![4] A later photo taken in 1918, after the group had renamed

---

[1] Kelly VanBuskirk, "St. Mary's Band: Going Strong after 115 Years," *Canadian Winds* 17, no.2 (Fall 2018) 3.
[2] Copies of all marches are contained in the author's private collection.
[3] Raymond Locat, *La Tradition Musicale à Joliette : 150 Ans d'Histoire* (Joliette, QC : Raymond Locat, 1993) 130.
[4] Steve Guidone, *Trail Maple Leaf Band 90th Anniversary Photo-History Album 1917-2007* (Salmon Arm, BC: Guidone, 2007) 8.

itself the Trail Maple Leaf Band, clearly shows younger players seated cross legged in front of the adults. [Fig. 9.4]

Even as the training of boys as wind musicians was increasingly being conducted in non-school settings, the country's rapid population growth demanded the construction of new schools. Catholic teaching orders, when they had the qualified personnel available, would find a place for a school band. In 1913, the Jesuits established Collège Sacré-Coeur in Sudbury, Ontario. By 1916, the college had a band.[5]

The Interwar Boys' Bands

The real growth of the youth band movement began in the years immediately following the Armistice. John Slatter, band director of Toronto's 48th Highlanders, established the Toronto Cadet Band in the 1920s and his brother Henry was the driving force behind the creation of the Orchard City Junior Band in Kelowna in 1925 as well as the New Westminster and District Boy Scouts Band in 1928.[6] Military bandmasters, like the Slatter brothers, many of whom had served as band boys in the British military, recognized the value of musical instruction and supported it whenever they could. Winnipeg was home to another of the country's early cadet bands, the Winnipeg Sea Cadet Band (1927), whose first members were taught by Captain Tommy James of the permanent force PPCLI Band. Neither was the importance of early training for young performers lost on community band directors of the period. Bandmasters were often under a contractual obligation to conduct one or more junior bands in addition to their responsibilities for the adult band. Charles F. Thiele, who had been appointed conductor of the Waterloo Musical Society in 1919 "…had the responsibility of training two bands under the aegis of the musical society, a senior and a boys band."[7] In the twin city of Kitchener his colleague George Henry Ziegler taught both junior and intermediate bands to ensure a steady supply of trained musicians for that community's adult band. Under Ziegler's leadership, the Kitchener Boys Bands won a string of first place finishes during the 1930s both at the CNE and elsewhere [Fig. 9.5]. By 1940 they were forbidden from further competition.[8] Captain George Brown, bandmaster of the Governor General's Foot Guards Band became conductor of the Ottawa

---

[5] Metro Kozak, "Sudbury," *Encyclopedia of Music in Canada* (Toronto: University of Toronto Press, 1981) 899.

[6] Kerry Turner and John White, "New Westminster and District Concert Band", *Canadian Winds* 10, no. 1 (Fall 2011) 32.

[7] John Mellor, *C.F. Thiele: Father of Canadian Band Music* (Waterloo, ON: Melco History Series, 1988) 21.

[8] Sybil Card Crawford, "George Henry Ziegler 1889-1981," *Waterloo Historical Society* 76 (1988) 54-71

Boys Band in 1934. Under his direction the Ottawa Boys Band appeared in communities across eastern Canada and the United States as well as making a series of radio broadcasts. The band was no stranger to competition as it "…captured first place at the Quebec Festival of Music and also at the Canadian National Exhibition in Toronto."[9]   Throughout Ontario, boys' bands were to be found in Stratford, Owen Sound, Brantford, Windsor, Guelph and Preston [now part of Cambridge].[10]   The impetus for many of these groups was not just the belief that it was important to maintain a steady stream of trained musicians for the local community band.   It was also felt that participation in a band was an ideal way of keeping boys "out of mischief".   The British Military Band tradition of social engagement resurfaced in Canada, especially during the Depression and set the foundations for the growth of today's school band programs.

Perhaps the most compelling evidence that bands served a societal function was that despite the hardships faced by many Canadian communities during the Great Depression, resources were made available for the formation of/or continued maintenance of boys' bands.   Sponsors often included commercial interests, municipal councils, service clubs or some combination of all three.   Their support extended not only to the many groups in Ontario but to youth bands in the Maritimes, such as the Moncton Boys Band.[11]   On the prairies smaller communities were especially active.   The North Battleford Boys Band was funded by the local Rotary Club and in Rouleau, a boys' band was formed in 1932 under the direction of Andrew King using instruments that had previously belonged to the Rouleau Ladies Band [see Chap.7].   The town's population at the time was only 1,100 souls yet the group's membership stood at a respectable twenty-five.[12]   In Calgary, several attempts to start a boys' band failed, primarily due to lack of financial backing for the purchase of instruments and uniforms.   Eventually the Calgary Native Boys Band was born and by 1936, under the direction of Wally Hayward, it had performed at both the B.C. Jubilee in Vancouver and the Montana State Fair.[13]   British Columbia fared quite well with boys' bands in Courtney (1924), Cranbrook (1931), Kamloops (1922), Kelowna

---

[9] James Milne, *A History of the Governor General's Foot Guards Band* (Ottawa: Unpublished history, 1988) 12.

[10] Mellor, *C.F. Thiele*, 101-103.

[11] Payson Rowell, "Codiac Concert Band: A Young Band with a Rich History," *Canadian Winds* 12, no. 1 (Fall 2013) 32.

[12] Mr. Deane Charles, telephone interview with the author, 29 March 2003.

[13] Norman Draper, *Bands by the Bow: A History of Band Music in Calgary* (Calgary: Century Calgary Publications, 1975) 53.

(1925), New Westminster (1926), Prince George (1938), Prince Rupert (1925), Quesnel (1935), Vancouver (1925) and Victoria (1928).[14]

The Kitsilano Boys' Band

There were many fine boys' bands in Canada during the 1930s but none achieved the stature and international acclaim equal to that of the Vancouver Kitsilano Boys Band. The Kitsilano Boys Band was formed in 1928 by Arthur W. Delamont. Born in England and raised in a family actively involved with Salvation Army bands, Delamont first organized the group as the General Gordon School Band. When its original members moved on to Kitsilano High School, the name changed to the Kitsilano High School Band. As more and more students were drawn from schools across the city it became simply the Kitsilano Boys Band.[15] Rehearsing twice a week in the basement of General Gordon School, the extra-curricular ensemble excelled rapidly. It performed at the CNE in Toronto in 1931 and at the Chicago World's Fair in 1933 where "…against seven accomplished bands, the Kitsilano Boys Band won the competition with 225 of a possible 240 [points]"[16] The band made frequent trips to England starting in 1935 and the following year played at London's Crystal Palace winning "…the "Class A Junior Shield" competing against thirty-three adult bands (called Junior by the prevailing system of categorization)."[17] [Fig. 9.6] In 1937 the band headed south to perform at the Golden Gate Bridge Fiesta in San Francisco.[18] Further trips to the United Kingdom took place in 1939 (interrupted by the outbreak of World War Two), 1950 (which also included a swing through Holland), 1953 and 1955. Not content with just one boys' band, Delamont was also responsible for the formation of the West Vancouver Boys Band in 1931 and the Royal City Junior Band of New Westminster in 1935. Of all the youth groups he led it was the Kitsilano Boys Band that set the standard. It finally ceased its operations in 1974 and Arthur Delamont passed away in 1982 at the age of ninety.

One of the frequent arguments used by contemporary band directors in defence of the inclusion of band programs in school curricula is that participation in musical study develops the whole person. It instills a sense of worth through hard work, self-discipline and the common pursuit of artistic excellence. The Kitsilano Boys Band was Canada's

---

[14] Dale McIntosh, *A History of Music in British Columbia 1850-1950* (Victoria: Sono Nis Press, 1989) 61.
[15] Gordon Laird, "The Kitsilano Boys Band," *Canadian Winds* 5, no. 1 (Fall 2006) 10.
[16] Ibid., 11.
[17] Ibid., 11.
[18] McIntosh, *A History of Music in British Columbia*, 34.

original inspiration for this line of thought as "…it created a host of good citizens, remarkable businessmen, actors, politicians, diplomats, theatrical producers, commercial artists, school teachers and religious leaders."[19]   It was also the training ground for generations of professional musicians who would become famous across North America as performers, conductors and arrangers.

During the interwar period, as the benefits of instrumental music performance became increasingly apparent, the first girls' bands began to appear. As noted previously [Chap.7] Kitchener's George Henry Ziegler had established the Kitchener Ladies Band in 1925. Although the group had adult members it is possible that some of its musicians were still in school. Many of the first participants had acquired their instrumental skills at Zieglers' Kitchener Conservatory of Music and so it is conceivable that some of these had not yet reached adulthood.   In 1935, Vancouver's Arthur Delamont, by then responsible for the creation of at least three successful boys' bands, appeared in a postcard labelled "Vancouver Girls' Band" [Fig. 9.7].   There are no other details and few other sources of information about the group's activities, membership or longevity.   In Fort William, Ontario [now part of Thunder Bay], we find photographic proof of the existence of the Fort William Girls Military Band directed by Amelia and Maurice Jackson. [Fig. 9.8]   The website www.fortwilliamgirlsmilitaryband.ca contains a series of photographs taken until at least the end of the Second World War that include the band performing for troop trains and returning veterans. [20]

The success of the youth bands was not lost on the newly formed CBA [Canadian Bandmasters' Association]. It was inevitable that the idea of school-based band programs would be revisited. The immediate question was what would be the role of the association in their development. On January 17, 1937 CBA secretary J. Andrew Wiggins expressed concern "…about the eventual establishment of bands in the school system and whether the CBA members would be able to qualify for teaching positions on staff."[21] He was just ahead of the country's largest school board: "…on March 7 [1937], the Board of Education in Toronto passed a resolution that three bands be organized in Toronto schools. According to this resolution, the instruments would be supplied to the students and a fee of 25 cents per lesson paid by the student."[22]   Similar initiatives were undertaken in two Alberta communities. The Edmonton School Boys band had been formed in 1936 under the direction of T. Vernon Newlove and in 1939 the Calgary Public Schools Band was

---

[19] Laird, "Kitsilano," 11.
[20] Fort William Girls Military Band at www.fortwilliamgirlsmilitaryband.ca accessed 17 June 2020.
[21] Frank MacKinnon, "History of CBA," *Canadian Band Journal* 14, no. 2 (Winter 1989) 21.
[22] Ibid., 22.

established.[23]   By 1938, the position of the CBA had become more proactive and at its seventh annual convention, which took place on July 10 of that year, it was proposed that "...all Boards of Education should promote the organization of school bands in order to make them more appealing."[24]   The association went one step further and discussed the possibility of setting up six-week summer courses that would certify successful candidates as school band teachers.[25]   It was an idea well ahead of its time and even though no concrete steps were taken to implement it then, it would be resurrected by the Ontario Department of Education in the 1950s and 1960s.

The boys' and girls' bands of the interwar era were a collaborative effort by communities across the country to engage youngsters in a constructive and creative way that sought to instill positive civic values through music.   Sponsors came from all segments of society: local governments, commercial enterprises, fraternal lodges, service organizations, churches and private citizens.   Together they provided many young people with valuable life skills that would remain with them into adulthood.   For those who chose to continue making music, especially for those of modest means, and during the Great Depression there were many, the youth bands were a crucial step on the way to musical careers.   Few, however, imagined just how quickly the skills they learned in those youthful groups would be once again put to use in the service of their country.

By 1939, Canada's boys' bands had nurtured the growth of a generation of musicians, many of whom were now in their late teens and early twenties.   With the outbreak of World War Two and the rapid demand for military musicians, many volunteered for active service.   The Royal Canadian Navy's H.M.C.S. *Naden* Band, formed at the Esquimalt Naval Base in September of 1940 was a destination for many former band boys.   Its first director, Lieutenant Henry Cuthbert, was a trumpet player who had conducted the Saskatoon Boys Band in the 1930s.   He encouraged many of his former musicians to join the navy as well as retired members of the Kitsilano Boys Band.   The remainder of the Naden Band's musicians were "...professionals from Calgary dance bands ...[and musicians] off the Empress ships."[26]

The Naden Band was just one service band.   Canada's former band boys would serve the nation in many, many more.

---

[23] Keith Mann, ed. "Edmonton Schoolboys Band Holds 60th Reunion," *Canadian Band Journal* 14, no. 4 (Summer 1990) 25.

[24] Frank MacKinnon, "History of CBA," *Canadian Band Journal* 14, no. 4 (Summer 1990) 26.

[25] Ibid., 26.

[26] Jack Mirtle, *The Naden Band: A History*. (Victoria, BC: Jackstays Publishing, 1990) 1.

CHAPTER NINE GALLERY

Figure 9.1. St. Mary's Band, St. John N.B., 1905. Bandmaster C.H. Williams. Established in 1903, this group was one of Canada's first youth bands not affiliated with any partricular school. Source: Doug Reece.

Figure 9.2. Parrsboro Citizens Band, Parrsboro N.S., 1910. Younger players were often part of the adult band, especially in smaller communities. Source: "PCB History," *Parrsboro Citizens Band* at www.sites.google.com

Figure 9.3. L'Union Musicale de Joliette, Joliette, Québec, 1912-1913. Bandmaster Emile Prévost. Prévost led the band for fifty years. Source: Maxime Perreault, L'Union Musicale de Lanaudière.

Figure 9.4. Trail Maple Leaf Band, Trail B.C., 1918. Bandmaster Frank Giovanazzi. Originally formed in 1910 as the "Italian Band" the group adopted its new name in 1918. Note the front row of boys with their instruments. Source: Trail Maple Leaf Band.

Figure 9.5.　The Kitchener Boys Band, Canadian National Exhibition, Toronto, 1939. Bandmaster George Henry Ziegler.　The band was a regular first place winner at the CNE's "Music Days" competitions.　Source: Robert Thiel.

Figure 9.6.　The Kitsilano Boys Band in front of Buckingham Palace, London, 1936. Conductor Arthur W. Delamont.　Perhaps the best known of Canada's interwar boys' bands, it was also one of the longest running, from 1928 to 1974.　Source: City of Vancouver Archives.

Figure 9.7.   Vancouver Girls Band, Vancouver, 1935.   Conductor Arthur W. Delamont.   The image is taken from a contemporary postcard.   Source: City of Vancouver Archives.

Figure 9.8.   Fort William Girls Military Band, Fort William (Thunder Bay), c. 1937. Conductors Amelia and Maurice Jackson.   Members of the band also functioned as a dance orchestra.   The ensemble performed regularly for troop trains passing through Fort William, now part of Thunder Bay, during WWII.   Source: https://fortwilliamgirlsmilitaryband.ca accessed 20 April 2022.

CHAPTER TEN

CANADIAN BANDS AND THE SECOND WORLD WAR

On September 1, 1939, at 0631 ZULU [military abbreviation for Greenwich Mean Time], the British Admiralty sent out an encrypted message addressed to "ALL AUTHORITIES AT HOME AND ABROAD". It was classified "MOST IMMEDIATE – TOP SECRET" and it contained only three words: "PREPARE FOR WAR". One of the overseas authorities included on the distribution list would most certainly have been Canadian Naval Headquarters in Ottawa [Fig. 10.1].[1] Even though Canada didn't officially declare war on Hitler's Germany until September 10, 1939, the momentum to join in support of the British Empire was unstoppable despite Prime Minister Mackenzie King's best efforts to delay it.

At the outset of the war, the Royal Canadian Navy consisted of six destroyers, four minesweepers, twelve naval reserve divisions in cities spread out across the country and two bases in Esquimalt, B.C. and Halifax, N.S. It had a total personnel strength of approximately 3,500 officers and men. Six bloody years later it was the world's third largest naval fleet after those of the U.S. and Great Britain with almost 100,000 men and women on active duty.

Canadian Army Bands in WWII

Canada's military bands experienced a similar growth in personnel during the conflict. In the army that growth initially came slowly. Permanent force bands maintained prewar routines in their respective depots and militia units were forbidden to take their bands on active strength. By 1940 however, the need for bands became clear and "…Lt. General McNaughton proposed…the organization of nine bands, one to be stationed at Borden, the other eight to circulate among the units of the two Canadian infantry divisions."[2] The process took longer than expected due to a lack of qualified directors and manpower shortages caused by the loss of prewar permanent force musicians who volunteered for active service overseas leaving vacancies in their respective bands. The Royal 22nd Regiment Band of Québec lost so many men to the war that it was forced to perform with

---

[1] Copy of message from the estate of Rear Admiral John A. Charles, CD, RCN.
[2] Canada, Department of National Defence, *History of Bands in the Canadian Army* (Ottawa: National Defence Headquarters, 1952) 14.

less than fifteen musicians. By the Fall of 1941 it had been able to increase its strength to twenty-two "...the bandmaster, Captain Belanger, one piccolo, four clarinets, two saxophones, two horns, four trumpets, three trombones, one euphonium, a tuba and three percussionists...by 1944, it had over forty members." [3] Another prewar permanent force band, that of the Royal Canadian Horse Artillery based in Kingston, was somewhat luckier. By 1940, the band was up to a strength of thirty musicians including the Director of Music [Fig. 10.2]. The growth in the total number of bands was steady and by 1944 there were "...ten full time bands [overseas] and in Canada...thirty-three full time bands plus a nucleus of permanent bandsmen in spare-time [volunteer] bands." [4] Many of the musicians that staffed these groups had been professional players before the war and the evolving nature of popular music was reflected in the activities of the wartime ensembles. As an example, the Royal Canadian Artillery Band "...in addition to being a military band, it had within its personnel a dance band, an "old time" band, a salon orchestra, a choir and instrumental and vocal soloists." [5] With such a range of abilities focused on maintaining troop morale, it is not surprising that bands were in demand.

The Royal Canadian Ordnance Corps Band performed "...during its six-month tour of North-West Europe [1944-45] 125 concerts, 75 dances, 24 ceremonial parades, 5 route marches." [6] In Italy, the Royal Canadian Army Service Corps [RCASC] Band was equally committed. In one month alone, June of 1944, the band under the direction of A. Hollick, a British Army bandmaster on loan to the Canadian Army, rehearsed three times yet performed thirty-one concerts, played for two dances and participated in two church parades. During that same period, they moved camp four times and for three days mid-month lost the Fifth Armoured Division to which they were supposed to be attached for a seven-day rotation. [7] By today's standards, itineraries such as these would be considered extreme: travelling in the backs of trucks, sleeping on stretchers or camp cots under tents or in makeshift barracks and eating army food. Despite all these privations, the musicians were still expected to perform at a professional level repeatedly, regardless of the

---

[3] Jack Kopstein and Ian Pearson, *The Heritage of Canadian Military Music* (St. Catharines, ON: Vanwell Publishing Limited, 2002) 85.

[4] Canada, Department of National Defence, *History,* 16.

[5] Canada, Department of National Defence, *History,* 18.

[6] Ibid., 18.

[7] A. Hollick, *RCASC Band War Diary, April 1944 to October 1945* (Unpublished document, 1945) The author obtained his copy from a second hand bookstore in Calgary that was subsequently destroyed in the 2013 flood. The diary was presented to its previous owner in 1977 by Major Al Brown who had been a member of the band during the war years.

conditions, which on occasion meant competing with distant artillery fire. This was the norm for the overseas army bands.

In addition to the thirty-three full time bands stationed in Canada, most of which were at training establishments and depots, there were volunteer bands led by full time musicians at operational bases. Some reserve bands, especially the more prestigious prewar militia bands, continued to operate including Gagnier's Canadian Grenadier Guards Band in Montréal, Ottawa's Governor General's Foot Guards Band and John Slatter's 48th Highlanders Band in Toronto. The Second World War was also the catalyst for the creation of the Canadian Women's Army Corps Band in 1943. This was initially a forty-one piece brass band with two additional saxophones but by April of 1945 "...the band, which now included reed instruments, was posted overseas and played numerous concerts in Holland and Belgium."[8] By the end of the conflict, Canadian Army bands, especially the overseas bands, were considered to be the equal of any bands in either the British or American forces. Despite a slow start, they had contributed to the "esprit de corps" that characterized the Canadian Army as a whole. The irony was that for the first time in our wind band story, the Second World War also helped create competing ensembles in both the Royal Canadian Navy and the Royal Canadian Air Force. These bands got off to a much better start than the army bands for the simple reason that the navy and the air force paid their musicians more.[9]

Royal Canadian Navy Bands in WWII

The Royal Canadian Navy, unlike the army, had no tradition of professional bands either in the regular force or the reserves prior to 1939. Yet by January of 1940, only four months after the start of hostilities, the H.M.C.S. [His Majesty's Canadian Ship] *Stadacona* Band had been recruited in Toronto, trained and posted to the Stadacona base in Halifax as an operational unit. The initial plan for the employment of naval bands was to perform "...three parades daily, noon day concerts and weekly dances for their ship's company, and in addition, civic engagements for charitable purposes."[10] In practice, the concert aspect of the navy's bands became their most popular function. The person responsible for the growth of these bands was Alfred Edward Zealley (1878-1961). As with so many of his contemporaries, Zealley had joined the British Army as a band boy and in 1898 had completed his training at Kneller Hall. After leaving regular service in 1908, he emigrated

---

[8] Kopstein and Pearson, *Heritage*, 89.
[9] Canada, Department of National Defence, *History*, 16.
[10] Jack Mirtle, *The Naden Band: A History* (Victoria, BC: Jackstays Publishing, 1990) xx.

to Boston and from 1910 to 1914 was bandmaster at Harvard University. He joined the Canadian Army in 1915 as bandmaster of the 75th Battalion, CEF, and returned to Boston in 1918. Between the wars he was involved with a variety of conducting activities "…the highlight being an extensive tour through the U.S.., Cuba and Mexico with the "Belleville Kilties" Band".[11]

In 1939 Zealley offered his services to Naval Headquarters in Ottawa promising to provide the navy with a band at no cost to the government. His offer "…was accepted and he was given the rank of Lieutenant RCNVR [Royal Canadian Navy Volunteer Reserve][12] [Fig. 10.3]. By 1942 he had overseen the creation of three more bands in Naden, B.C., St. Hyacinthe, QC and the largest, numbering over sixty full-time musicians at Cornwallis, N.S. [Fig. 10.4]. In November of that year, Zealley was appointed Director of Music for the Royal Canadian Navy and was instructed to establish an RCN School of Music in Toronto. Over a period of two years until its closure in December of 1944, the RCN School graduated more than 500 musicians "…for approximately 17 bands, including three cruiser bands at sea and the York Band."[13] Each of these bands was capable of subdividing itself to form dance bands, salon groups and in some cases, male choirs. One of the greatest contributions of the navy bands was that many were posted to smaller communities that had no prior tradition of professional wind instrumental music making. These included H.M.C.S. *Chatham* in Prince Rupert, B.C., H.M.C.S. *Avalon* in St. John's NFLD [not yet part of Canada at the time], H.M.C.S. *Shelburne* in Shelburne. N.S. and H.M.C.S. *St. Hyacinthe* in Québec.[14]

The instrumentation of most shore-based bands averaged from thirty-two to thirty-six players [with the exception of the Cornwallis band that was much larger]. The three ship-based bands, H.M.C.S. *Nabob* [aircraft carrier], H.M.C.S. *Ontario* and H.M.C.S. *Uganda* [later renamed *Quebec*], both light cruisers, each consisted of fifteen musicians. The Naden and Stadacona bands were also larger, possibly because the bases themselves were well established before the war. A photograph of the Naden Band taken in 1944 demonstrates why the navy bands became best known as concert organizations. Under the direction of Stan Sunderland the group consisted of two flutes, one oboe, two bassoons, nine clarinets, one bass clarinet, five saxophones, seven trumpets, four horns, four trombones, two euphoniums, two tubas, one string bass and three percussionists.[15]

---

[11] Ibid., xx.
[12] Ibid., xx.
[13] Ibid, xxi.
[14] Alfred Zealley, *Music Ashore and Afloat: Famous Bands of the RCN* (Unpublished copy, nd)
[15] Mirtle, *Naden Band*, 45.

Considering that many of the wartime naval bandsmen were professional musicians before the war, an ensemble of this size was ideally suited to the performance of any repertoire for band. By the end of the war in Europe [May 8, 1945], the Royal Canadian Navy's bands began to revert to their civilian status. The popularity and success of those bands however had convinced post war planners to include two in the navy's peacetime establishment: the bands of H.M.C.S. *Naden* and H.M.C.S. *Stadacona*.

Royal Canadian Air Force Bands in WWII

Like the navy, the Royal Canadian Air Force [RCAF] had no tradition of professional musicians in the service prior to the onset of hostilities. There was a volunteer band formed at RCAF Station Trenton in 1938 but it was made up of tradesmen who practised and performed in their spare time but were expected to work at their respective trades during duty hours [Fig. 10.5]. Full time professional bands were not authorized until 1940. Five bands were originally proposed, each with a leader and twenty-nine musicians consisting of seven clarinets, three saxophones, six cornets, three horns, three trombones, two euphoniums, three basses and two percussionists. At first, the Air Force only permitted these groups four hours of practice a week, the remainder of the time being filled with general aircraftsmen duties.[16] The first full time band, the RCAF Central Band, was formed in January of 1941 at RCAF Station Rockcliffe near Ottawa. The sixty-five piece ensemble eventually became the selection and testing centre for the sixteen part-time bands that were in existence by the Fall of that year.

The reputation for musical excellence that characterized both wartime and later peacetime RCAF bands had its origins in the RCAF overseas bands that left Canada starting in 1942. The RCAF Overseas Headquarters Band, a forty-piece ensemble under the direction of Flying Officer Martin Boundy was immediately successful "…playing 373 engagements in their first year overseas."[17] The demand for their services was such that three more bands were sent, each with thirty-three musicians: the Bournemouth Band under Bandmaster S.V. Vowden, the RCAF No. 6 Group Band under Warrant Officer Clifford Hunt and the Warrington Band conducted by Warrant Officer Howard Leroy. By 1944 all four bands were heavily committed to a wide variety of military and civilian activities including church parades, dance engagements, fund raising concerts and twice weekly radio broadcasts on the BBC. During their time in Britain, the RCAF overseas bands

---

[16] Kopstein and Pearson, *Heritage,* 100.
[17] Ibid., 102.

"...performed two thousand seven hundred and seventy-eight engagements...the Headquarters Band alone performed over eleven hundred times during its three years overseas."[18] Back in Canada the sixteen part time bands never achieved the same stature as the fully professional bands in Britain but they also contributed to the war effort. The RCAF Station bands were especially renowned for the dance orchestras they formed the best known of which was the twelve-piece Trenton group. Like the army, the RCAF also created an all-female band, the RCAF Women's Division Band authorized in 1942. Although it was a Drum and Bugle band, it too proved to be enormously popular and by the last year of its existence this part-time group was averaging thirty engagements, both military and civilian, a month [Fig. 10.6].

One of the unintended beneficiaries of the war years was the RCMP's part-time band in Ottawa. With so many service bands overseas or previously committed, there was "...a large void of musicians and ensembles able to provide patriotic music for official civic and government functions at home."[19] The RCMP Band [Fig. 10.7] filled that void with performances in different parts of Canada for parades and Victory drives. Some of these engagements included participation in radio broadcasts and movie newsreels, a summer concert season at the Supreme Court of Canada beginning in 1943 and performances for visits by various heads of state. Two of the most distinguished visitors in 1944 being U.S. President Franklin D. Roosevelt and British Prime Minister Winston Churchill.[20] There were, however, growing problems with this increased exposure. As absences from their full-time police duties grew ever more frequent and longer there was increased tension in those RCMP sections staffed by band members. Personnel remaining grew understandably resentful because of increased workloads brought on by the band's growing popularity. It would not be until 1959 that a solution would be found; the establishment of a full-time professional RCMP band.

The war affected the boys' bands as much as the adult ones. Just as a generation earlier adult community bands rebadged themselves to become military bands, so too some prewar boys' bands became cadet bands. One such example was the North Battleford Rotary Boys Band that became a sea cadet band for the duration of the war.[21] Others adapted by opening up their memberships to girls. In the early 1940s, the Guelph Boys and Girls Band, sponsored by the Canadian Women's Service Force, numbered over forty-one

---

[18] Ibid., 103.
[19] Darren Wayne Oehlerking, "The History of Instrumental Wind Music within the Royal Canadian Mounted Police Band" (D.M.A. thesis, University of Iowa, 2008) 38.
[20] Ibid., 40.
[21] Katelyn Hannotte, "North Battleford City Kinsmen Band at 65", *Canadian Winds* 13, no. 2 (Spring 2015) 29-31.

individuals [Fig. 10.8] and the same city's Police Boys' Band had at least one female member by 1943.[22] Elsewhere in the country, newly established youth bands had also opened up their memberships to boys and girls: Gordon Olsen's Vancouver Junior Band in 1944 and Regina's Queen City Band in 1945.

Other, more significant changes were underway. Although the community operated and sponsored youth bands were still the dominant form of instrumental instruction for young people, a gradual shift had begun to take place during the war. The CBA's attempts in the late 1930s [see Chap. 9] to encourage the growth of the band movement in the schools was inching closer to reality as instrumental music instruction was slowly being transformed from an extra-curricular activity into one that was an integral part of the school day. One of the earliest curricular school band programs (other than those that existed in various forms in the religious colleges and private schools) first emerged in British Columbia. The precedent was set in the small community of Oliver in the province's southern interior. By 1941, band classes had been scheduled for three periods a week during the school day. It was the result of a fortunate combination of "...serious transportation problems for students who lived long distances from the school, and a sympathetic school administration."[23] Once the example had been set the movement gathered momentum and similar programs followed. The real impetus that year for the growth of curricular band programs came not from the west but from the city of Barrie in Ontario where a history and English teacher convinced an equally sympathetic administration to integrate band into the grade nine course of studies at Barrie Collegiate Institute.

The start of the Second World War also marked the end of an era. The founding figures of the Canadian band movement, Charles O'Neill, R.B. Hayward, J.J. Gagnier, John Slatter and C.F. Thiele were all in their senior years. There was a need for fresh blood and ironically it was the war that provided it. Unlike the army which sought experienced bandmasters from the British, the navy and the air force found their leaders at home. Most of these were young men, many still in their twenties, largely untested and unknown. By war's end they had established their credentials and it was primarily from the air force that this new leadership of the Canadian band movement emerged. Three names in particular are worth noting because of the enormous contributions they made to the continued growth and development of wind bands during the postwar years. The first two were conductors, Warrant Officer Clifford Hunt and Flying Officer Martin Boundy. Hunt and Boundy

---

[22] Robert F. Hamilton, *Guelph's Bands and Musicians* (Guelph, ON: Hamilton Art Studio, 1996) 8.
[23] Dale McIntosh, *A History of Music in British Columbia 1850-1950* (Victoria, BC: Sono Nis Press, 1989) 173.

would lead military, community, college, youth and school bands for the remainder of the twentieth century. In doing so they would inspire many others from coast to coast. Both men were elected presidents of the American Bandmasters Association [Hunt 1972-73, Boundy 1983-84][24] and served twice each as presidents of the Canadian Bandmasters Association [Hunt, 1954 and 1959, Boundy 1951 and 1970]; these were measures of the esteem in which they were held by their colleagues from across North America. The third individual was a bassoonist but is best remembered as a beloved teacher and arranger. His name first appears during the war as a credit on a manuscript arrangement of *The Airmen's Prayer,* an air force band staple performed at church parades and ceremonies of a remembrance nature. Tucked away in the top right corner of each manuscript march size card, under the names of the composer and lyricist are the words "arr. by Cpl. K. Bray."[25] After he left the RCAF, Kenneth Bray pursued a distinguished career in music education at all levels, from the early grades through his work introducing the Kodaly Method to Ontario schools to his later years as a highly respected professor of music at the University of Western Ontario in London, Ontario. He co-authored, along with D. Bruce Snell, two texts for senior high school students entitled *For Young Musicians*, Vols.1 and 2 (Waterloo, ON: Waterloo Music Company, 1961, 1967, rev. ed. 1995) and was a prolific arranger.[26] Two of his most popular arrangements for band were a collection of national anthems, *O Canada, God Save the Queen* and the *Star-Spangled Banner* (Toronto: Gordon V. Thompson, 1957) and *Nine Hymn Tune Settings* (Toronto: Gordon V. Thompson, 1964). Both of these settings were fixtures in high school band music folios for generations of Canadian band students.[27] There were of course many other service musicians who also made significant contributions but few received the postwar recognition awarded Hunt, Boundy and Bray. What all of the country's Second World War musicians had in common, however, was their influence on their largest audiences, the soldiers, sailors, airmen and airwomen of the Canadian military.

Canada's population in 1939 was just over 11 million people. By the end of the war over 1.1 million of its citizens, mostly men between the ages of eighteen and forty-five,

---

[24] "Past Presidents," *American Bandmasters Association* at www.americanbandmasters.org accessed 08 April 2019. This particular list is a who's who of the American band movement including some of its most celebrated composers.

[25] Copies of the *Airmen's Prayer* are in the author's private collection.

[26] Wallace Laughton and Betty Nygard King, "Kenneth Bray," *The Canadian Encyclopedia*, May 9, 2007 last edited December 13, 2013 at www.thecanadianencyclopedia.ca accessed 09 April 2019.

[27] Ken Bray began teaching at the University of Western Ontario in September of 1969. One of his assignments was a first year under graduate theory class attended by a very insecure student by the name of Charles E. Charles. To this day the author believes the only reason he passed that year was because of Ken Bray's warmth, patience, support and good-humour.

had served in uniform.[28]   When not in direct combat zones, they would have heard the music of the military bands in makeshift army camps, on naval bases and air stations.   The bands were omnipresent and often performed two or three times a day.   With the end of the war the troops came home and went on to parent the largest cohort of children in Canadian history, the "Baby Boom".   When those boomers started reaching high school age in the late 1950s and early 1960s, they enthusiastically embraced wind band programs, in some cases taught by former wartime musicians like Martin Boundy, Howard Leroy and Ken Bray.   The fact that their parents showed little reluctance in supporting their offspring's musical activities begs the question: did the parents' own exposure to wind bands during the war contribute to the support that would create one of the most exciting and productive periods for high school bands in our wind band story?

The contribution of Canadian military bands and military musicians to not just the growing school band movement but to an increasingly confident national musical culture didn't end with the cessation of hostilities in 1945.   Veterans returned home to a war weary nation ready to resume their peacetime lives but it was not to last.   By 1948 Churchill's "Iron Curtain" had descended across Eastern Europe and Canadians found themselves facing a new enemy in a new kind of war.   As in the past, when Canada's armed forces found themselves facing a potential external threat, the bands once again were unintended beneficiaries and as a result the 1950s became a "Golden Age" for Canadian regular force bands.

---

[28] "Military History of Canada during World War II," Wikipedia at www.wikipedia.org accessed 09 April 2019.

CHAPTER TEN GALLERY

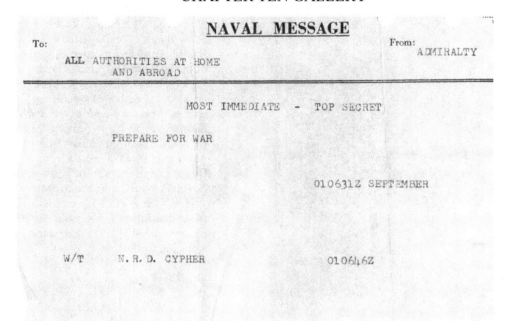

Figure 10.1.   "PREPARE FOR WAR" Source: Estate of Rear Admiral J.A. Charles, RCN

Figure 10.2.   Royal Canadian Horse Artillery Band, Camp Petawawa, 1940.   Director of Music Captain F.W. Coleman.   The RCHA Band was one of the first prewar permanent force bands to reach effective strength after the start of WWII.   Source: Royal Canadian Horse Artillery Association, Kingston.

160

Figure 10.3.   Lieutenant Alfred E. Zealley, RCNVR, undated photo. Known as "The Father of Canadian Navy Bands", Zealley had been a British Army bandmaster, director of the Harvard University Band, leader of the "Belleville Kilties" Band and coauthor of a book entitled *Famous Bands of the British Empire*.   His offer to provide the RCN with bands at no cost to the government was quickly accepted. By the end of the war, he had helped establish the RCN School of Music at H.M.C.S. *York* in Toronto and seventeen full-time bands across the country and at sea.   Source: Jack Kopstein Collection.

Figure 10.4.   The H.M.C.S. *Cornwallis* Band, Cornwallis N.S., 1944.   This was the largest of the navy's bands and at full strength it numbered over sixty musicians.   During the war the Cornwallis Naval Base itself was the largest in the British Commonwealth with a capacity for training 10,000 new recruits at a time.   Source: HMCS-CFB *Cornwallis* Military Museum.

Figure 10.5. RCAF Station Trenton Band, 1938. This was a volunteer band whose members were expected to perform their regular tradesmen duties during the day and rehearsed during off-duty hours. Source: National Air Force Museum of Canada.

Figure 10.6. RCAF Women's Division Band, 1945. Although a Drum and Bugle group, it along with its sister ensemble the Canadian Women's Army Corps Band, helped put to rest the fiction that women were less proficient wind instrumentalists than men. Source: National Air Force Museum of Canada.

Figure 10.7. Royal Canadian Mounted Police Band, Ottawa, 1940. Director Joseph T. Brown. This was a part-time ensemble whose members were expected to perform regular police duties during the day and rehearse in their off duty hours. Their increasingly busy schedule of performances during WWII created tensions between musicians and those in their respective sections left behind who were expected to do the work of missing members while the band was engaged in a wide range of public appearances and war bond parades. The final solution was the creation of a full time professional RCMP Band in 1959. Source: Photo courtesy of Peter Carss.

Figure 10.8. Guelph Girls and Boys Band, early 1940s. Bandmaster Sid Ecott. Sponsored by the Canadian Women's Service Force, this was one of the early examples of a mixed youth band in Canada. The "pillbox" style of hat was very popular during the 1940s and appears often in photos of youth bands taken during the period. Source: Robert Hamilton, *Guelph's Bands and Musicians,* 1996.

CHAPTER ELEVEN

CANADIAN MILITARY BANDS IN THE COLDWAR ERA

The Golden Age of Regular Force Bands (1947-1968)

With the end of the Second World War, the Canadian military and the country as a whole were eager to return to the stability of their prewar lives. By March of 1947 "…all of Canada's full-time Active Force [Army] bands were reduced to nil strength."[1] Important lessons however had been learned by all three services; the contributions of the bands to the maintenance of morale, not just amongst servicemen and servicewomen, but to the civilian population at large had been clearly demonstrated. Despite the reductions of 1947, the army, navy and air force managed to keep some of their bands by the administrative manoeuvre of reconstituting them under a peacetime establishment. The army began by reinstating three bands, the RCHA [Royal Canadian Horse Artillery], the RCR [Royal Canadian Regiment] and the R22eR [Royal 22nd Regiment]. A fourth, the PPCLI [Princess Patricia's Canadian Light Infantry] joined them later that summer. The navy kept two professional bands, those at H.M.C.S. *Naden* in Esquimalt, B.C. and H.M.C.S. *Stadacona* in Halifax, N.S. The air force held on to the Central Band in Ottawa and added two more "…in 1946, Flight Lieutenant Hunt organized the RCAF Training Command Band at RCAF Station Downsview [Toronto] followed in 1947 by the Tactical Air Command Band…"[2]

The army however, struggled to fill vacant positions as wartime musicians sought new opportunities in civilian life. As the decade came to a close, the future of Canada's full-time army bands looked as though it would revert to the lean days of the prewar period. All of that changed with an enormous bang on August 29, 1949. It was on that day in the remote Semipalatinsk region of Kazakhstan that the Soviet Union [Russia] successfully tested its first atomic bomb. The acquisition of a functioning nuclear weapon inaugurated an arms race between the United States and the Soviet Union that was to last for four decades until the collapse of the Berlin Wall in 1989, a period known as the "Cold War". Although other countries would eventually join the nuclear club, Britain, France, India, Pakistan and China, it was the rivalry between the two superpowers that was to redefine

---

[1] Canada, Department of National Defence, *History of Bands in the Canadian Army* (Ottawa: National Defence Headquarters, 1952) 21.
[2] Jack Kopstein and Ian Pearson, *The Heritage of Canadian Military Music* (St. Catharines, ON: Vanwell Publishing Limited, 2002) 107.

global defence strategy in the postwar period.[3]   A doctrine emerged that was appropriately enough called MAD, Mutually Assured Destruction, which would initiate profound changes in military practices that had existed for centuries.   It was these changes that would breathe new life into Canadian Army bands.

To give the reader some idea of just how monumental these changes were, we need only examine them in the context of the life of one of the twentieth century's greatest statesmen. In 1898, Winston Churchill was a young cavalry officer at the Battle of Omdurman in the Sudan.   At the time, the most effective form of offensive warfare was, as it had been since Roman times, the cavalry charge.   Less than half a century later on August 6, 1945, just a few months shy of Churchill's seventy-first birthday, it was the airborne atomic bomb.   A shift of this scale necessitated similarly extraordinary leaps in the associated fields of military planning and preparedness.

In the past when nation states went to war against each other, the process of recruiting, training, mobilizing and deploying sufficient forces to the battlefield had always taken months to achieve.   Even during the First World War, with the extensive use of railways, it still took weeks to call up reserves and move them in the millions to the front lines.   With the advent of nuclear weapons and the development of long-range bombers, reaction times had been reduced to a matter of hours.   By the late 1950s, the introduction of ICBMs [Intercontinental Ballistic Missiles] further reduced that time to a matter of minutes.   There was no longer time to mobilize reserve forces.   A nation's first and only line of defence was its regular forces.   As a result, the 1950s witnessed the largest peacetime buildup of active duty military forces in Canada's history, before or since.   As our study has repeatedly shown, whenever there was an increase in defence spending during times of perceived or real danger, military bands also received a share of those increases.

Initially finding enough musicians to staff the four existing army bands was a challenge.[4]   The creation of a fifth band, the First Canadian Infantry Battalion Band at Camp Valcartier [near Québec City] in 1951 only made a desperate shortage of qualified musicians worse.   "In August 1952, there were thirty-three vacancies for bandsmen to staff at least five bands."[5]   These were not large bands to begin with.   The scale of issue for army bands in 1951 included one piccolo, one flute, one oboe, one Eb clarinet, ten Bb clarinets, two alto saxophones, one tenor saxophone, one baritone saxophone, five Bb

---

[3] Canada could have been a member had it chosen to do so.   The ZEEP [Zero Energy Experimental Pile] reactor went critical on September 5, 1945 at the Chalk River Ontario nuclear laboratory.   It was the first operational reactor outside of the U.S.   See R.E. Green and A. Okazaki, "ZEEP: The Little Reactor that Could," *CNS Bulletin* 16, No. 3 (Autumn, 1995) at www.cns-snc.ca accessed 03 July 2019.

[4] Kopstein and Pearson, *Heritage*, 107.

[5] Ibid., 109.

cornets, four horns, two tenor trombones, one bass trombone, one euphonium, two basses and two percussionists.[6] The solution to the problem was found that same year overseas, at first in the Netherlands, liberated by Canadians in 1945, and then in England. Dutch musicians were given permission to emigrate to Canada following a handover of Canadian equipment to Holland. When the Minister of Defence, Brooke Claxton was asked by his Dutch counterpart what Canada wished in return, Claxton replied "bandsmen."[7]

In January of 1953 permission was also granted to enlist professional musicians in the United Kingdom. By the time this European musician recruitment program ended in 1967, over two hundred and fifty Dutch and two hundred British musicians had joined Canada's regular force bands. Highly trained in Dutch conservatories or graduates of Kneller Hall, they further contributed to the professionalism and proficiency of the country's postwar military bands.

The first of the newly formed postwar bands was the previously mentioned First Canadian Infantry Battalion Band. Shortly after its formation in 1951 under the baton of Captain James Gayfer, it left for a thirteen-month rotation with the Canadian Army in what was then called West Germany.[8] Upon its return the band was stationed at Camp Borden, Ontario. In 1952 the first of the Dutch draft had begun to arrive and with them the army's bands began to fill the vacancies that had been plaguing them. Assured of a stable source of qualified musicians the army then began an aggressive campaign to increase its number of bands adding two more in that year alone: The Royal Canadian Artillery Band in Halifax and the Royal Canadian Corps of Signals Band at Vimy Barracks in Kingston. No sooner had the Signals band been settled, it was posted to Korea to entertain Canadian troops, only returning to Kingston in May of 1954.

The first active service Canadian Army band to benefit immediately from Dutch and British musicians was the Royal Canadian Engineers Band established at Vedder Crossing, B.C. [now part of the city of Chilliwack], in 1953. Under the direction of World War Two veteran Albert Brown, the Engineers band was authorized an effective strength of fifty-two musicians '…two flutes, one Eb clarinet, two oboes, sixteen Bb clarinets, two alto and two tenor saxes, one baritone sax, two bassoons, four French horns, eight Bb cornets, five trombones two euphoniums, two tubas and three percussionists."[9] After the band's six

---

[6] Canada, Department of National Defence, *History*, Appendix "D".

[7] Kopstein and Pearson, *Heritage,* 109.

[8] From the end of the Second World War until the collapse of the Berlin Wall and the implosion of the Soviet Union in 1991, Canada maintained an entire army brigade as well as air force squadrons at bases in West Germany. It was an obligation entered into by the terms of the 1949 NATO agreement that was respected by successive Liberal and Conservative governments.

[9] Kopstein and Pearson, *Heritage,* 116.

month tour of duty in West Germany in 1954, where it performed regularly across the Netherlands and once in Luxembourg, it returned to Vedder Crossing to become actively involved in musical activities throughout British Columbia.   In 1955 two more regular force bands were created; the Royal Canadian Dragoons Band and the Band of the Black Watch [Royal Highland Regiment of Canada].   Both ensembles were eventually posted to Canadian bases in West Germany for extended overseas postings, the Dragoons from 1959-1961 and the Black Watch from 1962-1965.   When in Canada they were stationed at Camp Gagetown N.B. and Montréal respectively.   The following year saw the formation of the last two new army bands, the Royal Canadian Ordnance Corps Band in Montréal and the Lord Strathcona's Horse Band in Calgary.   By 1957, the Canadian Army supported twelve full-time professional bands with an average strength of fifty to fifty-five musicians in each.   They were to be found in seven of ten provinces on bases from Chilliwack to Halifax with one on permanent duty with NATO forces in West Germany from 1955 until 1968 [Fig. 11.1].

Although there were 106 thirty-piece bands authorized for the militia as of December 6, 1951, many were classified as being non-effective, essentially non-existent.[10]   These reserve bands, like their community band cousins, were facing the challenges of changing public tastes and competition from new technologies.   Postwar prosperity also gave greater numbers of Canadians access to their own motor vehicles which, combined with the nation's road building frenzy of the 1950s drew more and more people away from their communities on weekends and the summer months.   By 1968 the number of active militia bands had dropped to below fifty.

The Royal Canadian Air Force maintained a total personnel strength in the 1950s roughly equivalent to that of the army but it only supported three bands, the Central Band in Ottawa, the Training Command Band at Downsview [Toronto] and the Tactical Air Command Band, later to be known as the Northwest Command Band in Edmonton.   These were superb concert organizations whose performance standards attracted the country's finest musicians.   In 1958 the Downsview band, under the direction of Flight Lieutenant Clifford Hunt consisted of "…two flutes, two oboes, two bassoons, seventeen Bb clarinets, one alto and one bass clarinet, two alto and two tenor saxophones, three cornets, two trumpets, four horns, five trombones, two euphoniums, two tubas, two string bass and percussion."[11]   Ottawa's Central Band [Fig. 11.2] enjoyed a similar complement of musicians while the Edmonton band was a little smaller with forty-two bandsmen.   In

---

[10] Canada, Department of National Defence, *History,* 23.
[11] Kopstein and Pearson, *Heritage*, 123.

addition to staffing its three bands, up to ten RCAF musicians were also attached to the NORAD [North American Air Defense Command] Band in Colorado Springs, Colorado. This was an elite group of musicians drawn from all three U.S. services, army, navy and air force as well as the RCAF. Known as the "Cavalcade of Music" it toured extensively in Central and North America in the 1960s and 1970s. It appeared at Montréal's EXPO 67 during centennial year and performed at both the CNE in Toronto and Vancouver's PNE. In its heyday in the 1960s, membership included some of the finest service musicians in the combined forces of Canada and the United States. The group's popularity waned in the 1970s and in 1979 its operations were terminated. Similar cost-cutting measures had already started in Canada. In 1965, the Downsview band was declared surplus and the RCAF reduced its support to just two bands, the Central Band in Ottawa and the Edmonton band which was renamed the Training Command Band and transferred to its new home in Winnipeg.

As with the army and the air force, the Royal Canadian Navy was also a beneficiary of the agreement to recruit foreign musicians for its bands. Those that joined the navy however, were drawn almost exclusively from the United Kingdom and most were former members of the Royal Marines Band Service.[12] These joined the existing establishment of naval bandsmen with the main bands at Esquimalt and Halifax. A smaller group was maintained at the navy's recruit training centre H.M.C.S. *Cornwallis* situated in Nova Scotia's Annapolis basin. In addition to fulfilling its own musical commitments, Halifax's Stadacona Band was also responsible for providing small ship's bands [12-15 piece] for the aircraft carriers H.M.C.S. *Magnificent* [Fig. 11.3] and H.M.C.S. *Bonaventure*. By 1955 the navy's bands were enjoying the same level of support as those in the army and the air force. The RCN's *Manual of Drill and Ceremonial* contained a section on bands which authorized an instrumentation of forty-five musicians: three flutes, two oboes, one Eb clarinet, twelve Bb clarinets, one alto and one bass clarinet, four saxophones, four cornets, two trumpets, four horns, three trombones, one euphonium, four basses and three percussionists [Fig. 11.4].[13]

Foreseeing the possible challenges of maintaining a steady supply of trained musicians to keep its bands up to strength, the Royal Canadian Navy established the RCN School of Music at Esquimalt in 1954. Modelled on the Royal Marines School of Music in the U.K., the school was designed to train new recruits with little or no previous musical experience

---

[12] The Royal Marines Band Service provided (and still does) bands to the U.K.'s Royal Navy. Since Canada has never maintained a force comparable to the Royal Marines, bands for the Canadian navy have always been attached directly to that service.
[13] Kopstein and Pearson, *Heritage,* 112.

for service in the bands. Bandsmen Apprentices, as they were called, signed on for a seven-year term of service. After a fifteen-week basic training course at H.M.C.S. *Cornwallis*, they would undergo two years of intensive musical training at the school by which time they would be ready for the navy's bands. By 1961, as postwar conditions improved in both the Netherlands and England, the supply of trained musicians from those countries that had helped bolster Canada's military bands in the 1950s began to dwindle. In response, the army and the air force turned to the RCN School of Music for new recruits. That year the school was renamed the Tri-Service School of Music and in 1968, on the heels of unification, it became CFSMUS [Canadian Forces School of Music]. During the 1960s, musician candidates were often in their late teens with little formal music education beyond high school band. The military musician course of study was comprehensive including classes in aural training and theory as well as instruction on a primary instrument in private, small ensemble and large ensemble settings [Fig. 11.5]. The Bandsmen Apprentice program at the Tri-Service School of Music in Esquimalt gave talented and motivated young instrumentalists of modest means an opportunity to pursue a career in music without the benefit of expensive and limited [1960s] post-secondary programs of study. Many graduates of the school, like Halifax's Jim Forde, went on to successful careers as performers, conductors, composers, arrangers, teachers and musical entrepreneurs, not just in the military but in the larger civilian community.[14]

In 1967 Canada celebrated 100 years of Confederation. The centennial year was a period of intense national pride marked by celebrations that ranged from the Montréal World's Fair EXPO 67, to locally organized events including the dedication of innumerable new arenas, schools, theatres and community centres. The Department of National Defence was equally involved and focused most of its resources on a travelling spectacle known as the Canadian Armed Forces Tattoo 67. It was a mixture of pomp, pageantry and history lesson that from March 31 until October 11 gave a total of 157 performances in forty-five Canadian communities from coast to coast. In the Spring and Fall, smaller venues were served by two travelling arena shows that numbered approximately 300 performers each. They travelled on two specially outfitted trains, the red (CPR) and the blue (CNR) which were "...home, workshop and community centre for ...a six-week period."[15] From May 25 until September 9, the two joined forces and were augmented by a further 1000 personnel to form the stadium ensemble which gave forty-eight

---

[14] Jim Forde, e-mail correspondence with the author, 22 January 2019.
[15] Keith Allan Wilson, *The Making of a Tattoo: Canadian Armed Forces Tattoo 1967* (Victoria, BC: Friesen Press, 2017) 63.

performances in Victoria, Vancouver, Ottawa, Montréal, Toronto and Hamilton.[16]   Many of the participants were musicians from the regular force bands who provided the members of the static pit band (30), herald trumpets and marching massed bands.   One scene "…meant to evoke the mood of the Boer War, involved a massed band of 350 playing popular band selections of the time."[17]   Some of these musicians were detached from their parent units for up to six months but the bands they had left were still expected to continue operating during the centennial year.   Despite being shorthanded they maintained busy schedules performing in community parades, outdoor concerts, charitable fundraising events and military ceremonies.   In some cases, such as the navy's H.M.C.S. *Cornwallis* Band, reserve musicians were employed to fill vacancies created by the Tattoo.[18]   In addition to both the Tattoo and local commitments, one band was also on permanent station at EXPO 67 and the Canadian Guards Band of Petawawa was required in Ottawa during the summer months for the daily "Changing of the Guard" ceremony on Parliament Hill.

The Legacy of the Postwar Regular Force Bands (1968-1994)

By 1968, the golden age of Canada's regular force bands was drawing to a close.   In retrospect it was inevitable.   The immediate postwar period was one of unprecedented economic growth; a prosperity that sustained increases in defence spending made necessary by the threats of imminent nuclear war and a seemingly endless string of communist successes in the developing world.   As the defence budget grew, so too did the number of bands supported by it.   In 1958, the Department of National Defence had 1011 full-time bandsmen on the payroll making it the country's largest single employer of musicians.[19] By the mid 1960s however, the Defence Department had started looking for ways to trim spending under the leadership of a dynamic young MP by the name of Paul Hellyer.   The solution was "The Canadian Forces Reorganization Act" which came into effect on February 1, 1968.   This resulted in the army, navy and air force being merged into one force, the Canadian Armed Forces, with a single unified command structure.   Unification achieved a primary objective, to eliminate the triplication of support and logistical services that had previously plagued the Department of National Defence.   One of the casualties however was the army's bands.   Seven were reduced to nil strength, leaving only five:

---

[16] Keith Allan Wilson, *The Making of a Tattoo,* 42.

[17] Ibid., 49.

[18] The author was a musician in the Royal Canadian Navy Reserve in 1967 and spent one month with the Cornwallis Band in July of that year.

[19] Kay Kritzweiser, "These are airmen who fly on wings of song," *The Globe Magazine* (November 22, 1958) 13.

RCR (London), PPCLI (Calgary), R22eR (Québec), RCA (Montréal) and Vimy (Kingston). The navy lost the H.M.C.S. *Cornwallis* Band but kept its other two, those at Naden (Esquimalt) and Stadacona (Halifax). The air force Central Band remained in Ottawa as did the newly named Air Command Band in Winnipeg.

The commitment to music made by the Defence Department during the immediate postwar period was very much in keeping with the Canadian tradition of military band engagement with local communities that stretched back to the days before Confederation. As Bernard Ostry pointed out in his study *The Cultural Connection: An Essay on Culture and Government Policy in Canada*:

> The importance of music and theatre was recognized early, not only in relieving the tedium of military routine but in promoting a corporate spirit and sense of pride, and in fostering cheerful relations between garrisons and civilian populations. For years the Department of National Defence was alone among federal departments in developing a conscious, consistent and imaginative cultural policy and providing the funds to make it work.[20]

Military musicians contributed well beyond their official duties in the surrounding communities. At the national level, no one story better illustrates this involvement than that of Victoria's "Symphony Night". Rear Admiral John A. Charles, CD, RCN [the author's father] was appointed Canadian Maritime Commander Pacific in 1966. In this capacity he was the operational commander of Canadian military forces and their support units on the West Coast. One of these units was the H.M.C.S. *Naden* Band. Shortly after the Admiral's arrival, his headquarters staff approved a request for an evening performance by the band. Within days, his staff also received an urgent request from the Director of Music of the Naden Band to meet personally with the Admiral to explain to him why the band was unable to fulfill the commitment. It was a courageous move when one considers that in the naval hierarchy, the band's director, a lieutenant, the second lowest commissioned rank in the service, was pleading with a rear admiral, functionally the second highest rank in the navy. At the meeting, the band's director was asked why the band could not perform as requested, especially since the Commander of all Canadian Forces on the Pacific coast had effectively ordered it to do so. A somewhat shaken bandmaster

---

[20] Bernard Ostry, *The Cultural Connection: An Essay on Culture and Government Policy in Canada* (Toronto: McClelland and Stewart, 1978) 41.

responded: "But sir, its Symphony Night!".[21] This meant nothing to Rear Admiral Charles at the time but he quickly learned, as did general officers across the country whose commands included regular force bands, the full extent to which their musicians were involved with local musical activities at multiple levels.   In the case of the Victoria Symphony, over one half of the orchestra's woodwind, brass and percussion sections were serving sailors in the navy band.   From that point on, until his transfer back to Ottawa in 1969, Rear Admiral Charles' office always kept a copy of the Victoria Symphony's schedule on hand.

As noted in the introduction to this study there were thirty orchestras active in Canada in 1955.   Of these, only two were fully professional, those in Toronto and Montréal.   At least ten were semi-professional in which musicians were paid per service.[22]   One of these was the Edmonton Symphony Orchestra.   A program from the 1955-56 season contains the names of the orchestra's members.   Of the twenty-seven listed in the brass, woodwind and percussion sections, twenty-one were serving in the Tactical Air Command Band as was the entire string bass section.[23]   Across the country, wherever a regular force band and a symphony orchestra co-existed, whether in Victoria, Calgary, Edmonton, Winnipeg, London (Ont.), Kingston, Ottawa, Québec, Fredericton or Halifax, many in the woodwind, brass and percussion sections were serving members of the Canadian military.   Even the string sections were beneficiaries; many of the British and Dutch musicians who joined had been cross-trained in their countries of origin.   It was not unusual for units like the U.K.'s Royal Marines to insist that their musicians play both a wind and a string instrument [strings were needed for the more intimate setting of shipboard mess dinners].   Consequently, these musicians could also fill vacancies as violinists, violists, cellists and string bassists.   Their extra-curricular activities were not just limited to playing in the local symphony.   They were teachers, both private and at conservatories or post-secondary institutions, arrangers, composers and conductors.   Extensive as the musical activities of the 1951-1968 cohort of military musicians were while they were still in uniform, it pales in comparison to what many achieved after they retired from active service.   It would be impossible to do justice to all but a brief mention of several may give the reader some appreciation of the enormity of their contributions to Canada's growing musical culture.

---

[21] My father passed away in September of 2010. Whenever I went to visit him during the last decades of his life, he would tell me this story. Sitting in his easy chair in the log house he built with his own hands, surrounded by his beloved forest at Otter Point, he would always start the same way "…did I ever tell you the story…". He would chuckle and laugh and at the end would always finish off with "…bands, caused me nothing but trouble. Everybody wanted one but nobody wanted to pay for it!" [sound familiar?]

[22] Ernest MacMillan, *Music in Canada* (Toronto: University of Toronto Press, 1955) 68-77.

[23] Annotated copy of program courtesy Michael Scott.

Chief Petty Officer Ronald MacKay joined the Royal Canadian Navy in 1946 after finishing high school. He was originally destined to be a cook but his early musical training in the Dunnville (Ont.) Boys Band led to a speedy remuster to the bandsman trade as a French hornist. With the exception of a brief training interlude at the Tri-Service School of Music in Esquimalt, his entire career was spent with the H.M.C.S. *Stadacona* Band in Halifax. In 1964 he was engaged as the first professional conductor of the Truro Concert Band which rehearsed on Tuesday evenings. Shortly thereafter, the principal of Truro Junior High School enticed MacKay to come up earlier in the day and lead an after-school rehearsal of the school band as well as a second one on Saturday mornings.[24] In 1966 he took his release from the navy and started a second career as a music teacher. He began at Truro Junior High School but in 1970, with the opening of the Cobequid Education Centre, he devoted more of his energies to the high school level band. He was a tireless and enthusiastic advocate for music in the schools and led by example. On his retirement from the classroom in 1991, his colleague Donna Hargreaves wrote … "He created an instrumental program that led the way for others of its kind in Nova Scotia, and set a performance standard for high school concert bands throughout the province."[25] Like Joseph Vézina in Québec before him, Ron MacKay wasn't just satisfied with two careers. After 1991 he travelled the Maritimes as an adjudicator, clinician and conductor. He taught at Nova Scotia Teachers College as well as at St. Mary's, St. Francis Xavier and Dalhousie Universities.[26] His dedication to music and the wind band was such that right up to the year of his death in 2008 he remained the principal conductor of the Halifax Concert Band.

Out west, another ex-military musician from the postwar era was also a pioneer but he chose to nurture the love of wind bands and their music in an entirely different segment of the general population. In 1953, the First Canadian Infantry Battalion Band [later redesignated as the Canadian Guards Band and moved to Camp Petawawa in 1956], was based at Camp Borden. Under the direction of Captain James Gayfer, the ensemble numbered forty-six musicians, one of whom was a cornet player by the name of Band Corporal A.H. Pinchen.[27] Arthur Harry Pinchen was born in Toronto in 1935 and in early childhood moved to Merritton, Ontario. Both his grandfather and father were cornet players and both had heard the legendary Herbert L. Clarke perform accompanied by the Anglo-Canadian Leather Company Band. His father had also played with the Thorold

---

[24] Ken Henderson, "Truro District Schools Band Program," *Canadian Winds* 5, no. 2 (Spring 2007) 62.

[25] As cited in Henderson, "Truro District Schools" 64.

[26] Ibid., 63.

[27] Band membership list contained in an undated concert program c. 1954 courtesy of Ed Barlow.

Concert Band so it was inevitable that young Harry would also take up the instrument, which he did at the age of ten. By his late teens he was an accomplished player but in Canada in 1953 there was no Canadian university offering undergraduate degrees in performance, so Harry Pinchen joined the army.[28] After nine years of service in two bands ending with the Lord Strathcona's Horse Band in Calgary, Harry Pinchen was honourably discharged in 1962. In 1964 he relocated to Edmonton and shortly thereafter was encouraged by another former military musician to conduct a recently formed community band. The new group was financially supported by the Cosmopolitan Society of Edmonton, a local service club and in 1967 was formally named the "Cosmopolitan Music Society".[29] Under Harry's direction the society flourished with both youth and amateur adult instrumental programs numbering over 400 participants. These included four concert bands, two jazz bands, a string program and a jazz dance program with groups rehearsing on average once a week. The dramatic increase in Edmonton's curricular school band programs in the 1970s, with up to four rehearsals a week, forced the society to abandon its youth element. It was at this point that Harry Pinchin "...conceived the idea of developing beginning adult classes for persons who had never played band instruments."[30] The success of the initiative was far reaching. By 2003, the Cosmopolitan Music Society was sponsoring three bands and a choir with a membership of over 200 adult participants.

In addition to Harry Pinchen's activities with adult bands through the society, he also spearheaded a recording project that made Canadian music for band widely available to general audiences. He collaborated with CBC Records in the release of two recordings entitled *Concert in the Park* (CBC Enterprises, 1988) and *Snake Fence Country* (CBC Records, 1997). With Pinchen conducting the Edmonton Wind Sinfonia, these two discs represent some of the finest collections of wind band music ever assembled by Canadian composers including works by Howard Cable, Stephen Chatman, Donald Coakley, Robert Farnon, James Gayfer, Pierre Mercure, Godfrey Ridout and Healey Willan.

The hundreds of Dutch and British musicians who joined the Canadian military in the 1950s were equally engaged in enriching our national musical culture. Like Ron MacKay and Harry Pinchen, many were enthusiastic advocates of wind bands after they completed their military service. The contributions of two in particular deserve some mention.

---

[28] Arthur Harry Pinchen, *Count Every Star: The Memoirs of Arthur Harry Pinchen* (Edmonton: Privately published, 2017) 3-4.
[29] Audrey Shonn, "Edmonton's Cosmopolitan Music Society: 40 years and still blowing strong," *Canadian Winds* 2, no. 1 (Autumn 2003) 11.
[30] Ibid., 12.

Henry Bonnenberg, a Dutch national, joined the Canadian Army in 1953 at the age of thirty-nine.   A clarinet graduate of the Amsterdam Conservatory and further studies in prewar Vienna, he served in the same band as Harry Pinchen for three years.   In 1958 he took his release from active service and accepted the position of music teacher at Ottawa's newly opened Laurentian High School.   Within ten years the Laurentian band program would go on to become one of the city's finest.[31]   Although "Hank" as he was known to his students would retire from the classroom in 1979, he certainly didn't slow down. Starting in 1980 he presented a wildly popular series of ten-week long evening courses entitled "The Enjoyment of Music with Henry Bonnenberg" at the privately owned Neils Lund Music Studio [Lund was himself a former percussionist with the RCAF Central Band].[32]

One British musician, after his years in the RCAF, went on to international acclaim as soloist, clinician, conductor and arranger with some of the finest performing wind bands and jazz groups in North America.   Born in Edinburgh, Scotland, Bobby Herriot began his musical studies with several local brass bands.   He received his formal training at Kneller Hall, the Royal College of Music and the Royal Academy of Music.   After serving in the band of the "Blues and Royals" [one of the more prestigious London regiments] he emigrated to Canada in 1957 and joined the RCAF.   Postings with Edmonton's Tactical Air Command Band and then the Central Band in Ottawa were followed by a transfer to the NORAD Band in Colorado Springs.   Bobby left active service in 1966 and after a brief stint in Vancouver that included lecturing at UBC, he settled in Toronto in the early 1970s. In constant demand, he appeared with some of North America's biggest names in jazz, including Buddy Rich, Stan Kenton, Xavier Cugat and Lionel Hampton.   He rejoined the Canadian military (militia) as Director of Music of the 7th Toronto RCA Band in 1976 where he served until his final retirement in 1990.   Through the remainder of that decade and into the 2000s he conducted two community groups, the Thornhill Community Band and the Hamilton Concert Band.   He was also an active member of the Canadian Federation of musicians serving at one point as Vice-President from Canada of the American Federation of Musicians of the United States and Canada.[33]

Bobby Herriot, like Ron MacKay, Harry Pinchen, Henry Bonnenberg and hundreds of other ex-military musicians in the postwar bands, fostered the growth of and love for wind

---

[31] W.O. Ketchum, "Faces of Ottawa: Henry Bonnenberg," *Ottawa Journal* (21 June 1969) at www.newspapers.com accessed 10 June 2019.

[32] Advertisement from the *Ottawa Journal* (25 January 1980) pg. 29 at www.newspapers.com accessed 19 June 2019.   The author resided in Ottawa until 1990 and can remember hearing on several occasions of the course's popularity on local radio and TV.

[33] "Bobby Herriot," *The Hamilton Concert Band* at www.hamiltonconcertband.com accessed 19 June 2019.

bands in a way that continues to resonate today. Their impact is to be found in recordings, compositions, arrangements, scholarships and above all in the lives of the thousands they mentored.

The Voice of the Army Band

Ironically the same cannot be said for the military bands in which they played. There was only one Canadian military band from that era that is still remembered today: it was an exceptional ensemble made up of some of the country's finest wind performers and it enjoyed enormous popularity across Canada and parts of the United States. It was in fact the best army band the army never had! Its musicians were not attested members of the Canadian military nor did they wear uniforms but in every other respect, it was an army band. The ensemble was created by the CBC in 1950 at the express request of Brooke Claxton, then minister of national defence [the same Brooke Claxton who arranged for the immigration of Dutch and British bandsmen to join the Canadian Army]. It was intended as a recruiting vehicle for the army at the start of the Korean conflict and was originally called "The Voice of the Army Band."[34] The radio broadcasts for which it was established were modelled on similar shows given by U.S. service bands and a gifted young CBC conductor from Toronto was chosen to lead it. His name was Howard Reid Cable [Fig. 11.6]. The program ran for two full seasons of thirty-nine weeks each during which time Howard Cable honed his skills as a master composer/arranger for the concert band. By the end of the Korean War the show had proven to be so successful that the CBC decided to continue running it for two more summer seasons. Speaking of the period immediately after the Korean War, Howard Cable himself remarked:

> We were on two seasons on radio and one on television with the Cable Concert Band, which was a superior band than anything around here. I would get calls from Don Hunsberger from Eastman and [Frederick] Fennell saying, "Who is in that band? What is going on? We never expected a Canadian band to sound like that."[35]

---

[34] Michael Purves-Smith and Jacqueline Dawson, "An Interview with Howard Cable," *Canadian Winds* 4, no. 2 (Spring 2006) 73.
[35] Howard Cable as cited in John Reid, ed.by Barb Hunter, "The Life and Music of Howard Cable," *Association of Concert Bands Journal* (June 2014) 20. Copy of the article given to the author by Howard Cable 6 November 2014. High praise indeed considering that Frederick Fennell established the Eastman Wind Ensemble in 1952.

It was during these radio years that Cable's best-known early works for band were composed. The show's final summer season was also picked up and broadcast in the U.S. by the Mutual Broadcasting Network and it was from there that *Newfoundland Rhapsody, Quebec Folk Fantasy* and *Snake Fence Country* were first heard by executives from the New York publisher Chappell. The rest as they say, is history. Howard Cable's association with military bands didn't end there. From 1962 to 1966 he was "...the civilian associate conductor and [Canadian] arranger of the NORAD Band in Colorado...".[36] In Canada he was an invited clinician and lecturer at the Canadian Forces School of Music after its move to CFB Borden in 1988 until its closure in 1994 and in the early 1990s he was also a guest rehearsal conductor of the 7th Toronto RCA Band whenever the band's regular director was unavailable.[37]

The "Voice of the Army Band", which became the "Cable Concert Band", made one final television appearance on the CBC shortly after the unification of the Canadian Forces. In 1970, the Howard Cable Concert Band was resurrected for a musical variety special entitled "A Little Bit of Omm-Pa!". Directed by the legendary Norman Campbell, the show featured Howard Cable conducting a forty-two piece ensemble consisting of some of Toronto's finest musicians. The performances included three of Cable's own compositions: *Marchmanship* (Chappell, 1954), one movement from the *Stratford Suite* (Chappell, 1964) and his *Newfoundland Rhapsody* (Chappell, 1956) in a modified arrangement that included Catherine McKinnon singing a newly introduced setting of the song *Cape St. Mary's*. The remainder of the program was a potpourri of marches, dances, solos and a "Concert in the Park" scene with Cable and a smaller band of twenty-five pieces dressed in fanciful "turn of the century" [1900] community band costumes [Fig. 11.7].[38] The entire production is a forceful remainder of Howard Cable's vision of the concert band as a medium of popular entertainment; a vision totally consistent and entirely faithful to the almost two centuries old military band tradition that it was originally created to promote.

Post-Unification (1968-1994)

The period between unification in 1968 and the even more draconian reductions of regular and reserve force bands in 1994, was one of greater inclusion, standardization and

---

[36] Ibid., 19. The NORAD Band's American arranger at the time was Warren Barker.
[37] Michael Lawson, former Director of Music of the 7th Toronto RCA Band, telephone interview with the author 18 July 2019.
[38] Copy of DVD *A Little Bit of Omm-Pa* (CBC, 1970) courtesy Lori Fox Rossi, November 2014.

increased engagement with the ever-growing number of post-secondary music schools across the country. After the initial cutbacks, the nine remaining regular force bands had their authorized strengths reduced from their pre-unification levels of 47-55 musicians down to 35. Only one band, Ottawa's Central Band was allowed an additional ten musicians. In 1971, eight more positions were allocated to the Central Band in the form of a "Serenade of Strings," a string ensemble with piano whose primary responsibility was the provision of musical support for formal dinners and receptions at Rideau Hall, the official residence of the Governor-General. Even before unification, reserve bands had also felt the effects of government cutbacks. In 1965, budgetary pressures within the militia affected the most famous of the prewar bands, Toronto's 48th Highlanders. The unit had both a military band and a pipe band. The military band was "struck off strength…the Pipe band would continue, but having two bands was regarded as a luxury."[39]

Despite the reductions, the early 1970s saw Canadian military bands, both regular force and reserve experience a series of evolutionary changes that would dramatically expand their recruiting base, improve their musical proficiency and ultimately ensure their survival in the face of challenges yet to come. The single greatest change was the decision to open the musician trade to women. The modern reader may ask "Why did it take so long?" The answer lies in a military policy that at the time, fifty years ago, was already itself over a hundred years old. Since the Crimean War, the role of bandsmen on the battlefield was that of stretcher bearers; an occupation that not only placed them in the middle of combat operations but also required a certain degree of physical strength. Right up to the end of the Second World War, this was an accepted part of being a musician in both the British and Canadian armies. By the mid-twentieth century however, advances in the medical treatment of traumatic injuries as well as technological improvements in methods of casualty evacuation made the policy obsolete. The reduction in the number of bands assigned to field units made it even more so. Although the regular force officially opened its bands to women in 1971, it wasn't until "…four years later the first woman entered the branch: she was pianist Lynn Hong who joined the Central Band's "Serenade of Strings"."[40] The delay between the permission for the recruitment of women as musicians and the actual admission of a qualified candidate had nothing to do with institutional foot dragging and everything to do with the fact that the regular force bands were full. Surplus musicians from the seven army and one navy band that had been declared redundant in 1968 were spread throughout the remaining bands. Many of the surplus navy musicians from the

---

[39] George W. Beal, *Family of Volunteers: An Illustrated History of the 48th Highlanders of Canada* (Toronto: Robin brass Studio Inc., 2001) 120.

[40] Kopstein and Pearson, *Heritage*, 181.

Cornwallis Band were posted to the Royal Canadian Regiment Band in London, Ontario, and on the west coast, most members of the now defunct Royal Canadian Engineers Band from Chilliwack were amalgamated into the Naden Band.[41] A photograph of the R22eR Band taken on January 22, 1971, at the opening of Québec City's "Grand Théâtre" shows an ensemble of fifty-three musicians, almost twenty more than its post-unification authorized limit [Fig. 11.8]. Reserve and militia bands had far more flexibility in the recruitment of women. By the summer of 1975, a naval reserve composite band, training at CFSMUS [Canadian Forces School of Music] in Esquimalt, B.C. and made up of musicians from eight naval reserve divisions from across the country, was almost one quarter female.[42] Initially there were quotas for all three reserve elements, land, sea and air as to how many females could serve but by the mid-1980s these had been abandoned and reserve bands were increasingly fully integrated [Fig. 11.9]. Within ten years, all three reserve components had bands with female directors: Joan Riley at Montréal's 438 Air Reserve Squadron Band, Jill Pensa with the H.M.C.S. *Carleton* Band in Ottawa and Rita Arrendz at Toronto's Queen's Own Rifles Band.[43]

The second change had to do with the role of CFSMUS. Just as Kneller Hall had centralized and standardized the training of British Army bandmasters in the mid-nineteenth century, CFSMUS also created a clearly defined path for all future directors of music of regular force bands. Prior to the establishment of its predecessor, the Tri-Service School of Music, all Canadian Army band directors were sent to the U.K.'s Kneller Hall for the British Army's three-year bandmasters' course. The last Canadians to graduate from Kneller Hall did so in 1965. From that point on, future directors for all three services (regular force) were trained in Canada. After unification the bandmasters' course was renamed the Trade Qualification 7 Course. It condensed the British model into an intense year long course of study that included theory, harmony, aural training, music history, conducting and orchestration as well as instruction in military writing, administration and supply procedures.[44] The "7's" course as it was called would go on to train a new generation of musical leaders who would guide Canada's regular force bands into the twenty-first century.

---

[41] The author spent four months with the Naden Band in 1971. At that time the ensemble numbered over sixty musicians.

[42] The author was a Petty Officer 2nd Class in the band that summer.

[43] The author also served as a reserve summer instructor at CFSMUS from 1984 to 1991 where he met all three.

[44] The first six trade qualifications were a mixture of recruit training, military leadership and musical proficiency exams that were roughly equivalent to RCMT grades 8, 10 and ARCT.

In the mid-1970s CFSMUS had also begun to broaden its responsibilities to include the training and assessment of reserve force musicians. By the time CFSMUS moved to CFB Borden in late 1987, it was the only authority for granting reserve musicians the qualifications necessary for promotion to the rank of sergeant and above. Potential reserve directors of music, many of whom were school music teachers in their civilian lives, could only be appointed after a successful assessment at Borden. The CFSMUS facility at CFB Borden was a newly refurbished former elementary school whose music facilities, rehearsal halls, offices and practice rooms were equal to or superior to those found in many of the nation's smaller post-secondary music schools. With instructional staff, both regular force and reserve, as well as TQ7 candidates and regular force musician trainees, the school was home to over thirty military musicians who could perform as a viable concert band ensemble. Yet even as CFSMUS was attempting to ensure that musical standards for all Canadian Forces bands, regular and reserve, were uniformly high, there were changes going on in the broader Canadian musical community that would have profound implications for the school itself.

In 1960 there were only a handful of Canadian universities offering undergraduate music degrees. By the end of the decade "…approximately thirty universities were offering music instruction."[45] The rapid growth in the number of post-secondary music programs was matched by an equally explosive growth in the number of baby boom applicants eager to enter those programs. The result was thousands of talented and trained young instrumentalists looking for gainful summer employment in the 1970s and 1980s. The reserves and especially the naval reserve, were the first to recognize and tap the potential. In 1976, Lieutenant-Commander Jack McGuire, recently retired conductor of the regular force Stadacona Band, accepted the position of Staff Officer, Naval Reserve bands. He organized the long serving Naval Reserve Composite Band, later to be known as the National Band of the Naval Reserve, a group of forty or more students drawn from naval reserve units across the country. They would gather every summer in Halifax from late May until the end of August. The ensemble was a regular fixture at the Nova Scotia International Tattoo which debuted in 1979 and would then spend the remaining summer months performing in and around the capital area. The band's final obligation each year would be to travel across the country to Esquimalt to perform at the annual Reserve Naval Officers Graduation Parade.

---

[45] J. Paul Green and Nancy F. Vogan, *Music Education in Canada: A Historical Account* (Toronto: University of Toronto Press, 1991) 412.

Initially the response of the militia was more localized with fulltime summer band concentrations being held in the Atlantic and Québec militia regions. When a national program emerged, it proved to be mutually beneficial to regular force bands as well as post-secondary students seeking summer employment as musicians. The Changing of the Guard was, and is, a popular summer tourist attraction on Parliament Hill in Ottawa. Originally performed by the band and units of the regular force Canadian Guards from CFB Petawawa, it is a ceremony modelled on that performed at Buckingham Palace in London. With unification in 1968 and the disappearance of the Canadian Guards through force reductions, other units had to fill the void. During the 1970s, regular force bands were assigned to participate on a rotating basis so that Ottawa's Central Band would not have to shoulder the entire season on its own. One of the unforeseen results of this policy was that the band branch incurred enormous additional costs for the provision of temporary duty accommodations and meals. In order to curtail those costs, the band of the Ceremonial Guard was established in 1981. Directed by a regular force musician officer, the ensemble was designated as a primary reserve unit of the Canadian Forces and since its inception has been enormously popular. Members are selected each year by audition from across the country with successful candidates being guaranteed up to four months employment as musicians from May until the end of August. In addition to daily performances of the Changing of the Guard ceremony from mid-June until late August, the band also performs concerts in and around the national Capital region and for diplomatic and state occasions as required [Fig. 11.10]. A similar ceremony held at "La Citadelle" in Québec City provided additional summer employment for musicians attached to Québec based militia units in a band known as "La Garde en Rouge".

Even though the creation of the Band of the Ceremonial Guard relieved some of the pressure on the regular force bands starting in 1981, the regular force bands still remained highly committed to a broad range of musical activities in their respective communities. Each band was stationed on military bases with large concentrations of other military units as well as being in or near large urban centres. The only band that had been relocated since unification was that of the Royal Canadian Regiment which was transferred from London, Ontario's Wolseley Barracks in 1970, to CFB Gagetown. As a result, regular force bands were spread almost equidistantly across the country: Stadacona Band (Halifax), RCR Band (Gagetown), R22eR Band (Québec), RCA Band (Montréal), Vimy Band (Kingston), Central Band (Ottawa), Air Command Band (Winnipeg), PPCLI Band (Calgary) and Naden Band (Esquimalt). In addition to their military duties, the bands also continued to perform school concerts, benefits in support of local charities and make appearances at events in support of the Canadian Armed Forces. The pre-1968 multi-year postings to Canadian Forces bases in Europe were replaced by six-week tours on a rotational basis, often in the Spring or Fall.

By the early 1990s, the Canadian Forces Band Branch, regular force and reserve, authorized and volunteer, had recovered from the challenges of unification almost a quarter century earlier. They were highly skilled ensembles, well equipped, musically versatile and very much in demand. Their members, both male and female, were involved in all aspects of music, in uniform and in civilian life.

The Royal Canadian Mounted Police Band

Not one of these bands however, achieved the star power in the 1970s and 1980s as did the country's only other taxpayer funded brass-reed band. During the 1950s, the Royal Canadian Mounted Police operated two part-time bands, one in Ottawa and the other in Regina. Since their establishment in 1938, the Force had experienced persistent difficulties in attracting and retaining qualified musicians. Inspector Ted Lydall, director of the "N" Division band (Ottawa) since 1951 had been lobbying tirelessly for the creation of a professional band modelled on those in the Canadian military. In 1959 he was successful and the RCMP consolidated the Regina and Ottawa bands into a fifty-one piece ensemble stationed in Ottawa. Under Lydall's direction the new full-time RCMP Band toured the country extensively often performing traditional commercially available military band literature "…transcriptions, marches, standard wind band repertoire and lighter fare."[46] By the mid-1960s the ensemble was still struggling to remain at full strength. Lydall petitioned his superiors to modify the acceptance regulations for musicians, easing some of the medical and age restrictions. When that proved unsuccessful, a further concession was sought to reduce the amount of time musician recruits were required to complete basic police training from a period of six months to two. With both of these compromises granted recruiting improved and by 1967 the instrumentation of the band was as follows "…1 flute, 1 oboe, 9 clarinets, 1 bassoon, 1 bass clarinet, 1 alto saxophone, 1 tenor saxophone, 1 baritone saxophone, 10 trumpets, 3 horns, 5 trombones, 3 euphoniums, 4 tubas, 4 percussion."[47] With its larger brass section it was an ensemble ideally suited for parade performance. All that was about to change in November of that year.

---

[46] Darren Wayne Oehlerking, "The History of Instrumental Wind Music within the Royal Canadian Mounted Police Band" (D.M.A. thesis, University of Iowa, 2008) 56.
[47] Ibid., 61.

Changes which were brought about when Inspector Ted Lydall retired from the RCMP after the bands' successful Centennial Tour of Canada, ending with a three-week engagement at EXPO 67 in Montréal. His replacement was W. Bramwell Smith, an Ottawa native who had served as trumpet soloist with the U.S. Marines' "President's Own" Band in Washington, D.C., from 1949 to 1957. After leaving the Marine Corps, Smith worked as a freelance musician in the U.S. capital for several years before accepting a teaching position at the American University until his return to Canada in 1967. Smith was a gifted musician, born showman and entertainer. His vision for the band was as a world class concert organization focused on reaching out to the "Baby Boom" generation. To this end, he increasingly abandoned the commercially available band literature of the day and relied more and more on his own staff arrangers, recruited specifically for the purpose of providing the band with up-to-date arrangements of the latest "pop" favourites. The approach certainly proved to be effective with younger audiences but for some of the older generations of listeners it was too much. Smith's insistence that the band was a concert aggregation rather than a marching unit bred further resentment from traditionalists within the Force.[48] Older members of the band, unhappy with the direction the ensemble was taking, remustered back to regular police duties.[49] This in turn created vacancies in the group that the new director filled with younger players, some fresh out of newly established post-secondary music schools focusing on Jazz and improvisational studies, such as Toronto's Humber College. The final touch was the addition of two sound engineers for "N" Division. With the purchase of over twenty microphones and a full audio mixing board, the transformation of the RCMP Band was complete.[50] Audiences loved it.

One of the RCMP Band's most popular programs in the 1970s was the Winter Concert Series at Ottawa's National Arts Centre. The series consisted of four concerts on the first Sunday of each month from January to April and they were free of charge. Houses were consistently full and each successful concert guaranteed even more enthusiasm for the next. Below the surface however, tensions were rising. Smith's stage persona was electric. He was a talented musician and he had created a first-class performing ensemble whose sole purpose was to please audiences. In doing so he ignored or resisted attempts by his superiors to direct the band's activities in support of the RCMP's public image as defenders

---

[48] The author can remember overhearing a comment made in the 1980s by a member of the RCMP Band to the effect that when Smith assumed the leadership of the band he said "…throw away the Stetsons boys, you won't need them anymore!".

[49] Oehlerking, "History" 70.

[50] Ibid., 70.

of law and order, stability and tradition. Bram Smith's band was young, hip and brash, everything the RCMP was not. It was an untenable position and in December of 1975, he resigned.

His replacement was Kenneth Moore, former solo trumpet of the RCAF Downsview band and former Director of Music of both the Canadian Forces Central Band and Kingston's Vimy Band. If the RCMP brass felt that Moore would "...restore a sense of dignity and respect they found lacking under Smith..."[51], they were right. He didn't however, reverse the focus on popular music or the reliance on special arrangements. By 1977 the band's instrumentation had evolved to reflect its greater emphasis on popular literature. It included "...2 flutes, 2 oboes, 8 clarinets, 3 alto saxophones, 2 tenor saxophones, 4 horns, 6 trumpets, 4 trombones, 2 euphoniums, 2 tubas, 1 electric guitar, 1 electric bass, 1 piano and 4 percussion.[52] The band continued to tour the country extensively and in 1986, travelled to Vancouver five times between June 25 and October 10, to perform at EXPO 86 [Fig. 11.11]. That same year Ken Moore retired and was replaced by the group's last director, long serving member Charlie Hendricks.

Although the ensemble remained as musically vibrant and versatile as always, it was no longer a brass-reed band in the conventional sense. A concert program given in 1985 contained fourteen selections, only three of which were commercially available scores. The remainder were "specials", arrangements by the band's staff arrangers of recent movie, T.V. and popular music releases.[53] It was "...a stage band with a concert band instrumentation."[54] The problems facing the band however went much deeper. There was a perception amongst the RCMP's senior leadership that members of the band "...lacked knowledge and pride of RCMP traditions and values."[55] A survey completed in 1988 revealed that twelve members of the band had "...little or no training in RCMP rules and regulations."[56] The response was rapid. Although the offer was voluntary, the band agreed to go to Depot in Regina for a six-week "refresher" training course that had nothing to do with music and everything to do with learning the basic skills needed to be a "Mountie".

The early 1990s were marked by dramatic cuts to spending across all Federal government departments. The RCMP was not immune and an initial attempt was made at savings by cutting the band's strength in half; from forty-six to twenty-three [Fig. 11.12].

---

[51] Ibid., 86.
[52] Ibid., 86.
[53] Program courtesy of Dana Kaukinen, former member of the RCMP Band.
[54] Oehlerking, "History" 115.
[55] Ibid., 101.
[56] Ibid., 101

It was a short-term solution which proved to be entirely unsatisfactory and so, by the end of 1993, the decision was made to terminate the band's operations entirely. The RCMP Band's final concert took place in Victoriaville, Québec, on December 14, 1993, with the closing selection, fittingly enough, being a piano solo entitled *The Party's Over*.[57] As of the writing of these pages [2022], almost twenty-nine years have passed since the RCMP Band's unfortunate demise but from 1968 to 1993, it was proof that live performances by wind bands could still reach and engage large audiences of Canadians of all ages, from coast to coast to coast. The band achieved a degree of popularity not seen since before the Second World War and in doing so provided a brilliant finale to the story of the RCMP's bands and their 120-year contribution to Canada's musical history.

To say that 1994 was a bad year for Canada's military bands, both regular force and reserve, would be an understatement. The Department of National Defence, like the RCMP, was under intense pressure from the government of the day to drastically reduce its budget. The Forces Reduction Plan [FRP] eliminated thousands of positions in the regular forces and bands were an easy target. The nine regular force bands were reduced to four. Only the Stadacona (Halifax), RCA (which in 1995 was moved to Québec and renamed the R22eR), Central (Ottawa) and Air Command (Winnipeg) bands were left standing. The reserve bands weren't spared either. The naval reserve cut its eight authorized bands down to four, the air reserve lost one of its two bands and Toronto's four remaining militia bands, the 7th Toronto RCA, the GGHG, The QOR and the Royals were all limited to twenty-five musicians each.[58] The Canadian Forces School of Music at CFB Borden was partially closed leaving only a skeleton staff to administer summer training for reserve musicians. In one respect this last cut was entirely understandable. The regular force "Bandsman Apprentice" program of the 1960s attracted candidates with little formal musical training. By the early 1990s, most trainees at the school had at least one post-secondary degree or diploma in music, some had more than one. There was little need to train potential military musicians who already had years of formal musical education.

Soon enough however, the "Decade of Darkness", as it was called by General Rick Hillier, former Chief of the Defence Staff, would come to an end. When it did, Canada's military bands would once again emerge, this time into the twenty-first century, leaner, more versatile and better musically than ever before.

---

[57] Ibid., 110.

[58] Michael Lawson, Director of Music 7th Toronto RCA 1991-1995, telephone interview with the author 18 July 2019. An interesting footnote is that in 1994, the directors of two of Canada's finest militia bands, Toronto's 7th Toronto RCA and Vancouver's 15 RCA were both former members of Arthur Delamont's Kitsilano Boys' Band.

CHAPTER ELEVEN GALLERY

Figure 11.1. Princess Patricia's Canadian Light Infantry Band, Soest, West Germany, 1957-1959. Director of Music Captain Herb Jeffrey. From the early 1950s until 1968, the Canadian Army maintained a professional band on permanent station with Canadian Forces, Europe. Source: Princess Patricia's Canadian Light Infantry Regimental Museum and Archives.

Figure 11.2. RCAF Central Band, Ottawa, c. 1965. Director of Music Flight Lieutenant Ken Moore. With over 60 musicians, the Central Band was the crown jewel of not just the air force's bands but all of Canada's regular force bands prior to 1968. With its own staff arrangers it was a superbly balanced concert organization. Note the presence of three string basses in addition to three tubas and harp. Source: Author's collection.

Figure 13.3. Royal Canadian Navy ship's band on the flight deck of the aircraft carrier H.M.C.S. *Magnificent*, c. 1955. The RCN posted 12 - 15 piece bands on its aircraft carriers and light cruisers. The last ship to carry a band on permanent deployment was the carrier H.M.C.S. *Bonaventure*, decommissioned in 1970. Source: Jack Kopstein Collection

Figure 11.4. H.M.C.S. *Stadacona* Band, Halifax, c. 1965. Director of Music Lieutenant William Gordon. This was the navy's largest band with 55 musicians. It was also the source of the 12-15 musicians who were assigned to the Halifax based ships' bands. Source: Jack Kopstein Collection

Figure 11.5. Small ensemble practice, Tri-Service School of Music, Esquimalt B.C., c. 1965. Air force instructor with navy and army trainees.   The school was renamed the Canadian Forces School of Music in 1968 and would continue to operate until its partial closure in 1994. Source: Jack Kopstein Collection.

Figure 11.6. Howard Cable, Toronto, 1950s CBC publicity photo. Cable was selected to conduct the "Voice of the Army Band" at the start of the Korean War, which then became the Howard Cable Concert Band in 1953. It proved to be enormously popular and was the inspiration for the composition of some of his most famous works for wind band. Cable's association with the military continued through the 1960s as a civilian conductor and arranger for the NORAD Band in Colorado Springs. During the late 1980s and early 1990s he was also a guest rehearsal conductor with Toronto's 7th Toronto Royal Canadian Artillery Band. Source: CBC Still Photo Collection.

Figure 11.7.   Howard Cable conducting the CBC's *Summer Showcase* Band, c. 1953.
Conductor and musicians are dressed in costumes meant to evoke an early twentieth century band
concert in the park.   A similar scene was recreated one more time in 1970 for a CBC TV musical
variety show entitled *A Little Bit of Concert Omm Pah*   Source: Howard Cable/CBC Summer
Showcase.

Figure 11.8.   La Musique du R22eR, Québec, 1971.   Director of Music Major Jean-François
Pierret.   The ensemble numbers 53 musicians, almost twenty more than its authorized post
unification (1968) limit.   Source: La Musique du R22eR, Québec.

Figure 11.9.   H.M.C.S. *Carleton* Naval Reserve Band, Ottawa, c. 1985.   Director of Music Lieutenant Commander David Yensen.   Reserve and militia bands were the first to accept female musicians and by the mid 1980s all restrictions had been lifted.   Source: Author's collection.

Figure 11.10.   Band of the Ceremonial Guard, Ottawa, 2005.   Director of Music Captain Brian Greenwood.   The Band is joined by members of the United States Marine Corps Albany Band. Source: Photo courtesy CWO (Ret'd) Tom Peet.

Figure 11.11. RCMP Band at EXPO 86 in Vancouver, 1986. Director of Music Inspector Ken Moore. It was Canada's most dynamic and popular professional wind band in the 1970s and 1980s. Source: Photo courtesy of Dana Kaukinen.

Figure 11.12. RCMP Band, Ottawa, 1993. Director of Music Charlie Hendricks. A final effort was made to save the band from budget cuts by cutting its strength in half, effectively making it a large stage band. It wasn't enough and in late 1993 the band's operations were terminated altogether. Source: Photo courtesy of Dana Kaukinen.

CHAPTER TWELVE

BARRIE SET THE BAR

By the mid 1950s, the Canadian Bandmasters Association had made the conscious decision to redirect some of its organizational efforts towards the emerging school band movement. Older generations of very successful community band directors were reluctant to abandon a reliable source of young musicians for the adult bands, namely the locally sponsored boys' and girls' bands. It was evident to most however, that in the future it would be the schools that could attract a much larger field of aspiring players at a fraction of the cost. As with almost all significant changes to a large institutional structure, the CBA needed a rallying figure to focus on the need for a new direction and to inspire the membership with the potential inherent in that new direction. That standard bearer emerged in the small city of Barrie, Ontario (population 18,000 in the 1950s), on the shores of Lake Simcoe.

William Allen Fisher (1905-1989) was born in Coburg, Ontario, and completed a Bachelor of Arts degree in English and History at Queen's University in Kingston. After a number of brief teaching assignments in Fort Frances, Prescott and Timmins, in 1937 he accepted the position of History Department head at the original Barrie Collegiate Institute (BCI). Although he had no formal music training other than playing clarinet in a town band and sax in a dance band at Queen's, he nevertheless had both the vision and the drive to found a school string orchestra that in 1939 was replaced by the Barrie Collegiate Band. He remained as its director until his retirement in 1972. [Fig. 12.1].

By 1941, having established his classroom management credentials in his English and History classes, W.A. (as he was affectionately known by generations of his students), convinced his school administration of the value of instrumental music in the daily curriculum. Consequently, BCI became one of the first high schools in Canada to integrate formal band classes into the grade nine daily schedule [Ontario high schools in the 1940s consisted of grades 9 to 13]. Within four years W.A. had established an ensemble that was recognized by the Ontario Department of Education as a worthy ambassador for instrumental music education in the province's schools. In 1946, the BCI Band undertook a week long concert tour of eastern Ontario, to be followed in 1947 and 1951 by similar tours of Central and Northern Ontario respectively. Barrie band members were billeted in the homes of local students with the result that friendships were formed and the performances often served to inspire young people in the communities visited (and their parents) to start their own band programs.[1]

The reputation of the BCI Band was such that by 1947 it was the only Ontario band to represent the province at an International Festival of School Music held at the Montreal Forum. There were six other Canadian bands, all from Montréal and thirty-seven from the United States.[2] The culmination of W.A.'s efforts in those early years was the 1948 performance of the Barrie Collegiate Band at the Music Educators National Conference of America in Detroit. This was followed by appearances in Chicago at the Midwest Band and Orchestra Clinic in 1952 and 1955, both with trumpeter Rafael Mendez as soloist. In 1958 the BCI Band became the first Canadian high school band to compete at the *WereldMuziekConcours* in Kerkrade, Netherlands. W.A. returned a second time in 1970 to even greater success at the head of an eighty-two piece ensemble – now renamed the Barrie Central Collegiate Band; a name change made necessary by the opening of Barrie North Collegiate in 1957.

On December 14, 1967, the Barrie (Central) Collegiate Band performed for the third and last time at the Midwest under the guest batons of four of Canada's most celebrated musicians and with renowned saxophonist Paul Brodie as soloist [Fig. 12.3]. Two newly published Canadian compositions for band were featured: Howard Cable's *Scottish Rhapsody* (MCA Music, 1966) and William McCauley's *Metropolis* (also known as *Big City Suite*, Oxford University Press, 1967). Both men were present that evening and conducted their own works. The final two guest conductors were Robert Rosevear, founder of the University of Toronto Concert Band and Wing Commander Clifford Hunt, Royal Canadian Air Force, Supervisor of Music for the Canadian Armed Forces. The Barrie band's performance that day, in celebration of Canada's centennial year, was a tribute to both W.A. Fisher and the members of the band. They were "Canada's Band" [Fig. 12.4].

The key to the success of the Barrie band was W.A. Fisher himself. He was described by his son Mark Fisher, a member of the band and graduate of the class of 1959, as "...one of a kind, insistent, diligent, demanding, but not overbearing or tyrannical. He had a way with words and loved to talk. Students admired him for his history and English classes just as much as the music. He was simply willing to put in the time."[3] More than anything it was the time he devoted to his students. The Saturday trips to Toronto, 114 kilometers

---

[1] J. Paul Green and Nancy F. Vogan, *Music Education in Canada: A Historical Account* (Toronto: University of Toronto Press, 1991) 271.

[2] Ibid., 351.

[3] Mark Fisher, e-mail correspondence with the author 27 February 2016.

to the south on a two-lane highway before the construction of the 400 Freeway, were the stuff of legend. He would load up his own car and drive students to private lessons at the Royal Conservatory of Music, in private homes or at the University of Toronto. Wherever possible he would ensure that the teachers were members of the Toronto Symphony Orchestra. While students were taking lessons, W.A. would visit various music retailers that stocked band music: Gordon V. Thompson, Whaley-Royce, J.M. Greene and Boosey and Hawkes. He would also deliver instruments that required repair to Martin Zweng, a master repairman, insisting that minor work be done before the drive home.

W.A. wasn't the only one making those weekend runs to Toronto. By 1972, the year he retired, almost half the Barrie band's members were taking private lessons. Some were driven by their parents, those that were old enough drove themselves and an adventurous few would take the Gray Coach bus to downtown Toronto (and grab lunch at the original Swiss Chalet within walking distance of the bus depot).[4] During the summer months, teachers from the TSO would even come to the school in Barrie to give multiple lessons.[5]

During the 1950s, full band rehearsals would last two hours and take place twice a week on Monday and Thursday evenings from 7:00 to 9:00 PM. By 1965 a third two-hour practice had been added on Sunday afternoons. Most striking of all, the band rehearsed through the summer months and students performed regularly at local tourist destinations including the Bigwin Inn, Britannia Lodge and Gull Lake in Gravenhurst. The season ended at the annual band competitions at the CNE in Toronto. There were also other options for W.A.'s students to improve their musical skills during the summer holidays.

In 1960, Ben and Sheila Wise established a summer arts camp for older students on the shores of Lake Manitouwabing in Ontario's Muskoka region. Known as the Interprovincial Music Camp (IMC), it soon became a magnet for talented and enthusiastic musicians from grades 8 to 13 (Ontario) from the Toronto area, eastern Ontario and Barrie. The camp was held during a ten-day period at the end of August just before the Labour Day weekend. On arrival students were assigned a large ensemble based on their technical ability. They would spend up to five hours a day rehearsing with that ensemble as well as spending an hour a day in individual practice. During the evening hours they attended recitals given by instructional staff drawn from college and university faculties from across Canada and the United States. IMC's popularity grew and camp attendance peaked during

---

[4] John Ramsay, BCCI class of 1975, interview with the author 16 May 2019. John went on to complete a Master's degree in performance on French horn at Julliard and then performed with both the TSO and the CPO before completing his education studies in the 1990s. Both his parents were members of the Barrie band in the early 1940s and between his two older siblings and himself there is an unbroken fourteen year stretch of membership in the band from 1961-1975.

[5] Ramsay, interview with the author 16 May 2019.

the 1970s and 1980s at approximately 375-400 campers per session. These in turn were divided into band and orchestral ensembles. The opportunity for like-minded young musicians to experience a highly enriched atmosphere of musical study with leaders in the field was invaluable.[6] It left participants primed for their return to school in the following weeks and ready to assume leadership roles within their own school band programs. Those students from Barrie Central Collegiate who attended IMC were no exception. They would contribute yet another level of experience and skill to W.A.'s band.

The Barrie Collegiate Band set the bar early on, not just for schools in Ontario but across the country. By 1955 it was already a shining example of what a Canadian high school band could do. An example duly noted by a relatively recent graduate of the Royal Conservatory of Music of Toronto who would become one of Canada's most famous composers of wind band music. In 2006, Jacqueline Dawson and Michel Purves-Smith wrote an article entitled "An Interview with Howard Cable" for the Spring issue of *Canadian Winds*.[7] At one point, when asked about the circumstances surrounding the composition of one of his best-known works, *Newfoundland Rhapsody*, Howard Cable made the following comment about its suitability for school bands:

> I was spoiled forty years ago by [W.] Allen Fisher and the Barrie Collegiate Band. That was my early notion of what high school bands could do, but there was only one Barrie band. Then there was the North Toronto Band with Bob Krueger. I had these two great high schools to work with, but I didn't realize that there were hundreds of others that couldn't play like that.[8]

The Barrie Collegiate Band would continue to play like that and *Newfoundland Rhapsody* would remain in its repertoire for years. Between 1962 and 1975, the band recorded four vinyl LPs, one of which, produced in 1969, was entitled, "Classics for School Band". It included performances of Vaughan Williams' *Folk Song Suite* and Dello Joio's *Scenes from the Louvre*. It also included *Newfoundland Rhapsody*.[9]

---

[6] Anne Fleming-Read, Director of IMC, e-mail correspondence with the author 30 May 2019.

[7] Michael Purves-Smith and Jacqueline Dawson, "An Interview with Howard Cable," *Canadian Winds* 4, no. 2 (Spring, 2006) 72-77.

[8] Ibid., 74. When John Ramsay was asked who were Barrie's arch rivals at the annual Kiwanis Music Festivals in Toronto, he answered without hesitation "North Toronto".

[9] See "Barrie Central Collegiate Band" at *Barrie Historical Archives at* www.barriearchive.ca. The site contains photos of the album covers and by clicking on the photo the reader will be able to listen to the recordings.

From the very start, Canadian music had a place in concert programs. In April of 1945, at a Victory Bond drive held in the city's arena, the Barrie band performed Montréal bandleader Guiseppe Agostini's *The Three Trumpeters* (Belwin, 1939). Two years later at the Montréal International Festival of School Music, Charles O'Neill's *Souvenir de Québec* and J.J. Gagnier's *Hands Across the Border* were both featured.[10] W.A. was always on the lookout for new music for band but he must have been conscious of the need to find materials that would also challenge his students. He commissioned several new works, two of which, Bernard Bogisch's *Huronian Episode* (1970) and James Gayfer's *Wells of Marah* (1971), were written by military band directors whose careers had been spent with professional ensembles. Both of these compositions are technically demanding and beyond the reach of most high school bands. He was also fond of transcriptions and used them frequently. W.A.'s formative musical experiences were in the interwar period when the community band was king and transcriptions of orchestral favourites were a pillar of their repertoire.

One of the best examples of the genre, and one that he used in the Class A Challenge Class at the 1965 Kiwanis Music Festival in Toronto was Brahms' *Academic Festival Overture* (Fischer, rev. ed. 1943) [Fig. 12.5].[11] It is an advanced level work whose themes lend themselves ideally to the wind band idiom. W.A. Fisher was a firm believer that good music was good music, whether played by an orchestra, band or keyboard.

The modern reader may assume that there must have been some added advantage to the music program at Barrie Collegiate that allowed its students to excel for over three decades. There wasn't. For that reason, it is worth examining W.A.'s classroom routines and procedures. Students started their instrumental music study in grade 9. There were seven academic classes during the school day with each one lasting approximately 45 minutes for an entire school year. Music was timetabled into this schedule four times a week. At the end of grade 10, classes might be working on senior band repertoire and in grade 11 most students were in the senior band. By the 1960s, Royal Conservatory of Music of Toronto (RCMT) grade six level performance was the minimum standard needed to make the senior band and most grade 12 and 13 students were playing at a grade eight level or higher. It didn't matter whether students entering the program had previous piano experience or no musical training at all, W.A.'s passion and personality, enhanced by the time and energy he devoted to them, instilled a love of music that was infectious.

---

[10] Mark Fisher, "Montreal 1947," *Notes in Time: A History of W.A. Fisher and the Barrie Collegiate Band* (Barrie: online publication, 2021)

[11] Mark Fisher, e-mail correspondence 27 February 2016.

W.A. was always able to provide for a balanced instrumentation in his ensembles. Particularly talented and motivated students were often directed towards the double reeds or French horn but every section was filled by a judicious combination of begging, pleading, coercion and, occasionally, "lying". More importantly, W.A. had the enormous good fortune to be teaching at a time when the schools were full and he was able to direct students towards instrumental choices that would complement a balanced band. Three photos posted on the now defunct Barrie Central Collegiate Band website in 2016 show the band in 1948, 1956 and 1958; in each case it is an ideally balanced ensemble. By the mid 1960s it could boast over ninety members including 8 horns, 3 oboes, 3 bassoons, 3 string bass and 6 tubas and they could all play!

The icing on the cake was provided by the Ontario Department of Education. Ontario's secondary schools offered grade 13 up to 2003, a fifth year of high school. The Ontario Grade 13 Music course of studies however, was included in the Barrie grade 12 band program, first introduced by W.A. in 1953. Before 1968, and the phase-out of province wide departmental exams, band students could write the Grade 13 Music departmental exam in grade 12, leaving them free to pursue their preferred academic courses the following year. At BCCI, they invariably continued to perform in the band program. The requirement of nine departmental papers or credits for graduation also meant that some students returned for a sixth year to make up missed subjects or to improve their marks. For band students this meant spending another year under the baton of W.A.[12] The practical result was that the core of the band's senior membership included students who had been playing for five and six years.

Middle school or Junior High School band programs in Ontario had not yet achieved the widespread acceptance during W.A.'s tenure at Barrie that they enjoyed in the United States. Consequently, there were no "feeder" schools for Barrie. Yet such was the success of the program that parents sought private instrumental instruction, in addition to piano lessons, for their children in order to ensure their entry into the band as early as grade 9. Ultimately this became an intergenerational enterprise as the sons and daughters of former band members took their turn under W.A.'s direction.

As with every great band in our story, sponsorship in the form of financial support was a contributing factor in W.A. Fisher's success. The Barrie Collegiate Band was fortunate in having not one, but two parent associations: The Band Parents Association and The Band Mothers Association. Postwar Barrie was a prosperous community and by the mid 1950s was home to a number of successful business enterprises. Since Barrie Collegiate Institute

---

[12] Mark Fisher, e-mail correspondence with the author, 10 June 2021.

was the city's only high school until 1957, it was not uncommon that owners and senior managers of these firms were often former BCI students, in some cases ex-members of the band and had children in the band. With men like Jack Nixon, a local real estate developer and student band president in 1943-44, Ross, his brother whose three sons were all members of the band, Bob Hunter, president of Lufkin Rule Company of Canada [manufacturers of Lufkin Tape Measures] and Bill Caldwell, owner of Moldex Toilet Seats [Canada's largest toilet seat maker in the 1960s], the Band Parent Association was led by Barrie's entrepreneurial elite. Other members of this exclusive club also included Leighton Clarke, owner of the Clarke and Clarke Tannery as well as Ron Stewart, federal Member of Parliament and director of Stewart Wholesale.[13] These community leaders used their business skills to raise money for the Barrie Collegiate Band and raise money they did. The lotteries they organized were at one point so lucrative that they managed, on two separate occasions, to offer first prizes of a Cadillac automobile and a Winnebago motor home. One example of the results of these fundraising efforts occurred in 1962, when the band appeared at the Seattle World's Fair. The entire ensemble plus parent chaperones could afford to travel across the country in its own CN rail cars, with dining car, making stops in Vancouver, the Okanagan and Edmonton along the way.

The Band Mothers Association was led by Eva Fisher, W.A.'s wife. She was a tireless supporter of the band and it is doubtful W.A. could have been as successful as he was without her. Under her direction the band mothers held a wide range of activities including rummage sales. They focused their attention on providing members of the band with not one, but two sets of uniforms: the red blazer and white skirt or trousers for the Senior Band's concert dress and the matching "Black Watch" tartan blazer and tie used as concert dress by the Junior Band and by the Senior Band as its travel dress. There was also one other initiative that both parent associations sponsored and that was the Canadian Artists Series. These were concerts given three times a year in the school auditorium by visiting artists including the legendary Oscar Peterson as well as the Toronto Symphony Orchestra, the Canadian Opera Company and Ottawa's National Arts Centre Orchestra. Perhaps one of the best measures of the success of the Barrie Band Parent Associations was the fact that between 1948 and 1970, the Barrie Collegiate Band was invited to and attended eight international conferences or competitions.[14]

There was nothing magical about W.A. Fisher's formula. His dedication to his students and his passion for music, plus the unique set of circumstances that existed in postwar

---

[13] Mark Fisher, e-mail, 10 June 2021.
[14] "W.A. Fisher Retirement Reception Programme-Barrie Central Band," *Barrie Historical Archive* at www.barriearchive.ca accessed 14 June 2019.

Ontario, made the achievements of the Barrie (Central) Collegiate Band possible. Nowhere was this more apparent than in the well over one hundred first place awards won by Barrie's musicians at the annual Kiwanis Music Festivals held in Toronto. These first-place certificates were not just for full band performances but also for solo and small ensemble classes that W.A. encouraged his students to enter. By the late 1960s these same certificates adorned the walls of the band room but only first place finishes were displayed. As the years progressed from the late 1940s on, the goal of an ever-growing number of high school bands in Ontario was simply to "beat Barrie". Even though the intensity of such competitions came to be frowned upon, Barrie did not always win, for as Fisher himself admitted "…it gets harder every year."[15] In fact, this is the legacy of W.A. Fisher and the bands that he and his three successors, Morley Calvert [Fig. 12.2], Douglas Hall and Lisa Perry led until the final closure of Barrie Central Collegiate in June of 2016.[16] For elsewhere in the province, whether in Ottawa, Toronto, London, Sudbury, Kingston or Windsor (or throughout Canada for that matter), equally passionate teachers, when presented with the same opportunities as those in Barrie, produced high school bands in the 1960s and 1970s that have rarely been equalled anywhere in the country since.

Notes in Time: A History of W.A. Fisher and the Barrie Collegiate Band

In June of 2021, Barrie's Mark Fisher, son of W.A. Fisher, completed a comprehensive study of the Barrie Collegiate Band under his father's direction entitled *Notes in Time: A History of W.A. Fisher and the Barrie Collegiate Band* (Barrie, Ont.: privately published, 2021). It is an exhaustively researched account that traces the growth of the Barrie Collegiate Band from its earliest years until the school's closure in June of 2016. The author's informal first-person narrative is as much a social history as musical memoir and richly details the people, places, events and challenges that influenced and nurtured what was one of Canada's most accomplished high school wind bands for over half a century. Illustrated with well over 200 photographs and multiple references to repertoire performed by the ensemble, it is a valuable research tool for anyone interested in this chapter of our Canadian wind band story. Readers wishing to obtain a copy should contact Mark Fisher directly at *mwfisher51@gmail.com.*[17]

---

[15] Mark Fisher, e-mail correspondence, 27 February 2016.

[16] In a fitting tribute to the man who built the Barrie band, the school building itself was demolished with the exception of the auditorium which bore his name. That chapter too came to an end in October of 2021 when the auditorium itself was also demolished.

[17] Mark Fisher, e-mail correspondence with the author, 15 June 2021.

CHAPTER TWELVE GALLERY

Figure 12.1. William Allen Fisher (1905-1989). Band Director, Barrie Collegiate Institute from 1941 to 1972. "W.A." as he was affectionately known to his students devoted enormous amounts of time to their development and in so doing created an ensemble that was invited three times to the Midwest Clinic in Chicago and completed eight international trips under his baton. The band was a frequent winner at the Toronto Kiwanis Music Festival and became the focus for many other high school bands to simply "Beat Barrie!". Source: Image courtesy of the Barrie Historical Archive.

Figure 12.2. Morley Calvert (1928-1991). Band Director, Barrie Central Collegiate Institute from 1972 to 1985. By the time Calvert arrived in Barrie he was already a highly respected music educator having taught in Montréal area schools since 1952. During the 1960s he was also director of the McGill University Concert band, the Lakeshore (Community) Concert Band and the Montreal Citadel Band of the Salvation Army. His composition for brass quintet entitled *Suite from the Monteregian Hills* (Berandol, 1961) had established him as a serious composer of wind music. Source: Image courtesy of the Barrie Historical Archive.

Figure 12.3. The Barrie (Central) Collegiate Institute Band, in front of the newly built school auditorium, 1968. Band Director William Allen Fisher. This was the band that performed at the Midwest Band and Orchestra Clinic in Chicago on December 14, 1967 [see Fig. 12.4]. Source: Image courtesy of the Barrie Historical Archive.

The Mid-West Salutes Canada In Her Year of Centennial Celebration

THURSDAY EVENING, DECEMBER 14, 1967

8:00 P. M. -- CLINIC CONCERT

BARRIE COLLEGIATE (HIGH SCHOOL) BAND, BARRIE, ONTARIO, CANADA
W. ALLEN FISHER, Director

TITLE	COMPOSER	PUBLISHER	YR. PUB.	GRADE	TIME
Star Spangled Banner Conducted by Dr. Raymond F. Dvorak.		Kjos			
Stratford Fanfare		Leeds			
O Canada		Leeds			
Concerto For Two Trumpets, Finale	Vivaldi	Colombo	65	4	3:15
Chaconne from D-Minor Partita	Bach	Bourne	67	3	7:45
An Age of Kings Conducted by Professor Rosevear, University of Toronto.	Sir Arthur Bliss	Chappell	67	3	4:05
The Silken Ladder	Rossini	Boosey Hawkes	38	5	6:00
Remarks by Superintendent J. M. Ramsay.					
Metropolis Conducted by the Composer, Professor W. A. McCauley, York University.	McCauley	Oxford	67	3	6:30
Proscenium Overture Conducted by Wing Commander C. O. Hunt.	Whear	Ludwig	67	4	6:00
Rondino Guest Saxophone Soloist: Paul Brodie, Toronto, Canada.	Jack Goode	Kjos	67	3	5:00
Scottish Rhapsody Conducted by the Composer, Howard Cable.	Howard Cable	MCA	66	4	7:45
Huronian Carol		Waterloo			4:30
Pines of The Appian Way, from Pines of Rome	Respighi	Colombo	51	5	4:10

Figure 12.4. Concert Program, Midwest Band and Orchestra Clinic, Chicago, December 14, 1967. The guest conductors that evening included three of Canada's most distinguished leaders in the wind band movement: Howard Cable, Robert Rosevear and Wing Commander Clifford Hunt.   Source: Midwest Archives, Special Collections in Performing Arts, University of Maryland Libraries.

Figure 12.5. Last page of the 2nd and 3rd Clarinet part to Brahm's *Academic Festival Overture* (Carl Fischer 1915, rev. ed. 1943). This was one of W.A. Fisher's favourite transcriptions and was performed by the Barrie band at the 1965 Toronto Kiwanis Music Festival. Source: author's collection.

CHAPTER THIRTEEN

THE EMERGING SCHOOL BANDS

The Booming Fifties and Sixties

A better title for this chapter could have been "The Emerging Publicly Funded, Student Population Viable, Qualified Teacher Led and Curricular School Bands".   It was abandoned for being too unwieldy but it is also much more accurate.   All of these conditions were critical for the evolution of Canada's school-based wind band programs and because education in Canada is an area of provincial responsibility, the emergence of school band programs was anything but uniform.   For that reason, it took upwards of thirty years for the country's school bands to reach their current level of widespread distribution. This segmented development might have made the study of postwar school bands next to impossible were it not for J. Paul Green and Nancy F. Vogan's exhaustive study *Music Education in Canada: A Historical Account* (Toronto: University of Toronto Press, 1991), a source which was consulted extensively in the preparation of the present chapter.

During the immediate postwar period, prewar youth bands continued to thrive and in western Canada new ones such as Calgary's Lions Club Band (1949), the Calgary Boys and Girls Band (1954), the Saskatoon Lions Band (1954) and the Victoria Boys Band [Fig. 13.1] all found eager new recruits as well as appreciative audiences.   The Guelph Police Boys Band was probably representative of many youth groups that performed well into the 1950s.   Although the band faced ongoing financial problems, it nevertheless won a string of festival first prizes between 1949 and 1952.[1]   A photograph of the group taken at the CNE in 1950 shows a forty-three piece ensemble that includes thirteen clarinets, one alto saxophone, twelve cornets, four alto horns, three trombones, four baritones, five basses and one percussionist.   Of particular interest is the twelve-year old trumpet prodigy Frederick Mills seated next to Bandmaster Ted Denver.[2]   By that time however, in Ontario at least, the era of the community sponsored youth bands was rapidly coming to an end.

---

[1] Robert F. Hamilton, *Guelph's Bands and Musicians* (Guelph, ON: Hamilton Art Studio, 1996) 3-11.
[2] Ibid., 15B.   Fred Mills was to go on to become one of the founding members of the world famous "Canadian Brass".

School Bands in Ontario

In 1946, Ontario was the country's most prosperous province and Toronto its most populous community.   With the Barrie model already well established, North Toronto Collegiate became the city's first high school to establish a curricular music program [Fig. 13.2].   Unlike Barrie, it focused on orchestral music.

> Music, like other optional subjects, was scheduled every day in a forty-five minute period in classes of approximately thirty-six students…[there were] separate classes for strings and winds in grade nine…in grade eleven, wind and string players were grouped together.[3]

Toronto was the epicentre of curricular music programs because it had satisfied the conditions necessary for growth: it had the financial base to support them, there were enough students to fill those optional courses and initially there were qualified teachers to teach them.   By 1949 "…all secondary schools in Toronto had launched instrumental music courses."[4]   At first orchestral and band programs were on an equal footing with successful orchestral programs operating at Riverdale Collegiate (Ken Bray), North Toronto (Jack Dow) and Oakwood Collegiate (Bruce Snell).   Malvern Collegiate was the outlier, focusing on band classes alone.[5]   Rapid growth came at a price, there was a problem finding enough qualified teachers.

The University of Toronto had only begun to offer a degree program in school music in 1946 and its first graduates didn't complete their musical studies until 1950. By then the demand for teachers had far exceeded the supply "…the expansion of instrumental music was not confined to the city of Toronto; curricular programs also spread rapidly throughout the metropolitan Toronto area and the industrial central region of the province."[6]   From there they appeared further afield: Owen Sound, Ottawa, St. Catharines and Sudbury.   It became necessary for the province's Department of Education to operate summer schools through its music branch to qualify enough music educators to meet the needs of an ever-expanding number of high schools offering music programs.   The vast majority of those musicians who qualified through these summer programs were former military or

---

[3] J. Paul Green and Nancy F. Vogan, *Music Education in Canada: A Historical Account* (Toronto: University of Toronto Press, 1991) 355.
[4] Green and Vogan, *Music Education*, 358.
[5] Ibid., 358.
[6] Ibid., 359

community bandsmen.[7] With ever greater numbers of potential teachers coming from wind band backgrounds, it was inevitable that they would choose to work with the ensemble they knew best.

One Ontario community that was to benefit enormously from the ex-service musician teacher pool was Ottawa. The National Capital and its surrounding communities drew from two regular force bands to fill its high school music teacher vacancies in the 1960s and 1970s: the Canadian Guards Band, based in Camp Petawawa and the RCAF Central Band whose home was RCAF Station Rockcliffe in the city's east end. In the 1960s former Guards musicians Peter Manley, Henry Bonnenberg, Art Very and Ron Milne accepted teaching positions at Woodroffe H.S., Laurentian H.S. [Fig. 13.3], and Nepean H.S. Ex-RCAF bandsmen taught at Hillcrest H.S., St. Patrick's H.S. and at South Carleton H.S. in the nearby town of Richmond. Although most of these men had little formal university training in music education, they were fine musicians and their contributions to the success of their respective school band programs were significant.

There were other factors involved in Ontario's early embrace of school band programs. The province's public education system was divided into two panels, elementary (K-8) and secondary (9-13) [grade 13 was renamed OAC – "Ontario Academic Credit" in the late 1980s and discontinued altogether in 2003]. Secondary school principals had enormous latitude in hiring staff for non-academic positions, which music was, and so were free to engage former bandsmen, military and community, with little more than one summer's classroom preparation. In some cases, potential band teachers didn't even have that and were engaged on an annual Department of Education "letter of permission". Eventually the province's universities began to catch up and by the early 1970s the University of Ottawa, Queens' University and the University of Western Ontario had joined the University of Toronto in offering degree programs in music education. In doing so they could finally provide enough graduates to staff Ontario's high schools.

One further factor, already noted, was the "Barrie" effect: a school band program that was so successful that it served as an inspiration to others. The standard set by the Barrie Collegiate Band beginning in the early 1950s was on display annually at the Toronto Kiwanis Music Festival's Challenge Class for bands. Teachers from across the province could see and hear what was possible as could the parents of the students they taught and the administrators of their respective schools. In 1956, Donald McKellar began teaching at Wheable High School in London where he started the city's first curricular music program. He later wrote of one of the year's defining experiences "…I remember sitting

---

[7] Ibid., 361

watching the Barrie band in a concert. They were playing *God Save the Queen* [Canada's official national anthem at the time, *O Canada* was not officially proclaimed legally as such until 1980] and it was at that moment with tears in my eyes that I decided this is what I want to do."[8] McKellar was as good as his word. He later went on to complete post graduate study and from 1961 until 1991 taught at the Faculty of Music at the University of Western Ontario. He championed bands and band music and it was under his direction that the U.W.O. Symphonic Band toured extensively throughout southern Ontario.[9]

By the 1960s and early 1970s, Ontario's high school band programs were expanding rapidly. Of the provinces 359 secondary schools in 1954-55, only 89 offered curricular music and 178 supported an extra-curricular music program.[10] During the 1966-67 school year, the number of orchestra programs was 89 whereas the number of band programs had reached 270.[11] It didn't stop with the high schools. Success builds on success and it was inevitable that pressure would grow to extend instrumental music down to the lower grades. As luck would have it, the province's elementary panel was changing with a new found focus on the middle school model, usually consisting of grades 6 to 8. These were ideal candidates for band programs and by the early 1970s they too were increasingly common.

School Bands in Québec

School based bands had existed in French speaking Québec since before Confederation and were still very much in operation in the 1960s. They were generally extra-curricular in nature and were present in the religious colleges supported and operated by the male Catholic teaching orders. Whether in schools like Collège Bourget, in the small community of Rigaud near the Ontario border, or in Montréal at the venerable Collège Mont St. Louis, bands regularly participated in a range of student activities.[12] The province's oldest school band, La Société Sainte Cecile at Québec City's Petit Séminaire had been established in 1838 and remained in operation until 1967, making it the longest continually active school band in Canadian history. Since the Catholic Church remained largely responsible for

---

[8] Donald McKellar as cited by Mark Fisher, son of W.A. Fisher, e-mail correspondence with the author 06 March 2018.
[9] The author was a music undergrad at U.W.O. from 1969 to 1973. He was a member of McKellar's Symphonic Band in his second year.
[10] Green and Vogan, *Music Education*, 359.
[11] Ibid., 359. Though the source table only specifies "extra-curricular" programs, it is probably safe to infer that the growth of curricular band programs was similar.
[12] Two of the author's brothers, John and Christopher, were boarders at Mont St. Louis and Collège Bourget in 1960-61 and 1966-67 respectively. Both remember the existence of a school band. John and Christopher Charles, interview with the author 05 October 2019.

education in francophone Québec until the "Quiet Revolution" of the 1960s, the status quo as far as the management of band programs remained intact. As a result, the growing influence of American style curricular band programs during the immediate postwar period was felt most keenly in the province's English speaking "Protestant" school boards. As with Toronto in Ontario, French Canada's largest city, Montréal was the epicenter of the new movement. Extra-curricular programs had been in place since at least 1947 with instruments and instruction being paid for by the Montreal Protestant School Board. Even with the success of the International Festival of School Music that took place at the Montreal Forum that year, it would not be until 1952 that instrumental music was integrated into the school day at Westmount Junior High School. It was an initiative that only took place after two teachers, Gifford Mitchell and Morley Calvert went to observe the program at North Toronto Collegiate.[13] Once started, progress was steady "…the Westmount program was eventually extended to the senior high level, and thus it paved the way for other schools in the Montreal area, such as Montreal West, Westhill, and several in suburban West Island."[14] This growth was matched with an increase in music education courses at McGill University.

By the mid 1960s, the Parent Commission had made sweeping recommendations for changes in Québec's French language schools both at the elementary and secondary levels. These included an integral place for instrumental music. Université Laval, recognizing the implications of this new thrust made "…progressive changes…in music education [programs]."[15] By the 1970s the curricular model of instrumental music instruction was increasingly present across Québec in both French and English-speaking schools. Its acceptance was aided in part by the province's structure for public education which started high school in grade 7, an ideal fit for the introduction of band studies.

In 1976, Bernard Hébert was initially hired to teach guitar classes at L'Ecole Polyvalente Nicolas-Gatineau in Gatineau, Québec. At the time and until 1980, music and art were compulsory subjects at the "secondaire 1" [grade 7] level and were offered twice a week in fifty-minute classes. Students were expected to choose between guitar and wind instrumental classes which would last for half a year before alternating with art. By the following year, "secondaire 2" [grade 8], students were to choose between music and art for the entire year.[16] With every student given an exposure to the music classroom, it was inevitable that with sufficient numbers, the music program would thrive. Shortly after his

---

[13] Green and Vogan, *Music Education*, 353.
[14] Ibid., 353.
[15] Ibid., 354.
[16] Bernard Hébert, e-mail correspondence with the author, 17 November 2019.

arrival, Bernard, a trumpet major, helped pioneer an experimental program called "spécialisation musique". The goal was to attract highly motivated students and engage them at school with daily classes in a subject about which they were passionate: music. It was hoped that their enthusiasm for the subject would spill over to the rest of the curriculum. The first year was so successful, with participating students scoring at the top of their classes in all disciplines, that other departments, arts, dance and physical education were all clamouring for similar opportunities.[17] Although daily music classes were eventually abandoned, the positive impact of regularly scheduled instrumental music instruction had been clearly demonstrated. Polyvalente Nicolas-Gatineau soon became representative of what was happening across Québec [Fig. 13.4].

School Bands in Western Canada

Unlike in Ontario and Québec, the first successful curricular school bands in British Columbia emerged not in the major urban centres, but in smaller communities. This anomaly may be explained by the fact that during the 1950s Vancouver could already boast at least two highly visible and internationally respected youth band programs: the Kitsilano Boys Band and the Vancouver Junior Band established by Gordon Olsen in 1944. In 1954, the first British Columbia High School Band Conference was held at New Westminster Junior High School. Bands from seven schools were in attendance including Kelowna H.S., Oak Bay H.S., Kimberly H.S., Oliver Southern Okanagan H.S., Powell River H.S., Summerland H.S. and S.J. Willis Junior High School in Victoria. Representatives from another four school bands were also in attendance, Castlegar H.S., Gladstone H.S. [Vancouver], Trail H.S. and Victoria H.S.[18] One of the driving forces behind this first gathering was Victoria's Howard Denicke, born in Chilliwack and a product of the boys' band movement. He taught at both S.J. Willis Junior High School and Mountview High School in the 1950s and 1960s and served as president of both the British Columbia Music Educators Association and the local branch of the American Federation of Musicians. One other successful band program to emerge from the province's more remote communities was established by Dennis Tupman in Kitimat in 1964.[19] After leaving Kitimat, Tupman became a Fine Arts Principal for the Vancouver School Board.

At the time, some of British Columbia's school districts were structured in a three-panel format: elementary (K-6), junior high (7-9) and senior high (10-12). This format gave

---

[17] Bernard Hébert, e-mail, 17 November 2019.
[18] Green and Vogan, *Music Education*, 368.
[19] David Dunnet, telephone interview with the author, 02 March 2021.

junior high school principals a greater degree of independence than their Ontario counterparts which in turn gave them greater flexibility, both in terms of hiring music specialists and allocating financial and physical resources. As a result, curricular junior high music programs emerged earlier than in Central Canada.

Once again, finding qualified music teachers for the province's schools was a pressing issue that the University of British Columbia [UBC] was initially slow to recognize. UBC's Faculty of Education was established in 1955 and "...its first faculty included a number of music specialists."[20] It was through their efforts, in the form of workshops and summer courses, that the first formal attempts were made to provide professional training for the province's music teachers. It was not until 1967 that UBC established its own music department and with it a series of specially designed music education courses. Prior to that time, the province's school boards had to seek qualified individuals south of the border. Or, as was the case with Oak Bay High School's David Dunnet, they needed to attend American universities to obtain the necessary training to teach band classes in Canadian schools. Dunnet was a talented and passionate young musician who was conducting a youth band in Victoria at the age of fifteen. He graduated from Oak Bay High School in 1958 and enrolled in the music department at the University of Washington in Seattle for the simple reason that "...there were no other music education schools in Western Canada at the time."[21] After graduation he returned to his alma mater in 1963 as band director [Fig. 13.5]. In addition to spending twenty-eight years at Oak Bay H.S., he was also a part-time sessional lecturer in music education at the University of Victoria, a master teacher seconded to the university for two years and an active member of the British Columbia Music Educators Association from 1968 to 1993.[22] Dunnet was hardly alone and nor was his story restricted just to British Columbia. Across western Canada, music graduates from American universities, American citizens as well as Canadians, travelled north to fill teaching vacancies in the emerging school band programs.

The Prairies faced one other challenge, large enough student populations. In order for there to be an optional curricular instrumental music program, there had to be sufficient students, per grade level, to fill not only the music classroom, but also those other optional classes scheduled at the same time for students that chose not to take music. It is not

---

[20] Ibid., 375.
[21] David Dunnet, as cited in Gerald King, "David I. Dunnet: One of Canada's Finest Band Directors, Pt. 1" *Canadian Band Journal* 20, no. 1 (Fall 1995) 23.
[22] Gerald King, "David Dunnet: One of Canada's Finest Band Directors, Pt. 2," *Canadian Band Journal* 20, no. 2 (Winter 1995) 19.

surprising then that curricular music programs in Manitoba, Alberta and Saskatchewan first appeared in the larger population centres.

In 1951, Fred Merrett, director of the Salvation Army's Winnipeg Senior Citadel Band, started a band at the city's Technical Vocational High School, known locally as TecVoc. Initially the program was extra-curricular with two practices a week lasting approximately one and a half hours each.[23]   The TecVoc band was also active in the community in the early 1960s playing concerts as well as marching in an average of five parades a year: two football games, the Winnipeg Santa Claus Parade, the Red River Exhibition Parade and the University of Manitoba Freshman Parade.   The first recorded curricular school band in province was established in 1955 with the opening of Winnipeg's Elmwood High School; by the end of the decade, it had been joined by the Sisler High School concert band. Elsewhere in Manitoba, progress was slow because enrolments were insufficient to support curricular programs.   A survey of the status of instrumental music in Manitoba during the 1962-63 school year revealed nine schools with band programs.[24]   The Manitoba Schools Concert Band, formed that decade, provided further incentives for wind instrumentalists and by 1966 band programs were beginning to appear with increasing frequency, in some cases replacing existing orchestral programs.   An example of this trend was at Winnipeg's Grant Park High School.   In 1972 it still had a string program along with band classes, but by 1990 the orchestra was gone.[25]

The pace of growth was once again limited by the slow response of the province's post-secondary institutions to the growing demand for qualified music teachers.   Brandon College was the first to offer a Bachelor of Music degree in Manitoba but its small number of graduates could not meet the need.   Although the University of Manitoba opened a music school in 1964, its emphasis on theory, history, and piano and vocal performance were of little use in the band classroom.[26]   As in B.C., boards had to look south for their music teachers or find teachers already on staff who were prepared to be very flexible with their teaching loads.   The band teacher at Winnipeg's Andrew Mynarski Junior High School in the late 1960s also taught Physical Education.   When he left it was the art teacher who took his place.[27]

---

[23] Richard Dooley, interview with the author 13 October 2019.   Richard is an enthusiastic amateur musician.   He was born in Winnipeg in 1943 and attended TecVoc from 1958 to 1961.   After graduating from university, he taught social studies at Grant Park H.S. from 1972-2001 where he was an active faculty supporter of the school's music program.

[24] Green and Vogan, *Music Education*, 379.

[25] Dooley, interview, 13 October 2019.

[26] Green and Vogan, *Music Education*, 380.

[27] Dooley, Interview, 13 October 2019.   Richard also taught at Andrew Mynarski Jr. H.S. from 1968-1972.

Alberta's first curricular school band was established at Calgary's Balmoral Junior High School in 1950. Within two years, the Calgary Board of Education had given approval for the introduction of curriculum-based band and orchestra classes at both the junior and senior high school levels.[28] Initially progress was slow because of limited student populations. A 1958-59 survey found that "...music is not a part of the curriculum in 296 Alberta high schools. Only ninety-three high schools have found a place for music courses in the curriculum."[29] Calgary's population had grown to over 457,000 people by the time it celebrated its centenary in 1975. That same year "...15 high schools and 100 junior high school bands [were] operating within the public school system."[30] By 1978, Lethbridge, with a population of just over 50,000 inhabitants, offered band programs in all three of its high schools, one of which, at Lethbridge Collegiate Institute, was taught by Jerry Pokarny, an American from Montana.[31]

The Edmonton Schoolboys Band was founded in 1936 and the group received both financial and logistical support from the Edmonton School Board but by the late 1950s not only were academic credits being given to members of the Schoolboys band, but instrumental music was increasingly being offered in individual secondary schools. The first junior high school programs were started in 1961 and by the following school year, 1962-63, instrumental music classes were operating in thirteen of the city's junior high schools and five out of six secondary schools.[32]

As in the rest of western Canada, the province's universities were woefully unprepared for the surge in demand for instrumental music teachers. The departments of music at the University of Alberta in Edmonton and the University of Calgary, which didn't become an independent institution until 1966, were not even established until 1965 and 1968 respectively. Throughout the 1960s, music education courses were offered by each institution's Faculty of Education. The University of Lethbridge established its own music department in 1967, the same year it received its charter. Like so many other newly formed schools, it would not be until the early 1970s that its first graduates would be available to teach. Once again "...school boards hired teachers trained in the United States [like Jerry Pokarny] or others who had experience in community bands and orchestras."[33]

---

[28] Green and Vogan, *Music Education*, 382.
[29] Ibid., 385.
[30] Norman Draper, *Bands by the Bow: A History of Band Music in Calgary* (Calgary: Century Calgary Publications, 1975) 71.
[31] Greg Fisher, interview with the author 12 November 2019. Greg went to high school in Lethbridge from 1978 to 1981. He is presently manager of the Calgary St. John's Music Store.
[32] Ibid., 383.
[33] Green and Vogan, *Music Education*, 386.

Saskatchewan's community youth bands laid the groundwork for the province's first curricular school bands, especially in its two largest cities, Regina and Saskatoon. The Regina Lions Band, first established in 1945 as the Queen City Band and the Saskatoon Lions Band were both closely associated with local schools. In 1949, R.J. Staples was hired as a provincial music supervisor. At the time there were only two school bands in the entire province, "…by the time he retired [1969] there were over 150 bands."[34]

Finding qualified teachers was again a challenge. In addition to looking south of the border, at least three of Saskatchewan's rural school boards also turned their attention to an institution that had been training band directors for over a century, Britain's Kneller Hall. The Sturgis School Unit, a rural district, "…advertised for a band leader in England [in 1958] and subsequently hired Leonard Camplin, who served as supervisor [teacher] until 1961."[35] British Army bandmasters remained an option until at least 1975 when Michael Scholfield, bandmaster of the band of the Royal Green Jackets was engaged by telephone to teach at the Outlook School Unit, No. 32. It was an itinerant position serving four rural schools and the initial contact was made through another former British Army bandmaster who by that time was teaching in Canora, Saskatchewan.[36]

One of the most successful school band programs in the province was in neither Regina nor Saskatoon but in the community of Yorkton. The city's first band programs were introduced around 1965 when the local population was approximately 12,000 people. Ten years later there were no fewer than 300 band students "…in the separate, private and collegiate schools in the city."[37] By the 1980s, the junior high band programme "…grew so large that it boasted Canada's largest marching band from 1985 to 1989, numbering over 280 students."[38]

School Bands in the Maritimes

Curricular band programs in the Maritimes were the late arrivals in the ever-growing Canadian school band movement. Much like the "Barrie" effect in Ontario a decade

---

[34] Ibid., 389.

[35] Ibid., 389. Camplin evidently didn't find teaching music in rural Saskatchewan altogether to his liking. He joined the Canadian Army in 1961 and as a graduate of Kneller Hall's bandmaster course was appointed Director of Music of the Royal Canadian Engineers Band in Chilliwack. After his retirement in 1972 he was active as a conductor of several B.C. community orchestras including the Okanagan Symphony Orchestra, the Kelowna Philharmonic Festival Society and the Fraser Valley Philharmonic.

[36] Michael Scholfield, *OHMS; On Her Majesty's Service* (Victoria: Friesen Press, 2015) 210.

[37] Kerry Linsley, "Yorkton and District Band Programme," *Canadian Winds* 4, no. 1 (Fall 2005) 6-7.

[38] Ibid., 6.

earlier, one of the inspirational moments that led to the introduction of school bands in Truro, N.S., was a performance in the Spring of 1962 by London, Ontario's Catholic Central High School Band under the direction of Martin Boundy.[39]   So impressed were local audiences that the desire to start their own band program provided the momentum necessary to establish the Truro Junior High School Band two years later under the leadership of Ron MacKay.   At first it was an extra-curricular enterprise rehearsing on Tuesday afternoons and Saturday mornings but eventually became part of the school day. A similar pattern was followed at Middleton High School located in the Annapolis Valley. Instrumental music was initially offered during the school's activity period on Wednesday afternoons and on Saturday mornings and was directed by ex-RCAF musician Wilf Harvey. In 1967 he was hired as a full-time teacher and the band program was integrated into the regular curriculum.[40]   Once the precedents had been set, curricular band programs began to appear, not just at the individual school level, but on a district wide basis as well.   In 1969, Ken Elloway, former Director of Music of Halifax's Royal Canadian Artillery Band was hired as coordinator for instrumental music in the Dartmouth, N.S., school district.[41]

Newfoundland and Labrador joined Confederation in 1949.   Prior to that time, Canada's tenth province was a British Crown Colony.   Its school system, like Québec's, was denominational with Roman Catholic, Anglican, United, Presbyterian and Salvation Army churches all responsible for their own schools.   There was no coherent pattern to the growth of band programs although Salvation Army run schools were the first to offer instrumental instruction to support their own rich brass band traditions.   Otherwise it was up to individual teachers to manage whatever they could with the means they had at their disposal.   One such example was Leo Sandoval, a US serviceman posted to Newfoundland in 1955.[42]   He married a local girl, took his release from active service and began teaching at St. Pius X High School in St. John's in 1964.   He introduced American methods of teaching band classes, "…which became the model for several schools which began instrumental instruction in the 1970s."[43]   Cornerbrook, the largest community on the west coast of the island was inspired in much the same way.   The high school band from the Harmon U.S. Air Force Base in nearby Stephenville "…played frequently at the

---

[39] Ken Henderson, "Truro District Schools Band Program," *Canadian Winds* 5, no. 2 (Spring 2007) 62.
[40] Green and Vogan, *Music Education*, 395.
[41] Ibid., 395.
[42] As part of the 1941 Lend-Lease Agreement between Great Britain and the U.S., Great Britain gave the Americans 99 year leases on British territories, which included Newfoundland at the time, in return for vast amounts of wartime materials and warships.   Two bases in particular, Harmon Air Force Base and the US Naval Base at Argentia remained operational until 1960 and 1994 respectively.
[43] Green and Vogan, *Music Education*, 396.

Cornerbrook Rotary Music Festival and inspired the creation of local school band programs, notably at St. Michael's High School in 1962."[44]

By the late 1970s, from Mahone Bay on Nova Scotia's south shore to schools extending from Victoria to Courtenay on Vancouver Island, curricular band programs were flourishing. There were many variables affecting that growth, only some of which have been discussed here. These included student populations, scheduling, engaged administrators and local financial support. Important as they were however, the catalyst that brought them all together to make music was the teacher. A fact recognized by Green and Vogan: "…the most significant factor in the rise of instrumental music in Canadian schools has been the teacher, for in every province, two or three outstanding individuals have provided the leadership and set high standards for others to emulate."[45] The bands they taught and directed served as examples to countless other band students and their parents. Wherever and whenever a successful wind band appears in Canadian history, whether military, community, youth or school, the defining element in its success was and still is the person or persons leading it. Some teachers did much, much more.

Keith Mann (1939-2001)

In the early twentieth century it was largely the military bandmasters who fostered the growth of the country's band associations and regional federations. They lobbied for greater acceptance of and higher performance standards for the nation's military, community and youth bands. By the 1960s and 1970s, that torch had passed to the country's music teachers. One of the undisputed leaders of this new breed of band activists was born in the rural community of Alix, Alberta. Keith Mann was the eldest son in a farming family whose exposure to music as a child was piano lessons. Shortly after starting his career as an elementary school teacher in the early 1960s, the seed planted on hearing a concert by the Leduc Community Band as a young boy began to bear fruit. He gained a working knowledge of band instruments by studying old method books then aggressively scrounged enough old instruments to start a school band. He began the process at his first school in Spruceview but it was not until his transfer to Elnora where it really "took off".[46] In 1965, he left Elnora to complete a Bachelor of Education degree and in 1968 was hired as a music specialist in Innisfail, Alberta, where he was responsible for teaching instrumental music to grades five through twelve. From 1968 to 1978, the

---

[44] Ibid., 396.
[45] Ibid., 398.
[46] Marilyn Mann, widow of Keith Mann, interview with the author 14 November 2019.

town's high school band, known as the "Innisfail Imps", rapidly established itself as one of the finest school bands in the province, competing successfully against those from the much larger centres of Edmonton and Calgary.

Not content with working only during the school year, Keith Mann spent the summer months from 1968 to 1979 as Captain, then Major Mann, in the Canadian Armed Forces Primary Reserve on the Cadet Instructor List. In that capacity he served as director of the music program at the annual Royal Canadian Air Cadet summer camps held at CFB Penhold.[47] The camp offered four two-week courses per season as well as several longer leadership courses. Each two-week session included a 50-60 piece band and senior cadets in the leadership billets, under Major Mann's direction, provided individual and group instruction to younger cadets from across central and western Canada.

Keith Mann resigned from his position at Innisfail High School in 1978 to accept a faculty post at nearby Red Deer College to develop and build a new music program.[48] In addition to his instructional and administrative duties he also immersed himself in a range of advocacy activities that included acting as editor of the quarterly magazine *Canadian Band Journal,* which he had started in 1976. He also filled executive roles with the Canadian Band Directors Association (renamed the Canadian Band Association in 1986) and lobbied tirelessly for the inclusion of a concert band component to MusicFest Canada competitions, efforts which finally paid off in 1989. Having also resigned his commission with the cadet movement he spent his summers touring, first with Al and Gladys Wright's "American Collegiate Wind Bands" and then from 1985 until 1996 as conductor of "Canadian Youth on Tour" ensembles in western Europe. In 1990 he was appointed director of both the Red Deer Community Band and the Red Deer Royals Marching Showband. Under his leadership this latter group was able to win a silver medal at the 1996 World Association of Marching Showbands competitions held in Calgary.

Despite the many accolades he received for his work with bands, one of his greatest contributions lay in his activities in support of the Canadian band movement. He was a "…President of the Canadian Band Association, 1975-1978, …past Chairman of the North American Band Directors Coordinating Council and a voting member on the boards of the Canadian Music Centre, International Music Festivals and the John Philip Sousa Foundation."[49] Recognition of his accomplishments extended south of the border with his receipt of the Edwin Franko Goldman Award and an honorary membership in the American

---

[47] Marilyn Mann, interview with the author 14 November 2019.
[48] Marilyn Mann, e-mail correspondence with the author 11 May 2020.
[49] "Keith Mann Outstanding Band Director Award – In Honorarium," *MusicFest Canada* at www.musicfest.ca accessed 19 November 2019.

Bandmasters Association.[50] His persistence and determination inspired many others to get actively involved in the support of bands at every level and his tragic death in a motorcycle accident on May 11, 2001 was a loss for Canada's entire band community [Fig. 13.6]. Keith Mann was a musical titan and a worthy successor to the great pioneers of the Canadian band story: Joseph Vézina, Charles O'Neill and C.F. Thiele.

The Summer Camps

As Major Mann's activities in the 1970s at the CFB Penhold air cadet camps clearly demonstrated, the music didn't end with the summer holidays. The postwar period also saw the appearance of summer music camps or schools for young wind instrumentalists. These were both rural residential and urban day programs. What they all had in common was the desire to provide intensive musical training to enthusiastic and talented young musicians.   The camps' organizers could often engage highly skilled teachers and performers as faculty because the summer months were traditionally a lean time for many of the country's universities, colleges and symphony orchestras. The result was that many student musicians like those from the Barrie Collegiate Band at the Interprovincial Music Camp in the 1960s and 1970s could return to school in September, re-energized, practiced and eager to share their improved skills with their fellow classmates.

In 1946, Charles F. Thiele, conductor of the Waterloo Musical Society Band and president of the Waterloo Music Company, fulfilled a lifelong ambition by opening a summer music camp not far from the city of Waterloo.   Named "Bandberg", it was intended for under-privileged boys, ages 12-18, drawn from boys' bands across the region.[51]   Summer courses lasted for six weeks and Thiele drew on his own financial resources to pay not only for the construction of the camp but also for the purchase of the land, development of the infrastructure (roads, water, sewer and power) and even the provision of livestock to local farmers to feed campers and staff. Even though the camp was not officially opened until July of 1949, it had been accepting students every summer since its launch three years earlier.[52]   Bandberg remained in operation until 1954, the year of Thiele's death, when without his ongoing financial support nor that of any other municipal, provincial or private sponsor, it was forced to close its doors. It had, however, shown the way.

---

[50] Marilyn Mann, e-mail correspondence with the author 11 May 2020.
[51] John Mellor, *C.F. Thiele: Father of Canadian Band Music* (Waterloo, ON: Melco History Series, 1988) 89.
[52] Ibid., 112.

The Jeunesses Musicales du Canada opened a summer music camp at Mount Orford in Québec's Eastern Townships in 1951. Conceived as a training facility for aspiring young musicians in the classical orchestral tradition, by the late 1960s it had attracted internationally renowned artists as summer faculty including its namesake the Orford String Quartet as well as violinist Lorand Fenyves, cellist Paul Tortellier and flautist Christian Lardé.[53] Distinguished wind performers from the Montréal area filled out the ranks of the teaching staff providing a quality of instruction, both individually and in small ensembles, that nurtured generations of wind instrumentalists. The nearby town of Ayer's Cliff, a fashionable summer resort destination for wealthy Americans since the nineteenth century, was from 1958 to 1970, the home of the Monteregian Music Camp. Established by the Montréal music teacher Morley Calvert, its goal was to provide summer music training for high school students.[54]

Another camp that opened in the 1950s and that continues to operate to the present day is the International Music Camp (IMC). It was established in 1956 by Winnipeg's Fred Merrett and Dr. Merton Utgard of Minot, North Dakota and its name is appropriate considering its location in "…the International Peace Gardens straddling the border between the United States and Canada" [Manitoba and North Dakota].[55] The camp offered eight one-week programs for junior and senior high school students during the months of June and July [corresponding to the U.S. school calendar]. Throughout its history IMC has attracted not only a "who's who" of American wind band guest conductors but some of Canada's most respected wind band leaders including Martin Boundy (on at least ten separate occasions), Clifford Hunt, Robert Rosevear [Fig. 13.7], and more recently, Jeremy Brown and Fraser Linklater.[56] Not only does it offer sessions for band and orchestra musicians but it has also expanded its mandate to include a wide range of other musical and artistic fields. An advertisement for the camp in the Spring 1998 issue of the *Canadian Band Journal* makes reference to supplemental courses for piano, ballet, art, choirs, swing choir, guitar and handbells as well as an extensive list of other disciplines.[57]

---

[53] Irfona Larkin et al, "Summer Camps and Schools," *The Canadian Encyclopedia* edited 16 Dec 2013 at www.thecanadianencyclopedia.ca accessed 27 October 2019. The author attended the JMC camp for two summers, 1966 and 1967.

[54] Nancy McGregor, "Calvert, Morley," *Encyclopedia of Music in Canada* (Toronto: University of Toronto Press, 1981) 134.

[55] "Location," *International Music Camp* at www.internationalmusiccamp.com accessed 27 October 2019.

[56] *International Music Camp 1956-2005: Celebrating 50 Years of Service to Youth, Souvenir Booklet* (Minot, N.D.: International Music Camp, 2005) 38-39. Courtesy Brent Johnson.

[57] "International Music Camp (Advertisement)," *Canadian Band Journal* 22, no.3 (Spring 1998) 8.

In 1957, Edmonton's David J. Peterkin established the MusiCamrose summer camp for bands and orchestras. Originally sponsored by the Alberta government's Department of Culture, Youth and Recreation, it was transferred to the Alberta Summer Music Workshop Association in 1983 and in 2001 was moved from Camrose to Red Deer to become known as MusiCamp Alberta. These band camps, lasting one week, host two concert bands, for junior and senior level student musicians respectively. MusiCamp Alberta continues to operate and has added camps for jazz bands, strings and musical theatre studies in separate sessions.[58]

Starting with Ben and Sheila Wise's Interprovincial Music Camp (also known as IMC) in 1960 [See Chap. 12], the decade saw the creation of several new summer music camps in Ontario. These included the Ontario Youth Music Camp at Beaverton on Lake Simcoe which operated from 1963 until 1980 and the National Music Camp of Canada on Lake Couchiching, near Orillia, which opened in 1965 and continues to operate to the present day.[59]

Across western Canada, the 1960s witnessed the addition of a variety of summer opportunities for music students: the Okanagan Summer School of the Arts in Penticton B.C. (1960) and the Courtenay Youth Music Centre (1966) on Vancouver Island. Saskatchewan's Echo Valley School of the Arts at Fort Qu'Appelle opened in 1963 and remained in operation until 1989.[60]

In the Maritimes, summer music schools were offered primarily by the region's universities. These included the Mount Allison University Instrumental Music Camp in Sackville N.B., in operation from 1959 to 1989, the Acadia [University] Summer Music Institute in Wolfville N.S. which was established in 1967, the Memorial University Summer Instrumental Music Camp of St. John's N.L. in 1972 and in 1975, the University of Prince Edward Island's Youth Music Camp.[61]

If longevity is a measure of success, then one of Canada's most successful summer camps, along with the two IMCs, is Québec's Le Camp Musical d'Asbestos. Asbestos [renamed Val-des-Sources in October of 2020] is the name of the nearby community in the province's Eastern Townships whose entire economy was built on the mining of the now banned fibre-like fire retardant mineral. Established in 1961 as "Le Camp Musical de l'Harmonie d'Asbestos [music camp of the Asbestos community band], attendance was initially restricted to members of the town band. In 1966 admission was extended to all

---

[58] Joel Gray, Director MusiCamp Alberta, e-mail correspondence with the author 10 January 2023
[59] Larkin et al, "Summer Camps" 27 October 2019.
[60] Ibid.
[61] Ibid.

band musicians aged 10 and older. The camp remains active to the present day with its focus on wind band musicians, both students and adults. It attracts participants from across Québec.[62]

It didn't matter where they were, nor whether they were rural or urban, residential or day only, Canada's summer music camps and schools made a large, if little acknowledged contribution to the growth of the school band movement in the postwar period. Most wind instrumentalists who attended these camps received their initial instrumental training in school band programs. At camp they were exposed to a range of pedagogical experiences from private lessons and small ensemble performances to full band rehearsals and faculty recitals, most of which were largely unavailable during the regular school year. The large ensemble practices especially focused on preparing repertoire for performance in a matter of days rather than the weeks or months that many students were accustomed to in their respective school bands. Not only did this expose participants to a wider range of music literature but it also gave them deeper insights to wind band performance practice.

New Challenges in the 1980s

It couldn't last. The 1950s, 1960s and 1970s witnessed explosive growth in the number and quality of Canadian high school bands but by the late 1970s, the forces that were about to put the brakes on were beginning to be felt. The first of these was declining enrolments.

The students that filled those band classrooms in the immediate postwar period belonged to the "baby boom" generation; those born between 1947 and 1962. In many cases their fathers were veterans of the Second World War whose demobilization began in earnest in 1946. Once home, they just wanted to get on with the rest of their lives, especially since many had seen or knew of fellow soldiers, sailors and aircrew who had perished in the bloodiest war in human history. They sought stability and family was traditionally the way to do it. What made it all possible was that Canada, physically untouched by a conflict that had literally flattened most of Europe, was ideally positioned to capitalize on Europe's reconstruction. We had the resources, the human capital, the infrastructure and the factories. The 1950s were a period of sustained economic prosperity and anyone who wanted a good job could get one and raise a family. Birth rates soared and the nation's classrooms were full.

By 1980 the last of the baby boomers were completing their public education. Inner city schools were the first to start emptying out although the news of their decline was often

---

[62] "Le Camp," *Camp Musical d'Asbestos* at www.centreo3.com accessed 05 November 2019.

eclipsed by headlines of overcrowded suburban schools surrounding the country's largest cities. The math, however, was simple. If there weren't enough students to fill enough seats, the class couldn't be offered. Unfortunately, declining enrolments were just the start as the late 1970s and early 1980s also introduced an unexpected series of educational initiatives and practices that further reduced the number of potential music students for Canada's high school bands.

The release of the final report of the Bilingualism and Biculturalism Commission in 1969 clearly identified a problem with the provision of federal government services to Canadians. Whereas in Québec minority anglophone Quebecers could easily access services in English, the availability of those same services to francophones elsewhere in Canada was woefully inadequate. The passage of the Official Languages Act that same year provided a legislative framework for improvement with the aim of creating a fully bilingual federal civil service across the country. Although there was acrimonious debate on how to implement the legislation for serving federal employees, on one point there was complete unanimity: the best way to achieve this end for future generations was to start in the schools. French immersion programs were immediately popular across the country as parents would often line up for hours outside board and district offices to ensure that their children would be registered in the limited number of spaces initially offered. These were parents who valued education and who wanted the very best for their offspring. Many were also band parents.

The practical problem created by French immersion programs, at least as far as band classes were concerned, only became evident when students reached the middle school grades and the start of instrumental music options. Depending on the intensity of the immersion program offered, it was necessary that anywhere from 50% to 80% of daily instruction take place in French. If band was only available in English, then it had to compete with every other subject only available in English for a limited number of spots in the school day. If some of those competing subjects were from the core areas, such as math or science, then the chances of fitting band into the schedule were significantly reduced. French immersion remains as popular as ever almost fifty years after it was first introduced and by most measures it has been spectacularly successful. Unfortunately, band classes were casualties in many schools as enthusiastic and talented young people who would have previously chosen band as an optional subject were unable to do so.

The 1980s added a new subject to the curriculum that also enticed students away from band as a preferred option. In 1977, Apple, Commodore and the Tandy Corporation released their respective lines of Apple II, PET and TRS-80 models of personal home computers. It didn't take long for educational authorities to take notice and integrate computer classes into the school curriculum. They first appeared as optional courses, in some cases alongside other more traditional arts disciplines including visual art, drama and music. As the influence of computer technology spread, made even more appealing by the increased popularity of the first video games, more and more students shifted allegiance from band to computers.

Taken together, declining enrolments, French immersion and emerging computer technologies all played a part in slowing the growth of the school band movement in the 1980s. Their impact, however, was felt largely in the total number of programs, not necessarily their quality. Fewer students meant fewer band classes and on occasion, the entire closure of a band program. For many of those that remained however, performance standards stayed high. The real threat was yet to come.

This "grim reaper" of Canada's high school band programs in the 1970s and 1980s was introduced as an "improvement" but in fact played havoc with the quality of band programs from coast to coast. It was called semestering or block booking. The traditional high school timetable during the 1950s and 1960s consisted of seven or eight 40 to 50 minute classes a day plus lunch. These would include the compulsory core subjects: English/Français, mathematics, science, history/geography and physical education. There would then be a number of optional subjects which, depending on the province could be visual arts, drama, music, industrial arts (shop), home economics or even Latin. Classes lasted all year. Within this framework curricular band programs flourished. Although there were provincial variations, band classes were usually scheduled four to five times a week. If, in addition to regular curricular classes, extra before/after school band practices were also offered, students could be playing six, seven or more hours weekly not including private practice at home. Ottawa's Laurentian High School Band in the 1960s and 1970s, under the direction of ex-army bandsman Henry Bonnenberg, was a perfect example. Band was scheduled for each grade level in classes of 50 minutes duration, four times a week. The senior band also rehearsed daily from 8:00 AM to 9:00AM.[63] Collectively, members of the band were playing together on average over eight hours a week and Laurentian High School was only one of many. Across the country, band students enrolled in a traditional timetable could be practicing well over an hour a day excluding private practice at home. Not surprisingly, high school bands excelled.

Semestering changed all of that. Instead of offering every subject daily all year, the curriculum was modified so that by doubling the length of each class, from 40-50 minutes

---

[63] Glenn McCue, interview with the author 28 April 2016. Glenn was a student at Laurentian from 1969 until 1973 and played French horn in the senior band.

each to 75-90 minutes daily, the instructional material needed to be covered for successful completion of a given subject at each grade level could be completed in five months instead of ten. Four subjects would be taught in the first half of the year and a different four in the second half. Core subject teachers, mathematics, science, social studies and English/Français loved it! It meant that instead of having to prepare for seven or eight classes daily [or mark seven or eight different sets of tests, quizzes or papers a day], they only had to do a maximum of four. The problem was that any subject that was sequential, cumulative and motor skill developmental faced the prospect of five months of intense activity followed by five months [plus another two for summer holidays] of inactivity. Whatever skills a student may have acquired during semestered class time were inevitably lost over the extended period of non-class time until the following year. Music, physical education and second language teachers especially recognized immediately the threat semestering posed to their respective programs but since these weren't generally considered "real" subjects by their high school core subject colleagues, their protests carried little weight. From the early 1970s in British Columbia,[64] the mid to late 1970s in Alberta,[65] and the 1980s in Ontario, Québec and Nova Scotia,[66] traditional schedules were devoured by the semestering juggernaut.

Fortunately for many band programs across the country, there were also school based administrators, principals and vice-principals, who were both insightful and sympathetic enough to understand the implications of semestering for their music programs. They actively supported their music teachers by encouraging other staff members to voluntarily modify their teaching schedules so that band classes could function year-round. Calgary's Earl Paddock at William Aberhart High School [grades 10-12] was fortunate in that physical education was a compulsory subject for grade 10 students in Alberta schools. He arranged a back to back timetable for his grade 10 band classes so that students took band one day, phys.ed the next for the entire school year. He was able to extend curricular band classes at the grade 11 and grade 12 levels by making similar arrangements with grade 11 mathematics and grade 12 spares respectively.[67] Semestering took a little bit longer to reach Nova Scotia but by the late 1980s it had been adopted at Dartmouth, N.S.'s, Prince Andrew High School [renamed Woodlawn High School in August, 2022]. The school's music teacher, Chris deRosenroll, like Earl Paddock in Calgary, enjoyed the support of an

---

[64] David Dunnet, telephone interview with the author, 04 November 2019.
[65] Earl Paddock, e-mail correspondence with the author, 29 October 2019.
[66] Bernard Hébert, e-mail correspondence with the author, 14 November 2019 and Chris deRosenroll, e-mail correspondence with the author 25 September 2019.
[67] Earl Paddock, e-mail, 29 October 2019.

equally enlightened administrator. English was a compulsory subject in grade 10 and band classes were timetabled back to back with it. In grades 11 and 12 a very understanding registrar arranged for band students to coordinate their year with curricular spares, again enabling them to perform during class time all year [Fig. 13.8]. Elsewhere in the country, whether at Martingrove Collegiate Institute in Toronto or Polyvalente Nicholas-Gatineau in Gatineau, wherever music teachers were supported by understanding and flexible administrators, some form of accommodation could be found. Not every high school music teacher was that lucky.

In the absence of supportive administrators, many band teachers were forced to schedule music classes before and after school or during lunch breaks. Since these were credit courses there had to be sufficient hours allocated per week to meet provincial guidelines for course completion. Given that there were only so many lunch breaks or periods available before and after school hours, it became impossible for grade levels to rehearse separately. The result was that many credit band classes practiced with all grades together at the same time. This created conditions where in some cases over one hundred students were gathered together for band class. It was an environment that was hardly conducive to instruction at the individual or sectional level. What made retention even harder was that band classes now came into conflict with school clubs, sports teams and part-time jobs.

By 1990, semestering was a "fait accompli" in most Canadian high schools. Although some programs continued to thrive through the combined efforts of inspired teachers and enlightened administrators, many others saw the quality of previously existing bands slip dramatically. Newer suburban high schools never attained the levels of excellence that their older inner-city cousins once knew. The silver lining was that Canada's postwar high school bands had clearly demonstrated the value of curricular music programs. It was a lesson that the feeder schools, the middle schools and the junior high schools had learnt and it was to them that the torch had been passed. Semestering was a non-starter for younger students and it was there that the new growth took place.

CHAPTER THIRTEEN GALLERY

Figure 13.1. Victoria Boys Band, Victoria, 1957. Director David Dunnet. Most prewar and immediate postwar community-based youth bands attracted elementary age beginners. They were proof that instrumental music could be effectively taught in elementary schools. David Dunnet led the band for three years. Source: David Dunnet

Figure 13.2. North Toronto Collegiate Institute Band, 1956. Director Jack Dow. In 1946, North Toronto C.I. became Canada's first large urban high school to offer instrumental music as a curricular subject. North Toronto and Barrie were arch rivals at the annual Toronto Kiwanis Festival's Challenge Class for bands. Source: North Toronto Collegiate Institute Archives.

Figure 13.3. The Laurentian High School Band, Ottawa, 1969. Director Henry Bonnenberg. In addition to four band classes a week for each grade level during the school day, members of the senior band (above) also rehearsed every morning from 8:00 until 9:00. Not including individual practice at home, band students were together in ensemble seven or more hours a week. Henry Bonnenberg was a Dutch national who joined the Canadian Army as a musician in 1953. After his release in 1958 he started his teaching career at the newly opened Laurentian High School. Source: Ottawa Carleton District School Board, Corporate Records Division.

Figure 13.4. Senior Ensemble, L'École Polyvalente Nicholas-Gatineau, Gatineau, Québec, 2007. Director Bernard Hébert. Bernard Hébert was winner of the MusiCan Teacher of the Year award in 2007 in recognition of his outstanding contribution to music education. Source: photo courtesy of Bernard Hébert.

Figure 13.5. Oak Bay Secondary School Band, Osaka, Japan, 1970. Director David Dunnet. The band was followed on one occasion by a one-hundred-piece all-American Youth Band, two students per state, conducted by Frederick Fennell. Source: photo courtesy of David Dunnet.

Figure 13.6. Keith Mann (1939-2001) Largely self-taught, Keith Mann's career spanned all branches of the Canadian band movement. He taught band at the elementary, secondary and post-secondary levels, directed military/cadet bands as well as community-based adult and youth bands. He was the founding editor of the *Canadian Band Journal,* a tireless advocate on behalf of wind bands across Canada and active as a clinician, adjudicator and conductor. Past President of the Canadian Band Association he was also a recipient of the Edwin Franko Goldman Award and an honorary member of the American Bandmasters Association. Source: photo courtesy of Marilyn Mann.

Figure 13.7.   Professor Robert Rosevear conducting an International Music Camp summer student band, International Music Camp, International Peace Gardens on the border between North Dakota and Manitoba, July, 1968.   Source: photo courtesy of the International Music Camp.

Figure 13.8.   Prince Andrew High School Senior Band, Lieutenant Governor's Garden Party Halifax, 2000.   Director Chris deRosenroll.   Her Honour Myra Freeman with Chris deRosenroll on her left.   The photograph clearly illustrates the use of an accomplished school band in a venue that would have traditionally been served by a military or community band. Source: photo courtesy of Chris deRosenroll.

CHAPTER FOURTEEN

THE MARCHING BANDS

From the Imperial Trumpet Guilds and Louis XIV's "Grande Écurie" of the seventeenth century to the "Harmoniemuzik" formations of the eighteenth, from the British Army's regimental bands in the nineteenth to Canada's legendary community bands in the early twentieth centuries, outdoor performance has always been part of the job description for wind and percussion instrumentalists. Even as late as the 1950s, every self-respecting adult community band in the country accepted marching and playing as part of its performance responsibilities. So too did the school bands. In 1955, even the Barrie Collegiate Institute Band, by that time already one of Canada's finest concert groups, was still participating in local parades.[1]

Military bands have been marching and playing since their first appearance over two and a half centuries ago and continue to do so today. It many respects, it is their "bread and butter" gig. Admirals and generals may defer to their directors of music when it comes to programming for sit down concerts in schools, at charity events or other public venues but on the parade square they want good performances of their respective service's musical canon. The army, navy and air force all have a select repertoire of marchpasts, slow and quick, inspection tunes, general salutes and more that are unique to their environment. When performed in conjunction with a change of command, a graduation parade, a regimental birthday or solemn Remembrance Day ceremonies, they are part of a centuries' old tradition. This martial literature is multi-layered. Its notes can evoke years of happy and sad memories. Regimental and branch marchpasts carry in their melodic lines echoes of sacrifice, struggle and hard-fought battles by previous generations of soldiers, sailors, airmen and airwomen. Although parade ground formations are no longer a part of the modern battlefield, militaries around the world continue to train new recruits in elements of marching drill. Marching in step, accompanied by a band playing music that is both stirring and yet familiar has been universally shown to inspire unit cohesion and reinforce discipline [Fig. 14.1].

Shortly after the unification of the Canadian Forces in 1968, the Department of National Defence released a document entitled *CFP 201: Manual of Drill and Ceremonial*. It was an exhaustive resource on all matters pertaining to parade ground drill movements and

---

[1] See "Barrie Central Collegiate Marching Band parades on Dunlop Street heading east, (1955)" *Barrie Historical Archive* at www.barriearchive.ca

military ceremonies. The publication also included at least two chapters, in whole or in part, dedicated to the employment of bands. Although primarily intended for regular and reserve force bands, it also provided direction to the country's growing number of cadet bands.

The Cadet Bands

The Canadian Cadet Organization is one of Canada's largest federally sponsored youth programs. Its three component branches, the Royal Canadian Sea Cadets, Royal Canadian Army Cadets and Royal Canadian Air Cadets are open to young people ages 12 to 18.[2] The goal of all three is to encourage their members to become active responsible citizens in their home communities through participation in activities that teach teamwork, leadership and citizenship. Although cadets are not members of the Canadian Forces and are under no obligation whatsoever to serve, it is the military ethos, with its emphasis on loyalty, respect, fitness and discipline that serves as a model for development.[3] In addition to using uniforms and training materials borrowed from their respective parent services, Canada's cadets have also embraced the military band. The composition and skill level of these groups were and are as varied as the communities from which they come and range from beginner level ensembles to the equivalent of fine senior high school bands. During the year they rehearse and march with their corps or squadron one night a week and sometimes parade on weekends. Their directors can be local school music teachers, ex-military musicians or accomplished amateur musicians who are paid members of a subcomponent of the Canadian Armed Forces reserve known as the "Cadet Instructor Cadre". Just like their adult counterparts in the regular and reserve force bands, the cadet bands play the musical repertoire associated with their branch affiliation [often in simplified arrangements for younger players] as well as a broader range of literature determined by their technical proficiency and instrumentations.

Sea and Army cadet organizations have been in existence in Canada since the late nineteenth century but it was not until 1927 that Captain John Slatter, Director of Music of Toronto's 48th Highlanders established one of the country's first cadet bands, the Toronto Cadet Band. That same year also saw the creation of the Winnipeg Sea Cadet Band. Winnipeg's Sea Cadets subsequently adopted the name John Travers Cornwell VC [Victoria Cross] Sea Cadet Corps in honour of the Royal Navy's sixteen-year-old boy

---

[2] "About Cadets", *Canada's Cadet Organizations* at www.cadets.ca accessed 25 November 2019.
[3] "About Cadets" *Canada: Canadian Cadet Organizations* at www.cadets.ca accessed 25 November 2019.

seaman who, though mortally wounded, remained at his station during the Battle of Jutland in May of 1916. Under that name, the John Travers Cornwell VC Sea Cadet band has remained continuously active to the present day.[4] The Depression years however, saw little growth in the number of cadet bands as community efforts were focused on the support of the boys' bands. The Second World War changed that almost overnight. The New Westminster Junior Band served as a cadet "house" band on the west coast that provided musicians for all three services.[5] On the prairies it was not uncommon for the boys' bands to gravitate towards the navy. One such example was the North Battleford Rotary Boys Band which became a wartime sea cadet band.[6]

With the end of hostilities in 1945 and the gradual disappearance of the boys' and girls' bands, cadet bands remained active. In 1975, federal legislation that authorized the deployment of resources, both human and material, from the Department of National Defence in support of the cadet movement was amended. One word was changed; "boys" became "persons" and that opened up the doors and the bands to girls. The cadet bands flourished. They had a steady supply of new members that were attracted by a series of advantages that were unique to the cadet organizations.

There were and still are no registration fees nor annual dues required for membership in a cadet corps or squadron. Although families are expected to support local fundraising activities, there are no financial barriers to participation. For potential musicians, a further incentive was the provision of instruments at no cost. During the 1970s, 1980s and early 1990s, musical instruments surplus to the needs of regular and reserve force bands, when judged "serviceable", were redesignated "for cadet use" and made available nationally. In some cases, this meant that some very fine instruments, Conn brasses, Boosey and Hawkes "Imperial" tubas and euphoniums, Selmer saxophones, Buffet clarinets and Haynes flutes/piccolos could end up in the hands of very fortunate young musicians.[7] Enticing as these free instrumental loans were, especially for boys and girls of modest means, one of the real perks was the summer band camps.

Major Keith Mann's Air Cadet summer band camps at CFB Penhold were just the tip of the iceberg. In 1953 the Royal Canadian Sea Cadets established a Cadet Summer

[4] Phillip Bingham, Manitoba Navy League, e-mail correspondence with the author, 30 March 2022.

[5] Kerry Turner and John White, "New Westminster and District Concert Band," *Canadian Winds* 10, no. 1 (Fall 2011) 32-33.

[6] Katelyn Hannotte, "North Battleford City Kinsmen Band at 65," *Canadian Winds* 13, no. 2 (Spring 2015) 29-31.

[7] From 1988 to 1993, the author was a CFSMUS summer reserve instructor at CFB Borden. On two occasions during this period he visited the CF instrument storage facility housed at 1 CFSD [Canadian Forces Supply Depot] in Downsview. Shelf after shelf contained instruments marked "for cadet use".

Training Centre [CSTC] at H.M.C.S. Quadra near Comox, B.C. It was followed three years later by H.M.C.S. Acadia, located next to the Royal Canadian Navy's recruit training school at Cornwallis, N.S. Both camps offered courses for brass-reed band musicians of three to six weeks duration. These two facilities were joined in the 1960s and 1970s by H.M.C.S. Qu'Appelle near Fort Qu'Appelle, Saskatchewan, H.M.C.S. Ontario in Kingston and H.M.C.S. Québec in Sainte-Angèle de Laval, a camp intended exclusively for francophone cadets.[8] Air Cadet summer programs, which also included a band component were established at air bases across the country to serve as regional centres for cadet training: CFB Greenwood in Nova Scotia, CFB Bagotville in Québec, CFB Borden in Ontario and CFB Penhold in Alberta.[9] Similarly, Army Cadet band programs were established at the Blackdown Cadet Training Centre (CFB Borden), the Argonaut Cadet Training Centre (CFB Gagetown) and the Whitehorse (Yukon) Cadet Training Centre. There was even a facility created exclusively for musician training in 1982: the Mont St. Sacrement Cadet Music Training centre near Valcartier, Québec.[10] Even as the number of regular and reserve force bands dwindled, especially after the FRP [Forces Reduction Plan] reductions of 1994, the number of cadet bands remained steady. The net result was that the military marching band tradition, which had been a cornerstone of the wind band movement in Canada since before Confederation, remained very much intact [Fig. 14.2].

High School Marching Bands

Although the American model of music education exerted a strong influence on the development of Canadian curricular programs, the marching band component was not as enthusiastically received. The adoption of marching bands within Canadian schools was uneven at best. One early exception was Toronto's Malvern Collegiate Institute. In 1949, George McRae established the Malvern Collegiate Marching Band, an ensemble whose performance history is as colourful as it is long. The band played regularly not only for its own Malvern football games but for the City of Toronto finals in both football and soccer. Through the years it appeared in many of the city's most beloved parades: the annual Santa Claus parade, the Beaches Easter parade as well as Grey Cup parades and Remembrance Day ceremonies. It was a regular guest at numerous civic events including

---

[8] "Royal Canadian Sea Cadets-Summer Training," *Wikipedia* at www.en.m.wikipedia.org accessed 23 February 2020.
[9] "Royal Canadian Air Cadets-Summer Training," *Wikipedia* at www.en.m.wikipedia.org accessed 23 February 2020.
[10] "Royal Canadian Army Cadets-Summer Training," *Wikipedia* at www.en.m.wikipedia.org accessed 23 February 2020.

the opening of both Toronto's new city hall and Roy Thompson Hall. More recently the band led the Toronto Blue Jays on their first appearance up Bay Street.[11]

It is likely that similar programs existed in the southwest Ontario triangle formed by the cities of Toronto, Niagara Falls and Windsor, but the passage of over sixty years since the gradual integration of curricular band programs has left little easily accessible documentary evidence. Some photographs however do offer clues. School based extra-curricular bands were certainly active prior to and during WWII. A photo of the Assumption College High School Band of Windsor, Ontario, taken in either the late 1930s or 1940s, clearly shows a group of over forty-five musicians including a small colour party and marching glockenspiel.[12] The band itself was formed in the 1930s by Father Harrison and by the late 1940s was directed by Frank Menichetti, a former US Navy bandmaster. During the immediate postwar period, the Assumption College High School band participated in the annual CNE "Music Days", the Waterloo Band Festival and appeared frequently in parades and concerts in both Windsor and neighbouring Detroit.[13] A more recent example is on a dust jacket for a vinyl recording made in 1969 by the Catholic Central High School Band of London, Ontario [Fig. 14.3]. Produced as a tribute to their departing Music Director of over fifteen years, Martin Boundy, the cover image shows an eighty-three-piece band in concert formation wearing uniforms that positively scream "...made for marching!" The liner notes list some highlights of the ensemble's activities since its creation in 1954. One such event under Boundy's baton was a private performance for Pope Paul VI in 1964; an outdoor concert that took place in the courtyard of Castel Gandolfo, the pontiff's summer residence. It is unlikely the group had time to prepare the venue for a formal sit-down presentation but for a marching band it would have been very easy to arrange. Considering Boundy's wartime experience as leader of the RCAF Central Band, training and directing a band on parade would have posed little problem for him.[14]

The marching band concept seems to have been more enthusiastically embraced on the prairies. In the early 1960s, Winnipeg's TecVoc High School Band participated in a wide variety of outdoor sporting events and parades. To the west, in neighbouring

---

[11] Dianne Chadwick, "George McRae's 90th Birthday," *Malvern Musings* (Spring 2016) at www.malverncollegiate.com accessed 20 November 2019. See also Bob Watson and Volker Hosemann, "Malvern C.I.: A Musical History" at the same web address.

[12] John Mellor, *Music in the Park: C.F. Thiele Father of Canadian Band Music* (Waterloo, ON: Melco History Series, 1988) 102.

[13] Jack Kopstein, e-mail correspondence with the author, 27 June 2021. Respected Canadian military band historian Kopstein attended Assumption College High School from 1945 to 1949.

[14] "Liner Notes," *Catholic Central Band Presents*, Sound Recording (London, ON: Academy Records International 8041, 1969)

Saskatchewan, the Yorkton and District band program produced a succession of fine marching bands. In 1983 "…the [Yorkton] Marching 100 were first among forty-seven bands in the senior high school field competition in Regina."[15] One can safely assume that at least some of the other forty-six bands in the competition came from elsewhere on the prairies. Across the west, the influx of Americans, or Canadians who had received their undergraduate musical training at American schools, meant that newly hired teachers were receptive to including marching bands as part of their teaching loads. Calgary's Robert Eklund, just arrived from Great Falls College, Montana, in 1967 began the Central Memorial High School Golden Rams Marching Band in 1970. He would remain its director until his retirement twenty-eight years later. By that time, it had been the model for one of the country's most successful marching band programs, the Calgary Stampede Showband, established in 1971.[16] The Golden Rams, however, were not the city's only high school marching band. In 1986, Elmer Riegal established the Bishop Grandin Ghosts Marching Band which remains to this day one of western Canada's elite marching high school bands. Nor was the marching band vision limited to just the larger cities. Jerry Chatwin, a transplanted Texan, arrived in Magrath, Alberta, in 1988 and by the mid 1990s, the Magrath High School Marching Band, known as the Spirit of Alberta, was a frequent guest at marching venues in nearby Lethbridge.

Victoria's Dave Dunnet began teaching at Oak Bay High School in 1963 and marching band was an integral part of his program until his retirement in 1991. It was extra-curricular in nature with practices taking place twice weekly outside of regular school hours. Dunnet was a pragmatist; his band averaged three parades a year and his insistence on doing street events, as opposed to field routines, meant that he didn't have to spend time teaching his students how to do intricate field manoeuvres like countermarches.[17] He further simplified his job by insisting that his players only memorize one march per season. If there were to be more than one selection necessary, members of the Oak Bay High School Band would read them off of march cards.[18]

[Author's note: for modern readers unfamiliar with march cards, they were a staple of the band music publishing industry for over a hundred years starting in the last decades of the nineteenth century. They measured an average of 17cm x 13cm (7" x 5") and were designed to be carried while performing. With the exception of flutes and piccolos, they were attached to instruments by means of a metal clamp called a "lyre". Flute and piccolo

---

[15] Kerry Linsley, "Yorkton and District Band Programs, *Canadian Winds* 4, no. 1 (Fall 2005) 6.
[16] Robert Eklund, telephone interview with author, 03 February 2020.
[17] A countermarch is necessary for a band to reverse direction while still marching and playing.
[18] Dave Dunnet, telephone interview with author, 04 November 2019.

players had several options available to allow them to read music while marching. One was a wrist/elbow bracelet with lyre attached and another was a curved paddle-like device that fit under the left arm. Equipped with march cards, a good marching band could theoretically play anything, anywhere. In the early twentieth century a wide range of band music was published in march card size format. These included not just marches, but waltzes, solos, serenades, sacred airs, classical transcriptions and even operatic selections.[19] By the 1950s, the number of titles began to dwindle but the market still remained healthy. In Canada, the appearance of Ken Bray's arrangements of *O Canada*, *God Save the Queen* and the *Star-Spangled Banner* (Toronto: Gordon V. Thompson, 1958), published in march card size format, support the view that there were certainly enough high school marching bands nationwide to justify their release.]

University Marching Bands

Canadian college and university marching bands never achieved the same degree of popularity as did their cousins in the United States. One that did and that has shown remarkable longevity and vitality is the Western Mustang Band of the University of Western Ontario [now known as Western University] in London. It was originally formed in 1923 as a small fifteen-piece group to play at football games and promote school spirit.[20] For over a decade its participation in campus life was sporadic and haphazard as it went through a succession of leaders including a brief association with the Canadian Officer Training Corps. In 1933, former member, trumpeter Don Wright became the band's leader and under his direction the group thrived [Fig. 14.4]. One of the keys to that growth was the fact that Wright would arrange the music for his band, including currently popular jazz numbers that were unavailable commercially. By exploiting the strengths and weaknesses of his ensemble he created a consistently solid sounding band that made the group a resounding success at football games. With the outbreak of the Second World War and the suspension of all extra-curricular activities in 1939, the band fell silent until 1945. The immediate postwar period witnessed a renewed interest in the band and by the mid 1960s it had grown to between 65 and 80 members. There followed a period of decline through the 1980s which only began to reverse itself in the mid 2000s.[21] Since 2007, a series of much publicized appearances at music award shows, celebrity videos and upbeat festivals has raised its profile, so much so that it was featured in the opening scene of the 2019 Juno

---

[19] Examples of all these genres are to be found in the author's private collection.
[20] "Western Mustang Band," Wikipedia at www.en.wikipedia.org accessed 01 December 2019.
[21] "Western Mustang Band," *Wikipedia*.

Awards ceremony in London.[22]   Although other university marching bands have existed through the twentieth century, only one, the Queen's University Brass Band, first established in 1905, has had the kind of staying power exhibited by the Western Mustang Band.[23]   There is one other university marching band whose longevity earns it a place in our narrative, the University of Toronto's Lady Godiva Memorial Bnad [sic].   Established in 1949 by a group of engineering students, it has been an uninvited guest at many Toronto public events until it became an official entry at the city's 2007 Santa Claus Parade.   Until that time the group regularly crashed the event and had to be escorted away by the Toronto Police Service.   Bawdy and irreverent, the band is still very much a part of the wind band tradition; they perform with a brass/reed/percussion instrumentation supplemented by other percussive effects such as stop signs, fire bells, jugs and frying pans.[24]

Although many of the prewar adult community bands that survived the 1950s and 1960s chose to abandon their marching roots, there were some that did not.   These were generally located in smaller population centres.   In Ontario they included the Kingsville-Essex Associated Band of Kingsville, the Perth Citizens' Band, the Newmarket Citizens Band and the Chatham Band which had previously been known as the Chatham Kilties Band; a group once led by Sidney Chamberlain, one of the founding fathers of the Canadian Bandmasters Association.   Further west, the Grande Prairie Marching Band of Grande Prairie, Alberta, first established in 1916, served the local community albeit with a modified rehearsal year that ran from February to August.[25]

Adult Community Marching Bands

Even as community bands across the country were either disappearing altogether or just abandoning their marching commitments, the appeal of the street band was such that new groups began to appear in the 1950s, 1960s and 1970s.   Once again it was in Ontario's

---

[22] The Faculty of Music at Western University is one of Canada's largest and most respected post-secondary music schools, one whose primary focus is in the European art music tradition.   Its official name is the Don Wright Faculty of Music, named after an inspired and very generous band leader.   That generosity extended well beyond his alma mater; in 2004 he donated $1 million to the University of Victoria in support of a music education wing.   One of that university's large performing ensembles was named in his honour- the Don Wright Symphonic Winds.   For a fuller account of his extraordinary life, see "Don Wright (composer)" on *Wikipedia*.

[23] "Queen's Bands," *Queen's University: Queen's Encyclopedia* at www.queensu.ca/encyclopedia/q/queens.bands accessed 01 December 2019.

[24] "Lady Godiva Memorial Bnad," *Wikipedia* at www.en.wikipedia.org accessed 15 November 2020.

[25] "About Us," *Grande Prairie Marching Band Association* at www.gpmarchingband.ca accessed 13 November 2020.

smaller communities where the new growth was most evident; the Kincardine Community Band, the Acton Band and the Ayr-Paris Band all included participation in a wide range of outdoor street events as part of their yearly activities. Those ensembles affiliated with "uniform" sponsors, like the military bands, included marching as one of their primary responsibilities. One of the Maritimes' oldest community bands, the Bridgewater Fire Department Band, was one such group and over the course of the twentieth century was joined by the Calgary Fire Department's Cappy Smart Band, the Ceremonial Band of the Waterloo Regional Police Service as well as bands associated with Royal Canadian Legion branches such as those in Petawawa and Pembroke.

There is perhaps no adult community band in Canada that embraces the marching ethos more than the Concert Band of Cobourg. The community of Cobourg, Ontario, lies midway between Toronto and Kingston on the shores of Lake Ontario and can lay claim to a town band since the 1840s. By the 1960s, the group known as the Cobourg Kilties Band had ceased operations but in 1970 was reborn under the leadership of Roland White, an ex-member of the United Kingdom's Royal Marines Band Service. White modelled the newly reformed ensemble on those of his former military employer, renamed it the Concert Band of Cobourg and adopted uniforms inspired by those of the Royal Marines, complete with white pith helmets. That inspiration went well beyond the uniforms. A photograph of the band on parade that appears on the home page of their website (www.theconcertbandofcobourg.com) clearly illustrates the influence. The front rank consists of five traditional field drums fitted with drag ropes, bass drum and cymbals in the second rank followed by brass and woodwinds. White's vision and drive certainly worked. The band remains popular today both as a parade formation and as a concert ensemble performing for an annual series of summer band concerts during the months of July and August.[26] The Concert Band of Cobourg, with its synthesis of military tradition and Canada's own history of community band engagement with local populations, is a testament to the strength and resilience of the Canadian band movement stretching back over two centuries.

The Marching Showbands

Newer band traditions formed in the period shortly after the Second World War were soon to provide fresh recruits for the adult marching bands. The Hamilton Top Hat Marching Orchestra and the Red Deer Regents are adult marching bands whose

---

[26] "History," *The Concert Band of Cobourg* at www.theconcertbandofcobourg.com accessed 24 February 2020.

membership is drawn primarily from young people who had performed with and then aged-out of their respective community-based youth bands: the Burlington Teen Tour Band and the Red Deer Royals. Both of these youth bands, still active today, are part of an evolutionary step in our wind band story: the marching showband. This "evolutionary step" came not from the high schools nor the universities. It was the community-based boys' and girls' bands that provided the impetus for what was to become an entirely new manifestation of the wind band idiom. What distinguished these new forms from earlier generations of marching bands was their reliance on a totally memorized repertoire, allowing for a greater emphasis on complex field drills and greatly expanded percussion sections. One of the earliest and still most successful is the Burlington Teen Tour Band of Burlington, Ontario [Fig. 14.5]. The band made its debut on December 15, 1947, when "…75 members of the Burlington Boys and Girls Band [gave] their first performance under the leadership of former member of the wartime Army Show, Elgin Corlett, the band's founder and first music director."[27] By 1952, the membership had grown to 150 and in 1965 the group's name was changed to the "Burlington Teen Tour Band". The ensemble travelled extensively throughout Europe, Japan and much of the United States. It also appeared in five Rose Bowl Parades (Pasadena), three Orange Bowl Parades (Miami), two Cotton Bowls (Dallas) and three Hula Bowl Parades (Honolulu). Appearances overseas also included representing Canada at the 50th and 60th anniversaries of the D-Day landings and the 70th anniversary of the attack on Pearl Harbour. As if that were not enough, its reputation has made it a marching band stand-in for movies, television shows, commercials and music videos: a complete list can be found on the band's website.[28]

In 1966, the Optimist Club of Windsor sponsored the formation of the Windsor Optimist Youth Band, an ensemble open to young people aged 10 to 22. Although not as well-known as its cousin in Burlington, the group has competed internationally and continues to participate in an average of up to twenty parades a year. Past travel has included a 2003 appearance at the Calgary Stampede Parade and a 2007 trip to Disney World in Florida.[29]

Vancouver was home to a successful showband whose roots lay in a previously existing boys' and girls' band. This was the Vancouver Junior Band established by Gordon Olson in 1944. During the 1950s, the band travelled down the U.S. West Coast, to the Midwest and as far as the Eastern Seaboard. Later in the decade, the ensemble was hired to provide half-time shows for the British Columbia Lions football team at the old Empire Stadium,

[27] "History," *The Burlington Teen Tour Band* at www.teentourband.org accessed 01 December 2017.
[28] "About Us-TV and Silver Screen," *The Burlington Teen Tour Band* at www.teentourband.org accessed 01 December 2019.
[29] "About Us," *Windsor Optimist Youth Band* at www.woyb.ca accessed 14 November 2020.

an association that was to last for over twenty years. In 1962 the group purchased new uniforms modelled on those of London's Yeoman Warders at the Tower of London. In recognition of the new look, the band's name was changed to the British Columbia Beefeater Band. It subsequently made its first trip to Europe in 1967 and included performances at the Edinburgh Military Tattoo as part of the itinerary. Over the two decades that followed, international destinations extended to South Africa, Australia and engagements at the Royal Tournament, London and the Cardiff Searchlight Tattoo. When the B.C. Lions moved to their new home at B.C. Place Stadium in the 1980s, the Beefeater Band's relationship with the football club came to an end. By the 1990s, with costs escalating and no successor willing to assume leadership of the ensemble, the activities of one of the country's most colourful showbands came to an end.[30]

Gordon Olson came by his enthusiasm for marching bands honestly. His father, J.B. Olson, was the founding director of the North Vancouver Schools Band in 1939, an ensemble that would be led by Arthur Delamont from 1943 to 1953 and renamed the North Vancouver Youth Band in 1969. The group toured extensively across Canada, to Europe and Japan but it too was forced to cease its activities in 2011 as a result of declining enrolment and funding shortfalls.[31]

The real home of Canada's marching showbands, ironically enough, lay not in temperate Central Canada nor on the balmy West Coast but rather on the prairies. It was there that a succession of bands emerged during the postwar period that continue to thrill audiences to the present day. It all started in the Queen City of Regina, Saskatchewan.

Marion Mossing was born in St. John's, North Dakota, in 1885 and emigrated to Saskatchewan with her family in 1895. She studied music at Manitoba's St. Boniface College, married trombonist Bernard Mossing and together they raised a musical family. In 1946, she decided she was not going to allow herself to be consumed by grief over the loss of her eldest son, Basil, an RCAF pilot, in a wartime flying accident. She adopted the recently formed Queen City Band and according to her son Bob, she literally banged on doors across Regina looking for sponsors until the local Lions Club agreed to do so. From that point on, she devoted herself to its support and growth.[32] This was the genesis of the Regina Lions Band, an extraordinary success story that lasted for over seventy years. First

---

[30] "About," *British Columbia Beefeater Band* at www.beefeaterband.wordpress.com accessed 03 December 2019.

[31] "North Vancouver Youth Band," *Memory BC* at www.memorybc.ca accessed 21 October 2020.

[32] Roger MacPherson, "Women We Won't Forget. Remembering Great Saskatchewan Women: Marion Mossing (1885-1975)," *Pink Magazine* (Regina, SK: Dec 2016) [Freely distributed in southern Saskatchewan].

rehearsals took place in the kitchen of the Mossing home on Ostler Street and then, as the program grew, they moved to Strathcona School.[33]

In 1964, Bob Mossing took over the day-to-day operations of the group and by the late 1970s and early 1980s, it was Regina's premier performing ensemble. There were four bands. The senior band had three subcomponents: the marching band, the concert band and the jazz band. There was also an intermediate band, a junior band and a beginners' band. Practices took place once a week and band members would age out when they reached their nineteenth birthday although there were some exceptions. Membership was a privilege and appearances were important. Boys were expected to keep their hair neatly trimmed and it was locally understood that if a young man in Regina had short hair at the time, he was either in the RCMP or the Regina Lions Band.[34]

The band would practice its marching routines on weekends and during the winter months would use the facilities at the RCMP's Regina depot. These practices were in preparation for the following summer's marching shows as well as half-time shows for the Saskatchewan Rough Riders football team. At its peak, the group numbered about 120 performers and travelled widely with appearances at the Rose Bowl, the Orange Bowl, in Europe and Hawaii [Fig. 14.6]. As with all showbands, the music was memorized, allowing participants to concentrate on field formations. The costs of that music, most of which were "specials" [unpublished, specifically arranged for the group] continued to escalate and in the early 2000s, with numbers dwindling and operating expenses spiralling ever higher, it became increasingly difficult to support the band's activities using traditional forms of community-based fund raising. By the end of the first decade of the new century, the Regina Lions Band was gone.

Regina however, wasn't the only city in the province to sponsor a Lions band. The Saskatoon Lions Band, established in 1954, held its first concert in late 1955.[35] From humble beginnings, it too grew to encompass a program offering beginning instruction as well as four other bands, two concert bands, a parade band and a field showband. Like the Regina Lions Band, the Saskatoon Lions Band also represented the city across Canada, appearing at EXPO 67 in Montréal and at many competitions and sporting events.[36] In addition to the two "Lions" marching bands there was also the North Battleford City Kinsmen Band. Formed in 1949, the marching showband, known also as "Blue Thunder," has performed locally, nationally and internationally. It performed at Canada Day

---

[33] Bob Mossing, telephone interview with the author 19 December 2019.
[34] Mossing, interview 19 December 2019.
[35] "History," *The Saskatoon Lions Band* at www.saskatoonlionsband.org accessed 01 March 2020.
[36] "History," *Saskatoon Lions.*

celebrations in Ottawa in 1997 and at a marching showband competition in Germany in 2003.[37]

Although Alberta's marching showbands are somewhat younger than those of its neighbouring province to the east, they have been no less successful. The Calgary Schools Patrol Band was formed in 1959 under the auspices of the Calgary Police Service's Traffic Unit and was subsequently renamed the Calgary Schools Safety Round-Up Band and finally the Round-Up Band.[38] In 1971, Robert Eklund, a music teacher at Calgary's Central Memorial High School and director of its Golden Rams Marching Band, was approached by members of the Calgary Stampede Board and asked to form a city-wide marching band to support the Calgary Stampede's annual grandstand show. Known as the "Calgary Stampede Showband", the group grew rapidly in part because the pre-existing Round-Up Band (grades 8 and 9), proved to be an ideal training ensemble for the newly formed showband [Fig. 14.7]. The Calgary Stampede Showband was originally intended for older students in grades 10, 11 and 12 and above. This changed with the formation of the Calgary Stetson Showband in 1988. Participation in the Calgary Stetson Showband was limited to students in grades 10, 11 and 12 and the Calgary Stampede Showband subsequently expanded its membership to include the most advanced performers aged 16 to 21 years.[39]

One of the reasons for the success of all three showbands, the Round-Up Band, the Calgary Stetson Showband and the Calgary Stampede Showband was and remains the support they gave to the many school-based band programs that supplied their members. School based programs were always given precedence when there were performance conflicts. If a school band and a showband had a concert scheduled at the same time, the policy was that participation in the school event always came first. This policy guaranteed a great deal of loyalty from school band directors who in return were happy to encourage their students to join the after-hours showband program. It also benefited the schools. A showband has to sound good before it can look good and to achieve that end, the directors of the Calgary Stampede's showbands engaged a range of specialist instrumental coaches and clinicians who worked tirelessly on balance and blend, tone and tuning.[40] These were skills which once acquired from the showbands enhanced the quality of the school bands. The contribution of the city's showbands extended to post-secondary institutions as well.

---

[37] Keaton Brown, "The North Battleford City Kinsmen Band to celebrate 70th anniversary," *Battlefords NOW* (Aug 30, 2019) at www.battlefordsnow.com accessed 01 March 2020.

[38] Norman Draper, *Bands by the Bow: A History of Band Music in Calgary* (Calgary: Century Calgary Publications, 1975) 63.

[39] Robert Eklund, telephone interview with author, 03 February 2020.

[40] Eklund, interview.

During the late 1990s and early 2000s, the Calgary Stampede Showband became the largest single source of undergraduate instrumental music majors at the University of Calgary.[41]

The Red Deer Royals Marching Showband was formed in the mid 1970s and from 1978 to 1991 was led by Alexander "Jigger" Lee, a former Canadian Army band director. It was during this time that the band was provided with new uniforms by the Lions Club of Red Deer and began to travel nationally to EXPO 86 and the Kelowna Regatta as well as internationally to California, Alaska and Florida.[42] In 1991, Keith Mann assumed direction of the group. Having previously worked for five years with the Calgary Stampede Showband he was well acquainted with the challenges involved. By 1997, the Red Deer Royals, now parading with eighty-five members, had toured across western Canada and as far away as Australia and Europe. They had distinguished themselves in competition against groups from much larger centres, a tradition they continued after the untimely death of their conductor in 2001.[43]

By now the reader will know that within the world of Canadian wind bands, the lines that distinguish one kind of ensemble from another are often blurred or in some cases, non-existent. Such was the case with the Bishop Grandin Ghosts Marching Band. In 1976, Elmer Riegal began teaching music, grades 10 to 12, at Calgary's Bishop Grandin Catholic Senior High School [renamed Our Lady of the Rockies High School in October, 2021]. Ten years later he introduced a marching band component to the program. It complemented existing concert band classes but was offered on an extra-curricular basis before and after school, Wednesday evenings and at monthly weekend rehearsals.[44] Participating students received additional credits towards their high school diplomas. Riegal's tireless efforts and the dedication of the Band Parents Association rewarded band members with an ever-growing reputation for excellence both in competition and on tour. School authorities quickly recognized the program's popularity and it was opened up to students from across the Calgary Catholic School District which by 2000 numbered over 100 schools and at least six high schools. The Grandin Ghosts had essentially become a community-based ensemble with Riegal himself as its greatest advocate. He had become keenly aware of an increasing emphasis on the importance of physical education in the high school curriculum and saw in the marching showband the perfect combination: "…a union of athletics and art."[45]

[41] Eklund, interview.
[42] Michael Dawe, "History," *Red Deer Community Bands* at www.reddeerroyals.com accessed 02 March 2020.
[43] Marilyn Mann, "Royals," personal notes provided to the author 04 November 2019.
[44] Elmer Riegal, e-mail correspondence with author, 08 January 2020.
[45] Riegal, e-mail.

Despite the demise of several of the country's earliest and best-known marching bands, the movement has not just been marking time. New marching ensembles have taken their place. At the university level, the McMaster Marching Band, established in 2009 and UBC's Thunderbird Marching Band, formed in 2012 have emerged to provide musical support for their respective schools' athletics and spirit events. At the high school level, marching bands are now part of the music programs at North Toronto Collegiate, Burnaby North Secondary School and Victoria's Spectrum Community High School.

Marching bands and their community-based successors, the marching showbands, are an integral part of the wind band story in Canada. More than any other manifestation of the wind band model, they have remained true to the traditions first established by the regimental bands in the eighteenth century. Those bands and the militia, community and youth bands that followed in the nineteenth and twentieth centuries all recognized that the wind band was a dual personality performing ensemble: it had both musical and visual characteristics. The traditional marching bands were all concert groups as are the showbands of today; they could and did perform traditional concerts in traditional concert venues. What set them apart was that they also understood the importance of spectacle; the synthesis of live music, colourful uniforms and intricate field movements performed [most often] in outdoor spaces before large audiences drawn from all segments of the population, many of whom might never have otherwise attended an indoor wind band concert. The key to the appeal of this blend of sight and sound however was and is the music played by a wind band. It is an ensemble which has charmed Canadians for over 250 years, indoors and out, in large and small communities from coast to coast to coast.

CHAPTER FOURTEEN GALLERY

Figure 14.1. Canadian Forces Tri-Service School of Music Marching Band, H.M.C.S *Naden*, [Esquimalt B.C.] c. 1966. Army, navy and air force trainees en route to the Naden parade square for marching band practice. The School of Music is the white building in the background. Source: photo courtesy of Jim Forde.

Figure 14.2. Royal Canadian Sea Cadet Composite Band performing the "Ceremony of the Flags" on Parliament Hill, Ottawa, Spring 1987. Trumpet section has taken up positions in front of the band to perform the traditional navy "Sunset Bugle Call." The entire ceremony is timed so that the call actually occurs at sunset. Note the inclination of the sun and the length of the shadows. Source: Manitoba Navy League.

Figure 14.3.   Vinyl Recording Dust Jacket, Catholic Central High School Band, London, ON, 1969.   Director Martin Boundy [right rear in white dinner jacket].   Boundy was an ex-RCAF bandmaster, president of the CBA and conductor of the first National Youth Band of Canada in 1978.   The Catholic Central High School Band was a superb concert organization as well as a marching band.   Source: author's collection.

Figure 14.4.   University of Western Ontario Marching Band, London ON, 1938.   Director Don Wright.   One of Canada's longest continually active university marching bands, the group owed much of its initial success to its leader who prepared special arrangements of popular 1930s tunes.   Source: John P. Metras Sports Museum, Western University.

Figure 14.5.   Burlington Girls and Boys Band, Burlington ON, c. early 1950s.   Director Elgin Corlett.   This community-based group would change its name in 1965 to the Burlington Teen Tour Band and go one to become one of the country's premier marching showbands.   Source: photo courtesy of the Burlington Teen Tour Band.

Figure 14.6. Regina Pride of the Lions Band. Santa Claus Parade, November 13, 2005. Regina, Saskatchewan. Photo by Barb Koroluk. Note the marching brass section, bells front French Horns and bells front shoulder tubas. These instruments are a distinctive feature of the marching showbands. Source: photo courtesy of Bob Koroluk.

Figure 14.7. Calgary Round-up Band, Spruce Meadows, Alberta, 2018. Photo by Fox Creative Design Ltd. Originally formed in 1956 as the Calgary Schools Safety Patrol Band, it is one of Canada's oldest junior marching bands (grades 8 and 9). Source: photo courtesy of the Calgary Round-up Band.

CHAPTER FIFTEEN

THE COMMUNITY BAND RENAISSANCE

The 1950s Decline

The explosive growth of the school band movement in the 1950s and 1960s was matched by an equally significant decline countrywide in the number of adult community bands. This decline was due to a combination of unparalleled prosperity, technological change and demographic upheaval. The postwar economic boom lasting well into the 1960s gave many Canadians the economic freedom necessary to purchase their own homes, cars and the leisure time to enjoy them. The recently invented television found a place in many of those households and the increase in privately owned automobiles put more families on the roads. Although both developments drew audiences and performers alike away from the community bands, an equally potent distraction came from the surging baby boom. As its first wave reached adolescence in the late 1950s, the invention of the transistor radio and 45 RPM vinyl discs contributed to a rapid generational divergence of popular music tastes. Whereas previous vacuum tube radios were larger pieces of furniture most often placed in the living room where they were listened to by the entire family, transistor radios and 45 RPM record players were smaller, portable and could be listened to behind closed doors in the privacy of a teenager's bedroom. The music of the local community band simply had less appeal to youthful audiences than the vibrant new idiom of Rock n' Roll.

The disappearance of Canada's postwar community bands may have been dramatic but it certainly wasn't fatal. Many community bands established in the nineteenth and early twentieth centuries remained very much alive. These were generally to be found in smaller centres in most provinces with Ontario and Québec leading the country with the highest numbers of continuously active bands by virtue of their larger populations. Community bands with especially long-established traditions proved to be the most resilient. Ontario could claim at least nineteen community bands that survived the 1950s and 1960s including many of the province's earliest ensembles. Amongst them were the Perth Citizens Band, the Thorold Town Band, the Galt Kilties Band, the Newmarket Citizens Band, both the

Kitchener and Waterloo Musical Society Bands as well as groups from Brampton, Burlington, Oakville, Owen Sound and Peterborough.[1]

Many of Québec's earliest bands also remained active including Le Cercle Philharmonique de St. Jean, L'Harmonie Calixa Lavallée de Sorel, La Société Philharmonique de St. Hyacinthe, L'Harmonie de Coaticook, L'Harmonie de Granby, L'Harmonie de Loretteville and L'Harmonie de Montmorency (founded by Joseph Vézina in 1872).[2] The story was much the same across the Maritimes as both the St. John, New Brunswick, St. Mary's Band and the Bridgewater Fire Department Band from Nova Scotia's south shore continued to perform regularly. Two other bands from the region were able to hold on by virtue of their associations with local militia units. These were the Sackville Citizens Band which also functioned as the regimental band of the VIIIth Hussars of Sackville, New Brunswick, and the Middleton Town Band which paraded as the band of the West Nova Scotia Regiment.

The situation on the prairies was more precarious with only a few prewar community bands surviving the 1950s and 1960s. These included the Prince Albert Concert Band and the Calgary Concert Band, both of which continued to rehearse and perform on a regular basis. British Columbia's community bands fared somewhat better. The Kelowna City Band, the Nanaimo Concert Band, the Penticton Concert Band and the Trail Maple Leaf Band all remained active participants in local musical life.

The Night School Bands

Ironically, even in the midst of declining numbers, the seeds for new growth in the adult community band movement were to be found in the schools. Night schools to be exact. In 1948, a night school music class at Toronto's East York Collegiate Institute provided the initial membership for the East York Concert Band.[3] In addition to being one of the first still active community bands in Canada whose origins can be traced back to night schools, the East York Concert Band was a trailblazer in one other respect. An early photograph of the group on its website shows a mixture of adult men, boys and one female, an alto saxophonist. This is a significant detail considering that many prewar community bands that remained active in the postwar period didn't admit women until the 1960s.

---

[1] Graham Nasby, *Community Band and Orchestra Resources* at www.grahamnasby.com accessed December 2019.

[2] "Ressources- Harmonies ou autres ensembles seniors (civil et/ou municipal)," *Fédération des harmonies et orchestres symphoniques du Québec* at www.fhosq.org accessed December 2019.

[3] "About," *East York Concert Band* at www.eatyorkconcertband.ca accessed 30 August 2020.

Other night school bands followed. Ottawa's Nepean Concert Band started as a continuing education course at Merivale High School in 1975 as did the Ottawa Community Band at Highland Park High School in the late 1960s. The Halifax Concert Band was also the result of an initiative in 1973 by the Halifax City Schools continuing education music program under the direction of Chalmers Doane.[4] One of the most noteworthy early night school/continuing education community bands was established in West Montréal in 1967. The brainchild of Morley Calvert, the Lakeshore Concert Band was created for the express purpose of providing Calvert's former high school band students with an opportunity to continue performing in adult life "…to enjoy and develop their musical skills…[using] a continuing education evening course offered by the school board, with himself as director…"[5] Calvert was one of the first to recognize the coming wave; growing numbers of young, enthusiastic high school graduates from fine band programs who wished to continue playing even though their professional careers were not associated with music [Fig. 15.1]. The night school/continuing education bands of the 1960s and 1970s were soon joined by a flood of new community bands seeking to attract the ever-increasing numbers of former high school wind instrumentalists.

Two of the most helpful online sources consulted in the preparation of this chapter were Graham Nasby's *Canadian Community Band and Orchestra Resources* at www.grahamnasby.com and the "Ressources" link on the website of La Fédération des harmonies et orchestres symphoniques du Québec at www.fhosq.org. As of January, 2020, these two sites listed over 350 community bands across Canada and provided links to their respective websites or Facebook pages. A survey conducted by the author of all available online community band sources revealed that 209 included the year that the band was established. There is a clear pattern of incremental growth in the number of community bands nationwide starting in the 1960s.[6] In 1960 there were at least sixty community bands active in eight of ten provinces. By the end of the decade another fifteen had been added. The 1970s saw an increase of a further twenty-one and the 1980s added another thirty-three. The last decade of the century saw thirty-five join the list and since 2000, there have been forty-five more community bands established in ten provinces and one territory. The reader is reminded that these figures only reflect those ensembles that included historical information on their websites or Facebook pages. There were at least 140 that did not. It is also possible that there are even more community bands and

[4] "HCB History," *Halifax Concert Band* at www.halifaxconcertband.ca accessed 31 August 2020.
[5] Keith Field, "The Lakeshore Concert Band Celebrates 50 Years," *Canadian Winds* 16, no. 2 (Spring 2018) 3.
[6] Survey completed 02 September 2020.

ensembles nationwide that have no online presence at all. That doesn't mean that they don't exist, only that the larger band community has no way of knowing about them.

Most of these newly formed community bands, as well as the pre-existing "legacy" groups, focused their attention on amateur adult musicians of moderate ability. The generally accepted standard was "high school level or higher". These ensembles performed in the grade 3 or 4 range and admission was usually open to anyone on a "sit-in" basis. This was and remains by far the largest cohort of community bands active in Canada today, but it certainly isn't the only one.

The Adult Beginner Bands

The late twentieth century witnessed the appearance of a totally new type of community band, one whose focus was on a segment of the population that had largely been ignored for over two centuries, the adult beginner. By the early 1970s, Edmonton's Cosmopolitan Music Society [CMS] was thriving with over 400 participants, both youth and adults. There "…were four concert bands (Red, Gold, Blue and Green), two jazz bands (A and B), a new string program …[and] a cosmopolitan marching band was formed."[7] It was however, becoming increasingly clear to the society's director, Harry Pinchin, that the CMS "one night a week" program couldn't compete with the curricular school band "class almost every day" model available to youth members of the society. In 1974, CMS board members and sponsors reluctantly decided to become a fully adult amateur music society with a minimum age requirement of eighteen years. Membership plummeted and Harry Pinchin saw immediately that the loss of the youth program could be fatal to the Cosmopolitan Music Society. There is an old saying that states "…necessity is the mother of invention." Facing an existential threat, Harry Pinchin acted boldly. He explains:

> This was a huge gamble my friend. Unless we could encourage the involvement
> of a sufficient number of adult members the highly successful society risked
> failing. Recruitment efforts were increased but we needed more members. It
> was then that I came up with the idea of developing a "beginner adult band
> program". I can't say with a certainty that we were the first and only program to
> do this, but I can honestly say that I knew of no other at the time. It was ***not***
> [H.P.'s italics and boldened] patterned after any other known entity.[8]

---

[7] Audrey Shonn, "Edmonton's Cosmopolitan Music Society – 40 years old and still blowing strong," *Canadian Winds* 2, no. 1 (Autumn 2003) 11.

[8] Harry Pinchin, e-mail correspondence with author, 06 January 2020.

The rest as they say, is history. The Cosmopolitan Music Society's adult beginner band program proved to be enormously successful and "…numerous adult beginner band classes were conducted until once again there were three full concert bands."[9] Edmonton set the precedent and it wasn't long before others took notice [Fig. 15.2]. In 1988, the Calgary Music Society was formed by Dennis Orr, Rod Pauls and Dennis Jackson. It started out "…with just one band of thirty-nine members…each member needed to be a beginner, so anyone who had previous experience had to start on a new instrument."[10] By 1992, the society could claim a membership of over 200 and in 1995 it was renamed the "Westwinds Music Society".

In Red Deer, a community of just under 60,000, Keith Mann had been appointed director of the Red Deer Community Band Society in 1991. The following year, in an attempt to build the adult band, he decided to start an adult beginner band. Ads went into the local paper and on radio and Mann set up twenty chairs for the first meeting; forty five showed up and "…forty stuck with it and a new band was formed…[Keith Mann] had created an adult feeder program that created two additional adult concert bands and a jazz band."[11]

Adult beginner bands may have had their start in western Canada, but one of the most effective boosters for their further growth throughout the rest of the country came from the United States. In 1991, Dr. Roy Ernst, a professor at the Eastman School of Music in Rochester, New York, started a beginning band program for retirees. His initial impulse was to create an ensemble guided by the philosophy that "…anyone can learn to play music at a level that will bring a sense of accomplishment and the ability to perform in a group."[12] It was his belief that in order to achieve this end the learning environment had to be "…completely supportive and free of competition and intimidation."[13] That first band set in motion a movement that became the New Horizons International Music Association. Although its founder was inspired to create performance opportunities for those over the age of fifty, the response was so positive that the association modified its admission policies to include those who self-identify as "adults". By January of 2020, the association's website listed New Horizons programs across the United States, Canada and

---

[9] Shonn, "Edmonton's Cosmopolitan Music Society" 12.

[10] Tina Holgate, "Westwinds Music Society: 30 Years of Learning, Playing and Having Fun!", *Canadian Winds* 17, no. 2 (Spring 2019) 3.

[11] Marilyn Mann, "Royals," personal notes provided to the author, 04 November 2019.

[12] "Dr. Roy Ernst," *New Horizons International Music Association* at www.newhorizonsmusic.org accessed 04 September 2020.

[13] Ibid.

overseas in the United Kingdom, Australia and New Zealand.[14]   Most of these ensembles were concert bands but increasingly they have included orchestras, choirs and other musical groups.   In Canada, there are currently [2020] twenty-six New Horizons affiliated adult beginner bands: one in British Columbia, one in Manitoba, four in Nova Scotia, sixteen in Ontario and four in Québec.   These range from Prince George's Alban Classical New Horizons Band to the Wolfville New Horizons Band in Nova Scotia.   Numbers vary from chapter to chapter but in larger communities, programs support several ensembles at every skill level from beginner to advanced.   Canada's largest, the Toronto New Horizons franchise, consists of two beginner I bands, two beginner II bands, two concert bands (intermediate) and two advanced symphonic bands.   In nearby London, the New Horizons Band program is affiliated with Western University and was one of the first to be established in Canada (1999).   It offers a beginner I band, a beginner II band, an intermediate band and two advanced ensembles.[15]   In the Maritimes, there are also the "Second Chances" band programs which include adult beginner groups in St. John, Fredericton, Halifax and Charlottetown.

In addition to Alberta's musical societies, the New Horizons programs and the Second Chances bands, some adult beginner bands are also sponsored independently by community bands in B.C., Ontario and Québec.   These groups, much like those in the New Horizons programs, form the first step in a family of ensembles under the auspices of the senior-most community band.   They often include the adult beginner band itself, a junior band and a more advanced group.   Examples include ensembles in Victoria and Maple Ridge B.C.; in Newmarket, Cobourg, Wallaceburg and Woodstock, Ontario, and in the cities of Asbestos [Val-des-Sources] and Laval in Québec.   A survey of Ontario's community bands in 2009 found that 33% of respondents did not learn to play their instruments at school.   If these musicians' first steps were not taken in the context of a school-based band classroom, then they must have either been self-taught, taken private lessons or been a part of an adult beginner band.   Considering the number of community bands in Ontario alone, this speaks volumes to the growing importance of the adult beginner band movement.[16]   Nationwide, the author's 2020 survey of adult beginner bands suggests that there are no fewer than thirty-nine in existence.   The presence of intermediate and advanced ensembles in conjunction with most beginner bands further suggests that

---

[14] "What is NHIMA," *New Horizons International Music Association* at www.newhorizonsmusic.org accessed 04 September 2020.
[15] Ibid.
[16] Roger Mantie, "A Preliminary Study of Community Bands in Ontario," *Canadian Winds* (Spring 2009) 60.

retention is high and once adult beginners are exposed to music making in a wind band they continue as lifelong learners. Harry Pinchin's gamble to save Edmonton's Cosmopolitan Music Society in 1974 succeeded and in doing so nurtured the growth of adult beginner bands across Canada.

The "Premier League" Performance Ensembles

Beginner adult bands and a majority of the country's community bands did not address the needs of a growing pool of skilled high school performers seeking new opportunities in adult ensembles. The rapid increase in the number of post-secondary institutions offering degree and diploma programs in music was adding to those numbers. Many of these musicians were looking for musical groups that would further challenge and develop their already considerable musical skills. Most community bands active at the time, however, only performed repertoire at the grade 3 to 4 level. It was literature that could hardly be expected to engage the new cohort of advanced level players. The conditions were ripe for the appearance of a new type of community band, one focused on the highly motivated amateur instrumentalist searching for performance environments at the professional level.

In 1967, the same year that Morley Calvert established the Lakeshore Concert Band on Montréal's West Island, a group of students at Toronto's Northview Heights Secondary School formed a band. They had all met and first played together at Willowdale Junior High School and the name they chose for their new ensemble was a composite reflecting the two founding schools, the Northdale Concert Band [Fig. 15.3].[17] The group eventually abandoned its original student base to focus on adult participants and attracted an increasingly "…skilled group of dedicated amateurs and many music professionals."[18] By 2010, many of the band's members were music teachers at both the elementary and secondary levels as well as music students at York University and the University of Toronto. Leaders in the Canadian band community have conducted the ensemble including Howard Cable and Bobby Herriot (1988-89), John Herberman (1989-90) and Mark Hopkins (1990-94). From 1996 to 2010, the Northdale Concert Band was directed by Stephen Chenette, Professor Emeritus at the Faculty of Music, University of Toronto.[19]

---

[17] L. Rosenfield, 2002, "A History of the Northdale Concert Band," *The Northdale Concert Band* at www.northdaleconcertband.ca accessed 28 September 2020.
[18] Rosenfield, "Northdale Concert Band"
[19] Stephen Chenette, "Northdale Concert Band," *Canadian Winds* (Spring 2010) available at www.northdaleconcertband.ca accessed 28 September 2020.

What made the Northdale Concert Band unique amongst the country's "Premier League" of community bands was its commitment to a growing body of Canadian repertoire for wind band. 1986 was the "International Year of Canadian Music". The Northdale Band wanted to play a program of Canadian music on Canada Day at Vancouver's EXPO 86 but found that at the time the selection was limited. A grant application to the Ontario Arts Council was successful and six composers were commissioned to write new works for band: Louis Appelbaum (*High Spirits*), Howard Cable (*Ontario Pictures*), Donald Coakley (*Vive La Canadienne*), Elma Miller (*Processional*), Glenn Morley (*Fanfare for the Uncommon Man*) and Phil Nimmons (*Skyscape: Sleeping Beauty & the Lions*). Gary Kulesha also donated a seventh composition entitled *Christening and Finale*.[20] The EXPO 86 appearances were a great success but when these compositions were offered to established Canadian publishers, none were willing to accept them for publication "…so the Northdale Band started its own publishing company…with the goal of publishing the best in compositions and arrangements by Canadian composers."[21] As of 2020 the Northdale Music Press had nine works for concert band listed on its website.[22]

It was inevitable that with the ever-expanding numbers of skilled adult performers nationwide, especially in the major urban centres, there would be a corresponding growth in the number of quasi-professional adult ensembles. Throughout the 1970s and 1980s groups across the country joined this artistic "Premier League" including the London [Ontario] Concert Band, founded by Martin Boundy and Vancouver's Pacific Symphonic Wind Ensemble, formed in 1981 by Maurice Backun.[23] In Alberta, the Calgary Musicians Association Band, first established in 1947, became the Calgary Wind Symphony and the New Edmonton Wind Sinfonia, 1980, attracted many of that city's finest wind performers. The year 1985 saw the creation of the Winnipeg Wind Ensemble whose focus was professional level performances at venues such as the "…Prairies Performances Concert Series, Winnipeg New Music Festival, International Music Camp Concerts, Optimus International Band Festival and the Mennonite Schools Festival in addition to the presentation of an annual concert series."[24]

---

[20] Chenette, "Northdale Concert Band."
[21] Ibid.
[22] "Compositions," *Northdale Music Press Limited* at www.northdalemusic.com accessed 17 November 2020.
[23] "About Us," *Pacific Symphonic Wind Ensemble* at www.pacificsymphonicwindensemble.ca accessed 25 September 2020.
[24] "About," *Winnipeg Wind Ensemble* at www.winnipegwindensemble.ca accessed 28 September 2020.

Ontario's contribution to the list of "Premier League" performance ensembles kept pace with its growing population. In 1981, the Wellington Winds of Kitchener/Waterloo were formed originally in Guelph, a city that served as the seat for the province's Wellington County and the inspiration for the ensemble's name. The greater Toronto Area saw the emergence of the North York Concert Band, the Toronto Concert Band, the Hamilton Concert Band and the Thornhill Concert Band. In Ottawa, the Centralaires, established in 1993, was an elite concert band whose membership was drawn from former members of the RCAF Central Band, the RCMP Band, the GGFG [Governor General's Foot Guards] Band as well as local music teachers.

In Québec, L'Ensemble à Vents de Sherbrooke was formed in 1982 as a collaboration between L'Université de Sherbrooke and recent graduates of its music school as well as skilled musicians from the surrounding community. To the north in Québec City, L'Harmonie de Charlesbourg was established in 1993. Montréal had long supported some of Canada's finest community bands extending all the way back to Ernest Lavigne's Bande de la Cité in the late nineteenth century. The dawning twenty-first century witnessed a new generation of superb bands join that tradition including the whimsically named L'Orchestre à Vents Non Identifié [Unidentified Wind Orchestra], established in 2005 and L'Orchestre à Vents de Musique de Films [Film Music Wind Orchestra], 2000, whose name reflects its focus on the performance of music written for films, video games and television.

The new century also added ensembles elsewhere including the Halifax region's Sackville Concert Band in 2002 [Fig. 15.4], Calgary's Alberta Winds, established by Mark Hopkins in 2003 and in 2005, the Ottawa Wind Ensemble, led by former RCAF Central Band clarinettist Mark Rocheleau. The growing number of "Premier League" wind bands was originally fed by graduates of the nations' schools in the final decades of the twentieth century. Yet even as these groups flourished, one of the primary sources of that first wave of advanced performers was facing unforeseen challenges that would reinvigorate the community-based youth band movement.

The Re-emergence of the Community Based Youth Wind Bands

As noted in Chapter Thirteen, changes in education across Canada during the late twentieth century affected the number of high school bands adversely. The effects of semestering however, were far more damaging as it also affected the quality of those programs. Although there is no conclusive evidence to suggest a causative link, it is possible that it was this decline that encouraged the re-emergence of community-based youth wind ensembles created specifically to provide advanced performance opportunities for young musicians. The original community youth bands had largely disappeared during the 1960s and 1970s as instrumental music instruction was consolidated in the schools. By 1975, many of the country's high school band programs supported ensembles that could perform advanced level repertoire. This was literature, including transcriptions, that would challenge even the most talented and enthusiastic music students. With the dramatic drop in the quality of these programs brought on by semestering and other curricular changes, there was a growing need to provide enriched musical experiences for gifted young performers from local school bands.

The response varied by community and followed several different streams. Some of the pre-existing [and surviving] community-based groups like the Burlington Boys and Girls Band or the Regina Lions Band evolved towards the marching showband model. Others, like the West Vancouver Youth Band, originally established in 1930 and in continuous operation since, sponsored a family of bands and even a string group.[25] The senior most of these ensembles often attracted the finest student musicians from the local community. As the population grew so too did the pool of prospective skilled applicants. It should come then as no surprise that one of the most successful community-based youth band programs designed to develop superior musicianship in its members originated in Canada's largest city.

In 1990, Toronto's Colin Clarke formed the Brampton Youth Wind Ensemble; the newly formed group gave its first performance, with a total of twenty-two musicians, the following Spring.[26] By 1994, after successful festival and concert appearances the previous year, the ensemble was renamed the Toronto Youth Wind Orchestra. As the quality of its performances improved and its reputation grew, a second ensemble, the Toronto Youth Concert Winds was established in 1996. This group too, was subsequently renamed the Toronto Youth Wind Orchestra (TYWO) Concert Winds "…with a focus on younger students (grades 5 through 9) and their development as budding musicians."[27] A third group, the Toronto Youth Symphonic Winds, intended to fit between the two previously established ensembles, has since been added. One of the core objectives of the TYWO is "…to expose its musicians to challenging works that would not normally be played by high school bands."[28] A selected list of this repertoire is contained as an appendix to Mark Caswell's article on the TYWO cited below. The titles on that list

---

[25] "History WVYB," *West Vancouver Youth Band* at www.wvyb.ca accessed 22 October 2020.
[26] Mark Caswell, "The Toronto Youth Wind Orchestra," *Canadian Winds* 6, no. 1 (Fall 2007) 5.
[27] Ibid. 6.
[28] Ibid. 6.

include classics for wind band, transcriptions and compositions by some of Canada's most respected composers. Almost all of these works are technically, as well as artistically demanding and are usually associated with performances by professional or university level wind bands [Fig. 15.5]. Another Toronto area ensemble, also established to provide exposure to enriched repertoire is the Etobicoke Youth Band. Formed in 1982, the group has grown from a modest twenty-three participants to "…well over 100 students every year…[and] members range in between 12 and 18 [years old]."[29]

Motivated by the demand for enhanced student performance opportunities, similar ensembles have emerged across the country. The Winnipeg Youth Wind Ensemble was established in 2016 and open to young musicians up to and including grade 10.[30] L'Orchestre à Vents du Suroît Junior was also formed in 2016 under the umbrella of the adult L'Orchestre à Vents du Suroît from the Vaudreuil Soulanges region west of Montréal[31] and the Kitchener Waterloo Youth Concert Band was created in 2017 and opened by audition to musicians ages 11 to 21.[32]

The Honour Bands

In addition to community-based youth bands operating on a permanent, year-round basis, there are also a range of "Honour Bands" organized by provincial band associations. These ensembles generally gather each year for several days of intense musical study followed by a concluding concert, often under the batons of nationally and internationally renowned conductors and music educators. Admission requirements range from a letter of recommendation by a local school band director to formal auditions. In each case, the goal is to provide motivated and talented music students with the opportunity to experience performance challenges not available in their home schools.

The Alberta Band Association supports two honour bands, the Junior High Honour Band (grades 7 to 9) and the Alberta Wind Symphony for senior high students (grades 10 to 12). Both groups meet over a three-day period in the Fall and sessions conclude with performances at the annual Alberta Music Conference. Similarly, the Saskatchewan Band Association sponsors two honour bands at the junior and intermediate levels. The Manitoba Band Association first established its honour band programs in 1976 and it has now grown to include junior, intermediate and senior level ensembles. In 2019, the

[29] "About," *Etobicoke Youth Band* at www.eyb.com accessed 23 October 2020.
[30] "About," *Winnipeg Youth Wind Ensemble* at www.winnipegyouthwinds.com accessed 23 October 2020.
[31] "Nouvelles," *L'Orchestre à Vents du Suroît* at www.ovs.ca accessed 23 October 2020.
[32] "About the Band," *KW Youth Concert Band* at www.kw-ycb.ca accessed 23 October 2020.

province's senior honour band numbered sixty-two student musicians from twenty-six schools.[33] The Ontario Band Association is responsible for four honour bands, a necessity considering the province's population and geographical size. There are two elementary honour bands; the Eastern Ontario Elementary Honour Band for grade 7 and 8 students in the Kingston, Renfrew and Ottawa triangle and the Laurier OBA [Ontario Band Association] Elementary Honour Band which met in 2019 at Wilfred Laurier University in Waterloo. The Western OBA Intermediate Honour Band is open to students from grades 8 to 10 and gathers at the Don Wright School of Music at Western University in London. The senior level of the province's honour bands is open by audition to high school musicians from across Ontario. Its 90 odd members meet for four days of intense rehearsals followed by a concert at the annual Ontario Music Educators Association Conference each Fall.[34]

The Halifax region is within weekend commuter distance of all areas of the province of Nova Scotia, an advantage that allows the Nova Scotia Band Association to significantly expand the musical opportunities it can offer students in its honour bands. NSYWE (Nova Scotia Youth Wind Ensemble) students "…meet for three weekends of rehearsals and workshops in the fall, and again in the spring, with a concert at the end of each session. In this way, the NSYWE behaves more like a youth orchestra program than the more traditional, two to five day long, once a year provincial honour band."[35] The NSYWE is the more advanced of the association's two sponsored ensembles and is open by audition to approximately sixty instrumentalists of high school and university age. The Nova Scotia Junior Wind Ensemble is tailored for younger players, most of whom start instrumental music in grade 6.[36] As with all provincial honour bands, the goal "…is to provide a high-quality educational experience for talented young musicians in a manner and of a quality otherwise not available to them."[37]

The National Youth Band and the Denis Wick Canadian Wind Orchestra

The provincial band associations that sponsor the honour bands described in the previous paragraphs are all affiliates of the Canadian Band Association. It too supports its own honour band, open to candidates from across the country. The original idea for a

---

[33] "Honour Concert Bands," *Manitoba Band Association* at www.mbband.org accessed 25 October 2020.

[34] "Honour Bands," *Ontario Band Association* at www.onband.ca accessed 25 October 2020.

[35] Kevin Finch, "The Nova Scotia Youth Wind Ensemble," *Canadian Winds* (Fall 2016) 7.

[36] Finch, "Nova Scotia Youth," 7.

[37] Ibid. 7.

national youth band was proposed at a meeting of the Canadian Band Directors Association in Edmonton in 1976.   Two years later, the first National Youth Band of Canada (NYB) gathered in Toronto under the direction of Martin Boundy and performed at the 1978 CNE with the support of its musical director, Lt. Col. (Ret'd) Clifford Hunt.[38]   There followed a hiatus of thirteen years due to "…lack of federal funding, commercial sponsors and managerial infrastructure."[39] In 1991 the ensemble reconvened in Vancouver and in 1994, with sponsorship assured through an arrangement with MusicFest Canada, the NYB became the featured ensemble at the Musicfest Canada Finals.[40] The association with Musicfest Canada ended in 2001 and from 2002 until 2019 the NYB has attempted to align its schedule with music festivals in host provinces across Canada[41].   These arrangements also include the provision of rehearsal spaces, accommodation and transportation with university campuses proving to be ideal venues.   Applicants undergo a rigorous audition process and between 1998 and 2006, the ensemble consisted of an average of 54% senior high school students, 40% undergraduate music majors and between 6 to 8% of participants from other backgrounds.   Numbering between fifty and sixty instrumentalists, repertoire for each year's NYB is selected by its guest conductor with some input from the featured soloist who is sponsored annually by Yamaha Canada.   The NYB is a "flagship" initiative of the Canadian Band Association and since its inception has performed nationwide and been a training ground for many of the country's most talented young musicians as they start their musical careers [Fig. 15.6].

The NYB's decision to part ways with MusicFest Canada created a void in MusicFest's National Finals performance programming.   This void was filled by the creation of the National Concert Band which gave its inaugural performance under the direction of Jeremy Brown from the University of Calgary in 2002.[42]   Like the NYB, it is an honour band of 60 plus musicians open by audition to woodwind, brass and percussion instrumentalists aged 14 to 24 from across Canada.   The ensemble gathers in different cities yearly as part of MusicFest Canada's National Finals week for master classes, mini-concerts and formal performances.   The National Concert Band, now known as the Denis Wick Canadian Wind Orchestra, by virtue of the corporate sponsorship provided by the British manufacturer of brass mouthpieces and mutes of the same name, has been in continuous operation since its

---

[38] "CBA News: National Youth Band of Canada's 25th Anniversary," *Canadian Winds* (Fall 2016) 55.
[39] "CBA News: National Youth Band of Canada's 25th Anniversary," Canadian Winds (Fall 2016) 55.
[40] Ibid. 55.
[41] Jim Forde, NYB Manager 1998-2006, e-mail correspondence with the author, 22 January 2020.
[42] Mark Hopkins, "The National Concert Band/Denis Wick Canadian Wind Orchestra," *Canadian Winds* 11/1 (Fall 2012) 25.

inception. It is currently under the direction of Mark Hopkins of Acadia University and Gillian MacKay, University of Toronto.[43]

The adult community bands and the community-based youth bands that were part of the community band renaissance in the closing decades of the twentieth century were and still are part of a musical tradition that dates back to the nineteenth century. Even the provincial honour bands are somewhat reminiscent of the massed band concerts of a century ago when local groups would gather together to perform for local festivals or patriotic celebrations. There was however, one type of band that was entirely new. The first appeared shortly after the Second World War, nurtured by a community within a community, and its successors continue to contribute immeasurably to the growing stature and prestige of the wind band idiom. These are the university wind ensembles. Although university bands in Canada have existed since the beginning of the last century, their existence was largely informal, extra-curricular and restricted to performances in support of school athletics and social events. The new university ensembles are totally different.

The University Wind Ensembles

Frederick Fennell [founder of the Eastman Wind Ensemble in 1952] didn't invent the modern wind band, the British Army did.[44] What Frederick Fennell did do was recognize the possibilities inherent in the wind band beyond the utilitarian restrictions placed upon it by generations of military and then community paymasters. He foresaw and then went on to prove that the wind band was a large instrumental ensemble capable of serious musical expression. His example provided the philosophical and practical foundations for others to build on and in the decades that followed, the wind ensemble became a core curricular fixture in an ever-increasing number of Canadian post-secondary music schools.

In 1946, Robert Rosevear [Fig. 15.7] joined the Faculty of Music at the University of Toronto and pioneered Canada's first undergraduate music degree for prospective school

---

[43] "The Denis Wick Canadian Wind Orchestra," *MusicFest Canada* at www.musicfest.ca accessed 10 September 2021.

[44] The evolution of the modern wind band in Canada was largely a result of the influence of British regimental bands [see Chap.3]. A plausible case can also be made for the development of wind bands in the United States. One of the most influential American band leaders of the nineteenth century was Patrick Gilmore. Born in 1829 in County Galway, Ireland, he joined the British Army as a musician at the age of 16 and in 1849 was stationed in Canada. From there he took his release from active service, emigrated to Boston and by 1859 was leading his own "Gilmore's Band". It was his involvement with two enormous music festivals, the National Peace Jubilee in 1869 and the World's Peace Jubilee in 1872 that raised his profile nationally and established him as the foremost band leader of his generation. See William Carter White, *A History of Military Music in America* (New York: Exposition Press, 1944)

music teachers. Concurrently he established the Royal Conservatory of Music of Toronto Symphonic Band which he directed until 1950. That band in due course became the University of Toronto Concert Band which Rosevear led from 1962 until 1974.[45] His ground breaking work with both groups helped establish the viability of the Eastman Wind Ensemble model and it was soon copied elsewhere in the country. The number of Canadian university music schools grew rapidly during the 1960s, from at least ten awarding professional music degrees in 1965 to approximately thirty by the end of the decade.[46] Wind bands were part of that growth. Montréal's Morley Calvert established the McGill Concert Band in 1956 and remained its conductor until 1970.[47] The University of Saskatchewan's Varsity Concert Band, whose affiliation with the department of music began in 1961, was renamed the University Concert Band in 1967 and the following year was renamed again, the University Wind Ensemble.[48] The University of Manitoba had sponsored a band as early as the 1940s.

The first edition of the *Encyclopedia of Music in Canada* was published in 1981. It contained entries for forty Canadian universities with either faculties, departments or schools of music of which twenty-two included wind bands as curricular student ensembles. Of these, three, the University of Alberta, the University of Western Ontario and McGill University supported two wind bands each.[49] Not included in this tally were post-secondary community colleges, many of which also supported smaller music departments with wind bands.[50] This growth was driven not only by artistic vision but by necessity. The nation's high school band programs were producing ever more wind and percussion instrumentalists looking to further their musical studies. The traditional large instrumental ensemble for serious musical study had always been the symphony orchestra. The only problem was there are only so many positions available in an orchestra for wind players before it is no longer an orchestra. The wind band on the other hand was much more flexible; call it a wind ensemble and it has a limited number of spaces available; call it a symphonic band and each section can accommodate far more musicians. The university band became essential as a vehicle for program administrators to ensure that all

---

[45] Patricia Shand, "Robert Rosevear," *Encyclopedia of Music in Canada* [EMC] (Toronto: University of Toronto Press, 1981) 822.

[46] J. Paul Green and Nancy F. Vogan, *Music Education in Canada: A Historical Account* (Toronto: University of Toronto Press, 1991) 412.

[47] Nancy McGregor, "Morley Calvert," *EMC,* 134.

[48] Glen Gillis, "Bands at the University of Saskatchewan: A Brief History, *Canadian Winds* 4, no.2 (Spring 2006) 97.

[49] "Universities," *EMC*, 952.

[50] Patricia Rolston, "Community Colleges," *EMC,* 209.

music majors could obtain their large ensemble performance credits. It turned out to be a mutually beneficial arrangement. Academia's embrace of the wind band idiom within its core course of studies gave the ensemble an artistic legitimacy that it retains and continues to enhance to the present day.

Britain's Kneller Hall in the nineteenth century and the Canadian military's Tri-Service School of Music starting in the early 1960s, were both established in part to ensure that prospective bandmasters had the necessary training and skills to be effective musical leaders. By 1980, the dramatic increase in the number of wind bands affiliated with Canadian educational institutions, at all levels, from middle schools to graduate schools, created a similar challenge; how to ensure that band directors had the necessary skills to articulate and realize the artistic potential inherent in the ensemble. It was this need that prompted the creation of summer wind band conducting programs. One of the earliest and most successful was the Wind Conducting Diploma Program at the University of Calgary. In 1984, Vondis Miller, then Director of Bands at the University of Calgary, introduced an intensive nine-week course of study for wind band conductors. It consisted of three summer sessions of three weeks each during which time students pursued a "…course of instruction that included theory, composition, conducting, score study and lectures…in the evenings, students worked in front of the resident wind band on the scores they chose to conduct."[51] Guest faculty included some of the most respected names in the field of wind band conducting: Frederick Fennell, Craig Kirchoff, Frank Battisti, Eugene Corporon, David Whitwell and Timothy Reynish as well as composers Karel Husa, David Maslanka, Warren Benson and Ron Nelson.[52]

From 1984 to 1996 alone, the literature studied covered over four centuries of wind band music from Gabrieli's Sonate *Pian e Forte* (1597) to the music of Frank Ticheli and Canadian Gary Kulesha. The University of Calgary's Wind Conducting Diploma Program has attracted participants from around the globe, not just from academic backgrounds but from military and community bands as well.[53] The program's impact on the growth of the Canadian band movement has been especially noteworthy. In 2020, Dr. Mark Hopkins of Acadia University, a graduate himself, observed "…of the sixteen or so of us leading wind

---

[51] Jeremy S. Brown, "The Wind Conducting Diploma Program of Calgary, 1984-1996: A Touchstone of the Core repertoire for the Wind Band, *Canadian Band Journal* 22, no.2 (Winter 1997) 8.
[52] Ibid. 8.
[53] The author attended one session of the program during the summer of 1999 in order to obtain additional graduate credits towards a M.Mus degree. The guest faculty that year were Frank Battisti, Timothy Reynish and composer Ron Nelson.

band programs at universities in Canada, 7 – 8 of them came through that program in part or in whole."[54]

An online survey completed by the author in early January 2020 found at least forty-seven wind bands affiliated with post-secondary institutions across Canada. Many of these groups can rightly be classified as community bands in the sense that membership is not just limited to music majors but to the entire campus community at large. Of those university and college websites reviewed, twenty-two listed only one wind band associated with their respective programs, most of which were to be found in the smaller music schools or in smaller population centres. Some examples are the Brandon University Symphonic Band, Vancouver's Douglas College Concert Band, the Mount Allison Symphonic Band, the University of Guelph Concert Winds, the Lakehead University Wind Ensemble, the Keyano College Concert Band of Fort McMurray and Langley B.C.'s Trinity Western Concert Band. Two other groups worthy of mention are those of Peterborough's Trent University and Kingston's RMC (Royal Military College of Canada). The Trent University Music Society includes a concert band which is active within the community despite there being no curricular music program on campus. The volunteer brass reed band at RMC consists of over 40 officer cadet musicians who rehearse and perform on their off-duty hours. Considering the school's full-time enrollment of just over 1000 students, the band's membership represents at least 4% of the total student body. This in an institution originally established in 1874 where the formation of future military officers precludes any form of musical study.[55]

Eleven of Canada's larger music faculties sponsor two wind groups; a larger ensemble, usually open to the wider academic community and a smaller wind ensemble whose membership is limited by audition to music majors only. It is this second cohort, the wind ensembles, also known as wind symphonies or wind orchestras, groups generally open by audition to music majors or other highly skilled instrumentalists, that deserve special attention. They are for all intents and purposes professional ensembles; although the student musicians are not paid, they receive academic credit in return for their participation or fulfill a requirement to participate in a large ensemble. Auditions limit membership to the university's finest performers and the competition to belong can be intense. What makes the position of our finest university wind bands so enviable is that they can concentrate on the performance of the very best literature without having to "…create revenue with ticket sales."[56] Unlike many community bands, which often rehearse only

---

[54] Dr. Mark Hopkins, Acadia University, e-mail correspondence with author, 25 March 2020.

[55] The Band of the Royal Military College of Canada at www.rmc-cmr.ca accessed 21 May 2022.

[56] Dr. Gillian MacKay, University of Toronto, e-mail correspondence with author, 18 March 2020.

once weekly, university curricular bands practice two to three times a week and are limited to four performances a year with an additional festival appearance or school concert possible.   With the extra time allocated for rehearsals and fewer concert commitments, repertoire can be exhaustively studied.   Acadia University's Dr. Mark Hopkins notes "…the lovely thing about working in the university level is we are not supposed to behave like a business.   We can explore and shape the performance experiences our students get, we curate their formal musical experiences."[57]   His colleague, Dr. Gillian MacKay at the University of Toronto notes "…my job is to reveal to them [the players] the way to listen and play so that the composer's intentions are highlighted."[58]   Simply put, the luxury of being shielded from market forces means that university wind band directors do not have to compromise artistic vision in order to fill seats just to survive.   This not only gives these directors the freedom to perform new repertoire without worrying about pleasing audiences, it also permits emerging or overlooked literature to be shared by means of live performances or recording endeavours.   One such example is the *North Winds* series of CDs produced by the University of Manitoba Wind Ensemble under the direction of Dr. Fraser Linklater [Fig. 15.8].   The *North Winds* project '…was usually aimed at Canadian music for less experienced ensembles (younger school and community groups)."[59]   To be considered for inclusion, pieces "…had to be composed or arranged by Canadians, [and]…had not been recorded before."[60]   One final consideration was pieces "…by Quebec composers and women composers."[61]   The series is a valuable resource for school and community band directors seeking suitable Canadian repertoire for their own ensembles.   Without the creative freedom and resources available at the university level, it may well not have happened.

From adult beginner bands to our finest university ensembles, the past six decades have seen an explosive growth in the number of community wind bands nationwide.   They offer performance opportunities to all ages, at all levels of society and in venues ranging from elementary schools to long term care facilities for our seniors.   Almost everyone associated with these groups is a volunteer and some even pay for the privilege of playing.   All of this points to a musical idiom not in decline but still vibrant, relevant and full of promise.

---

[57] Hopkins, e-mail.

[58] MacKay, e-mail.

[59] Dr. Fraser Linklater, University of Manitoba (Ret'd), e-mail correspondence with the author, 8 June 2020.

[60] Linklater, e-mail.

[61] Linklater, e-mail.

CHAPTER FIFTEEN GALLERY

Figure 15.1.   Lakeshore Concert Band performing at St. John's United Church, Pointe Claire, Québec, 21 February 1969.   Morley Calvert Conductor.   This was one of the country's first adult bands created through night classes (1967) to provide performance opportunities for recently graduated high school music students.   Source: Lakeshore Concert Band.

Figure 15.2.   Cosmopolitan Music Society Adult Beginner Band, Borden Park Bandshell, Edmonton, 1980.   Harry Pinchin Conductor.   The first CMS adult beginner band in 1975 proved to be enormously successful and was soon followed by many others across the country. Source: The Cosmopolitan Music Society, Edmonton.

Figure 15.3. Northdale Concert Band, Ontario Place, Toronto, August 1980. Carl Hammond, Director. Perhaps more than any other adult community band in Canada, the Northdale Concert Band has championed new Canadian music for wind band through its own Northdale Music Press. Source: Northdale Concert Band.

Figure 15.4. Sackville Concert Band, Sackville N.S., 2016. Jim Forde Director. The ensemble also sponsors a Sackville 9AM band for adults wishing to renew their playing skills from high school as well as supporting a bursary program entitled "Keep The Music Alive." Source: photo courtesy of Jim Forde.

Figure 15.5.   Toronto Youth Wind Orchestra, Toronto, 2013.   Colin Clarke, Director.   An ensemble established to provide enhanced performance opportunities for talented and highly motivated young musicians.   Source: Toronto Youth Wind Orchestra.

Figure 15.6.   National Youth Band of Canada, Halifax, 2004.   Dr. Denise Grant, Director.   The NYB has provided superior performance opportunities for Canadian youth for over twenty-five years under the direction of some of Canada's most respected wind band specialists. Source: photo courtesy of Jim Forde.

Figure 15.7.   Professor Robert Rosevear, University of Toronto, c. 1968.   Pioneer of Canada's first university music education degree program at the University of Toronto in 1946, Rosevear conducted the University of Toronto Concert Band from 1962 until 1974.   He was a guest conductor at both IMC summer camps, the International Music Camp in Minot North Dakota and the Interprovincial Music Camp in Ontario's Muskoka region.   A tireless advocate of the wind band he was also a guest conductor of the Barrie Collegiate Band at the Midwest Convention in Chicago on 14 December, 1967.   Source: International Music Camp.

Figure 15.8.   The University of Manitoba Wind Ensemble, Winnipeg, 2016.   Dr. Fraser Linklater, Director.   This is the group that spearheaded the *North Winds* project, a series of CD recordings that featured music for less experienced school and community bands by Canadian composers.   Source: photo courtesy of Dr. Fraser Linklater.

CHAPTER SIXTEEN

A 2022 PROGRESS REPORT

It's been sixty-seven years since *Music in Canada* (Toronto: University of Toronto Press, 1955) was published. In the introduction it was noted that a chapter on bands had been planned but had to be abandoned even though there were over a thousand bands nationwide at the time. Canada's population in 1955 was approximately 15.6 million people.   By 2020 it had grown to over 37 million, a 237% increase.   One measure of our progress is to see if the number of wind bands has kept pace.

The Department of National Defence was the country's largest single employer of bands and band musicians in 1955 and it still is today.   As of January 2020, the Canadian Forces employed six full time professional bands with an average strength of thirty-five musicians each [Fig. 16.1]; seven regular force volunteer brass-reed bands, each with a regular force musician attached as its director; five part time naval reserve bands; one part time air reserve band and twenty-four part time militia [army reserve] bands.[1]   In addition to the direct sponsorship of these groups through the provision of salaries, instruments, music and uniforms, the defence department also indirectly supports the activities of cadet bands. Of the 451 Air Cadet squadrons across the country, 300 offer band as a program activity. The Sea Cadets list band as a program activity at 141 of their 222 corps and the Army Cadets include band at 188 of their 421 corps locations.[2]   These numbers are not definitive since the program activity listings for band from the online cadet directories don't identify what kind of band is supported by local groups.   Those army cadet corps associated with highland regiments as well as some air cadet squadrons host pipe bands.   Some are glockenspiel and drum bands or drum and bugle bands.   The majority however, are brass reed bands and they vary enormously in both skill level and size, ranging from small groups barely beyond the beginner stage to accomplished ensembles comparable to a good high school band.   They all provide young people between the ages of twelve and eighteen the opportunity to play in a wind band at no direct cost to themselves or their parents.   The Department of National Defence makes this possible by providing the funds to employ instructors at the corps/squadron level through the CIC [Cadet Instructor Cadre].   Taken

---

[1] "Bands Directory," *National Defence and the Canadian Forces* at www.cmp-cpm.forces.gc.ca accessed 09 November 2020.
[2] "Cadet Corps and Squadron Directory," *Canada: Canadian Cadet Organizations* at www.app.cadets.gc.ca accessed 03 February 2020.

together, full time, part time, volunteer and cadets, there were up to 600 military bands operational in Canada as of the beginning of 2020.

The community bands, once so prevalent in the 1950s went into decline later that decade and into the 1960s, but came back with renewed vigour beginning in the 1970s. Today, online searches have found websites or Facebook pages for over 350 community bands in ten provinces and one territory. They range in size from the fifteen or so enthusiastic members of the Northern Winds Community Band of Fort St. John, B.C., to the fifty or more equally enthusiastic musicians of L'Orchestre d'harmonie des Chutes in Lévis, QC. In addition to the adult community bands, there are also a dozen or so marching showbands that tour and perform regularly across Canada and internationally. Of course, marching bands and community bands were commonplace in 1955. University bands were not. There are now [2020] thirty-five Canadian post-secondary institutions sponsoring forty-seven wind groups, including a significant number from smaller centres. They all continue to engage our finest young musicians in the pursuit of musical excellence.

Instrumental music as a curricular subject in Canadian schools was still in its infancy in 1955 and rare outside of the province of Ontario. Much has changed. One thing that has not is that education remains an area of provincial responsibility and there still exists a patchwork of provincial and territorial guidelines affecting music programs. As a result, it is difficult to obtain an accurate picture of the total number of school bands, elementary, middle/junior high school or high school across Canada. What we can do is sample the programmes of regional music festivals, which attract many of these bands, to get a general idea of how many participate. From that information we can draw some conclusions as to total numbers. As part of the research for our wind band history, festival programmes for five Canadian cities were examined: Vancouver, Calgary, Toronto, Ottawa and Sherbrooke.

The 2019 Vancouver Kiwanis Music Festival took place from April 30 to May 3 and hosted thirty-six bands, of all levels, from the lower mainland.[3] The 2020 Alberta International Music Festival (Calgary) was held from February 12 to February 25 and took place as scheduled. There were also three additional days in April allocated to beginner bands but these were cancelled as a result of the worldwide COVID-19 pandemic. Entries for the two sets of dates however, included 124 school bands.[4] The 2019 Toronto Kiwanis Music Festival, one of the country's longest running annual music festivals dating back to

---

[3] Vicki Cummings, Director of Development/Group Festivals Administrator, Vancouver Kiwanis Music Festival, e-mail correspondence with the author, 26 March 2020.
[4] Alberta International Band Festivals 2020 (Calgary) Programme.

1944, scheduled twenty-three separate band classes that attracted 101 entries.[5]   Another long-established festival sponsored by Kiwanis Clubs International is Ottawa's Kiwanis Music Festival which took place from April 8 to April 13, 2019.   Drawing participants from across eastern Ontario and the Outaouais region of Québec, the 2019 festival hosted thirty-three school bands in twelve separate classes.[6]   Canada's largest annual music festival, attracting entries from across Québec, is Le Festival des harmonies et orchestres symphoniques du Québec held in Sherbrooke.   In 2019, over a four-day period from May 16 to May 19, the organizers welcomed 127 competitors from Gatineau in the west through Lanaudière, Montréal, Trois-Rivières, Shawinigan and Québec City to Jonquière in the Saguenay region.[7]

The total number of school band entries for the five festivals listed in the previous paragraph is 421.   The reader is reminded the survey sample did not include 2019 festivals in Victoria, Edmonton, Moose Jaw, Regina, Winnipeg, Charlottetown, Halifax and St. John's, nor did it include regional Musicfest competitions in Ottawa, Toronto or Vancouver.   If it did, it is possible that the total number of school bands participating in local festivals nationwide may well have exceeded 600. Beyond those school groups from across the country that attend festivals on a regular basis, one also has to consider those that do not.   Many of these opt out for financial or philosophical reasons or both.   Either their budgets cannot afford the registration fees or their geographical location makes transportation costs to an urban centre prohibitively expensive.   There are also many dedicated band teachers who do not feel the investment in time and money in preparing for a music festival is worth the return.   Some simply believe that too much emphasis on competition or the preparation of a limited repertoire may not be in their own students' best interests.   It is difficult to gauge how many schools nationwide fall into this group, but a conservative estimate would be that for every Canadian school band competing at a local music festival, there is at least one that does not.   If that is the case, then we safely place the total number of school bands, at all levels, at 1200 or more.

In addition to the school bands there are also the municipal, regional, provincial and national honour bands, which though of relatively short-term duration offer outstanding opportunities to a highly motivated number of wind and percussion instrumentalists. These are performers who most often began their musical studies in the schools but go on

[5] Pam Allen, General Manager, Toronto Kiwanis Festival, e-mail correspondence with the author, 19 February 2020.

[6] Kim Chadsey, Executive Director, National Capital Region Music Festival, e-mail correspondence with the author, 30 March 2020.

[7] Claudine Roussel, Directrice, Festival des Harmonies et Orchestres Symphoniques du Québec, e-mail correspondence with the author, 01 April 2020.

to further study and careers in music. They in turn inspire new generations of wind band musicians [Fig. 16.2].

The figures for military bands, community bands, marching showbands, university bands, honour bands and school bands tell a story. It is probable that the total number of wind bands in Canada at the start of 2020 exceeded 2400. This is significant because it means that the number of wind bands has grown at the same rate as our population. If anything, it is proof that the wind band is very much an active part of our day-to-day musical culture. It is popular, relevant and vital. One of the keys to that vitality is that the bands; military, community, marching, university and school do not exist in isolation. They are closely integrated sharing directors and musicians freely amongst themselves. Military reserve and cadet bands are often led by school band teachers who themselves belong to community bands. University music students may belong to militia bands or the Band of the Ceremonial Guard in order to earn money for their education and regular force military musicians are increasingly graduates of some of our finest music schools. As an example, in 2004, the Royal Canadian Artillery Band based at CFB Edmonton could claim that 85% of its musicians had a post-secondary education.[8] This interconnectedness makes the entire band movement stronger and more resilient.

One of the peculiarities of the Canadian character is that we rarely celebrate the achievements of our artists until they have been recognized beyond our borders. Since 1955, our wind bands have consistently shown the world that they rank amongst the best. In 1967, the Barrie Central Collegiate Institute Band was a featured ensemble at that year's Midwest Band and Orchestra Clinic in Chicago and the Oak Bay High School Band was one of several representing Canada at EXPO 70 in Osaka, Japan.

The year 1981 saw the first of the World Association for Symphonic Bands and Ensembles (WASBE) biannual conferences take place in Manchester, England. Featured ensembles came from ten countries and represented the highest standards of wind band performance practice. Every two years thereafter, WASBE conferences held around the globe continued to maintain that standard. Martin Eckroth directed the University of Saskatchewan Wind Ensemble, later renamed the Wind Orchestra, from 1982 to 2001. Twice during his tenure, the ensemble was invited to perform at WASBE conferences, Kerkrade, Holland, in 1989 and Schladming, Austria, 1997.[9] In 1999, at the WASBE conference held at San Luis Obispo, California, one of the invited groups was the University of Calgary Wind Ensemble under the direction of Dr. Glenn Price. At the 2005

[8] Warrant Officer Shawna L. Mochnacz, "The Royal Canadian Artillery Band," *Canadian Winds* 3, no. 1 (Autumn 2004) 7.
[9] Glen Gillis, "Bands at the U of Saskatchewan: A Brief History," *Canadian Winds* 4/2 (Spring 2006) 98.

conference in Singapore, Canada was represented by Vancouver's Pacific Symphonic Wind Ensemble [Fig. 16.3]. The 2007 conference in Killarney, Ireland, welcomed the City of Brampton Concert Band and in 2015, in San Jose, California, Canada scored a hat trick when three Canadian ensembles were honoured, the Pacific Symphonic Wind Ensemble for a second time, the University of Saskatchewan Wind Orchestra once again and the New Edmonton Wind Sinfonia.[10]

Our marching showbands have also distinguished themselves in some of the world's most colourful and competitive outdoor spectacles. The Burlington Teen Tour Band has participated in five Rose Bowl Parades (the most recent being in 2018), three Orange Bowl Parades and the 1974 Cotton Bowl Parade [Fig. 16.4].[11] The Regina Lions Band was a participant at both Rose Bowl and Orange Bowl Parades as well as at Honolulu's Hula Bowl.[12] Another frequent guest at Pasadena's Rose Bowl Parade has been the Calgary Stampede Showband which attended for a fourth time on January 1, 2019.[13] Our Canadian wind bands have won accolades from around the world in every sphere of wind band performance practice. We are just now coming to recognize and acknowledge their achievements.

In the late 1930s, Sir Ernest MacMillan taught orchestration to a young oboist out of Toronto's Parkdale Collegiate Institute. Recognizing an enormous talent, MacMillan used his position as Principal of the Toronto Conservatory of Music [now the Royal Conservatory of Music of Toronto] to grant the student a special degree...in Conducting and Bandmastership.[14] That student's name was Howard Reid Cable and his gift for composition and arranging placed him in the forefront of a long line of Canadian composers of music for wind band whose work is the subject of the second part of this book.

---

[10] "Past Conferences," *World Association for Symphonic Bands and Ensembles* at www.wasbe.org accessed 05 November 2020.

[11] "Honours and Awards," *Burlington Teen Tour Band* at www.teentourband.org accessed 10 November 2020.

[12] Bob Mossing, Director Regina Lions Band, telephone interview with the author, 19 December 2019.

[13] *The Calgary Stampede Showband* at www.foundation.calgarystampede.com accessed 10 November 2020.

[14] John Reid, Barb Hunter ed., "The Life and Music of Howard Cable," *ACB Journal* (June 2014) 19.

CHAPTER SIXTEEN GALLERY

Figure 16.1. Canadian Forces *Stadacona* Band, Halifax, November 2016. Director of Music Lieutenant Commander Patrice Arsenault. This photograph is rich in symbolism; military bands need to strike a delicate balance between appealing to contemporary musical taste along with promoting the traditions of their parent services. The location of this image brilliantly frames the two; in the foreground the ensemble itself, gathered informally, full brass-reed with guitar and electric keyboard clearly visible, in the background, a painting depicting Nelson's great victory at Trafalgar. A victory that set standards for duty and sacrifice which were embraced by the Royal Navy and subsequently adopted by the Royal Canadian Navy when it was established in 1910. Source: Canadian Forces *Stadacona* Band.

Figure 16.2. National Youth Band of Canada, Winnipeg, 2019. Dr. Mark Hopkins Guest Director. The NYB is a focal point for the efforts of band directors across Canada; it represents the potential possibilities for musical growth in students from middle schools all the way to the largest university music departments. Participants are given the opportunity of working with many of our leading wind band conductors during a week-long period of intense musical study. Source: Jim Forde.

Figure 16.3. Pacific Symphonic Wind Ensemble, Vancouver, 2019. David Branter Director. Established in 1981 by Maurice Backun, the PSWE attracts some of the finest wind and percussion musicians from B.C.'s Lower Mainland. The ensemble has represented Canada twice at the prestigious World Association for Symphonic Bands and Ensembles (WASBE) conventions, first in Singapore in 2005 and then again in San Jose, California in 2015. Source: Pacific Symphonic Wind Ensemble.

Figure 16.4. Burlington Teen Tour Band, Pasadena, California, 2018. Established in 1947 as the Burlington Girls and Boys Band, this group has distinguished itself as one of the country's finest musical ambassadors abroad. They have travelled throughout Europe, Japan and much of the United States and participated in five Rose Bowl Parades, three Orange Bowl Parades (Miami), two Cotton Bowls (Dallas) and three Hula Bowl Parades (Honolulu). Source: Photo courtesy of the Burlington Teen Tour Band.

PART TWO: AND THE CANADIAN MUSIC THEY PLAYED

CHAPTER SEVENTEEN

FIRST NOTES

After reviewing hundreds of band programs dating back to the late eighteenth century, it is apparent that most Canadian bands played very little Canadian music at all. Rather than focus on what was played, where and when, this second section seeks to identify what Canadian band music may have been played on the rare occasions when it was programmed. To begin, it is important to agree on what constitutes "Canadian" band music. Consider the definitions of "Canadiana", "Publications", "Creator", and "Subject of Interest" prepared by Library and Archives Canada. When applied to Canadian band music they refer to music written by a Canadian composer or arranger, or music written on a Canadian subject. A Canadian composer, or arranger, refers to any person who is a Canadian citizen, a permanent resident in Canada, a resident in Canada during the time in which a work was composed or a Canadian whose professional training took place largely in Canada but who took up residency elsewhere later in her or his life. A Canadian subject refers to any place, personality, group, activity, experience or theme that is generally acknowledged to be Canadian.[1]

Two works represent the earliest documented examples of music written in Canada, by a Canadian, expressly for wind band, the *Marche de Normandie* [Fig. 17.1] and *Royal Fusiliers Arrival at Québec, 1791* [Fig. 17.2] both by the Québec notary Charles Voyer de Poligny d'Argenson. Notably they were marches, the pre-eminent form of literature for use in official military functions.

There were two types of march in common use during the late eighteenth and early nineteenth centuries, the march itself and the quickstep or quick march. The march was destined for ceremonial parades of a stately or noble character and would be associated with what is today called a "Grand March".[2] The quickstep, known as a "pas rédoublé" was in double time and according to the nineteenth century French band historian Georges Kastner, was, by the mid 1800s, the most commonly used in Europe "…de toutes les marches, la plus commune, et celle qui s'applique au plus grand nombre des cas" [of all

---

[1] "Collection Development Framework," *Library and Archives Canada*, ed. 2005 at www.collectionscanada.gc.ca accessed 08 December 2020.
[2] Dominique Bourassa, "La Contribution des bandes militaires Britanniques au développement de la musique au Québec de la conquête à 1836" (M.Mus mémoire, Université Laval, 1993) 77.

the marches, the most common, and that which is used in the greatest number of cases][3]. In addition to popular titles such as *British Grenadiers, Grenadiers March, General Howe's March* and *Rule Britannia*, British bands frequently played *Auld Lang Syne* at farewell parades and departure ceremonies.

It was, however, the music played for social activities that represented the largest portion of the British regimental bands' repertoire. Cruises, regattas, balls, assemblies, religious ceremonies, public concerts and dinners were all venues at which regimental musicians were expected to perform. The program given by the Band of the Royal Fusiliers on 21 February in 1792 [see Chap.1, pg. 13] is representative of many given by the British regimental bands during the late eighteenth and early nineteenth centuries. It consisted of a variety of ensembles, including the whole band: duets, quartets, solos as well as accompanied vocal presentations. Particularly popular in the category of concerted works were the theme and variations forms which often allowed the bandmaster to demonstrate his ability as a soloist. As in England, the most frequently performed types of large ensemble pieces were transcriptions of currently popular vocal favourites:

> The instrumental works of the great German symphony composers – Haydn, Mozart and Beethoven, do not seem to have appealed to the military band arranger. It was rather to the field of vocal music that he turned. There we find transcriptions from the best-known oratorio choruses of Handel, and excerpts from the masses of Haydn and Mozart.[4]

The fact that regiments were in a constant state of rotation meant that music that had only recently appeared in Europe very quickly made its way across the Atlantic. One example in particular involved the band of the 32nd Regiment of Foot which arrived in Québec during the summer of 1830. On 25 April, 1832, at the Théâtre royal de Québec, the band performed the overtures to *La Cenerentola, Semiramide* and *William Tell*, all by Rossini, the last of which had only had its premiere three years earlier in 1829.[5] Similarly, the most fashionable dances of Europe were performed at the many midwinter balls that occupied the wealthy classes during the long Canadian winter: contradances, cotillions, quadrilles and waltzes. While dance masters saw to the importation and teaching of the

---

[3] Georges Kastner, *Manuel Général de Musique Militaire à L'Usage des Armées Françaises* (Geneva : Minkoff Reprint, 1973) 335.

[4] George Henry Farmer, *The Rise and Development of Military Music* (London: William Reeves, 1912) 100.

[5] Bourassa, "La Contribution," 86.

latest dances, it was the military bands that ensured that Canadian audiences heard the most fashionable dance music.[6]

Most of the information available to scholars about the music played during this early period comes to us through letters and press reviews. They certainly provide us with some detail about the types of music played, but rarely the actual titles of literature performed. In retrospect, the lack of "hard copies" isn't surprising because the entire repertoire was in all probability copied by hand. There were no English publishers of band music until 1845 and as a result:

> Printed music for military bands at this date [prior to 1845] was very scarce. The little there was came from the Continent, and this was arranged for instruments peculiar to their bands…Those regiments that had bandmasters capable of composing or arranging were the best off, but their manuscripts were jealously guarded.[7]

The band library was functionally irreplaceable. Bandmasters would obtain piano arrangements or possibly full scores of current musical favourites and write their own arrangements. Musicians would then either copy out their parts from that score or someone, possibly the bandmaster, would write them out for them. Whatever the case, there would only be one copy of each part in existence. It is understandable then, that when the regiment was recalled to England, the library went with it. By extension, since the British regimental bands were the only wind groups active during the late eighteenth and early nineteenth centuries in colonial Canada, any music written by Canadians which could have been performed by those bands probably disappeared when they left. That would certainly explain the almost complete musical void that exists between 1791 and the appearance of our own bands almost forty years later.

There are tantalizing glimpses. Frederick Henri Glackmeyer [see Chap. 1, pg. 14], ex-military musician and musical entrepreneur in Québec wrote *Chateauguay March* for a performance in 1818. Composed to commemorate the victory of British and Canadian forces at the Battle of Chateauguay in 1813[8], like much of the band music of the period, it

---

[6] Ibid., 86.

[7] Farmer, *Rise and Development*, 115. This was no doubt the start of the bandmaster/arranger tradition that persisted through the remainder of the nineteenth century and well into the twentieth. Much of the Canadian music to be examined in this part of our study was originally composed by bandmasters, both military and civilian for their own bands.

[8] Elaine Keillor, *Music in Canada: Capturing Landscape and Diversity* (Montréal and Kingston: McGill-Queen's University Press, 2006) 108.

has not survived. There is one Glackmeyer march however that did. The inscription on the manuscript reads "March [sic] composée pour le Rev. Monsignor Tabeau par Frederick Glackmeyer Professeur de Musique à Quebec". A second inscription in a different hand reads "pour la solennité de St. Pierre et St. Paul"[9]. It is an undated work in two-line piano score of fifty-eight measures duration following a simple binary AB format. Characterized by multiple repeated dotted eighth-sixteenth note patterns and scale-wise sixteenth note running passages, its eighteenth-century roots are clearly evident. Unfortunately, there is no indication that it was ever played by a wind band. If it had been then it is entirely possible that the sets of parts suffered the same fate as those belonging to the regimental bands. They went back to England.

Just before the final departure of the imperial garrisons, the presence of a British regimental band in Québec may have contributed to the composition of one of the seminal works of the Canadian band repertory, Antoine Dessane's *Pas Rédoublé sur les Airs de "Vive la Canadienne" et "God Save the Queen"*. Dessane was born in France in 1826 and at the age of ten became one of the youngest students to attend the Paris Conservatory. He was a gifted learner in a class that included César Franck and Jacques Offenbach and won two competitions, one in cello and one in piano.[10] In 1848, the year of revolutions in Europe, he accepted the position of organist at Notre Dame Basilica in Québec City. Although his primary responsibilities were for the provision of music for the church, including seven masses both for choir and choir and orchestra, he also wrote for piano, voice, a variety of small string ensembles, full orchestra and the *Pas Rédoublé*.[11] Composed in 1865 and scored for three clarinets in C, three cornets in Bb, one alto sax-tromba in Bb, one bass sax-tromba in C [similar to an alto horn and baritone horn respectively], tambourine, triangle and "Batterie", it is a work of symphonic proportions at 337 measures in length [Fig. 17.3].[12] Dessane skillfully uses a range of compositional techniques, including augmentation and fragmentation to weave a musical tapestry depicting the two themes in conflict much like the adversarial melodies in Beethoven's *Wellington's Victory*. The decisive winner is "Vive la Canadienne." Although there is no clear indication as to who the first performers were, it is possible that musicians from the regimental band in the Québec garrison may have participated in the premiere.

---

[9] The author obtained a photocopy of the work during his research visits to Ottawa in the early 1990s.

[10] Juliette Bourassa-Trepanier, "Dessane, Antoine," *Encyclopedia of Music in Canada* (Toronto: University of Toronto Press, 1981) 267.

[11] Bourassa-Trepanier, "Dessane," 267.

[12] A revised edition of the score to *Pas Rédoublé* is included in the anthology *Music for Winds I: Bands* published by the Canadian Musical Heritage Society (Ottawa, 1998)

The band of the "Children of Peace" in Sharon, Ontario under the direction of Richard Coates [see Chap. 2, pg. 22] is one other source of information about early Canadian band music. In addition to accompanying religious anthems and hymns in support of the sect's church services the band also participated at "...numerous local secular events, particularly political rallies."[13]   By 1833, the group had abandoned its string players and was a functioning ensemble of ten musicians. Newspaper accounts of the period report "...that the Sharon Band was playing arrangements of folk tunes, songs and dance tunes."[14] Included in these accounts were the Scottish folk song *The Bush Aboun Traquair* and the English ballad *The Frog He Would A Wooing Go/The Lovesick Frog.* Other sources from the Sharon collections include "...British military band music, quadrilles, waltzes, marches, quicksteps, solo songs and duets, some glees, and folk tunes."[15]

As noted in Section One of this study, one of the country's first militia bands was that of the Canadian Artillery formed in Québec in 1831. We now know of at least one work performed by the group thanks to the growing prosperity of Canada's mid-nineteenth century middle classes. They had the money and the leisure time to enjoy Europe's preferred home entertainment system: the piano. In mid to late nineteenth century Canada, the military bands were the most popular form of large ensemble secular music making and the music they played was often published in piano reductions to allow audiences to replicate for themselves performances heard in the country's public spaces.

The Piano Reductions

One of the earliest published reductions was *Marche de la St. Jean Baptiste* by Jean Chrysostome Brauneis. Although the title page reads "composée pour le Forté Piano," the timing of the publication, 1848, suggests otherwise. Brauneis died of cholera in 1832 but was, like Glackmeyer, an ex-military musician who founded the Canadian Artillery Band the previous year. For the music to have remained popular enough after his death to justify its publication some sixteen years later, it must have been played widely to still be recognizable. The Canadian Artillery Band became La Musique Canadienne in 1836 under the direction of Charles Savageau and was first reported to have performed at ceremonies celebrating the feast day of St. Jean Baptiste on 24 June 1842. It is likely that the band played this piece on that and subsequent occasions. Another contemporary example was the *Favourite Waltz* which appeared in the December 1838 issue of the

---

[13] Keillor, *Music in Canada*, 95.
[14] Ibid., 96.
[15] Keillor, *Music in Canada*, 98.

Montréal monthly magazine *The Literary Garland*. Underneath the main title is a citation that reads: "As performed by the band of the First Royals."[16]

Montréal bandmaster Henry Prince composed and arranged the *Mermaid Polka* in 1856 and dedicated it to "The Ladies of Canada"; further down the title page is the caption, "as played by Maffré and Prince's Quadrille band." In the trio section [Fig.17.4] there are references to solos for Cornet and Clarionet [sic]. Although we have no way of knowing what the exact instrumentation of the Quadrille band was, the inclusion of these two instruments strongly suggests a brass-reed model. Considering that Prince was also leader of the Volunteer Militia Rifles Band and a talented cornetist, having performed a solo from Bellini's *La Sonnambula* at a Grand Military Promenade Concert held in the city on 17 September 1857, further reinforces this interpretation.[17] Prince was also a publisher and by the 1860s he was producing a series of piano pieces called "Gems of the Day." One of these, the *Brigade March*, contained the following inscription under the title on the first page of music: "As played by the Band of the 47th Regiment". Although the series is undated, historical sources place the 47th Regiment in the Montréal garrison from 1863 to 1866.[18]

The 1860s also witnessed the appearance of piano reductions in English Canada. Toronto's A & S Nordheimer, established by brothers Abraham and Samuel Nordheimer in 1844, published a series entitled *THE BAND A Selection of Fashionable Dances for the Pianoforte* [Fig.17.5]. At the top of the title page sits a stylized crest reading "As performed by the Military Bands" under which is an engraving of a British regimental band in circle formation playing in a landscape dominated by what appears to be Windsor Castle. Across the bottom are lists of four galops, three waltzes and three quadrilles. The underlined title was the actual piece on subsequent pages.

In nearby Hamilton, Peter Grossman, German bandmaster and founder of the Independent Artillery Company Band in 1856 was also a music publisher and his imprint can be found on an arrangement for piano of *Stolen Kisses Galop*. The inscription immediately below the title reads "As performed by the Band of her Majesty's 1st Battalion, 16th Regiment. Once again, regimental sources tell us that the 16th Regiment was garrisoned in Canada between 1855 and 1857 and again, intermittently from 1861 to 1870."[19]

---

[16] Maria Calderisi, *Music Publishing in the Canadas, 1800-1867* (Ottawa: National Library of Canada, 1981) 22.

[17] Ibid., 62.

[18] "Infantry I: Regiments of Foot 1st through 50th," *British Regiments in Canada* at www.freepages.rootsweb.com accessed 17 December 2020.

[19] Ibid.

Piano arrangements of band favourites appear to have remained popular, especially in Québec well into the last decades of the nineteenth century. Lavigne & Lajoie, the Montréal music retailer established by Ernest Lavigne, published a series of selections entitled *CHOIX DE MORCEAUX executés par la Musique du 65éme bataillon (BANDE DE LA CITÉ)* [Choice of pieces performed by the band of the 65th battalion (Bande de la Cité)] [Fig. 17.6]. In 1889, Joseph Vézina wrote a march in tribute to the Voltigeurs de Québec, his former regiment, to celebrate their deployment during the Northwest campaign of 1885. *De Calgarry [sic] à MacLeod, Souvenir du Nord-Ouest* existed in manuscript form only [Fig.17.7] until a piano arrangement was published shortly thereafter [Fig. 17.8]. Similarly, Alexis Contant's march, *Vive Laurier*, composed in 1897, was performed by La Musique du Parc Sohmer prior to appearing as a piano transcription [Fig. 17.9].

The practice of arranging band music for piano performance persisted into the early twentieth century as evidenced by the appearance in 1907 of an arrangement of Job Nelson's *Imperial Native March*. Nelson, bandmaster of the prize-winning Port Simpson band that bore his name was a Tsimshian First Nation band leader who must have been blessed with extraordinary musical gifts. Born into the rich culture of the Pacific Northwest's indigenous peoples, he wrote a march that compares favourably with many of those composed by his American, British and European contemporaries [Fig. 17.10].

In at least one case, a piano reduction was accompanied by an arrangement for band. The patriotic fervour that followed Canada's participation in the Boer [South African] War was the spark for the composition of Arthur Wellesley Hughes' *Royal Canadian March* published in 1900 by Toronto's Whaley, Royce & Co. A later folio cover by the company listing music for band, includes the *Royal Canadian March* along with others from Canada, the United States and Great Britain.

The piano arrangement record demonstrates the popularity of bands in Canada during the mid to late nineteenth century. It is possible that the examples provided here only touch the surface of the total number of keyboard reductions that may have existed at one time. They also give us some idea of manuscript sources that in all probability were used by bands in Canada during the early years of the nineteenth century. By the mid 1840s however, Britain's military bands, both at home and abroad were beginning to realize the limitations of relying on labour intensive manuscripts to satisfy their voracious appetites for new repertoire. It was at this point that a former British Army bandmaster, and an active-duty bandmaster both had the same idea, military band journals.

CHAPTER SEVENTEEN GALLERY

March de Normandie

by Charles Voyer de Poligny d'Argenson,
ca. 1791

Figure 17.1. Modern transcription of *Marche de Normandie* by Charles Voyer de Poligny d'Argenson (d. 1820). Along with the *Royal Fusiliers Arrival at Quebec, 1791* [Fig. 17.2], it is the earliest known example of music written for wind band in Canada by a Canadian. Source: Music Division, National Library of Canada, Ottawa.

Figure 17.2.   Original manuscript of the *Royal Fusiliers Arrival at Quebec, 1791* by Charles Voyer de Poligny d'Argenson.   The caption at the bottom reads: "Presented to the Royal Fusiliers Regiment of London, Eng. — with the compliments of Madame Elmire C. Pourtier, Québec, Québec, 1929." Madame Pourtier, who was the composer's great great granddaughter also included a manuscript copy of the *Marche de Normandie* [Fig. 17.1] with her gift.   Source: Music Division, National Library of Canada, Ottawa.

Figure 17.3. First page of the score to *Pas Rédoublé sur les airs de Vive la Canadienne et God Save the Queen* by Antoine Dessane, Québec, 1865. Note the instrumentation of three clarinets in C, three cornets in Bb, saxo-tromba alto in Bb, saxo-tromba basse in G (Concert Pitch), tambourine, triangle and "batterie" (field drums). Source: Music Division, National Library of Canada.

Figure 17.4. Trio from a piano reduction of the *Mermaid Polka* by Henry Prince, Montréal, 1856. References to solos for cornet and clarionet [sic] suggest an original for wind band. The title page contains a dedication to the "Ladies of Canada" as well as the caption "As performed by Maffré and Prince's Quadrille Band". Source: Music Division, National Library of Canada.

Figure 17.5.   Title page from the A & S Nordheimer series entitled "The Band", Toronto, c. 1860.   Note the stylized crest at the top of the page "…as performed by the military bands." Subtitled "A Selection of Fashionable Dances for the Pianoforte," the inclusion of galops, waltzes and quadrilles give the reader some idea of the repertoire played by nineteenth century bands, both British and Canadian.   The underlined title, in this case *Drawing Room*, Quadrille, by Woodlawn signified which selection was inside the cover.   Source: Music Division, National Library of Canada.

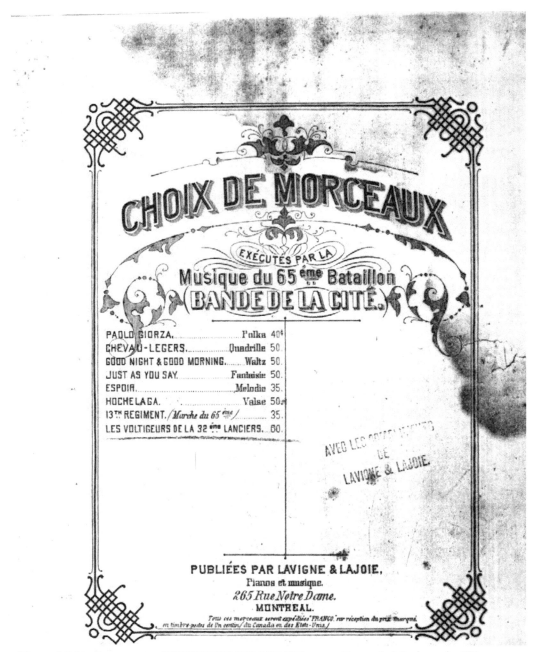

Figure 17.6.   Cover page, CHOIX DE MORCEAUX, executés par la Musique du 65éme Bataillon (BANDE DE LA CITÉ) [Choice of Pieces, performed by the Band of the 65th Battalion (BAND OF THE CITY), published by Lavigne & Lajoie, Montréal, c. 1885].   The list provides an insight as to the popular nature of band programs of the period: fashionable dances, quadrilles, polkas, waltzes as well as "fantaisies," "melodies," and marches.   Once again, the underlined title identifies the actual work contained within.   Source: Music Division, National Library of Canada.

Figure 17.7. Manuscript copy of the 1st Bb Cornet (Conductor) part to *De Calgarry à MacLeod* (*Souvenir du Nord-Ouest*) by Joseph Vézina, Québec, 1889. This would have been an original part probably used by members of the composer's "B" Battery Band. Note the use of cues to indicate the general outline of other band voices, a commonplace practice in much of the band music of the period. Source: Music Division, National Library of Canada.

Figure 17.8.   First page to the piano reduction of *De Calgarry à MacLeod, Souvenir du Nord-Ouest, Marche* by Joseph Vézina, Québec, 1889 [see Fig. 17.7].   Although there is no publication date given, it is likely that the above appeared shortly after the work's composition in 1889. Vézina's position as bandmaster [Chef de Musique] is clearly marked as is the band for which it was written, Batterie "B". R.C.A. [Royal Canadian Artillery]. Source: Music Division, National Library of Canada.

297

Figure 17.9. First page to the piano reduction of *Vive Laurier, Marche Brillante* by Alexis Contant, Montréal, 1897. "Exécutée avec grand succès par la Musique du Parc Sohmer" [Performed with great success by the band of Sohmer Park]. Source: Music Division, National Library of Canada.

The Imperial Native March.

By J. Nelson.

PIANO.

Entered according to Act of the Parliament of Canada in the year 1907 by J. Nelson at the Department of Agriculture.

Figure 17.10.   First page to the piano reduction of Job Nelson's *Imperial Native March*, published by Whaley, Royce &Co., Toronto, 1907.   The composer was bandmaster of the Port Simpson, B.C., First Nations band that won first prize at a band competition held at the Dominion Exhibition in New Westminster in 1905 [See Fig. 5.4].   Nelson must have possessed extraordinary musical gifts; he was born and raised in the rich culture of the Pacific Northwest Tsimshian peoples yet his march is easily equal in quality to those of his British, European and American contemporaries.   Source: Music Division, National Library of Canada.

CHAPTER EIGHTEEN

THE MILITARY BAND JOURNALS

The vast majority of the music performed by British regimental bands in Canada during the late eighteenth and early nineteenth centuries was read from hand written manuscript parts.   This was a time-consuming process that grew ever more onerous as the size and instrumentations of those bands evolved during the nineteenth century.   In 1844, the British publisher Jullien released the first "Jullien's Military Band Journal" under the editorial direction of Charles Godfrey, former bandmaster of the Coldstream Guards.[1] Within two years, Carl Boosé, a former bandsman in the German army and Bandmaster of the Scots Guards, recognising that established publishers were unwilling to take a chance on military bands, decided to publish his own arrangement of selections from Verdi's *Ernani*.   The response to this release was so positive that the instrument manufacturer T. Boosey & Co. "…undertook the publication of a periodical issue of these works [band arrangements] as *Boosé's Military Journal* [in] 1846, appointing Boosé sole editor."[2] Within two years, the enterprise proved to be so lucrative that two other publishers had hired bandmasters from the Coldstream Guards and Grenadier Guards respectively to edit their own journals.   All three were bandmasters of bands based in London, the finest in the British Army.   A series of quality arrangements by experienced writers, written for highly skilled musicians were now commercially available by subscription.   Although Jullien was eventually acquired by Boosey & Co., the potential in the emerging military band market soon attracted new publishers, Chappell in 1858, Hawkes, founded in 1865 and Lafleur.[3]

The terms *Military Journal*, *Army Journal* or *Military Band Journal* may seem confusing to the modern reader but when viewed in the context of the time, they made perfect sense.   The first part, "Military", "Army" and "Military Band" were necessary to distinguish the brass reed wind ensemble from the brass bands that were emerging across the British Isles in the mid-nineteenth century.   The military bands themselves could trace their origins back to the "harmoniemuzik" formations of the late eighteenth century and woodwinds were an essential part of their instrumentations.   This distinction between

---

[1] George Henry Farmer, *The Rise and Development of Military Music* (London: Wm. Reeves, 1912) 145.
[2] Ibid., 116.
[3] William H. Rehrig, *The Heritage Encyclopedia of Band Music: Composers and their Music*, Vol. 2 ed. By Paul E. Bierly (Westerville, Ohio: Integrity Press, 1991) 867.

"Military Band", meaning the brass reed band, and the "Brass Band", signifying brass instruments only was to persist well into the twentieth century.

The "Journal" part was a reflection of the geopolitical reality of the time. "The sun never sets on the British Empire" was an expression familiar to every Canadian schoolboy and schoolgirl in the years leading up to the First World War [1914-1918]. It was a patriotic boast that meant that British territorial possessions were so extensive, encompassing up to one quarter of the land surface of the globe, that during any given twenty-four-hour period, there was always an English-speaking colony or dominion experiencing daylight. Wherever there were British colonies, there were troops and the Royal Navy to police them. With those troops, there were also British regimental bands. In that most unique of military institutions, the British Army of Queen Victoria's reign, the officers posted to the far corners of the empire eagerly supported those bands. In return for their support, they demanded a steady diet of musical postcards that would remind them of home and their own status as "gentlemen". The practical problem facing bandmasters was where were they supposed to find the latest band editions in the markets of India, the teeming streets of Hong Kong, the bazaars of Egypt or the wilds of Canada? Obviously, they weren't. It was the journal publishers who found a solution. They proposed a subscription system whereby a regimental band might subscribe, on a yearly basis, to a series of up-to-date band arrangements released on average once a month. The publishers would then mail these anywhere in the world as part of the subscription service, exactly in the same way as magazine and newspaper subscriptions include delivery; hence the name, "Journal".

The size of the potential market for the journals grew with the growth of the British Empire. By 1903, there were 211 full time professional wind bands in the British Army alone.[4] At the outset of World War One there were a further fifty-three authorized bands posted to the battleships, battlecruisers, heavy cruisers and shore establishments of the Royal Navy.[5] Together there were over 250 active duty bands with a voracious appetite for new music; then add to that figure the territorial (militia) bands, civilian town and industrial plant bands and the bands overseas in Canada, Australia and elsewhere including the United States. As the popularity of the Military Band Journals grew, new issues, referred to as Supplementary Journals, available for purchase individually, also began to appear. Boosey's Supplemental Military Journal alone contributed over 500 titles to the

---

[4] Major (Ret'd) R.G. Swift, Bandmaster Course Director, Royal Military School of Music, Kneller Hall, correspondence with author, 17 May 1995.
[5] John Trendall, *A Life on the Ocean Wave; The Royal Marines Band Story* (Dover, U.K.: Blue Band Magazine, 1990) 41.

journal repertoire between 1846 and 1931. One particularly noteworthy example of these was Jacob Kappey's 1899 edition of Handel's oratorio *Messiah* which included all recitatives, arias and choruses [Fig. 18.1].

The repertoire of the journals fell into three general categories: arrangements of popular operatic selections of the day, orchestral transcriptions and descriptive pieces. The operas of Gounod, Donizetti, Rossini, Verdi and following him, Puccini, were favorites and often appeared in journal catalogues. With titles beginning with "Selections from" or "Reminiscences of", they were staples of the military band repertory. Journal covers also contained advertisements for instruments and "appurtenances" from those publishers whose activities included the manufacture of brass and woodwind instruments as well as references to upcoming arrangements of the latest "Continental successes". It appears that in the late nineteenth century the stages of Paris, Vienna and Milan were seen as the centres of musical culture for all tastes, not just those of the "leisure classes".

Transcriptions of orchestral favourites were equally popular with journal publishers. Overtures, symphonic movements, tone poems and dances all found themselves in the published literature. It must be remembered however, that these were never intended for serious audiences alone. The enormous range of orchestral forms that served as a source for these transcriptions is probably best associated with what is today known as "pops" programming. This included overtures by Mozart, Beethoven, Von Weber, Mendelssohn and Wagner. Symphonic movements and tone poems from the works of Berlioz, Grieg, Tschaikovsky, Liszt and Rimsky-Korsakov were equally well represented. Later journals published in the United States also included transcriptions of works by Saint-Saens, Dvorak, Mussorgsky and Brahms. Ballet suites and the waltzes of Strauss, Gung'l and Lehar were also featured.

A third popular category, and the only one that involved music specifically written for wind bands, was the descriptive piece. These were either drawn from folk sources or were originally composed to evoke the musical atmosphere of some far-off exotic part of the world. Dervish or Serbian Dances, Hawaiian or Persian Patrols, even battle scenes, were all exploited for their audience appeal. Of particular interest were the country "Reminiscences" published by several journals. These were medleys of folk songs from Ireland, Scotland, England and elsewhere that must have been especially popular judging by the number of editions produced. Published prior to the invention of the recording cylinder, they offer valuable insights as to what were considered to be genuine folk melodies at the end of the nineteenth century.

The success of the British Military Band Journals was far reaching. Shortly after the end of the American Civil War [1865], the number of American bands began to grow and

American publishers were quick to sense the opportunities. In 1876, A.E. Squire of Cincinnati published a popular collection of twenty-four pieces entitled the *Centennial Collection*. The instrumentation included the standard brass band of the period plus Db piccolo, Eb clarinet, solo, 1st, 2nd and 3rd Bb clarinets.[6] Parts were written so that the arrangements were functional with as few as five or six key players. Within a decade, American journals began to emerge from music houses Ditson, Cundy and Carl Fischer. Shortly thereafter, they began to appear in Canada alongside those from the British publishers. A concert program presented by the Governor General's Foot Guards Band of Ottawa in 1876 contains ten numbers. All selections save the Regimental March were drawn from Military Band Journals.[7]

The definition of "Canadian music" presented in the opening paragraphs of this section of the book also includes music by a non-Canadian composer as long as it deals with a "Canadian" subject. The Military Band Journals contributed to this growing body of Canadiana with titles like *Canada Fantasia* (early 1900s) and *Canadian Patrol* (1911) [Fig.18.2]. Both of these examples are medleys of what were considered to be popular Canadian songs of the period. The "Patrol" format especially was a favourite of British, Canadian and American band composers during the early years of the twentieth century. It was a musical attempt to give the impression of a band playing in the distance, approaching, passing by in review and then receding by means of a steady increase and then decrease in dynamic levels. Within this formal structure, melodies, most often folk songs, were used to give the work its descriptive nature. British and Canadian composers of the time usually included a number of French-Canadian folk songs, *Vive la Canadienne* and *O Canada* being two of the most popular as well as songs from England, Ireland and Scotland to represent the country's English-speaking citizens.

It was the appearance of the Military Band Journals, first in England and then in the United States, that did more than anything to standardize the instrumentation of the military band.[8] An early journal, Boosé's arrangement of the Overture from Mendelssohn's *Midsummer Night's Dream*, published in 1860, was scored for Db piccolo, oboes, 1st and 2nd bassoons, 1st and 2nd Eb clarinets, 1st, 2nd and 3rd Bb clarinets, althorn in Bb, 1st and 2nd pistons (Bb cornets), 1st and 2nd Eb trumpets [sounding a minor third higher than written], 1st, 2nd, 3rd and 4th Eb horns, 1st and 2nd tenor trombones [in tenor clef], bass trombone,

[6] Rehrig, *Heritage*, 855.
[7] Elaine Keillor, "Musical Activity in Canada's New Capital City in the 1870s," in *Musical Canada: Words and Music Honouring Helmut Kallmann*, eds. John Beckwith and Frederick A. Hall (Toronto: University of Toronto Press, 1988) 121.
[8] Rehrig, *Heritage*, 867.

basses and drums [Fig.18.3].   By 1899, Kappey's edition of *Messiah* included a two line conductor's score as well as parts for Eb piccolo/flute, oboes or clarionets [sic] in C, 1st and 2nd bassoons or bass clarionets [bass clef], 1st and 2nd Eb clarionets, 1st, 2nd and 3rd Bb clarionets, Eb alto clarionet and Eb alto saxophone [marked as tenor clarionet and tenor saxophone], 1st and 2nd Bb cornets, 1st and 2nd Eb trumpets, 1st, 2nd, 3rd and 4th Eb horns, 1st and 2nd tenor trombones [tenor clef], bass trombone, Bb baritone [treble clef], euphonion [sic], basses and drums.   The intense competition for market share forced Boosey's competitors, especially Hawkes and Son, to conform as a 1908 arrangement of *Trauermarsch* from Wagner's opera *Die Götterdämmerung* shows: three-line condensed conductor's score, 1st, 2nd and 3rd Db flutes, oboes, 1st and 2nd bassoons, Eb clarinets, solo, 1st, 2nd and 3rd Bb clarinets, alto clarinet and alto saxophone, tenor saxophone, 1st and 2nd Eb trumpets, 1st and 2nd Bb trumpets, 1st and 2nd Bb cornets, 1st, 2nd, 3rd and 4th Eb horns, 1st, 2nd and bass trombones, baritones in Bb [treble clef], euphonium, basses, timpani and drums [Fig.18.4].

American publishers were even more inclusive. Carl Fischer's 1900 edition of Haydn's *Military Symphony* [no. 100] arranged by Theo. Moses-Tobani was available with a two line condensed score and parts for flute in C, oboes or clarinets in C, bassoon, Eb clarinet, solo or 1st, 2nd, 3rd and 4th Bb clarinets, alto and bass clarinets [treble clef], soprano, alto, tenor and baritone saxophones, Eb cornet, solo or 1st Bb cornet, 2nd Bb cornet, 3rd and 4th cornets or trumpets in Bb, 1st, 2nd, 3rd and 4th Eb horns, 1st and 2nd trombones, bass trombone, baritone treble and bass clef, basses, timpany [sic] and drums [Fig.18.5]. The interwar period saw a final consolidation of the modern wind band's instrumentation on both sides of the Atlantic as military band journals published by both British and American publishers included all parts in modern use.

The popularity of both military bands and British brass bands led to a hybrid form of journal in the early 1900s published by Boosey & Company and its main rival, Hawkes and Son.[9] These were brass band journals, with complete sets of parts for brass band with supplementary parts for flute/piccolo, oboes, bassoons, Eb and Bb clarinets. Saxophones were expected to perform from Eb alto horn and Bb tenor horn parts to complete the woodwind section. It was a popular format, especially in those regions, like Canada, where the brass band formed the nucleus of most early wind bands. One striking example of this type of edition, with a Canadian connection, was *Sunset on the St. Lawrence* by Maxime Heller (Hawkes & Son, 1919). The name M. Heller was in fact a pseudonym for Frederick

[9] Boosey & Co. and Hawkes and Son merged in 1931 to form Boosey & Hawkes.

Harris, founder of Toronto's Frederick Harris Music Company who wrote the original melody in 1910 [Fig.18.6].[10]

The Military Band Journals, also known as the Army Band Journals, formed the core of Canadian band libraries for over a century. Although most, especially those published in England, contained very little in the way of identifiable Canadian music for band, one American journal in particular, the Carl Fischer Military Band Journal, did include Canadian band music through the activities of one of its most prolific yet reclusive editors, Louis-Philippe Laurendeau.

Louis-Philippe Laurendeau (1861-1916)

By 1910, Montréal was Canada's largest city, its commercial heart, a major trading centre and its southern suburb of Longeuil was home to Louis-Philippe Laurendeau. Virtually unknown today, he was the one individual who more than any other who put the "Canadian" in the American military band journals. Laurendeau was born in St. Hyacinthe, Québec, and little is known of his formal musical training other than that at one point he appears to have been bandmaster at a military school in nearby St. Jean.[11] After winning the *Metronome* magazine composition contest in 1895 with his *Intermezzo Twilight Whispers* [Fig. 18.7], he devoted himself entirely to composition and arranging. The New York based publisher Carl Fischer engaged him in an editorial capacity and for the remainder of his life he was to produce an enormous body of band literature: original compositions, transcriptions, a text on arranging and method materials for younger players. So great was his contribution, at one point representing over one quarter of Fischer's entire catalogue, that Laurendeau assumed the pseudonyms of Paul Laurent and G.H. Reeves.[12] Although it is not clear how much time he actually spent living in New York, by 1910 he was residing in Longeuil. In 1915 he moved to Montréal proper where he died the following year after a long illness at the age of fifty-five.

The most comprehensive listing of Laurendeau's prodigious body of work for band is to be found in William H. Rehrig's *The Heritage Encyclopedia of Band Music: Composers and their Music*, Vol. 1, ed. by Paul E. Bierley (Westerville, Ohio: Integrity Press, 1991).

---

[10] Marlene Wehrle, "Frederick Harris Music Co. Ltd.," *Encyclopedia of Music in Canada* (Toronto: University of Toronto Press, 1981) 416.

[11] "Mort de L.P. Laurendeau," *Le Passe-Temps* (Montréal, 26 février 1916). There had been a military band presence in St. Jean since the days of the St. John's band in the early 1850s but the particular institution with which he was affiliated is unknown.

[12] Robert Hoe, Jr., "Louis-Philippe Laurendeau," *The Heritage Encyclopedia of Band Music* Vol 1 (Westerville, Ohio: Integrity Press, 1991) 441.

We are indeed fortunate that American publishers were and still are obligated to deposit copies of new releases in the Library of Congress where they are now accessible to modern researchers. It was in this way that Bill Rehrig was able to confirm the existence of the titles included in Laurendeau's entry in the encyclopedia.[13] Ironically, that research also revealed that upwards of 75% of the British military band journals discussed earlier were also registered with the Library of Congress in an attempt to ensure copyright protection in the United States.[14]

Laurendeau wrote in all genres, of which the largest single category was marches. He wrote ninety-six under his own name, two under the pseudonym of Paul Laurent and one as G.H. Reeves. The vast majority were published by Fischer but a handful appeared in editions by Squire, Coleman, Cundy, Church and Mace Gay. Their titles reflect popular images, people and events of his day with names like *Moto Cycle, Wireless Message, Oregonia, Republic of Panama* and *Col. Roosevelt's Rough Riders*. Embedded in the list are marches inspired by his Canadian homeland: *Carillon, Marche Patriotique Canadienne-Francaise* (Fischer, 1907) [Fig.18.8], *Mount St. Louis Cadets* (Fischer, 1894)[15], *Laurentian March* [featuring *O Canada* in the trio section] (Fischer, 1908) and *Land of the Maple* [with the *Maple Leaf Forever*] (Fischer, 1912).

Laurendeau's second largest genre collectively was dances, of all kinds. He wrote at least thirty waltzes, seventeen galops, eight mazurkas, nine polkas and ten other dance forms all of which must have enjoyed enormous popularity during the late nineteenth and early twentieth centuries. The earliest of these appears to be *My Pretty Minnie, Song and Dance*, published by Cundy in 1887. By 1904, in his capacity as an editor for Carl Fischer, Laurendeau had arranged at least three Johann Strauss Jr. favourites for band, *Die Fledermaus* (1903), *Blue Danube* (1897) and *Roses from the South* (1900).[16] Fischer published Laurendeau's waltz *Prés Fleuris* [Flowery Fields] that same year, a mature work of 281 measures without repeats [Fig.18.9].

Concert works in a variety of forms fill out the remaining categories. Laurendeau wrote twenty overtures, eighteen medleys, twelve solos, five serenades, four fantaisies and thirty-eight other compositions. It is in the medleys that once again we find the influence of his French-Canadian roots. In 1893 Cundy published the folk medley *Shores of the St. Lawrence* which concluded with "Vive la Canadienne" and in 1908, on the occasion of the

---

[13] William H. Rehrig, correspondence with the author 27 July 1999.

[14] William H. Rehrig, correspondence with the author 23 January 1999.

[15] Named in all probability after Montréal's "Collège Mont St. Louis," a prestigious private school opened in the late 1880s on Sherbrooke Street.

[16] Copies of all three works in the author's private collection.

tricentenary of the establishment of Québec, Fischer released *Laurentian Echoes,* subtitled "A Potpourri of French-Canadian Melodies" [Fig. 18.10]. It consists of seven well known French-Canadian folksongs, "A St. Malo, beau port de mer," "A la claire fontaine," "En roulant ma boule," "Un canadien errant," "Lev'ton pied," "Quand Marianne s'en va-t-au moulin" and "Vive la Canadienne." The medley concludes with an *Allegro risoluto* rendition of Calixa Lavallée's *O Canada.* This closing section once again illustrates Laurendeau's mastery of the band idiom as multiple running lines in the upper woodwinds and descending sequential eighth note figures in the low brass combine to evoke a genuine sense of patriotic pride in the listener. One further measure of Laurendeau's skill was that a Carl Fischer band catalogue released in 1954, thirty-eight years after his death, still contained forty-nine of his original compositions for band.[17]

The *Heritage Encyclopedia of Band Music* confirms the existence of 284 Laurendeau works for band. It fails to mention the hundreds of his arrangements that also satisfy the requirements for being considered "Canadian." These cover the entire range of musical forms that were popular in his day, from sentimental songs like the *Angel's Serenade* (Fischer, 1898), *Good-bye* (Fischer, 1908) and *Simple Aveu* (Fischer, 1900) to lighthearted treatments of solos and duets with band accompaniment such as Ritter's *Long, Long Ago, Fantaisie for Clarinet* (Fischer, 1912) or Kling's *The Elephant and the Fly, Duo Characteristique for Piccolo and Trombone/Baritone* (Fischer, 1903). We also find amongst these arrangements some early examples of Christmas specials for band, especially *Around the Christmas Tree* (Fischer, 1911) and *Cantique de Noel* (Fischer, 1898). Laurendeau's most significant arrangements however, were the complete transcriptions of some of the cornerstones of the nineteenth century orchestral literature. These include but are not limited to *L'Arlesienne Suite* (Fischer, 1904), *Caprice Italien* (Fischer, 1903), *Danse Macabre* (Fischer, 1904), *The Flying Dutchman Overture* (Fischer, 1912), *1812 Overture* (Fischer, 1904) and the *Ride of the Valkyries* (Fischer, 1908).[18]

One measure of Laurendeau's genius for arranging was that he understood both the musical and business limitations of his art. Nowhere is this more evident than in his arrangement of Tchaikovsky's *Marche Slave* [Fig. 18.11]. Viewed from today's perspective, it is tempting to conclude that he never took full advantage of the broad range of tonal colours available in the modern wind band; a conclusion that is often reached based on his scores which contain multiple examples of doubled voices. The reasons for these choices however had more to do with practical considerations than any creative

---

[17] Catalogue in the author's collection.
[18] Copies of all works cited are in the author's private collection.

preferences. The instrumentation of the wind band at the beginning of the twentieth century was much more variable than it is today. Although there were far more adult bands at the time per capita than there are now, they generally numbered fewer musicians. In order to reach this potential market, Laurendeau had to create arrangements that would be accessible to almost any combination of instruments. To achieve this end, we find extensive doublings and cross-cues for instruments such as bassoons, oboes, bass clarinets and horns.

With *Marche Slave*, the success of the transcription is also due as much to the work itself as it is to the talent of the arranger. Its original orchestration is heavily weighted in favour of the winds. There are few strings-only sections and these are brief and often in unison. The rich sound of celli and basses is replicated in the fusion of low register clarinet and euphonium and throughout the transcription it is the clarinet section, supported by saxophones, that forms the glue holding the diverse elements together. Laurendeau exploits this strength to create a musical composition of superior quality with all the challenges of the original which continues to thrill audiences everywhere. Over a century after his death, Louis-Philippe Laurendeau's transcription of *Marche Slave*, first published in 1906, is still available today as a "Classic Band Edition" on the Carl Fischer website.[19]

Laurendeau didn't limit himself just to compositions and arrangements for accomplished ensembles. In 1897, the John Church Company published the *Up to Date Band Book*, a collection of twenty-four selections including marches, waltzes, serenades and other dance forms specifically created for "younger players." Instrumental ranges were limited, rhythms were relatively simple and formal structures uncomplicated. A note on the back cover proclaimed that the entire collection could be performed by as few as six players. These march size booklets were enormously popular because they allowed bands to perform outdoors in almost any venue. As both composer and arranger, Laurendeau was extensively involved in their preparation. His compositions were staples in at least six published by Carl Fischer including *The Majestic Band Book, The Elite Band Book, The 20th Century Band Book, Our Mascot Band Book, The Record Band Book* and the *New Era Band Book*.[20] His contribution as an arranger was equally prodigious. These included entries in the *Carl Fischer Concert and Operatic Band Book* (n.d.), which featured operatic selections from the works of Donizetti, Verdi, Bizet and others as well as his *Collection of Gospel Hymns* (Fischer, 1902).

---

[19] "Concert Band" in "Large Ensemble," *Carl Fischer* at www.carlfischer.com accessed 07 January 2021.
[20] All titles listed on the back cover of the *C.F. Standard March Book* (Fischer, n.d.) in the author's collection.

Internationally respected, Laurendeau shared his insights and experience with others by writing *The Practical Band Arranger* (Fischer, 1910). Subtitled "A Systematic Guide for Thorough Self-Instruction" it is a text that covers briefly the elements of harmony, instrumental ranges and characteristics, transposition and arranging from either piano or orchestral sources. The work, despite the name, is by no means exhaustive, especially in the chapter on woodwinds where Laurendeau only deals with piccolos and clarinets. For readers interested in learning more about the double reeds, alto and bass clarinets and the saxophone family he advised them to consult H. Kling's *Modern Orchestra and Instrumentation*, copies of which were also available from Carl Fischer. Although many of his observations with respect to brass instruments remain valid, one in particular is worth noting only because the instrument in question, the Eb alto horn is no longer in use "…the alto is in reality a substitute for the French horn, which instrument is so delicate that it is not well suited for the use of amateurs."[21]

His funeral notices in both Montréal's *Le Passe-Temps* (Montréal, 26 février 1916) and New York's *Metronome* magazine (March 1916) remarked on his talent and the respect in which he was held by his contemporaries. In Québec, the pride was palpable "…ses compositions et arrangements ont été jouées par les plus célèbres corps de musiques, non seulement du Canada, mais des Etats-Unis et même en Europe…l'auteur a été connu, applaudi et aimé [his compositions and arrangements were played by the most famous bands, not only in Canada, but in the United States and even in Europe…the author was known, applauded and loved].[22] His tributes in America were no less glowing "…as an arranger he stood at the head of his profession, he had mastered the difficult problems which confront the specialist in this particular branch of music and all arrangements bearing his name have become the standard of excellence as far as practical utility, skilful tonal blend and general musical effectiveness is concerned."[23]

Of all the Military Band Journals available in Canada at the dawn of the twentieth century, few were as popular as those published by Carl Fischer. Tucked away in the top right-hand corner of many of those yellowing sheets, whether as composer or arranger, is the name of Canada's Louis-Philippe Laurendeau.

There are some in the wind band community today who lament the military band journals, with their heavy reliance on transcriptions, as a squandered opportunity to create a unique repertoire for wind band. In doing so, they apply a twenty-first century perspective to nineteenth century practice. The modern reader needs to place themselves

---

[21] Louis-Philippe Laurendeau, *The Practical Band Arranger* (New York: Carl Fischer, 1911) 18.
[22] "Mort de L.P. Laurendeau," *Le Passe-Temps* (Montréal, 26 février 1916)
[23] "Death of L.P. Laurendeau," *Metronome* 32, no.33 (March 1916)

in the position of a late nineteenth century band director to fully understand why transcriptions were so popular. Recording technologies had not yet been invented so live performance was the only way to hear music of any kind. Furthermore, symphonic ensembles capable of playing the emerging orchestral canon were limited to the large urban centres of Europe and the United States whereas military brass reed bands were widespread. Military bandmasters sensed that "…the musical reputation of the military was measured by the effectiveness of its transmission of this music…[and] senior army bandmasters felt that great music was not compromised by transcription because it was so great…".[24] Simply put, most military band leaders of the late nineteenth century were convinced that the transcriptions they were programming represented the summit of musical art and any attempt to replace them with a literature written only for wind band was pointless.

Equally important is the recognition that what is now called "serious" music by twenty-first century listeners and performers was at the time of its composition "popular" music. Contrary to the generally held belief that great composers are rarely appreciated until after their deaths, the opposite was true. Nineteenth century opera composers, Rossini, Donizetti, Bellini, Meyerbeer, Weber, Verdi, Wagner and Puccini as well as its symphonists, Schubert, Mendelssohn, Schumann, Chopin, Liszt and Brahms were immensely successful.[25] They had legions of followers, champions as well as detractors and they filled opera houses and concert halls with audiences eager to hear their latest works. They were the "Pop" superstars of their time. The performance of transcriptions of nineteenth century operatic and orchestral literature had much more in common with school bands today performing arrangements of the latest Disney movie hits than any attempt to educate listeners through the performance of some work of "quality" literature.

---

[24] Trevor Herbert and Helen Barlow, *Music and the British Military in the Long Nineteenth Century* (Oxford: Oxford University Press, 2013) 192.

[25] Henry Pleasants, *The Agony of Modern Music* (New York: Simon and Schuster, 1955) 19.

CHAPTER EIGHTEEN GALLERY

Figure 18.1.   First page of the 1st clarinet part to Jacob Kappey's edition of the complete oratorio *Messiah* by Handel, published by Boosey. & Co., 1899.   This monumental transcription is a testament to the number and quality of wind bands across the English-speaking world at the time. The 1st clarinet part is twenty-two pages long, the 2nd bassoon or bass clarinet, sixteen and the 1st cornet, fourteen.   Source: author's collection.

Figure 18.2.   First page of the conductor's score to *Canadian Patrol* by A. Williams, published by Boosey & Co. in 1911.   Note the inscription and dedication just below the title.   The composer, Albert Williams had been Director of Music of the Grenadier Guards Band since 1897 and held a doctorate in music from Oxford University (1906).   Source: author's collection.

Figure 18.3. First page of the 1st clarinet part to the overture from *Midsummer Night's Dream* by Felix Mendelssohn, arranged by Carl Boosé and first published by Boosey & Co. in 1860. Source: author's collection.

Figure 18.4. Euphonium part to the *Trauermarsch* (Funeral March) from Wagner's *Die Götterdämmerung,* arranged by A.J. Stretton and published by Hawkes & Son in 1908. Nineteenth century operas were a favourite source of material for British military band journal arrangers. As the above example shows, technical skill was rarely a consideration as military musicians were expected to play anything put before them. Source: author's collection.

Figure 18.5. First page to the conductor's score, *Military Symphony* (no. 100) by Joseph Haydn, arranged by Theo Moses-Tobani and published by Carl Fischer in 1900. Note the three library stamps: "The Irish Regiment of Canada," "The Toronto Symphony Band" and the "411 Sqn. RCAF Concert Band (Aux)". U.S. publishers contributed equally to the military band journal repertory; note also the inscription just below the word "Conductor", *United States Mil. Band J'l*. Source: author's collection.

Figure 18.6.   First page to the solo cornet (conductor) part of *Sunset on the St. Lawrence* by M. Heller, published by Hawkes & Son in 1919.   "M. Heller" was a pseudonym for Frederick Harris, founder of Toronto's Frederick Harris Music Company who first wrote this melody in 1910.   Source: author's collection.

Figure 18.7. Solo Bb cornet (conductor) part to *Twilight Whispers* by L. P. Laurendeau, published by Carl Fischer in 1895. Source: author's collection.

Figure 18.8. Solo cornet part to *Carillon* by L.P. Laurendeau, published by Carl Fischer in 1907. Source: author's collection.

Figure 18.9. Solo cornet (conductor) part to *Prés Fleuris* Waltz by Louis-Philippe Laurendeau, published by Carl Fischer in 1904. Source: author's collection.

Figure 18.10.   Conductor's score to *Laurentian Echoes* by L.P. Laurendeau, originally published by Carl Fischer in 1908.   Laurendeau's "Pot-Pourri of French-Canadian Melodies" was in all probability written for Québec's tricentenary in 1908.   Along with Vézina's *Mosaique sur les Airs Canadiens*, it is one of the first arrangements for wind band to fully exploit French Canada's rich folksong repertory.   Source: author's collection.

Figure 18.11. Solo cornet part, with cues, to Laurendeau's arrangement of *Marche Slave* by Tschaikovsky, published by Carl Fischer in 1906. As with most transcriptions of the period it remains technically faithful to the original, with the only modifications, if any being to keys more suited to instruments of the band. Note the addition of rehearsal numbers which the reader may notice have generally been missing in the examples up to this point. Source: author's collection.

CHAPTER NINETEEN

THE BANDMASTERS

The Québec Bandmasters

One British regimental band tradition rapidly adopted by the first Canadian bands, militia, community and youth, was the practice of bandmasters arranging and composing music for their own ensembles. At first it was done out of necessity. Printed music for band was all but unavailable and even when it did begin to appear, first with the British military band journals and then in the 1880s with their American rivals, the composition of many early groups made their use impractical. As noted in previous chapters, most nineteenth century bands in this country, especially the community bands, had nowhere near a balanced instrumentation and when the varying skill levels of their members were considered, it was easy to see why the journal repertoire was woefully inadequate. Local bandmasters responded in the only way they could, by writing for their own groups. They knew the strengths and weaknesses of their musicians as well as the local audience for whom they played. Initially their compositions and arrangements were in hand written manuscript but by the last decade of the nineteenth century, particularly successful Canadian bandmasters were finding publishers ready to take a chance on the burgeoning band music market. This repertoire, created for specific wind bands by their own directors, dominated much of the literature produced for band in the late nineteenth and early twentieth centuries in Canada.

In French Canada bandmasters were highly respected and valued. They produced a substantial body of literature for wind band and much of this repertoire has been preserved in military, provincial and academic libraries in both Montréal and Québec City. One of the most prolific of the province's late nineteenth century bandmaster-composers was Joseph Vézina. As noted earlier [see Chap. 6], Vézina was entirely self-taught with the exception of six months private study in harmony with his friend Calixa Lavallée. Yet he still produced no less than fifty-four works for wind band.[1] These include twenty-five marches, eleven waltzes, eight polkas and galops, five overtures, fantasies and potpourris, one bolero, one mazurka and three works for solo cornet and band.[2]

---

[1] Jean Philippe Côté_Angers, "Joseph Vézina et L'Orchestre à Vent : l'expression d'un nationalisme musical canadien" (M.Mus. diss. Université Laval, 2010)
[2] Jean-Philippe Côté Angers, "Vézina", 123.

One of Vézina's earliest compositions was the *Canadian Rifles Waltzes* written in 1870 and dedicated to Colonel Charles-Eugène Panet, commanding officer of the 9th Batallion [Voltigeurs du Québec]. Vézina had been appointed bandmaster of the regimental band the previous year and at the time was only twenty-one years old yet the work still shows a remarkable degree of maturity. The 1880s were his most productive decade with the composition of twenty-seven works in all genres with three for solo cornet and band. One, *Première Neige,* [First snowfall] *Polka*, is unique in that the composer provides the option of an alternate solo part, for flute/piccolo as well as cornet, even though the dedication reads "…À mon frère Ulric, Solo cornettiste au 8e C.R. [To my brother Ulric, solo cornet of the 8th Canadian Rifles] [Fig. 19.1]." Composed in October of 1889, it is a relatively short work of only ninety-one measures in simple AB form yet its contrasting sections, lightly textured accompaniment and dance like solo part all display an effortless mastery of the band idiom. By this time in his career, Vézina was a well-established musical figure in his native Québec and could afford the services of a professional copyist. Directions on the autograph score state "…copiez les deux premières mesures de cette partie [copy the first two measures of this part]."[3]

Perhaps his best-known work and one of the few to have been published in an edition for band was his *Mosaique sur les Airs Canadiens*, composed especially for and premiered at "La Convention nationale des canadiens français" which took place at the Québec Skaters Pavilion on 24 June, 1880. It is a medley of French-Canadian folksongs that introduced a new "chant national" by his friend and former private teacher Calixa Lavallée entitled *O Canada* [Fig. 19.2]. Some of the ten songs Vézina employed included: "Par derrière chez ma tante," "À St. Malo," "Marianne," À la Claire Fontaine" and "Le Drapeau de Carillon."[4] Although it is a relatively lengthy work, at 278 measures, it is sequential in nature, avoids excessive chromaticism and is heavily scored throughout with few exposed or solo passages. More than anything, its value lies in its symbolism: the first public performance of what was to become Canada's national anthem a century later.

It was Vézina's success as musical director of this festival that helped solidify his position in Québec city's musical life. For the remainder of the decade his compositional output kept pace with his other roles as bandmaster, teacher and musical organizer [see Chap.6]. One work produced during this period and also worthy of mention was *La brise: The Québec Yacht Club Waltz.* Originally composed in 1886, Vézina transcribed the work for symphony orchestra and presented it at an artistic festival organized by Lord Grey, the

---

[3] Copy of Vézina's score in the author's collection.
[4] Copies of sets of parts in the author's collection.

Governor General in 1907. It was subsequently submitted, though not accepted, by his son, Raoul, to the organizing committee of a concert dedicated to the work of Canadian composers that took place at Carnegie Hall on 16 October, 1953.[5]

Montréal was equally blessed with bandmasters who also composed and arranged. Although Ernest Lavigne's piano scores published as part of his series *Choix de Morceaux* [see Fig. 17.6] contained titles that probably originated locally, "Hochelaga Valse," "Espoir Melodie," and "13th Regiment (Marche de la 65éme)", there is no indication as to who the composers are; Lavigne only takes credit as arranger.

Joseph-Laurent Gariépy was a cornet virtuoso and bandmaster of the Victoria Rifles Band in the early 1900s and a contemporary of Lavigne's. Although little is known about him, he produced a series of manuscript sets of parts with titles like *Collége de Montréal, Jolly R.Y.G. Time, Ovila Ski March* and *Polonaise Caprice*. He also wrote a series of *Marches Canadiennes* which featured settings of popular French-Canadian folksongs. Another contemporary was the Belgian born bandmaster François Héraly who moved to Canada in order to lead the Sherbrooke band. From there he relocated to Montréal and at one point conducted the Sohmer Park Band as well as the St. Pierre-Apôtre parish Temperance Band.[6] It was these experiences that provided the inspiration for two of his undated manuscript compositions for band: *Mes Adieux à Sherbrooke* and *Souvenir de Montréal*.

Jean-Joseph Goulet was one of the twenty string players from the Conservatoire de Liège engaged by Ernest Lavigne for the Sohmer Park's ill-fated 1891 season. He remained in Montréal, became first concert master of the Montréal Symphony Orchestra in 1894, conducted "La Musique du Parc Sohmer" from 1911 to 1914 and then increasingly devoted his energies to the wind band. He taught at the Collége Mont St. Louis and for many years was Director of Music of the regimental band of les Fusiliers Mont-Royal. Copies of thirteen Goulet compositions, seven marches, two tangos, a bolero, a minuet, and two solos with band accompaniment show that there is a direct correlation between Goulet's works and the ensembles for which they were written. These include *F.M.R. Marche Régimentaire* [Fusiliers Mont Royal regimental march] (1932), *Les Anciens de Mt. St. Louis* [Old Boys of Mt. St. Louis] (n.d.), *General Gibson's March* (1933) and *Le Prince Beaudoin de Belgique, Marche* [Prince Beaudoin of Belgium, march] (1934). Even his *Le Petit Chardonnet, Caprice pour Piccolo* [The Little Goldfinch, Caprice for Piccolo] (1932) carries the inscription "…execution par Lucien Rochon au Collége de Mt. St. Louis en

---

[5] Jean Philippe Côté Angers, "Vézina" 102.
[6] Gilles Potvin, "Héraly, François J.A.," *Encyclopedia of Music in Canada* (Toronto: University of Toronto Press, 1981) 426.

novembre 1933… [performed by Lucien Rochon at Mt. St. Louis College in November 1933]".[7] Goulet served as president of the Canadian Bandmasters Association from 1933 to 1934 and in this capacity, he would have known bandmasters outside of Québec including Reg Hinchey, a CBA president and conductor of the Belleville Municipal band. That acquaintance may have been the inspiration for his *Souvenir de Belleville, Bolero* (n.d.). Popular in nature, it is a colourful work with some fine examples of soli writing in all voices and challenging technical passages in the upper woodwinds [Fig. 19.3].

Several municipalities in the Montréal region had long been known for their bands and in the first decade of the twentieth century, the bandmasters of two of them, those in St. Jean and St. Hyacinthe were also respected composers. Unlike Vézina, Gariépy and Goulet, these two, Norbert Boisvert and Léon Ringuet appear to be amongst the first Québec bandmasters whose compositions were to appear in published wind band editions. Ironically, their publishers were all American.

Norbert Boisvert was a native of Angeline, in Rouville county, Québec. He trained for a career in dentistry at the Université de Montréal but changed his plans shortly thereafter and moved to Boston to study cornet under T.V. Short and Signor Liberati [see Chap. 4] where he subsequently played with several American bands before returning to his native province.   Upon his return he assumed the leadership of "Le Cercle Philharmonique" in St. Jean sur Richelieu where he died in 1947.[8] While Boisvert was still at the head of one of the country's oldest continuously active community bands, Carl Fischer published four of his compositions between 1910 and 1913: *Richelieu March* (1910), *Salute to Montreal March* (1911), *Fickle Beauty, Polka Caprice* (1911) and *Peace Centennial* (1913). The influence of Sousa is clearly evident in the two marches and the American march king, in return, was obviously aware of Boisvert's work having included *Richelieu March* in one of his own 1910 programs [Fig. 19.4].[9]

Unlike Norbert Boisvert, Léon Ringuet began his musical studies early, trained for a career in music, studying both piano and organ in Montréal and in 1880 moved to St. Hyacinthe where he died in 1932. For fifty years he was organist-choirmaster at the cathedral, conducted the Société Philharmonique de St. Hyacinthe [see Fig. 5.2] and served as bandmaster of the 84th Infantry Battalion band.[10] He wrote at least eight published marches for band including *"Hockey" March* (Coleman, 1908), *Jean* (Gaston Ringuet, nd),

---

[7] All works cited in the author's collection.

[8] Robert W. Hoe, jacket notes to *Heritage of the March, Volume 54: Marches of Québec*, La Musique du Royal 22e Régiment/LCol C.A. Villeneuve (Robert W. Hoe Foundation: Heritage of the March, nd)

[9] Paul E. Bierley, correspondence with author, 17 March 2002.

[10] Gilles Potvin, "Ringuet, Léon," *Encyclopedia of Music in Canada* (Toronto: University of Toronto Press, 1981) 811.

Joliette March (Missud, 1903) and *Philharmonic March* (Fischer, 1900).[11]   There can be little doubt that his association with the Société Philharmonique provided the inspiration for titles like "Philharmonic", or "Joliette", the name of a thriving community with its own band north of Montréal.   If the reader is Canadian, the name "Hockey" requires no explanation whatsoever [Fig. 19.5].

Jean-Josaphat Gagnier was born in 1885 in Montréal, the oldest of twenty-seven children of whom seven were professional musicians.   In 1913 he accepted the position of Director of Music of a militia unit, the Canadian Grenadier Guards Band.   He was to hold this appointment until 1947.[12]   Under his leadership this ensemble attracted the city's finest musicians and it performed locally, on radio and was a guest band at Toronto's CNE "Music Days" on three separate occasions.[13]   He was a prolific composer writing for band as well as orchestra, small ensembles, choir and solo voice.   Those compositions for band preserved in manuscript form, of which there are no fewer than nine, were intended for performance by a skilled ensemble, presumably his own, especially his *Eglogue II "Pan aux Pieds de Chèvre [Goat footed Pan]"* (1932) which is scored for full band plus harp and celesta.   Four of Gagnier's works for wind band were published, all by American publishers: *Hands Across the Border, March* (Remick, 1939), *Skip Along March* (Fischer, 1934), *Toronto Bay, Valse* (Fischer, 1933) and *La Dame de Coeur, Overture* (Fischer, 1935).   These last two are worthy of note; the first because of its connection to Toronto and the second because it reflects Gagnier's growing interest in the field of music for a wider audience including school bands.   The dedication to *Toronto Bay, Valse* [Fig. 19.6] reads "…respectfully dedicated to the citizens of Toronto, Ontario, Canada.".   From its lilting introduction marked *A la barcarolle* to the valse themes with their reliance on a broad spectrum of solo, soli and tutti textures, *Toronto Bay* is a concert work firmly rooted in nineteenth century form yet intended for popular twentieth century tastes.   *La Dame de Coeur, Overture* [Fig. 19.7] on the other hand, "…was conceived with band competitions in mind…[and] was premiered at the American Bandmasters Association convention in Toronto in 1934."[14]   It is a highly dramatic work, semi-descriptive in character in which Gagnier demonstrates his mastery of compositional technique.   His themes are subjected to a variety of transformations involving changing metres, movement to related keys as

---

[11] William H. Rehrig, *The Heritage Encyclopedia of Band Music: Composers and their Music*, Vol. 2, ed. Paul E. Bierley (Westerville, Ohio: Integrity Press, 1991), 633.

[12] Gabrielle Bourbonnais, "Notes biographiques," *Inventaire sommaire du fonds J.J. Gagnier* (Montréal : Bibliothèque nationale du Québec, 1989) 11-12.

[13] Ed. Terziano, ed. *The Little Town Band That Grew and Grew* (Huntsville, ON: Forester Press, 1986) 31.

[14] Timothy Maloney, ed., *Music for Winds I: Bands* (Ottawa: Canadian Musical Heritage Society, 1998) xiv.

well as contrasting instrumental combinations. *La Dame de Coeur* is a major concert work that places Gagnier, the Montrealer, at the forefront of the bandmaster-composers of his generation in Québec, his only real competition coming from his fellow founding member of the American Bandmasters Association downriver in Québec City.

Joseph Vézina's successor in 1912 as Director of Music of Québec's permanent force "B" Battery Band was Charles O'Neill. He remained as its leader until his retirement from the Canadian Army in 1937 and although he composed a significant body of published music for wind band during that period, it is unlikely that it was all intended initially for just this group. His earliest published score was *Land of the Maple and Beaver* (Hawkes, 1918), a patrol featuring settings of "O Canada" and "Vive la Canadienne". He wrote several other works while still in uniform including two marches, *Emblem* (Waterloo, 1930) and *Nulli Secundus* (Waterloo, 1931) as well as the whimsical Entr'acte *Mademoiselle Coquette* (Fischer, 1933). Perhaps his best-known work during this period and one that would have definitely been associated with the Royal 22nd Regiment Band was *Souvenir de Quebec* (Fischer, 1930) [Fig. 19.8]. A medley of French-Canadian folksongs very much in the tradition of Vézina's *Mosaique* and Laurendeau's *Laurentian Echoes*, O'Neill's treatment of his melodic materials moves beyond mere functional arrangement into the realm of composition. He treats each folksong in ways that reflects both the meaning of the lyrics and enhances the musical content through the use of a wide variety of compositional techniques. His artistry was a turning point in the treatment of Canadian folksongs in band music and helped set the stage for those who would follow including Howard Cable and Morley Calvert.

Charles O'Neill was also a gifted arranger and two of his early published arrangements may well have been played by his Royal 22nd Regiment Band: Labelle's *O Canada, Mon Pays, Mes Amours [Land of All that I Love]* (Leo Feist, 1928) and Wagner's *Entry of the Gods into Valhalla* (Fischer, 1930). Jean Baptiste Labelle's (1828-1898) musical setting of words first written by Georges Etienne Cartier, is scored by O'Neill for solo cornet and band [Fig. 19.9]. It is an arrangement that expresses an almost prayer-like sense of longing through the interplay of solo and accompanying voices whereas the Wagner transcription is a faithful reproduction, technically demanding but retaining all the intensity of the original score.

Highly respected as an adjudicator at both the Canadian National Exhibition and at the United States National Band Contests, O'Neill worked for six consecutive years with both

John Philip Sousa and Edwin Franko Goldman.[15]   His reputation for fairness and integrity was such that he was elected president of the American Bandmasters Association in 1933. More than anything, it was his support for the growing school band movement that culminated in a string of works focused on younger musicians: *Silver Cord Overture* (Schirmer, 1933), *Remembrance Serenade* (Fischer, 1935), *Builders of Youth* (Fischer, 1937), *Three Graces Overture* (Fox, 1939), *Aladdin's Lamp* (Fischer, 1940), *Fidelity Overture* (1940), *Nobility Overture* (Remick, 1945) and *Sovereignty Overture* (Remick, 1949).

After his retirement from the army, O'Neill accepted positions at the University of Wisconsin and at the State Teachers College in Potsdam, New York, where he served as director of the music school until 1948.   When he returned to Canada, he spent a further six years as professor of theory and composition at the Royal Conservatory of Music in Toronto before retiring a third and final time in 1954.   He subsequently settled in Québec City where he died in 1964.

Although Charles O'Neill also wrote for orchestra, small ensembles and choirs, his main focus was the wind band for which he composed no fewer than twenty-four published scores.   These included marches (of which two, *Marche "Royal 22eme"* and *RCMP March* remain the official regimental marches of their respective units/service), ten overtures, entr'actes, serenades, a fantasy as well as numerous arrangements.   One of the most obvious measures of his popularity was that these compositions were published by at least seven publishing houses in both Canada and the United States: Waterloo, Fischer, Rubank, Remick, Boston, Schirmer and Fox.[16]   Not only was he recognized for the quality of his work in support of wind bands, he was also favourably compared to many of the most outstanding wind band composers of his time.   His *Builders of Youth Overture* was "…written expressly for school bands" and dedicated to "…the school music directors and supervisors of the United States of America."[17]   It alone proved to be so popular that it was performed at least four times by the Goldman Band between 1938 and 1941.[18]   One of these was at a concert on 19 July, 1938, that was dedicated exclusively to the

---

[15] Victor Falardeau and Jean Parent, *La Musique du Royal 22ᵉ Régiment : 50 Ans d'Histoire* (1922-1972) (Québec : Editions Garneau, 1976) 53.
[16] Rehrig, *Heritage,* 566.
[17] Charles O'Neill, "Introductory notes" to *Builders of Youth Overture* (New York: Carl Fischer, Inc., 1937)
[18] Rita Schmidt, e-mail correspondence with author 07 March 2002.

performance of original works for wind band by such names Holst, Wagner, Respighi, Strauss, Prokofiev as well as O'Neill and Goldman himself.[19]

It is probable that there were other Québec bandmaster-composers whose works have not been included in this chapter. Their compositions may exist only in manuscript form or were self-published and have not as yet been uncovered. One example of this latter scenario is an unknown musician, J.H. Larivière. He self-published five marches in 1908, possibly in celebration of the province's tercentenary. Québec roots are clearly evident in the titles: *Marche Au Fort Chambly, La Citadelle de Québec, Marche Je Me Souviens, Marche Sur Le Richelieu* and *Marche Sur L'Yamaska*.[20]

Québec's contribution to the creation of a Canadian wind band literature (especially if the works of L.P. Laurendeau are included), was enormous, out of all proportion to its population. Equally important was the influence Québec based musicians had on their counterparts in English Canada. Most didn't act in isolation but freely shared their enthusiasm and skills with bandmasters across the country.

The English Canadian Bandmasters

On May 8, 1974, a resident of Bathurst, N.B., wrote a letter to what was to become the Music Division at the National Library of Canada. He wished to inform library personnel that he had acquired a "Score Book" written by William E. Delaney, bandmaster of the 75th Battalion Band of Lunenburg, N.S., dated from October 21, 1884 to December 31, 1891 with some entries dating to as late as 1908. The writer went on to describe the contents which included sixteen hand written compositions for wind bands of eighteen to twenty-four musicians. Of these, thirteen were listed as being composed by Delaney himself, five being of a patriotic nature: *Our Canadian Heroes* (n.d.), *Hail: Empire Not Obscured by Sunset* (1898), *Prince Tommy* (n.d.), *Our Citizen Soldiers, March* (1899) and *Fair Canada Valse* (n.d.).[21] The whereabouts of the score book itself is now unknown but the list sheds some light on the work of at least one bandmaster in the Maritimes at the end of the nineteenth century. Band leaders in smaller communities often had to write for their own ensembles especially when they required literature of a patriotic or dedicatory nature.

---

[19] Douglas Stotter, "The Repertoire and Programs of Edwin Frank Goldman and the Goldman Band," *Journal of Band Research* 36:2 (2001) 13.

[20] All works in the author's collection.

[21] Copy of the letter provided to the author by Dr. S. Timothy Maloney, Head Music Division, National Library of Canada, July 1991.

One other bandmaster who wrote extensively for his own ensemble was Sergeant Harry L. Walker, NWMP. He assumed the leadership of the Regina depot band in 1891. Born in 1840, he originally came west with the Wolseley Expedition in 1870 and had been a bandmaster in Winnipeg prior to joining the force in 1878.[22] At one point he left the NWMP and from 1887 to 1891 directed community bands in both Qu'Appelle and Moose Jaw. On his re-enlistment in Regina, he found himself with an ensemble that rarely exceeded fifteen musicians. In almost complete isolation while on the prairies he was forced to write or arrange much of the music played by the bands he led. Contemporary press accounts dating from 1874 to 1893, in the *Winnipeg Free Press* and later in the *Regina Leader* and the *Regina Standard*, suggest that he composed over thirty-nine works for band consisting primarily of popular forms of the day: waltzes, marches and quadrilles.[23] Most of his manuscript compositions have yet to be discovered but two appear to have been published: *Riders of the Plains Waltz* and *Dinsmore Galop* [Fig. 19.10].

Unlike in Québec, the number of manuscript compositions available for study from English Canadian bandmasters is limited. By the last decade of the nineteenth century increasing numbers of English Canadian bandmasters were able to find publishers for their music. Perhaps because of the burgeoning American band music market, publishers, both Canadian and American were eager to find composers to fill their catalogues.

Ironically, one of the country's earliest bandmaster-composers made an international reputation for himself not as a bandmaster nor as a composer but as a renowned virtuoso. His name was Herbert L. Clarke. Born in Woburn, Massachusetts, in 1867, Clarke's family moved to Toronto in 1880 when his father was appointed organist-choirmaster at Jarvis Street Baptist Church. One year after his arrival, the self-taught cornetist was accepted into the last chair position of the Queen's Own Rifles Band.[24] By 1886 he occupied the solo cornet position and within two years had been engaged to teach and conduct the Taylor Safe Works and Heintzman Piano Company bands in Toronto. It was while he was still in the city that his name first appears as an arranger on two marches: *Orange March* (Whaley, Royce & Co.,1890) and *12th of July March* (Whaley, Royce & Co., 1890).

---

[22] Jack Kopstein and Ian Pearson, *The Heritage of Canadian Military Music* (St. Catharines, ON: Vanwell Publishing Ltd., 2002) 158.

[23] Professor H. Bruce Lobaugh, University of Regina, interview with the author, 12 July 1994.

[24] Edward B. Moogk, "Clarke, Herbert L.," *Encyclopedia of Music in Canada* (Toronto: University of Toronto Press, 1981) 200. It is worth noting that the age limit for entry into the militia at the time was eighteen. Clarke must have made a very favourable impression.

Shortly thereafter he returned to the U.S. and by 1891, at the age of twenty-four, was cornet soloist with Gilmore's band. Two years later he was holding the same chair in Sousa's band. Herbert L. Clarke spent the next two and a half decades in America establishing his reputation as the foremost North American cornet virtuoso of his generation. He composed over thirty solos, duets and trios with band accompaniment, eighteen marches and six other works during his lifetime of which six were completed while he was engaged as conductor of the Anglo-Canadian Leather Company Band in Huntsville, Ontario, from 1918 to 1923.[25] One of these, *Flirtations, Trio for Three Cornets* (Fillmore, 1923) may well have been written to include Clarke's patron, the businessman Charles Orlando Shaw, as one of the soloists [Fig. 19.11]. Understandably enough, he was the intended soloist for many of his works and Sousa programmed no fewer than twenty-five of Clarke's compositions a total of 155 times between 1892 and 1919.[26]

Throughout his time in Huntsville, Clarke continued to write and arrange including a complete transcription of Tchaikovsky's "Danse de la Fée Dragée" [Dance of the Sugarplum Fairy] from the *Nutcracker Suite*. Although he was born and died in the United States, Herbert L. Clarke's contribution to music in Canada was substantial and he more than satisfies the conditions necessary to be considered "Canadian." He was performer, teacher, arranger, composer as well as conductor and the wind band was at the centre of all his musical endeavours.

By 1894, the name Arthur Wellesley Hughes begins to appear on band music published both in Canada and the United States. Born in the Kingston area of eastern Ontario in 1870, Hughes left home early and by 1890 appears briefly as bandmaster of the Perth Citizens Band.[27] From there he left to lead the Sudbury Citizens band and then disappears only to reappear in 1912 as a musician with the Downie and Wheeler Circuses in the U.S..[28] World War One brought him home to Canada and in 1915 he was serving as bandmaster of the 76th Battalion Band (C.E.F.).[29] After the war he returned to the United States once again playing horn and steam calliope with a succession of circuses culminating with two years in the Ringling Brothers, Barnum and Bailey Circus from 1924 to 1926.[30]

[25] Willliam H. Rehrig, *The Heritage Encyclopedia of Band Music: Composers and Their Music*, Vol. 1 ed. by Paul E. Bierley (Westerville, Ohio: Integrity Press, 1991) 146.
[26] Paul E. Bierley, letter to the author, 17 March 2002.
[27] Daphne Overhill, *Sound the Trumpet: The Story of the Bands of Perth 1852-2002* (Perth, ON: A. Rosenthal, 2002) 53.
[28] Rehrig, *Heritage*, 359.
[29] Kopstein and Pearson, *Heritage*, 46.
[30] Rehrig, *Heritage*, 359.

For the purposes of this chapter our study will limit itself to those works Hughes composed prior to the end of the Great War while he was still serving as a Canadian army bandmaster.   They consist of four dances, seventeen marches and three undated arrangements.   Of these the earliest authenticated date is for the march *Reign of Peace* (Whaley, Royce & Co., 1894).   For the next twenty years he would produce a succession of marches clearly inspired by his activities in Canada with titles such as: *United Empire, March* (Whaley, Royce & Co., 1897), *Hail! Edward VII, March* (Whaley, Royce & Co., 1901), *In Old Quebec* (Whaley, Royce & Co.,1908), *Fort Garry March* (Whaley, Royce & Co., 1911) [Fig. 19.12] and *Red Deer March* (Whaley, Royce & Co., 1911).   The three undated arrangements, also marches, suggest an association with Ontario's Orange Lodges in the late nineteenth century: *No Surrender, Boyne Water* and *Protestant Boys*.   One of the most stirring of Hughes' marches was *St. Julien*, first published by Cundy in 1918 and re-released by Carl Fischer in 1969.   It is noteworthy for two reasons, the opening theme is in a minor key, unusual for marches of the period and the low brass theme in the trio is both powerful and immediately appealing [Fig. 19.13].

Toronto was home to many fine bands at the start of the twentieth century, none more so than that of the 48th Highland Regiment of Canada.   John Slatter had been appointed its Director of Music in 1896 and remained in the position until his retirement in 1946.   Born in 1864 in London, England, he had been a band boy in the Royal Navy at age eleven and by age seventeen was playing euphonium with the First Life Guards Band.[31]   In 1884 he emigrated to the United States and joined the Victor Herbert Orchestra in New York City. He was playing with the Detroit Symphony Orchestra in 1896 when he was offered the bandmastership of the 48th.   Although not as prolific as Delaney, Hughes, Walker or Clarke he nevertheless composed or arranged ten works for band.   His marches especially reflect his British military associations: *Cock O' the North* (R.S. Williams, n.d.), *Rise Sons of William* (Waterloo, n.d.) and *Under the British Flag* (R.S. Williams, 1908).   He arranged at least four other marches.   Perhaps the best known of which was Alexander Muir's *The Maple Leaf Forever*, included in the *National Airs and Regimental Marches Band Book* published by R.S. Williams in 1910.

Slatter's one concert work, *Canadian Patrol*, was and remains one of the most unique compositions in the historical Canadian band repertory.   As noted previously, "Patrols" were a popular compositional form in the early twentieth century with no fewer than three

---

[31] George W. Beal, *Family of Volunteers: An Illustrated History of the 48th Highlanders of Canada* (Toronto: Robin Brass Studio, 2001) 118.   There is some confusion as to what he played.   Beal, who is a non-musician writing a regimental history, states cornet, Jack Kopstein, author of Slatter's entry in the *Encyclopedia of Music in Canada* is sure it was euphonium and trombone.

bearing the title *Canadian Patrol*: those by Herbert L. Clarke (MS, 1895), John Slatter (R.S. Williams, 1911) and Albert Williams (Boosey & Co., 1911). Slatter's version, subtitled "The Passing of a Jolly Canadian Sleighing Party," follows the formula closely integrating a number of Canadian folksongs into the overall texture which also includes an original theme meant to portray an outdoor winter scene. The Canadian content consists of "Vive la Canadienne," a short reference to "O Canada" and brief fragments of "Maple Leaf Forever". It also includes "British Grenadiers," "St. Patrick's Day" and "The Campbells are Coming," all of which were intended to depict the English-speaking heritages of Canada's population at the time. It is the recurring melodies that are most striking: "Merrily We Roll Along" and "Jingle Bells." The final *decrescendo* features a contrapuntal treatment of "Jingle Bells" and the "Maple Leaf Forever" in the oboe and clarinets followed by a *pianissimo* melodic statement integrating "Merrily We Roll Along," "Maple Leaf Forever" and "O Canada." Reflecting the patriotic sentiments of the day and his own British roots, Slatter appends an eight-bar coda in the form of a *tutti* statement of "Rule Britannia" [Fig. 19.14]. Ironically the presence of "Jingle Bells" in the thematic mix would automatically identify John Slatter's *Canadian Patrol* as a "seasonal" or "holiday" selection for the modern band director, a role the composer himself probably never intended.

Toronto was also home to the Queen's Own Rifles band conducted by Richard Benjamin Hayward. Like so many of his contemporaries, Hayward was born in England [London, 1874] and joined the British Army as a band boy at the age of twelve. He graduated from the Royal Military School of Music [Kneller Hall] bandmaster's course in 1904 and served as the director of the Band of the Royal Irish Rifles. He retired from active service in 1919, moved to Canada in 1921 and accepted the position of Director of Music of the Queen's Own Rifles Band in Toronto, an appointment he held until 1928. A founding member of the American Bandmasters Association, he served on its board of directors for five years and was elected its president in 1940-1941. He had eleven works for band published in the United States by both Carl Fischer and Schirmer, including three overtures, *Corsair's Bride* (Fischer, 1937), *Mountain Valleys* (Fischer) and *The Norsemen* (Schirmer, 1940) [Fig. 19.15].[32] He also composed a cornet solo *Anita* (Fischer, 1935), a suite, *In a Spanish City* (Fischer, 1933), *Eventide Reverie* (Fischer, 1933), *Three Characteristic Dances* (Fischer, 1934), a march and a descriptive piece published by Boosey & Hawkes entitled *Zingaresca*. There was one undated manuscript composition, *Fantasie "Sabbath Evening in Camp"* as well as two "novelties", *The Band That Jack Built*

---

[32] Rehrig, *Heritage*, 328.

(Fischer, 1937) and *Barnyard Competition* (Fischer). Just as the name "novelty" suggests, these last two were light hearted descriptive pieces intended entirely for entertainment purposes.

Although not technically a bandmaster, William Ramsey Spence's long association with his home town band, the Perth Citizens Band, earns him a place in this chapter. Born in Montréal in 1859, he studied piano and organ with W.O. Pelletier and Vichtendahl. From 1880-1897 as well as 1901-1911 he was "...organist at two Anglo-Catholic churches in that city. He was also a fine cellist and at different times during these periods was a member of both the Montreal Symphony Orchestra and a professional chamber group."[33] From 1911 until 1913 [possibly 1914] Spence served as organist to the court of Emperor Franz Josef II in Vienna. Growing international tensions that eventually led to the outbreak of World War One forced him to return to Canada. With the support of his brother, he obtained a position as organist and choirmaster at St. James Anglican Church in Perth, a small agricultural community southwest of Ottawa where he remained until his death in 1946. Over his lifetime, Spence wrote a hundred and ninety-two works for choir, piano and organ which appeared in editions published by Oliver Ditson, Theodore Presser and Arthur P. Schmidt.[34] The majority were choral compositions including ninety-seven anthems, canticles and a cantata and almost all were of a religious nature. He also composed five unpublished pieces for band. These consisted of four marches, *Fraternity*, *International Parade*, *Marche Militaire*, *To the Front* and one waltz. All five were written for the Perth Citizens Band.

It is the waltz, *Moonlight on the Rideau* that is worthy of mention.[35] It was written in 1936 and arranged for the Perth Citizens Band by J.J. Gagnier of Montréal. Gagnier must have been impressed with the work because he made a second arrangement, copies of which are on deposit at La Bibliothèque nationale de Québec in Montréal. This second arrangement, copied professionally, must have been used for recording/broadcasting purposes because each part is stamped *Société Radio-Canada* [Canadian Broadcasting Corporation]. It is a work of refined simplicity with long sustained legato lines. The scoring of the Trio, which progresses from a delicate *pianissimo* to a *fortissimo tutti* by means of the addition and manipulation of instrumental ranges is somewhat reminiscent of Ravel's *Bolero*.

---

[33] Patricia Bernard Williamson, "William Ramsey Spence: A Case Study" (M.A. thesis, Carleton University, 1993) 2.

[34] Ibid., 7.

[35] "Rideau" refers to the Rideau Canal, a branch of which runs through Perth.

The bandmaster composers listed above were by no means the only ones. They have been included primarily because their compositions, whether in published or manuscript form are still readily accessible in militia or community band libraries, museum collections or provincial archives. Many other bandmasters produced only one or two compositions, usually marches, few of which were ever published. Those that were include *Maple City March* (Waterloo, 1938) by Sidney Chamberlain, bandmaster of the Chatham Kilties band and former Ottawa bandmaster Arthur Clappé's *G.G.F.G. Two Step* (Clappé, 1906).

It wasn't just bandmasters writing music for their own ensembles. As the market for band music grew during the last decades of the nineteenth century, composers of all genres joined in if publishers were prepared to pay. The well-established British Military Band Journals weren't generally inclined to seek out Canadian contributors, as they relied on their own large supply of composers and arrangers. It was the American publishing houses and then our first Canadian ones that nurtured an ever-expanding body of literature for wind band.

CHAPTER NINETEEN GALLERY

Figure 19.1. First page, solo piccolo part to the author's revision of *Première Neige* [First snowfall], *Polka* by Joseph Vézina, 1889. Of the composer's three works for solo instrument and band, this is the only one that provides two options, for solo cornet or solo flute/piccolo. The 1880s were Vézina's most productive decade as a composer possibly because of his association with the full time "B" Battery Band, R.C.A. [see Fig. 4.2]. Source: author's collection.

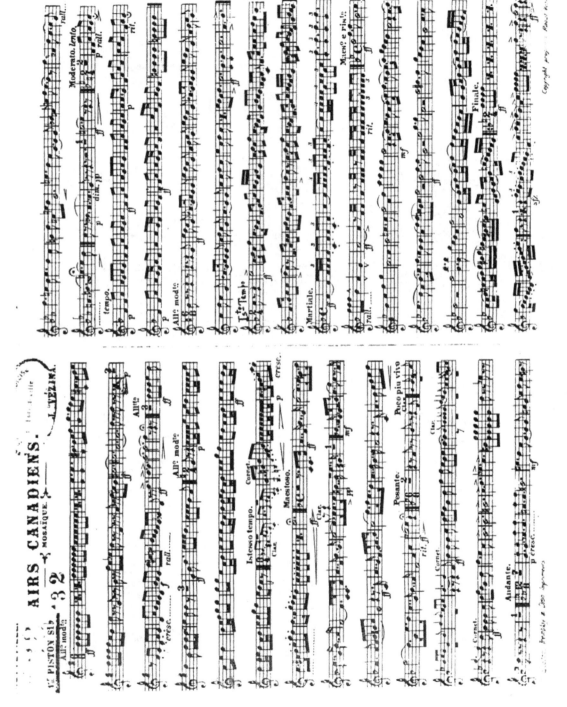

336

Figure 19.2. First cornet part to *Mosaïque sur les Airs Canadiens* by Joseph Vézina, 1880, in a published edition by his son Raoul Vézina. The concluding measures, starting with the *Martiale* fanfares [page 2] introduced a new "chant national" by Calixa Lavallée entitled "O Canada." Source: author's collection.

Figure 19.3.   First clarinet part to *Souvenir de Belleville* by J.J. Goulet, arranged by E. R. Hinchey, c. 1935.   Belgian born Goulet was one of the string players invited by Ernest Lavigne to join the Sohmer Park Band for the ill-fated 1891 season.   He remained in Montréal and became the first concertmaster of the Montréal Symphony Orchestra.   Despite being a fine violinist, he devoted most of his career to wind bands as conductor, teacher and composer, serving at one point as president of the Canadian Bandmasters Association (1933-1934).   E.R. Hinchey was one of the early members of the Belleville Kilties Band (1908-1910) and director of Belleville's municipal band during the 1930s.   Source: author's collection.

Figure 19.4.   Solo cornet (conductor) part to *Richelieu March* by Norbert Boisvert, published by Carl Fischer in 1910. Source: author's collection.

Figure 19.5.   Solo cornet part to *"Hockey" March* by Leon Ringuet, published by Harry Coleman, Philadelphia, 1908.   Source: author's collection.

Figure 19.6. First page to the solo or 1st cornet part of *Toronto Bay Valse Scherzo* by Jean Josephat Gagnier, published by Carl Fischer in 1933. Gagnier and his Canadian Grenadier Guards Band were frequent visitors to the Canadian National Exhibition and its "Music Days". Source: author's collection.

Figure 19.7. First page of the solo and 1st cornet part to *La Dame de Coeur* [Queen of Hearts] *Overture* by Jean Josephat Gagnier, published by Carl Fischer in 1935. The work was premiered at the annual convention of the American Bandmasters Association held in Toronto in 1934. The composer's manipulation of the work's three principal themes, through the use of changing metres, movement to related keys and contrasting solo, soli and *tutti* passages creates a richly textured concert work. Source: author's collection.

Figure 19.8. First page of the conductor's score to *Souvenir de Quebec* by Charles O'Neill, published by Carl Fischer in 1930. Source: author's collection.

Figure 19.9. Solo cornet part *to Land of All That I Love* by J-B Labelle, arranged by Charles O'Neill, published by Leo Feist in 1928. Source: author's collection.

Figure 19. 10. Solo cornet part to "Dinsmore" Galop by Harry Walker, published by Whaley, Royce & Co., 1891. Source: author's collection.

Figure 19.11. First page of the conductor's score to *Flirtations, Trio for Three Cornets* by Herbert L. Clarke, published by Henry Filmore in 1923. Clarke directed the Anglo Canadian Leather Company Band from 1918 to 1923. It is possible that he wrote this work during this period and that one of the other intended soloists may have been his patron, Charles Orlando Shaw. Source: author's collection.

Figure 19.12. Solo cornet part to "Fort Garry" March by Arthur Wellesley Hughes, published by Whaley, Royce & Co., in 1911. Source: author's collection.

Figure 19.13. Solo cornet part to *St. Julien March* by A.W. Hughes, published by Cundy-Bettoney in 1918. Source: author's collection.

Figure 19.14.   Solo cornet part to *Canadian Patrol* by John Slatter, published by the R.S. Williams & Sons Co. in 1911.   The "patrol' format was a popular compositional form in the early twentieth century and Slatter's, with its use of "Jingle Bells" and "Merrily We Roll Along", in addition to "The Maple Leaf Forever" and fragments of "O Canada," is unique in the Canadian wind band repertory.   Source: author's collection.

Figure 19.15. Solo or 1st clarinet part to the *Norsemen Overture* by Richard Benjamin Hayward, published by G. Schirmer in 1940. After retiring from the Canadian Army (militia) in 1928, Hayward continued as the director of wind instrument instruction at the Toronto Conservatory of Music and assumed the leadership of the Toronto Concert Band. A founding member of the American Bandmasters Association along with fellow Canadians J.J. Gagnier and Charles O'Neill [see Fig. 8.13], he served as the association's president from 1940 to 1941. Source: author's collection.

CHAPTER TWENTY

THE PUBLISHERS

Boston, Massachusetts, in the 1880s was alive with the sound of band music. Patrick Gilmore had organised two enormous music festivals in the city in 1869 and 1872 prior to moving to New York and establishing the 22nd Regiment Band. The surrounding New England states were home to a number of outstanding professional bands: the American Band of Providence under the direction of David W. Reeves; the Salem Cadet Band directed by Jean M. Missud and the Brockton Band conducted by Mace Gay.[1] In 1888, the Boston based publisher W.H. Cundy approached one of the city's brightest musical lights to write three band overtures. He was a French Canadian by the name of Calixa Lavallée. Although best known to the modern reader as the composer of our national anthem *O Canada*, Lavallée was a talented musician and gifted writer highly respected by his peers. He was also the first in a long line of Canadian composers who had to either relocate to or publish in the United States to achieve any measure of financial success.

Calixa Lavallée (1842-1891)

Calixa Lavallée was born in Verchères, Québec, where his father, an enthusiastic amateur musician, worked for a time with the organ builder Joseph Casavant and was conductor of the band of the Société Philharmonique de St. Hyacinthe. Lavallée's musical gifts were recognized early on and at the age of thirteen "…he gave his first piano recital at the Theatre Royal in Montréal where his family now made its home."[2] He was a fast learner and though he specialised on the piano he was also "…an accomplished violinist and a creditable cornetist."[3] By the late 1850s, the urge to travel prompted him to relocate to New Orleans where he was engaged as a tour accompanist. With the start of the American Civil War, he enlisted in the Union Army as a musician and was quickly appointed bandmaster of a Rhode Island regimental band. His military service was short lived and by 1863 he had returned to Montréal to teach and perform. Ever restless, he

---

[1] William Carter White, *Military Music in America* (New York: Exposition Press, 1944) 111. It is worth noting that both Jean M. Missud and Mace Gay were also active in the band music publishing business, and that Mace Gay in particular was an early sponsor of L.P. Laurendeau and A.W. Hughes.
[2] Helmut Kallmann, *A History of Music in Canada 1534-1914* (Toronto: University of Toronto press, 1960) 134.
[3] Ibid., 134.

headed south again in 1865 to work as a touring musician for five years before returning to Canada. With the financial support of a group of friends he left in 1873 for Paris where he studied at the Paris Conservatory with Bazin, Boieldieu, Jr. and Marmontel.[4] Once home, his experiences in France had convinced him of the need for a national "conservatoire" for the training of musicians and he worked tirelessly to achieve this end. He received little official support and despite winning local acclaim for his composition of the French Canadian "chant national" *O Canada* in 1880, he realised that his efforts were futile in the face of bureaucratic indifference. That same year, at the age of thirty-eight, he left one final time for the United States. Settling in Boston, he was quickly appointed organist of the Roman Catholic cathedral and acting director of the Petersilea Conservatory.[5] Ironically, it was only in the U.S. where his talents as church musician, teacher, performer and composer were fully appreciated. By 1887, he had been elected president of the American Music Teachers National Association and was considered a champion of American music. His health had always been frail and he died after a lengthy illness on 31 January, 1891.

Calixa Lavallée was a prolific composer who wrote at least three comic operas, two orchestral suites, a symphony with chorus, three band overtures, over twenty works for piano, music for choir, solo voice and a small number of works for chamber ensemble. Excluding those that remained in manuscript form, the remainder were published in Boston. He had a gift for writing lyrical and accessible melodies in all genres, sacred and secular, choral and instrumental and although his creative output was primarily of a lighter nature, it was nevertheless recognised by his contemporaries as the work of a "…genuinely creative artist, a pure musical genius."[6]

Lavallée's three band overtures commissioned by W.H. Cundy in 1888 were *The Bridal Rose*, *King of Diamonds* and *The Golden Fleece*. Of these, *The Bridal Rose* appears to have been the most popular having been performed by Sousa on at least one occasion in 1893 [Fig. 20.1].[7] One further measure of its popularity is that it has been revised and re-released at least once, in 1931 by Cundy-Bettoney. More recently, Howard Cable revised *King of Diamonds* (Severn Music, n.d.) in an edition for modern Canadian wind band.[8] All three overtures are "light classic" in character; they display skilful use of harmony and rhythm with melodic lines that are immediately appealing and highly operatic in nature.

---

[4] Ibid., 136.
[5] Ibid., 139.
[6] Augustus Stephen Vogt as cited in Kallmann, *A History*, 143.
[7] Paul E. Bierley, letter to author 17 March 2002.
[8] The author provided Howard Cable with a set of parts from a 1914 arrangement in August 2014.

Two other Lavallée works originally composed for other media have also been arranged for band. His *Marche Indienne* (Ditson, 1891) first appeared as part of a "melodramatic musical satire" entitled *TIQ* in 1883 and that same year the *Mouvement à la Pavane* was published for piano solo by White, Smith and Company.[9] This second work was arranged for band by Montréal's J.J. Gagnier for an all Lavallée concert given by the Canadian Grenadier Guards Band on 13 July, 1933 [Fig. 20.2]. The performance was part of the celebrations surrounding the return of the composer's body, forty years after his death, to rest in the city's Church of Notre Dame.

By the early to mid 1890s the names of Canadian composers begin to appear in band music published in the United States by Mace Gay, W. H. Cundy, Oliver Ditson, John Church, Jean Missud and Harry Coleman. Examples include A.W. Hughes' *Salute to Mars, March* (Gay, 1895) and *Corinthian March* (Gay, 1895). L.P. Laurendeau, before he was fully engaged with Fischer, was also associated with several other American publishing houses. Cundy published *Advance Guard March* (1893), *Company B March* (1892), *The Lime-Kiln Club's Soiree* (1891) and *Shores of the St. Lawrence* (1893). Mace Gay released *Brocktonian* March (1894) and *The Conqueror March* (1894) and Harry Coleman, *Country Life, A Bucolic Sketch* (1896) and *Manfred March* (1894).[10]

In 1888, the Toronto firm of Whaley, Royce & Company was established. Within two years it was printing its own music as part of a growing range of services that included '…band instruments, pianos and organs, sheet music, and general musical merchandise; …the manufacture of brass and percussion instruments [and] published music."[11] As noted previously some of its earliest band scores were originally produced to be performed in conjunction with Ontario's Orange Lodges and three of the names associated with these arrangements have already been discussed in previous chapters, Herbert L. Clarke, John Slatter and A.W. Hughes. In addition to the early Orange marches the company also published in 1890 the *Imperial Band Book No. 1*; a collection of pieces for band that included *Greeting to Toronto Polka* by Herbert L. Clarke.[12] By the end of the decade the firm had published music for band by T. Baugh, *Canadian Medley March* (1890), Harry L. Walker, *Dinsmore Galop* (1891) [see Fig. 19.10], H.L. Clarke and A.W. Hughes' *Reign of Peace March* (1894), *United Empire March* (1897) and *Hail! Edward VII March* (1901).

[9] Timothy Maloney, ed., *Music for Winds I: Bands,* vol.21 (Ottawa, ON: The Canadian Musical Heritage Society, 1998) xii. A revised edition of the score to Gagnier's arrangement is included in this anthology.
[10] Copies of all titles in the author's collection.
[11] Helmut Kallmann, "Whaley, Royce & Co.," *Encyclopedia of Music in Canada* (Toronto: University of Toronto Press, 1981) 994.
[12] Maloney, *Music for Winds I*, xiii. A revised edition of the score is included in the anthology.

The first decade of the twentieth century saw Whaley, Royce & Co. rightfully claiming to be "Canada's Greatest Music House". It carried band music from British and American publishers as well as its own, which were generally limited to selections, mostly marches, of a patriotic nature. A.W. Hughes was a major contributor: *Dufferin March* (1910), *Etoile March* (n.d.), *In Old Quebec March* (1908), *Fort Garry March* (1911) and *Red Deer March* (1911). A front cover published by the company in the 1930s contains a list of twenty-one "PATRIOTIC MARCHES-75¢ Net Each Number".[13] It is probably safe to assume that many of these were written by Canadians for Canadian bands. The back cover contains lists of available overtures, operatic selections, fantasias on popular and national airs and waltzes but these are drawn almost entirely from British and American military band journals of the period. By the time this cover appeared however, Whaley, Royce & Company had lost much of its market dominance to newer generations of Canadian band music publishers.

Following Whaley, Royce & Co., was Toronto based R.S. Williams & Sons, Limited. Although the firm's list of band publications was far more modest than that of Whaley, Royce & Co., it was no less influential. With John Slatter as their primary contributor, R.S. Williams focused primarily on the military market with titles such as *Cock O' the North, Scottish March* (1908) and *Under the British Flag* (1908). The company's most significant contribution came in 1911 with the publication of the band book *National Airs and Regimental Marches* [Fig. 20.3]. The vast majority of the contents are regimental marches, but the first page includes a "General Salute", an "Inspection March" and an arrangement of "The Maple Leaf Forever." The "Inspection March" was in fact one of the first band arrangements of *O Canada* published in English Canada and along with *The Maple Leaf Forever* arrangement would be performed by generations of military and cadet bands into the twenty-first century [Fig. 20.4].[14]

Charles Frederick Thiele (1884-1954)

By far the most successful Canadian band music publishing enterprise of the twentieth century began in earnest in 1919 with the arrival in Waterloo, Ontario, of Charles Frederick Thiele. Two years later he formed the Waterloo Music Company and the key to the firm's

---

[13] The most effective way of dating the document is contained in the list of "Marches and Two-Steps" at the top of the page. *Standard of St. George* by Alford, which appears at the bottom of the middle column, was written in 1930 but Alford's final marches, *By Land and Sea* (1941), *Army of the Nile* (1941) and *Eagle Squadron* (1942) do not.
[14] The author served in the King's Own Calgary Regiment Band as both Assistant Director and Bandmaster from 1990 to 2005. Both arrangements were played regularly.

initial success was the growing demand for "Music Cue Sheets", prepared for silent movies that enabled theatre musicians to provide appropriate background music for the latest Hollywood releases.   Thiele recognized immediately the possibilities in Canada and organized his newly-established business accordingly.   Sensing intuitively, however, that "…it was a business that was limited in scope…he began to broaden his field and import sheet music from as many as twenty different music publishers in the United States: music for orchestra, band, organ and choir."[15]   His experience with bands in particular had taught him the difficulty in obtaining recent publications of band music from either the U.S. or Britain so in 1925, "…Thiele made the monumental decision to become a publisher of music, by Canadian composers."[16]

Thiele began modestly enough with a series of classroom texts entitled *The Singing Period* and *Songs for Today* that were rapidly accepted by educators across the country. Then in 1928, he accepted the financial responsibility for two ailing publications, the *Canadian Bandsman and Musician* and *Musical Canada*.   He agreed to become the managing director of both and promptly amalgamated them under the name of *Musical Canada*.   It was a shrewd business move and with this arrangement in place, his company was well protected from the double shock of the 1929 Wall Street crash and the advent of the "Talkies".

> While Thiele's takeover of the Canadian magazines *Canadian Bandsman* and
> *Musical Canada* were correctly described as an act of generosity motivated by a
> singular desire to assist Canadian musicians, it could be argued that his generosity
> had also been motivated by business interests. A born entrepreneur, he now
> controlled two of the most influential and popular musical magazines read by the
> majority of Canadian musicians and musical educators. Promotion of sheet
> music, instruction books and instruments sold by his company could now be made
> through the medium of *Musical Canada*.[17]

Under his baton, the Waterloo Musical Society Band was recognized as one of the finest community bands in Canada [see Chap. 7] and it was inevitable that in an environment as rich in band activities as Ontario was at the time new compositions would appear.   Thiele

---

[15] John Mellor, C.F.Thiele: Father of Canadian Band Music (Waterloo, ON: Melco History Series, 1988) 30.
[16] Ibid., 31.
[17] Ibid., 36.

hired a staff writer in the person of the legendary A.W. Hughes, who had already written scores of works for Whaley, Royce & Co., as well as American publishers Cundy, Barnhouse and King. From 1930 until 1934 Hughes produced eight titles for Waterloo including *Specialty Overture* (1931) [Fig. 20.5], *Novelty Overture* (n.d.) and *Rose Festival Waltz* (1931) as well as five marches: *Canada, Land of Liberty* (1932), *Canadian Patriots* (1930), *Hospitality* (1930), *In the Lead* (1930) and *Mediterranean* (n.d.). Charles O'Neill, a personal friend and fellow founding member of the Canadian Bandmasters Association in 1931 also contributed at least three marches, *Emblem* (1930), *Nulli Secundus* (1931), and perhaps one of the finest Canadian marches ever written, *Mon Ami* (1943). Increasingly, concert works were being added to the catalogue. O'Neill also wrote *In the Moonlight, Serenade* (with bell obbligato) (1927) [Fig. 20.6] and *Knight Errant Overture* (1928).

As one of the founding members of the Canadian Bandmasters Association, Thiele actively encouraged and supported his fellow bandmasters in their own compositional efforts. He published a march, *Maple City March* (1938) and an overture, *Friendship Border* (1949) by Sidney Chamberlain, bandmaster of the Chatham Kilties Band as well as Reg Hinchey's *International Patrol* (1946) and *Marche Athene* (1943). Other contributors included Bill Clancy, bandmaster of the Brantford Band, *Carleton March* (1943); Odile Hudlot, bandmaster of L'Union Musicale de Trois-Rivières, *Trois-Rivières Tricentenaire* (1936) and *Cap de la Madelaine Tricentenaire* (1951); Fred Moogk's *On Parade March* (1933) and three marches by William Sheppard, bandmaster of the New Hamburg Citizens Band: *Pro Patria March* (1936), *C.B.A. March* (1943) and *Silver Trumpets March* (n.d.)[18].

Thiele himself, both as arranger and composer provided a further ten titles including two concert overtures, *Characteristique* (1938) [Fig. 20.7] and *Veteran* (1934), two medleys, *Land O' the Heather* (1943) and *Land O'the Shamrock* (1941) as well as six marches. The front cover of an undated Waterloo "Band Edition" folio from the period contains listings for fifty titles published by the company including overtures, selections and miscellaneous works. Of these, sixteen were either arranged or composed by Canadians. The Waterloo Music Company was to remain a publishing powerhouse for band music, even after Thiele's death in 1954, well into the 1960s and 1970s.

Another Canadian publisher to emerge in the 1930s, who would also survive into the decades following the Second World War was Toronto's Gordon V. Thompson. Although the original band catalogue contains only four marches composed by Thompson himself

---

[18] All titles cited in the author's collection.

during and after the First World War, the company itself, like the Waterloo Music Company, continued to operate after his death in 1965 with a band series published well into the 1970s. Thompson was born in 1888 and the primary musical influences in his youth were "...singing at the missionary meetings of which his mother was an ardent supporter."[19] His earliest published works, *10 Life Songs* (Revival Publishing Bureau, 1909) were religious in nature but during the First World War he shifted his attention towards the composition of patriotic songs. Without competition from American rivals [the U.S. did not enter the conflict until 1917] these proved to be enormously popular and four were arranged for band: *Where is My Boy Tonight* (1915), *Red Cross Nell and Khaki Jim* (1916), *For the Glory of the Grand Old Flag* (1918) and *Land of Glad Tomorrows* also subtitled *Canada, Our Own Home Land* (1927). These were all released by the American publisher Leo Feist for whom Thompson worked as Canadian representative until he purchased the rights and set up his own company in 1932.

American publishers, like Leo Feist, also contributed to the growing body of literature for band by Canadian composers. Central Canada's big three, J.J. Gagnier, Charles O'Neill and R.B. Hayward, all founding members of the American Bandmasters Association enjoyed widespread name recognition south of the border and it was inevitable that they would pursue opportunities there. As noted in previous chapters all three worked closely with major U.S. publishers including Fischer, Remick, Boston and Schirmer. By the late 1930s the focus of their works began to shift towards an emphasis on the growing school band movement in the United States, a shift best exemplified by O'Neill's *Builders of Youth Overture* (Fischer, 1937) [Fig. 20.8].

Arthur Wellesley Hughes left Canada shortly after the end of the First World War and spent a decade in circus bands in the United States. During this time, he wrote several works inspired by his experiences under the big top, *Circus Echoes Galop* (Barnhouse, 1928) and *Unique Overture* (King, 1929) as well as a number of marches. After leaving the Waterloo Music Company in 1934, he returned to the United States a final time and continued to compose a series of marches for the Cundy-Bettoney Company including *Carry On* (1940), *Our Commonwealth* (1940), *Our Pilot* (1940) and *Veteran Brigade* (1940).

One Canadian composer from the interwar period who went on to making a lasting contribution, right up to the present day, was George Douglas. Born in Glasgow, Scotland, in 1890 he emigrated to Canada and settled in Swan River, Manitoba, where he taught violin and his wife, Beatrice, taught piano. In the 1920s they moved to Winnipeg and

---

[19] Helmut Kallmann, "Thompson, Gordon V.," *Encyclopedia.* 913.

George "...opened up a music store in the ethnic St. John's north end of Winnipeg, hence the St. John's store name."[20] During the Depression he and his wife operated the store and supplemented its income by serving as a local post office outlet.[21] During that time George Douglas also co-wrote two volumes of the *Douglas Band Folio*, published by the Cleveland based Sam Fox Publishing Company (Volume 1, 1929; Volume 2, 1933) [Fig. 20.9]. Between the two volumes, Douglas contributed fifteen works including seven marches, two waltzes, two serenades, one reverie, a galop and two "characteristiques". The *Douglas Band Folios* proved to be popular during the 1930s with titles like *Athabasca March*, *Idle Thoughts Serenade*, *Dance of the Stars Novelette* and *Dawn Break Reverie* [Fig. 20.10].

One other option was to self-publish. During the first decade of the twentieth century at least four composers released band arrangements of their own works: J.H. La Rivière's five marches possibly composed in 1908 in celebration of Québec's tercentenary [see Chap.19]; A. Clappé's *G.G.F.G. Two Step* (1906); Albert Ham's *Canada, Marche Militaire* (1908) and A. Glen Broder's *Ride of the R.N.W.M.P.* (1906) [Fig. 20.10]. The "A" in this last composer's name stands for "Annie," making her work the first example in Canada of published music for band by a female composer. Annie Glen Broder was born in 1857 in Agra, India, the daughter of a British cavalry officer. She was educated as a pianist at the National Training School for Music, Royal College of Music and wrote a highly respected text on accompanying entitled *How to Accompany*. She moved to Canada in 1902 and settled in Calgary in 1903 where she taught piano and became a prominent member of the city's musical establishment. She passed away in Calgary in 1937. The composer deliberately obscured the fact that she was a woman in this self-published work by the use of initials rather than her full name both in the composer and copyright credits. An accomplished musician, she relied on the Toronto bandmaster John Waldron to complete the arrangement for band. The formal structure of the work however, clearly reflects Broder's familiarity with her subject. It is entirely functional, intended to "...accompany the changing cadences of galloping, trotting and cantering horses...".[22] Despite these utilitarian considerations, it is an exciting composition full of melodic and metrical contrasts.

Along with George Douglas, Winnipeg was also home to the Princess Patricia's Canadian Light Infantry Band which in 1924, under the direction of Captain Tommy

---

[20] George Douglas, President of St. John's Music and grandson of George Douglas, letter to author 10 May 1999.

[21] Ibid.

[22] Timothy Maloney, ed. *Music for Winds I: Bands*, vol 21 (Ottawa: The Canadian Musical Heritage Society, 1998) xv. The opening theme and *presto* section parallel the twin movements of walk and canter used by cavalry regiments as part of a formal parade march past.

James, performed at the British Empire Exhibition in London where it premiered a work entitled *Hudson's Bay Company Patrol "IN CANADA"* [Fig. 20.11]. The reception was sufficiently positive for the venerable Hudson's Bay Company to actually publish it under its own name in 1929. Arranged for band by William Delaney, the Lunenburg bandmaster who had relocated to Winnipeg in 1910, *IN CANADA* integrates eight Canadian folk songs into the patrol format so popular during the early twentieth century. The cover page contains a synopsis which reads:

> A descriptive number, depicting the approach, passing by, and gradual disappearance in the distance, of a Fur Brigade of canoes on the Red River, prior to the advent of steam locomotive power in the West. The following songs being sung to the rhythmic swing of the paddles:

> "THE RED RIVER VALLEY."
> "JOHNNY CANUCK."
> "VIVE LA CANADIENNE."
> "THE MAPLE LEAF FOREVER."
> "EN ROULANT MA BOULÉ."
> "ALLOUETTE."
> "THE LAND OF THE MAPLE."
> "CANADIAN BOAT SONG."

> Snatches of the foregoing songs are heard towards the end of the number, which concludes, after a momentary pause, with the inspiring strains of

> "O CANADA."

What makes *IN CANADA* unusual is that unlike all previous Canadian Patrols, including those already cited by H.L. Clarke, John Slatter and Albert Williams, there are no British, Scottish or Irish tunes included to represent the country's English-speaking population. The eight melodies listed above are all native to popular Canadian musical culture, both French and English, as it existed at the time.

Figure 20.1.   First page of the solo cornet part/Conductor to *The Bridal Rose Overture* by Calixa Lavallée, published by W. H. Cundy in 1888. Source: author's collection.

358

Figure 20.2. First Clarinet part to J.J. Gagnier's arrangement for band of *Mouvement à la Pavane* by Calixa Lavallée, first written for piano and published in 1883. The work was arranged for band on the occasion of an all Lavallée concert given by the Canadian Grenadier Guards Band in Montréal on July 13, 1933 to celebrate the return of the composer's body to his hometown for final burial. It exhibits a degree of chromaticism not generally associated with original music for band during the late nineteenth century. Source: author's collection.

Figure 20.3. Front cover of the *National Airs and Regimental Marches* band book published by the R.S. Williams & Sons Co. in 1911. Source: author's collection.

Figure 20.4. First page, solo cornet, of the *National Airs and Regimental Marches* band book [see Fig. 20.5 above]. The "Inspection March" represents one of the first examples of the use of "O Canada" in arrangements intended exclusively for the use of Canadian military bands. Source: author's collection.

Figure 20.5. First page of the solo cornet/conductor part to *Specialty Overture* by Arthur Wellesley Hughes, published by the Waterloo Music Company in 1931. Source: author's collection.

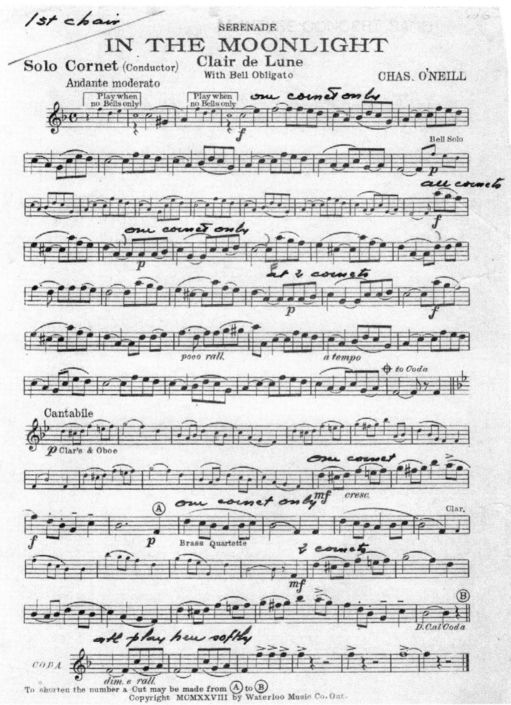

Figure 20.6. Solo cornet (conductor) part to *In the Moonlight, Serenade* by Charles O'Neill, published by the Waterloo Music Company in 1928. Source: author's collection.

Figure 20.7. First cornet (conductor) part to *Characteristique Overture* by Charles Frederick Thiele, published by the Waterloo Music Company in 1937. Source: author's collection.

Figure 20.8. First page of the condensed score to *Builders of Youth, Overture* by Charles O'Neill, published by Carl Fischer in 1937. After retiring from the Canadian army in 1937, O'Neill taught at several U.S. post-secondary institutions. He was highly respected as an adjudicator and clinician and had already served as president of the American Bandmasters Association from 1933 to 1934. He was to compose at least nine concert overtures, published by Fischer, Remick, Waterloo, Boston and Schirmer, most of which were intended for school groups. Source: author's collection.

Figure 20.9. Front cover of the *Douglas Band Folio*, Vol. 2, [C Flute] published by the Sam Fox Publishing Co. in 1933. Source: author's collection.

Figure 20.10. First clarinet part to *Dawn Break, Reverie* by George Douglas, published as part of the *Douglas Band Folio*, Vol. 1, by the Sam Fox Publishing Co. in 1929. Source: author's collection.

Figure 20.11. Solo cornet part to *The Ride of the R.N.W.M.P.* by A. Glen Broder, arranged for band by John Waldron and self-published in 1906. This work represents one of the first examples of music published for wind band in Canada by a female composer. Annie Glen Broder was an accomplished pianist, author and music critic for the *Calgary Herald*. Her *Ride*, with its use of both duple and triple meters, reflects a detailed knowledge of the various paces used in mounted parades. Source: author's collection.

Figure 20.12. First page of the condensed score to the *Hudson's Bay Company Patrol, In Canada*, arranged by W.E. Delaney, published by the Hudson's Bay Company in 1929.

CHAPTER TWENTY-ONE

THE CANADIAN MUSIC CENTRE COMPOSERS

In 1959, the Canadian Music Centre [CMC] was established by a small group of serious composers with the goal of providing a venue for the "…dissemination and promotion of Canadian concert, operatic, educational and church music."[1] Starting with a select group of well-established names, most of whom had received their formal musical training prior to the outbreak of WWII, the CMC has grown from its modest one office beginnings in Toronto to five regional centres in Montréal, Toronto, Calgary, Vancouver and Halifax. From only twenty founding members it now boasts over 900 associate composers, all of whom must apply for acceptance.[2] One of the original goals of the CMC was to maintain a central repository of associate composers' works that would be available on loan to encourage their performance nationwide. In 2021, the CMC website's search engine listed over 600 entries under the keywords "concert band/wind ensemble".[3] These entries included not only music for wind band but works for band and choir, band and solo instruments (including strings as in Oskar Morawetz's *Memorial to Martin Luther King for solo cello, winds, percussion and piano* (1968) or John Fodi's *Concerto for Viola and Two Wind Ensembles* (1972) and music for orchestral winds [no saxophones].

Howard Cable (1920-2016)

One of the most prolific Canadian writers for wind band to appear in the 1950s and an early associate composer of the CMC was Howard Cable. His name first appeared on *Jingles All the Way, Fantasy* (Mills Music, 1947), a series of radio jingles arranged for band in the style of various classical composers including Tschaikovsky, Bach, Strauss, Rossini, Mendelssohn and Wagner. It was followed within ten years by a succession of works in which Cable established his mastery of the band idiom: *Saturday's Game, March* (Chappell, 1952), *Three Candy Cornets, Cornet Trio* (Chappell, 1955), *Snake Fence Country* (Chappell, 1955), *Quebec Folk Fantasy* (Chappell, 1956), *Here Comes the Band, March* (Chappell, 1956) and *Newfoundland Rhapsody* (Chappell, 1956). Subsequent

---

[1] Patricia Shand, "Canadian Music Centre," *Encyclopedia of Music in Canada* (Toronto: University of Toronto Press, 1981) 146.
[2] "What is the CMC," *Canadian Music Centre* at www.cmccanada.org accessed 07 February 2021.
[3] Survey conducted by author at "Search Library," *Canadian Music Centre* at www.cmccanada.org accessed 01 February 2021.

publications with Chappell included: *Marchmanship March* (Chappell, 1959), *Cortege* (Chappell, 1959) and *Stratford Suite* (Chappell, 1964).

The 1960s saw Cable devote much of his energy to arranging with his name appearing on band releases of Broadway, television and "pop" favourites: *The Sound of Music* (Williamson, 1961), *Barbados* (Chappell, 1963), *Downtown* (MCA, 1965), *Brazilian Festival* (CA, 1966), *Toy Tiger* (Northern, 1966), *Theme from "The Virginian"* (Northern, 1968), *Ask Not* (Frank, 1971) and the *Hans Christian Anderson Suite* (Morris, 1972). In addition to serving as a civilian associate conductor and arranger for the NORAD Band from 1962 to 1966 he also composed *Scottish Rhapsody* (MCA, 1966) which he conducted at the 1967 Midwest Band and Orchestra Clinic [see Chap. 12]. He was one of the country's most successful composers for wind band but he wasn't the only one.

Other CMC members of the period were highly respected composers of music for orchestra, chamber ensembles, choirs, solo voice and keyboards. Their contributions for band may not have been as numerous nor as well-known as Cable's but they were equally significant. Early associate composers, including Dr. Healey Willan, one of English Canada's most respected musical figures, contributed with his *Royce Hall Suite* (Associated, 1952), *Centennial March* (1967) and the posthumously published *Elegie Heroique* (Boosey & Hawkes, 1971). John Weinzweig, one of the founding members of the CMC, composed *Band Hut Sketches* (1944) and *Divertimento No. 5 for Trumpet, Trombone and Wind Ensemble* (1961). His most successful work for wind band, however, was *Round Dance* (Leeds, 1966) [Fig. 21.1]. Other composers in those early years were Gerhard Wuensch, *Caribbean Rhapsody* (1959), *Symphony for Band* (1960) and *Variations and Fugue on a Mozartian Theme for Band* (1986); François Morel, *Diptyique for orchestral winds* (1954), *Aux Marges du Silence* (1982), *Aux Couleurs du Ciel* (1988) and *De subitement lointain* (1989) and Harry Freedman, *Laurentian Moods* (1951), *A la Claire Fontaine* (1970), *Blanche comme la Neige* (1970), *Echo Prelude* (1970) and *Etude No. 2* (1970). Two other composers from this first cohort, Robert Fleming and Louis Applebaum, worked for both the National Film Board [NFB] and the CBC. Robert Fleming wrote *Jamboree* (1956) and *Three Scenarios for Band* (1974). Louis Appelbaum, in addition to working for both the NFB and the CBC was for many years musical director of the Stratford Shakespeare Festival. It was this experience that led to the composition of the *Suite of Miniature Dances* (1953). Later works for wind band included *Celebration*

York (1985), *High Spirits a Short Overture for Concert Band* (1986) and *Passacaglia and Toccata for Concert Band* (1986).[4]

James Gayfer (1916-1997)

Most of these early CMC associate composers concentrated their creative efforts on more traditional venues for musical composition: the symphony orchestra, chamber ensembles, choral and keyboard music. There was however one other, like Howard Cable, who focused his energies largely on the wind band. This was James McDonald Gayfer. Born in Toronto, he completed a doctoral degree in music at the University of Toronto in 1950. He also joined the Canadian Army in 1942 as a bandsman and by 1951 was Director of Music of the First Canadian Infantry Battalion Band at Camp Borden, Ontario.[5] A champion of music for band, he wrote extensively for winds; initially for professional military bands but after his retirement from active service for both school and community groups. His first major release was *Royal Visit, Grand March* (Boosey & Hawkes, 1959), "Composed for the occasion of the visit of her Majesty Queen Elizabeth II and His Royal Highness Prince Philip to Canada 12th-16th October, 1957"[6]. This was followed by several marches, *The Canadian Infantryman* (Waterloo, 1960), *Royal Canadian Dental Corps March* (Waterloo, 1960) and *Silver and Green* (Whaley, Royce & Co., n.d.).

After leaving the army Gayfer accepted a teaching position at Southwood Secondary School in Galt,Ontario, [now part of Cambridge] and it was here that he wrote the pastorale *Green Fields and White Hawthorne (A Country Ballad for Band)* [Fig. 21.2]. A commission from the Barrie Central Collegiate Band resulted in the *Wells of Marah* in 1971 and in 1975 his tone poem *Canadian Landscape* (Boosey & Hawkes, 1975) was published. There followed a series of manuscript scores, now on deposit at CMC, including *Streight, From Canada, Ceremonial March* (1974), *Celebration of Wisdom* (1976), *Fanfare, Toccata and March* (1978) and *On Parliament Hill* (1983). Very much a traditionalist, Gayfer's *Green Fields and White Hawthorne* and *Canadian Landscape* are two of the finest examples of lyrical writing in the Canadian wind band repertory. He died in Lindsey, Ontario, in 1997.

The late 1960s and 1970s welcomed a new generation of CMC associate composers, a handful of whom would contribute to an ever-growing body of literature for winds.

---

[4] "Composer Showcase-Appelbaum, Louis" *Canadian Music Centre* at www.cmccanada.org accessed 07 February 2021.
[5] Mark Miller, "Gayfer, James" *EMC.* 370.
[6] James M. Gayfer, *Royal Visit, Grand March* (Boosey & Hawkes, 1959) from the author's collection.

Perhaps the most prolific of these was Donald Coakley. The CMC online catalogue [2021] contains sixteen titles for band by Coakley, most of which are now available from Toronto's Eighth Note Publications.[7] Born in 1934 in what is now Cambridge, Ontario, his musical education in the United States included study with Vincent Persichetti at the Philadelphia Conservatory of Music. He returned to Canada and was Assistant Co-ordinator of Music for the Scarborough Board of Education for twenty-three years.[8] A composer in all genres, his experience as a music educator gave him insights to the needs of bands and student level ensembles whom he acknowledged as "… the largest single market for music in the country."[9] Starting in 1970 with *Cantos* (Eighth Note, 1970), the decade saw the release of *Lyric Essay* (Eighth Note, 1975), *A Canadian Folk Rhapsody* (Eighth Note, 1976) and *Songs for the Morning Band* (Ricordi, 1977). For the remaining years of the twentieth century, his many compositions for wind band ranged from the Grade 1 level *Land of the Silver Birch* (Eighth Note, 1982) [Fig. 21.3] to the Grade 5 level *Vive la Canadienne* (Northdale, 1986), originally commissioned by the Northdale Concert Band for its Canada Day appearance at Vancouver's EXPO 86.

Another newcomer was Alfred Kunz. Although much of his "… creative output has been choral, his music covers all genres of writing. Since 1980 he has written numerous orchestra, concert band, string orchestra and choral music for school room use."[10] His concert band scores, many of which draw on the Canadian folksong tradition range in difficulty from *Eskimo Lullaby* (1981), rated at a Grade 1.5 level, to *Canadian Trilogy* (1982) at Grade 4 [Fig. 21.4]. There are no fewer than twelve Kunz scores in the CMC catalogue and most were composed in the early 1980s. In addition to other folk adaptations, *Donkey Riding* (1982), *Land of the Silver Birch* (1981), *Red River Valley* (1982) and *She's Like the Swallow* (1982), he also wrote a number of lighthearted works intended for audience appeal: *Lake Huron March*, (1982), *Overture for Fun* (Oktoberfest) (1984) and *Shine on Me!* (1982).

Gary Kulesha is rightfully described in his CMC biography as "…one of Canada's most active and visible musicians."[11] Prior to appointments as Composer in Residence to the Kitchener-Waterloo Symphony (1988-1992), the Canadian Opera Company (1993-1995) and Composer-Advisor to the Toronto Symphony Orchestra, Gary Kulesha wrote a considerable body of music for wind band. Starting in 1975 with *Variations for Winds*

---

[7] "An Interview with Donald Coakley," *Canadian Winds* 2, no. 2 (Spring 2004) 64.

[8] Ibid., 60.

[9] Donald Coakley, "An Interview", *CW*, 63.

[10] "Composer Showcase-Kunz, Alfred," Canadian Music Centre at www.cmccanada.org accessed 08 February 2021.

[11] "Composer Showcase-Kulesha, Gary" *CMC* at www.cmccanada.org accessed 08 February 2021.

(1975) and *March in F* (1975), the decade that followed welcomed *Ensembles for Winds* (1979), *Concertino for Flute and Wind Orchestra* (1980), *Two Pieces for Band* (1982) and *Overture for Concert Band* (1983). In 1986, he donated *Christening and Finale* to the Northdale Concert Band. Since then, he has been a Composer in Residence at the Banff Centre for the Arts and with the National Arts Centre Orchestra in Ottawa.

There were many other composers who wrote music for wind band during those years. Included is Godfrey Ridout, whose *Fall Fair* for orchestra (1961), arranged for concert band by Earl Fralick, was performed by the New Edmonton Wind Sinfonia at the 2015 WASBE Conference in San Jose California. Ridout's later contributions for band were *Partita Academica* (1969) and *Tafelmusik* (1976). Other CMC contributors were Morley Calvert, *Romantic Variations* (Gordon V. Thompson, 1975) and *A Song for our Time* (Gordon V. Thompson, 1980); Jack Sirulnikoff, *Polka Dots* (1967) and *Variations on a Rollicking Tune* (E.C. Kerby, 1977) [Fig. 21.5]; Clifford Crawley, *Tyendinaga: Legend for Concert Band* (1978) and William McCauley, *Canadian Folk Song Fantasy* (Southern, 1972) [Fig. 21.6]. By 1979 the number of CMC associate composers had grown from the original twenty to 159 and the number of circulating scores in its library to over 6500.[12] At least sixty of those composers had written music for wind band.

The 1980s saw the CMC add music for wind band by female Canadian composers starting with Anita Sleeman's *Cantus* (1981) and *Carol of the Bells, A Fantasy on the Christmas Carol* (1989). She was joined by American born and Eastman School of Music trained oboist Elizabeth Raum who writes "…for a wide range of musical media in extremely diverse styles, featuring an audience friendly musical language."[13] By 2008 Raum had written three operas, an oratorio, other choral and vocal works, ballets, orchestral music, solo concertos, chamber music, film and video soundtracks and eleven works for band or band and soloist.[14] Her works for wind band range from music for junior level ensembles, *Bushwakked* (1982), to intermediate level groups, *Sodbuster* (1999) and *A Prairie Alphabet Musical Parade* (2002) to challenging advanced level compositions, *Echoes of Fort San* (1987) and *One Hundred Years of Fanfares* (2005) [Fig. 21.7]. Although not all her compositions are available from the CMC, those that are represent a significant contribution to the Canadian repertoire for winds.

The growing number of Canadian composers writing music for band, much of which was unpublished, created a problem for the CMC. How was it to promote the use of its materials in the schools? In 1973, the Canadian Music Educators Association (CMEA)

---

[12] Shand, "Canadian Music Centre," *EMC* 147.
[13] Jennifer McAllister, "An Interview with Elizabeth Raum," *Canadian Winds* 6, no. 2 (Spring 2008) 65.
[14] Ibid., 67.

and the CMC agreed to jointly sponsor the John Adaskin Project whose aims were to acquaint teachers "…with music suitable for school use …[and] to promote the publication of additional Canadian repertoire and to encourage composers to add to that repertoire."[15] The first part of this initiative was the publication in 1978 of Patricia Martin Shand's *Canadian Music A Selective Guidelist for Teachers* (Toronto: Canadian Music Centre, 1978). This comprehensive reference work provided information on suitable published materials available for Canadian schools. It included sections on music for choirs (unison and mixed voice), bands, orchestras, string orchestras and chamber ensembles, both wind and mixed.[16] The chapter on bands included a brief synopsis of fourteen works by ten composers, eight of whom were associate composers of the CMC, as well as a supplementary listing of nine recently published marches.[17] This relatively small number of wind band entries was a function of the limited number of Canadian publishers of band music active at the time, a topic which will be discussed at greater length in Chapter Twenty-Three. Recognizing that the vast majority of the CMC's holdings were unpublished and existed in manuscript form only, a second volume was released by the same author in 1987. It was entitled *Guidelist of Unpublished Canadian Band Music Suitable for Student Performers* (Toronto: Canadian Music Centre, 1987) and it drew on the CMC's extensive and growing manuscript collection of music for wind band. Compositions were arranged by level of difficulty: easy, medium and difficult. There were only three in the easy category but twenty-six in the medium category including works by Calvert, Coakley, Gayfer, Kulesha, Riddle, Sirulnikoff and Weait. Stylistically, the music ranged from the traditional forms and tonalities employed by Morley Calvert and James Gayfer to Richard Evans' whimsically named *Mrs. MacTwivley's Tuning her Knickers (In Concert)* with its unconventional technique of assigning each instrument only one note, resulting in a composition without "…melodic, harmonic or rhythmic organization."[18] The final section contained analyses of thirty-four advanced level works for wind band by Canada's most esteemed composers including Murray Adaskin, John Beckwith, Alan Bell, Robert Fleming, Godfrey Ridout, John Weinzweig and Gerhard Wuensch. Both volumes are still available for review today at all regional offices of the CMC and together they bear eloquent testimony to the contribution of the Canadian Music Centre to a significant body of wind band literature during the first thirty years of its existence.

---

[15] Patricia Martin Shand, *Guidelist of Unpublished Canadian Band Music Suitable for Student Performers* (Toronto: Canadian Music Centre, 1987) iii.

[16] Patricia Martin Shand, *Canadian Music A Selective Guidelist for Teachers* (Toronto: Canadian Music centre, 1978) iii.

[17] Ibid., 103.

[18] Shand, *Unpublished Canadian Band Music*, 17.

Perhaps the greatest testament to the quality of music produced during this period is to be found in S. Timothy Maloney's *Canadian Wind Ensemble Literature* (DMA thesis: Eastman School of Music, University of Rochester, 1986). It is a monumental work and after providing a historical perspective followed by a review of the contemporary repertoire, Dr. Maloney included an in-depth analysis of seven representative works: Pierre Mercure's *Pantomime* for orchestral winds; John Weinzweig's *Divertimento No. 5 for Trumpet, Trombone and Symphonic Wind Ensemble*; Harry Somers' *Symphony for Woodwinds, Brass and Percussion*; Oskar Morawetz's *Memorial to Martin Luther King for Solo Cello and Wind Orchestra*; Sydney Hodkinson's *Cortege: Dirge Canons for Band*; Ka-Nin Chan's *Foung* and Brian Cherney's *In the Stillness Between*. All seven composers were associates of the CMC.[19]

By the end of the 1980s another twenty-five associate composers had joined the roster of those whose music for wind band had been acquired by the CMC and with them a trend began to emerge that has continued to the present day. Although there were more and more composers joining the ranks of the organization there were very few who wrote more than one or two works for wind band. Of the twenty-five CMC composers in the 1980s cohort, only five, Tibor Polgar, Brent Dutton, Michael Colgrass, Elizabeth Raum and Derek Healey have written five or more works for band since being accepted as associate composers.[20] The last decade of the twentieth century was much the same. Of the thirty-three composers whose wind band compositions were first acquired in the 1990s, only three have written five or more works for band: Arsenio Giron, Michael Purves Smith [Fig. 21.8] and Sid Rabinovitch. The survey results for the period from 2000 to the present day show a similar pattern; only three composers of forty-seven admitted are actively invested in composing for band [having written five or more scores]: John Palmer, Christopher Nickel and Alan Gilliland.

At first glance it appears that interest in writing for wind band by the CMC's ever-growing list of associate composers is waning. Not so. It should be noted that the quality of music for band by those who continue to write for the idiom, whether they do so only once or twice or more often, remains as high as ever. The eligibility requirements for potential associate composers are extensive. They demand lists of completed works, performance histories, proof of public performance by three different ensembles or

---

[19] S. Timothy Maloney, "Canadian Wind Ensemble Literature (DMA thesis: Eastman School of Music at the University of Rochester, 1986).
[20] Survey by author, 01 February 2021.

individuals and a personal CV that includes references to training, awards and grants.[21]   It is a very high bar and Canada's bands are the beneficiaries of the process since the selection process ensures only the most talented and passionate creative artists are accepted.

This is the lasting legacy of the Canadian Music Centre.   It has been the guardian for over sixty years of serious contemporary music making in this country.   Band directors from across Canada can easily access over six hundred titles in a variety of twentieth and twenty-first century styles, for all grade levels, at reasonable cost with just the click of a key or a phone call.

---

[21] "Become an Associate Composer," *Canadian Music Centre* at www.cmccanada.org accessed 09 February 2021.

CHAPTER TWENTY-ONE GALLERY

Figure 21.1. First page of the condensed score to *Round Dance* by John Weinzweig (1913-2006), arranged for band by Howard Cable and published by Leeds Music (Canada) in 1964. Weinzweig, like so many of his generation had served as a bandsman in the military (RCAF) during WWII and was familiar with the wind band idiom. One of his earliest scores was entitled *Band Hut Sketches* (1944). *Round Dance* is available for rental from the CMC at https://cmccanada.org/shop . Source: used by permission of the copyright holder CMC, Toronto.

Figure 21.2.   First page of the 1st clarinet part to *Green Fields and White Hawthorne, A Country Ballad for Band* by James McDonald Gayfer (1916-1997).   Full score and parts are available on a rental basis from the CMC.   Source: manuscript copy of *Green Fields and White Hawthorne* presented to the author by James Gayfer in August of 1993.

LAND OF THE SILVER BIRCH

Clarinet 1

setting by Donald Coakley

02005   © 1993 by D. Coakley Published by COMPRINT

Figure 21.3. Clarinet 1 part to *Land of the Silver Birch* by Donald Coakley, originally published by Comprint in 1993. There have been many arrangements for band of this classic Ontario summer camp song but few have been as effective as the one above by Donald Coakley. Scored for a Grade 1.5 level ensemble it engages all sections in developing the main theme in a setting that is both exciting and meditative. *Land of the Silver Birch* is now available from Eighth Note Publications in Toronto. Source: reproduced by permission of Eighth Note Publications.

Figure 21.4.   First page of the score to *Canadian Trilogy* by Alfred Kunz, published by the author in 1982. It is a Grade 4 level work featuring "The Banks of Newfoundland," "Un Canadien Errant" and "Nova Scotia Song."   Source: Copyright by Alfred Kunz, 1982.   Used by permission.

Figure 21.5. Flute part to *Variations on a Rollicking Tune* by Jack Sirulnikoff, originally published by E.C. Kerby in 1977. The rollicking tune of the title is the Newfoundland classic "I'se the B'ye". Rated as a Grade 3 level composition, the arrangement embodies all the humour of the original folksong and has been performed widely across Canada. It has also been recorded by the University of Manitoba Wind Ensemble as part of the *North Winds – Canadian Band Music Project*. Score and parts are still available from Counterpoint Music Library Services. Source: reproduced by permission of the copyright holder Counterpoint Music Library Services.

Figure 21.6.   First page of the condensed score to *Canadian Folk Song Fantasy* by William McCauley (1917-1999), published by Southern Music Publishing Co. in 1972.   Canada's centennial year, 1967, provided McCauley with the inspiration for two fine compositions for wind band, the *Canadian Folk Song Fantasy*, above and *Metropolis*, also known as the *Big City Suite*. *Metropolis* was performed by the Barrie (Central) Collegiate Band under the direction of the composer at the Midwest Convention in Chicago in December, 1967.   "Overture on Canadian Folksongs" (McCauley, William) Copyright © 1972 Southern Music Pub. Co. Inc. Copyright © Renewed.   Used By Permission.   All Rights Reserved

One Hundred Years of Fanfares

Commissioned by the Saskatchewan Band Association
For the Canadian Band Association National Youth Band of Canada
On the Occasion of Saskatchewan's 100th Anniversary of Confederation with Canada.

© Elizabeth Raum 2005

Figure 21.7. First page of the score to *One Hundred Years of Fanfares* by Elizabeth Raum. Commissioned for the National Youth Band of Canada, it is an advanced level work. Score and parts are available for rental from the CMC. Source: score graciously provided to the author by Elizabeth Raum.

382

Figure 21.8. First page to the score of *The Cremation of Sam McGee* for narrator and wind ensemble by Michael Purves-Smith. Source: Copyright by Michael Purves-Smith, 2004. Used by permission.

CHAPTER TWENTY-TWO

OTHER VOICES

As significant as the contribution of the Canadian Music Centre was and is to the growth and development of a distinctly Canadian literature for wind band, it was not the only voice. The modern wind band serves two purposes, its traditional role as a medium of light musical entertainment and a newer role as an idiom worthy of serious artistic expression. The Canadian Music Centre was created to serve the latter and subsequently had little place for those who embraced "light music' and its associated forms. Of all those forms, none was more synonymous with the wind band than the march.

The patriotic fervour that accompanied Canada's participation in the Second World War carried on into the 1950s as established publishers continued to provide the nation's many military and community bands with new music. Two examples include Ralph Whetstone's *Swords and Daggers March* (Waterloo, 1955) and James Gayfer's *Canada Overseas March* (Whaley, Royce & Co., 1954).[1] The most prolific of the published postwar march composers however, was Maurice DeCelles, a Trois-Rivières native who wrote at least six marches, three of which, *Alouette, Marche Patriotique* (Canadian Music Sales, n.d.), *Cadet Roussel, Marche* (Canadian Music Sales, n.d.) and *Vive la Canadienne, Marche Patriotique* (Canadian Music Sales, 1955) were included in Patricia Martin Shand's *Canadian Music: A Selective Guidelist for Teachers* (CMC, 1978). One other Québec based composer was Montréal's Robert Ryker who wrote three marches, *Marche "Canadienne"* (Montreal Music Supply, 1958), *March to the Copper Country* (Montreal Music Supply, 1958) and *Marche "Le Royal"* (Montreal Music Supply, 1958), the first two of which were also reviewed in Shand's *Selective Guidelist*.[2]

The 1960s were dominated musically by one event, Canada's Centennial Year. Although there had been several march releases earlier in the decade including Maurice Zbriger's *Lord Nuffield March* (MS, 1960), arranged for band by Montreal bandleader Guiseppe Agostini and Henk Uitvlucht's *A Mare Usque Ad Mare* [From Sea to Sea] (Waterloo, 1965), it was the centenary (1967) that was the catalyst for several new outstanding Canadian marches. Three were composed for the 1967 Canadian Armed Forces Tattoo [see Chap. 11], Ron McAnespie's *Century of Progress* (Boosey & Hawkes,

---

[1] Although Gayfer was an associate composer of the CMC, this march does not appear on its library list.
[2] Unlike other march titles cited, Ryker's works are printed on concert size sheets in professionally hand copied manuscript format.

1967) and Ron Milne's *Marche Cartier* (B & H, 1967) and *Marche Vanier* (B & H, 1967). One other Canadian march that received enormous public exposure was *CA-NA-DA, A Centennial Song* (Centennial Commission, 1967) by Bobby Gimby, arranged for band by Ken Bray. By the end of the decade, the appetite for marches, especially those printed in march size formats for adult ensembles such as Ron McAnespie's *Symbol of Unity* (Boosey & Hawkes, 1969) was waning, as were the number of Canadian publishers willing to publish them.

Howard Cable was Canada's best known postwar bandmaster and a champion of "light music" programming. He was not alone. A fellow Torontonian and contemporary, Robert Farnon (1917-2005) was equally successful in England and has often been referred to as "A forgotten Canadian." Farnon was born in Toronto, studied composition with Louis Waizman and had his first symphony, entitled *Symphonic Suite,* premiered by the Toronto Symphony Orchestra in January, 1941. He joined the Canadian Army in 1943 and directed both the Army Show and the Canadian Band of the Allied Expeditionary Forces. Shortly after the war, he relocated to England where he remained for the rest of his life with the exception of several brief visits to Canada in the 1960s and 1990s. He died at his home in Guernsey at the age of eighty-seven.[3] He was a gifted composer and arranger and worked with some of the most famous names in show business: Tony Bennett, Peggy Lee, Lena Horne, Frank Sinatra and Sarah Vaughan. His talent for creating melodies that were both warm, playful and immediately appealing made his compositions attractive choices for Chappell's Army Band Journal which published no fewer than eight during the 1950s and 1960s including *Excerpts from the Works of Robert Farnon* (1952), *Derby Day* (1957), *Dominion Day* (1958), *Royal Occasion* (1957), *Seashore* (1961), *Westminster Waltz* (1965) and *Toronto City* (1966).[4] Farnon continued to write through to the end of the century completing scores for over forty movies and television series as well as several more works for band including *Bandutopia* (Jenson, 1986) and *An Irish Posy* (Jenson, 1983). His final composition for band was a commission for the Roxbury High School Band of Roxbury, New Jersey, entitled *The Gaels: An American Wind Symphony.*

One other contemporary of both Cable and Farnon was the polish born, naturalized Canadian, Walter Eiger (b. 1917). He studied music in France at the Université de Grenoble and at the École normale de musique in Paris. One of his early works, *Overture*

---

[3]Betty Nygaard King and Barry J. Edwards, "Robert Farnon" *The Canadian Encyclopedia.* Historica Canada. Article published 20 February 2007. Last Edited 04 March 2015 at www.thecanadianencyclopedia.ca accessed 11 February 2021.

[4] William H. Rehrig, *The Heritage Encyclopedia of Band Music: Composers and their Music*, Vol 1, ed. by Paul E. Bierley (Westerville, Ohio: Integrity Press, 1991) 230.

on Canadian Folktunes, was originally written for orchestra and subsequently performed by the Vancouver, Toronto and Québec symphony orchestras as well as at New York's Radio City Music Hall.[5]   In 1975, the composer revised the score for concert band and it was published by the Texas based Southern Music Company in 1980.   The six French Canadian themes he employs are subjected to a variety of compositional techniques, both harmonic and contrapuntal, which give the *Overture on Canadian Folktunes,* at 346 measures in length, the scale and scope of a major level 5 symphonic work for winds [Fig. 22.1].

Canada's legacy music publishers, Waterloo, Boosey & Hawkes (Canadian Branch) and Gordon V. Thompson continued to include works for band in their catalogues during the 1960s.   One of the composers they sponsored had extensive experience with Canadian military bands and was more than familiar with the musical vocabulary necessary to reach popular audiences.   This was Kenneth Campbell, a talented arranger and former member of the RCAF Central Band in Ottawa.   It was his association with the national capital region that inspired his *Capital City Suite* (Gordon V. Thompson, 1962), a work whose three movements, "Legislation," "River by Night" and "Confusion Square" [Fig. 22.2] evoke images of dignity, serenity and chaos respectively.   The first movement is relatively easy but the extreme instrumental ranges, key signatures, chromaticism and tempi in the last two place the work at a Grade 5 level.   Thompson also published Campbell's *Puppet Parade* (1963), a concert march stylistically similar to those of the British light classicists Eric Coates and Ronald Binge.   Easily accessible to a good high school band, it, like his earlier *Capital City Suite* were both included in Shand's *Selective Guide List.*

Gordon V. Thompson continued to publish music for band into the 1970s and 1980s with Peter Riddle's *Farewell to Nova Scotia* (1978), Morley Calvert's *Romantic Variations* (1975) and *A Song for our Time* for S.A.T.B. Choir and Band (1980), Thomas Legrady's *Le Facteur* (1983) and *J'Entends le Moulin* (1983) as well as three arrangements by Charles "Bud" Hill.   These consisted of *Theme from Ontario Place* (1971), *The Homecoming* (1975) and a medley of three French Canadian folksongs, *Canadiens Ensemble-Canadians Together* (1980).   *The Homecoming* proved to be enormously popular; the arrangement captured much of the languid tranquility of fellow Torontonian Haygood Hardy's score, first composed for a "Salada Tea" commercial in 1972 and then released as a single in 1975.   Charles Hill had been a music educator for thirty-three years in the Toronto area, member of the low brass section of the Hamilton Philharmonic and

---

[5] "Walter Eiger," In *The Canadian Encyclopedia*. Historica Canada. Article published 19 March 2007. Last edited 16 December 2013 at www.thecanadianencyclopedia.ca accessed 27 September 2021.

tubist with several Toronto bands, one of which was the Royal Regiment of Canada Band. It was his association with this group that led to the composition of the delightfully playful *Brutish Tubadiers*, for tuba section and band. The regimental march of the "Royals" is *British Grenadiers* and Hill skillfully integrated the theme into this work which was declared the winning composition, CBA Ontario Chapter, Canadian Composition Contest 1987-1988.[6]

The Waterloo Music Company went into a slow decline after the death of its founder C.F. Thiele in 1954 and increasingly limited itself to the publication of educational musical materials. In the late 1970s however, it engaged Robert McMullin to write four works for band: *Autumn Morning* (1978), *Pet Rock* (1978), *Plus Fours* (1978) and *Prairie Sketches* (1960) [Fig. 22.3]. This last composition had originally been commissioned in 1958 for school orchestra by the Ontario Music Educators Association and premiered the following year by the CBC Symphony Orchestra; it was subsequently arranged for band by James Hargreaves.[7] One of the company's last successful band releases was David Roe's *Three Canadian Folk Songs* (1983), a compilation of "I'se the B'y That Builds the Boats," "D'où Viens-tu Bergère" and the "Huron Carol" in settings for young band.

Bernard (Ben) Bogisch was one of the Dutch musicians who emigrated to Canada in 1953 to swell the ranks of Canadian Army bands. A graduate of the Kneller Hall Bandmasters course and former Director of Music of the Royal Canadian Dragoons Band and the CF Naden Band, Bogisch was a consummate musician and talented composer with a fondness for lush chromatic harmonies.[8] In 1969, his *Chebucto, Overture for Windband* (Boosey & Hawkes, 1969), the first in a string of works for wind band and wind band and solo instruments was published. By then, his reputation was enough to earn him a commission from William Allen Fisher and the Barrie Central Collegiate Band which resulted in *Huronian Episode* (Boosey & Hawkes, 1970).[9] Initially B & H agreed to publish it but unfortunately the editors changed their minds and chose to release the work on a rental only basis, ensuring it never got the distribution it deserved.[10] While still on active duty, Bogisch wrote two official marches, *Duty Above All* (1966) and *Canada North* (1972) as well as three Inspection Marches, *Bonavista* (1972), a medley of Newfoundland

---

[6] Charles Hill, letter to the author 22 December 1997.

[7] Bernard Deaville and Betty Nygaard King, "Robert McMullin." *The Canadian Encyclopedia*. Historica Canada. Article published 22 November 2007. Last edited 15 December 2013 at www.thecanadianencyclopedia.ca accessed 13 February 2021.

[8] In 1971, the author spent four months, May-August, on active duty with the CF Naden Band, Captain Bernard Bogisch, Director of Music.

[9] Both works were included in Patricia Martin Shand's *Selected Guidelist for Teachers*.

[10] Bernard Bogisch, letter to the author, 24 August 1997.

Folksongs and two Québec folksong medleys, *Les Habitants* (1974) and *Les Voyageurs* (1974).[11]

After his retirement from the Canadian Forces in 1983, Bogisch accepted no less than twelve commissions from regular Canadian Forces bands for works for concert band or solo instrument(s) and concert band. Of those, six (including *Bonavista*), were accepted for publication and released by the Dutch music company Molenaar: *Chance Encounter* (n.d.), *Noël Chez Nous* (1999), *Sci-Fi Suite of Dances* (1999), *Suite Acadienne* (1997) and *Turkey Talk* (1997). All are still in print and available at the company's website.[12] His remaining compositions, the special commissions, are discussed further in Chapter Twenty-Four.

One other composer, like Bogisch, who shifted his allegiance to the Dutch Molenaar was Thomas Legrady. Legrady was born in Budapest in 1920, was a graduate of the Bartók Conservatory and moved to Canada in 1956. He settled initially in Montréal where he taught music at both Loyola College and McGill University; he subsequently relocated to Toronto and from 1972 to 1985 taught woodwinds at Etienne Brulé High School.[13] Although he had published two works with Gordon V.Thompson in 1983, he chose then to go to the Netherlands and it was there that a further six compositions for band were released and are still listed as current: *The Wise Teddybear, Solo Trombone and Band* (1983), *Spring Festival* (1987), *Tubantella, Solo Tuba and Band* (1987) [Fig. 22.4], *Hungarian Gala and Dance* (1989), *At the Stadium* (n.d.) and *Mediterranean Suite* (1991).[14] A composer in multiple genres, orchestrator and pedagogue, Legrady also authored a beginning band method in French entitled *V'la le Bon Vent* (Toronto, 1979).

The activities of Ontario's music publishers paled in comparison to what was going on in French Canada. Québec had long recognized that its artists were one of the most effective means of protecting its unique francophone culture in an overwhelmingly anglophone North America and the province actively supported the arts sector as well as its music publishers. Throughout the 1970s, 1980s and 1990s, Orchestration Cartier, Les Éditions F.H.Q. [La Fédération des Harmonies du Québec], Les Éditions D'armony and Les Éditions S. Emery published collectively over seventy-five works for band. The most

---

[11] Ibid.

[12] "Composer-Arranger-Bernhard Bogisch," *Molenaar Music* at www.molenaar.com accessed 13 February 2021.

[13] Durrell Bowman, and Stanley L. Osborne, "Thomas Legrady." *The Canadian Encyclopedia*. Historica Canada. Article published 07 February 2006. Last edited 10 December 2013 at www.thecanadianencyclopedia.ca accessed 13 February 2021.

[14] "Composer-Arranger-Thomas Legrady," Molenaar Music at www.molenaar.com accessed 13 February 2021.

active of these was Orchestration Cartier whose catalogue from the mid 1990s consisted of twenty-eight titles of which all but one were arrangements of popular music written and performed by the province's best known vocal artists.[15] These included Gilles Vigneault's *Mon Pays*; Robert Charlebois's *Lindberg*; Stephane Venne's *Le Temps est Bon*, *Sur la Rue de la Montagne* and *Les Enfants de L'Avenir* and two selections by the songwriting team of Robitalle and Gagnon originally performed by Ginette Reno: *Je T'ai Fait une Chanson* and *Des Croissants de Soleil*. Another noteworthy inclusion was a band arrangement of *Une Colombe* [A Dove] by Marcel Lefebvre and Paul Baillargeon. The original song was the first single on Céline Dion's album *Mélanie* and she performed it in front of an audience of 65,000 at Montréal's Olympic Stadium on 10 September, 1984, to welcome Pope John Paul II to the city.

Rival Les Éditions F.H.Q. included fifteen titles in its catalogue from the same period including arrangements of popular songs by Vigneault, *Avec les mots du dimanche* and *Tam Ti Delam*; Charlebois, *La marche du Président* and Diane Juster's *Je ne suis qu'une chanson*. There was also an arrangement of traditional material entitled *Pot pourri folklorique* by Georges Codling, long time conductor of Sorel's Harmonie Calixa Lavallée as well as *Fantaisie* by CMC associate composer Réjean Marois. The 1997 catalogue from Les Éditions D'armony listed eleven titles of which four were transcriptions of works by Ravel, Satie, Saint-Saens and Tchaikovsky. That same year, Les Éditions S. Emery issued a temporary price list containing over twenty-five entries ranked by level of difficulty; easy, intermediate and difficult with only three being original compositions, the remainder were arrangements of popular, classical and Christmas titles.

Even though there is a temptation to minimize Québec's contribution to the wind band repertory during the closing decades of the twentieth century because of its largely "popular" nature, this would be a mistake for two reasons. The first deals with the arrangers. Six titles in the Orchestration Cartier catalogue were arranged by the noted American arranger Robert Lowden and a further two by CMC associate composer Maurice Dela. Canadian composer André Jutras added his name to two works in the F.H.Q. catalogue as did François Dompierre, a highly respected composer of music for film. Claude Sheridan, long time conductor of L'Union Musicale de Shawingan and professor of music at Le Conservatoire du Québec à Trois-Rivières contributed three arrangements and one original composition to the S. Emery catalogue. The quality of the arrangements themselves are worthy of study. The second reason is the music. Little known outside of Québec, it retains a freshness and vitality not usually associated with most English

---

[15] Copy from the author's collection.

language "pop" songs of the period. Vigneault's classic *Mon Pays* [My Country], arranged by Miville Bois, is a perfect example [Fig. 22.5]. From the slow recitative like opening to a lilting chorus in triple time, it is a musical evocation of skating on an outdoor rink in Winter that simply transcends any type of categorization.

One final observation has to do with "seasonal" or Christmas music. Québec's French Catholic past has given it a special attachment to old French "noëls" of which "Il est né le divin enfant" [He is Born the Divine Child] and "Venez divin Messie" [O Come Divine Messiah] are perhaps the best-known.   There are at least three different arrangements of these two melodies in the Québec literature studied for this section; two are listed in the 1997 D'Armony list, *Venez divin Messie* and *Variations stylistiques sur "il est né le divin enfant"*. *Il est né le divin enfant,* arranged for easy level band by Pierre-Marc Charbonneau was also published by Les Éditions S. Emery in 1997.

Even as Ontario's legacy music publishers, Whaley, Royce & Co., the Waterloo Music Company and Gordon V. Thompson were taking their final bows in the last decades of the twentieth century, a new generation of publishers were emerging ready to take their places. The E.C. Kerby Ltd. Publishing company was established in 1971 in Toronto and named after Elvira Columbo Kerby.[16] It was the original home of Donald Coakley's earlier works including *Lyric Essay* (1978), *Songs for the Morning Band* (1980) and *Canadian Folk Rhapsody* (1982) and fellow Canadian Jack Sirulnikoff's *Variations on a Rollicking Tune* (1977) [Fig. 21.5].   Unfortunately, the company was sold in 1989 and its catalogue assigned to Boosey & Hawkes which closed its Canadian branch in 1994.[17]

In 1986, Toronto's Northdale Concert Band performed at EXPO 86 in Vancouver and as part of its Canada Day performance premiered six new commissioned works for band by some of the country's most respected composers, all of whom except one were associates of the CMC.   Failing to find a Canadian publisher willing to take a chance on these new works, the group established the Northdale Music Press for the express purpose of championing new Canadian music for band.

In Edmonton, two music educators, Brian Appleby and Scott Rogal teamed up and formed Apro Music with the intention of providing music "by educators, for educators." Their music is directed exclusively at the middle/junior high school level ensemble, never exceeding a difficulty level of grade 2.   It found a ready market and by the end of the 1990s, the company had released twenty-nine titles ranging from beginning band compositions like *Good King Wenceslas* (1990), arranged to be playable by a first-year

---

[16] Marlene Wehrle, "E.C. Kerby Ltd.," *The Canadian Encyclopedia*. Historica Canada. Article published 07 February 2007. Last edited 13 December 2013.

[17] Ibid.

band after only three months experience, to the grade 2 level *Sunset Point Celebration* (1989) [Fig. 22.6].[18]

Another small western publisher focused almost exclusively on materials for young bands was Larry Dureski's Upstage Innovations. Based in Cranbrook B.C., the company catalogue has grown since its inception in 1997 to include over twenty-five works for early concert band [Grades .5 to 1.0]. Larry has been an elementary band teacher in the community since 1990 and each title is class tested by his grade six students.[19] First releases like *Miser's March* (Cranbrook, BC: Upstage Innovations, 1998), which used a maximum of six notes (thus earning the title "Miser") were ideal for beginners and are especially well-suited to elementary band classes [Fig. 22.7].

Nova Scotia's Ron MacKay, after twenty years as a musician in the Royal Canadian Navy and a further twenty-five as one of Nova Scotia's most successful and influential music educators, embarked, at age 63, on a third career as clinician, conductor, consultant and teacher at the Nova Scotia Teachers College in addition to St. Mary's, St. Francis Xavier and Dalhousie Universities.[20] In 1996, he also started his own publishing company, "ronmacmusic." Ron had always recognized the need for graded repertoire for his school bands and between 1970 and 1991 had produced a succession of manuscript arrangements that he subsequently began to transcribe onto computer files. By 2000, from modest beginnings starting with *Meet the Band* (1970), *4H Club Theme* (1972), *Bernie's March* (1972) and *A Little Bit of Canada* (1985), his company's catalogue had grown to include twenty-eight titles with both arrangements and original compositions including *Annapolis Royal March* (1996), *Cape Breton Trilogy* (1998), *Cape Blomidon Overture* (1999) and *Avondale Overture* (2000). Ron continued to write until just before his death in 2008 and the ronmacmusic catalogue, still very much active [2021], now contains no fewer than fifty-eight arrangements and thirty-two original compositions for wind band [Fig. 22.8].[21]

Another of the country's new publishers of band music, Eighth Note Publications, was also established in 1996 by David Marlatt, a recent graduate of what was then known as the University of Western Ontario [now Western University] together with Kenneth Bray, one of Canada's most revered music educators. The collaboration began with a fourteen-piece catalogue of arrangements for brass quintet with the first concert band score following shortly thereafter.[22] In 2002, biographies of four contributing composers,

[18] "Concert Band," *Apro Music* at www.apromusic.com accessed 16 February 2021.
[19] Larry Dureski, telephone interview with the author, 03 March 2021.
[20] Mark Hopkins, "In Memoriam-Ronald MacKay 1928-2008," *Canadian Winds* 7, no. 1 (Fall 2008) 53.
[21] Karen MacKay, daughter of Ron MacKay, e-mail correspondence with the author, 17 February 2021.
[22] "CBA 2019 Canadian Composers Award," *CBA ENews February 2019* dated 16 February 2019.

Kenneth Bray [d. 1999], David Marlatt, Donald Coakley and Jeff Smallman included listings for a total of twenty-four works for concert band. Since then, the company's growth has been exponential; the 2021 online catalogue lists a staggering 405 titles for concert band ranging from music for beginning band [grade 0.5] to advanced level ensembles [grade 5+].[23]

There were also American publishers. Just as the country's eminent interwar bandmasters, O'Neill, Gagnier and Hayward published extensively with U.S. publishers, recent Canadian composers have done likewise. In 1979, Vancouver's Stephen Chatman, a CMC associate composer, wrote *Grouse Mountain Lullaby* for publication by the New York based publisher Edward B. Marks. This was followed by *Mountain Sojourn* in 1984 and *Walnut Grove Suite* in 1995. These last two were subsequently acquired by Toronto's Eighth Note Publications in 2004. Similarly, Toronto native John Herberman's *Delamont Overture*, composed in honour of the noted musical pedagogue Gordon Delamont, was published by the William Allen Company in 1989. Like Chatman before him, later compositions for band, *The Fisher Who Died in His Bed* (1995) and *Couchiching Suite* (2010) were published in Canada by the Northdale Music Press and Eighth Note Publications respectively. By 1998, Newfoundland's Jim Duff, also a CMC associate, had published six titles with the Alfred Publishing Co., *Newfoundland Folk Song, A Seaside Ballad, Terra Nova Overture, Greenwood Overture, March and Interlude* and *Petty Harbour Bait Skiff* and four titles with CPP/Belwin, *Cape St. Mary's, Big Band Boogie, Galactic March* and *Rockarama*.[24] University of Toronto graduate Douglas Court moved to Florida in 1985 and began publishing with the Curnow Music Press in 1994. He has written extensively for young bands with titles such as *Land of the Silver Birch*, *A New World Adventure* and *Kawartha Legend*.[25]

An equally successful composer was Québec's André Jutras. A graduate of Université Laval, he played English horn in L'Orchestre symphonique de Québec from 1985 to 1991 and from 1991 to 1994 was staff conductor with the Calgary Philharmonic Orchestra as well as guest conductor with many other Canadian orchestras.[26] In 1985 Oklahoma based C.L. Barnhouse Company published his Christmas medley *C'Est Noel*, subtitled "A French Canadian Yuletide Celebration." Once again, the principal theme is the Québec favourite "Il est né le divin enfant" followed by varied treatments of "Sainte Nuit" [Silent Night] and

[23] "Concert Band," *Eighth Note Publications* at www.enpmusic.com accessed 16 February 2021.
[24] Jim Duff, letter to the author 27 January 1998.
[25] "Douglas Court," Wind Music Sales at www.windmusicsales.com accessed 18 February 2021.
[26] "Our Composers-Andre Jutras," *C.L. Barnhouse Company* at www.barnhouse.com accessed 17 February 2021.

"Les Anges dans nos Campagnes" [Angels we have Heard on High]. Barnhouse followed with the release of *Three Folk Miniatures* (1986), a saxophone solo with band accompaniment entitled *Daydreams* (1988) [Fig. 22.9], *Moventa* (1989), *Latin Sun* (1991) and *They Came Sailing* (1994). There was a brief hiatus before two more works appeared; *Inversia* (2003) and *Célébration Folklorique* (2010). A more recent Canadian addition to the Barnhouse catalogue has been the Toronto native and University of Toronto graduate David Eastmond. Beginning with his debut score, *A Sailor's Tale* (2005), Eastmond has produced four more, all at the intermediate band level [Grades 2.5 – 3.5]: *Exultia* (2006), *Kanata Spring* (2007), *St. Lawrence Chronicles* (2008) and *With One Courageous Voice* (2019).

In 1987, New York based music publisher Bourne Co. released a new work for young band (Grade 1+) by little known Québec music educator Arnold MacLaughlan. Entitled *A French-Canadian Suite* it was an arrangement of three French Canadian folksongs: "Le Jolie Tambour," "C'est la Belle Françoise" and "À Saint-Malo, Beau Port de Mer." MacLaughlan's use of texture, voicing and ranges created a work of remarkable musical sensitivity while at the same time allowing all members of the ensemble the opportunity to perform the melody at least once [Fig. 22.10]. Eventually others sat up and took notice. A guide to music for beginning band written by Thomas L. Dvorak, Richard L. Floyd and edited by Bob Margolis, *Best Music for Beginning Band: A Selective Repertoire Guide to Music and Methods for Beginning Band* (Brooklyn, NY: Manhattan Beach, 2000) contained the following summation: "…This is music perfectly conceived for young band. It is in all ways musical, filled with a gold mine of educational opportunities, and will be a real test for even the most mature Grade I bands."[27] It would take another American, Michael Burch-Pesses to remind us once again of this hidden Canadian jewel on page 98 of his *Canadian Band Music* (Galesville, MD: Meredith Music Publications, 2008).

As stated previously, the definition applied to Canadian band music in the present study also includes music written by non-Canadians as long as their compositions deal with a Canadian "subject", which includes any person, place, group, activity, experience or theme that is generally acknowledged to be "Canadian." Previous chapters have noted that Canadian composers, Vézina, Laurendeau, Clarke, Delaney and Hughes had been doing this well before the end of the nineteenth century. The early twentieth century however witnessed a growing number of band music composers from both Europe and the United States integrate Canadian themes into their own music for band.

---

[27] Thomas L. Dvorak, Richard L. Floyd, ed. by Bob Margolis *Best Music for Beginning Bands: A Selective Repertoire Guide to Music and Methods for Beginning Bands* (Brooklyn, NY: Manhattan Beach Music, 2000) 86.

CHAPTER TWENTY-TWO GALLERY

Overture on Canadian Folktunes

B♭ Clarinet 1.

WALTER EIGER

Figure 22.1.   First clarinet part to Walter Eiger's *Overture on Canadian Folktunes* for concert band.   The work was originally written for orchestra but subsequently transcribed by the composer for band.   "Overture on Canadian Folktunes" (Eiger, Walter) Copyright © 1980 Southern Music Pub. Co. Inc. Copyright © Renewed. Used By Permission.   All Rights Reserved.

Figure 22.2. First page of the score to "Confusion Square," third movement of the *Capital City Suite* by Ken Campbell, published by Gordon V. Thompson in 1962. Campbell was a prolific RCAF Central Band arranger whose fluency with the wind band idiom is evident in this one of only two published works. Although the first movement, "Legislation" is relatively easy, the last two movements require the skills of an advanced level ensemble. Score and parts are available for rental through Counterpoint Music Library Services. Copyright U.S.A. MCMLXII by Gordon V. Thompson Limited, Toronto, Canada. Reproduced by permission of Counterpoint Music Library Services, agent for the publisher Warner-Chappell Music Canada, owner of the Gordon V. Thompson catalogue.

PRAIRIE SKETCHES

Figure 22.3.   First page of the 1st clarinet part to *Prairie Sketches* by Robert McMullin, arranged for band by Jim Hargreaves and published by the Waterloo Music Company in 1974.   McMullin wrote four works for band for Waterloo in the 1970s.   Mayfair Music obtained the Waterloo Music Company catalogue when the company was dissolved and scores and parts for works for band are still available through Mayfair's order service.   Used by permission of Waterloo Publishing. A division of Mayfair Music Publications, 26037 Woodbine Ave., Keswick, ON, L4P 3E9.

Figure 22.4. Solo tuba part to *Tubantella* by Thomas Legrady, published by Molenaars in 1987. The title is a delightful play of words on the actual musical form of the "Tarantella". Legrady had two works for band published by Gordon V. Thompson in 1983 but since has had six released by the Dutch based Molenaars, all of which are still available in their online catalogue. Source: Copyright 1987 by Molenaar N.V., Wormerveer, Holland. Used by permission.

Figure 22.5. First clarinet part to *Mon Pays* by Gilles Vigneault, arranged for band by Miville Bois, published by Les Éditions Solset (Orchestration Cartier) in 1976. Québec based publishers produced over 70 titles for wind band during the last three decades of the twentieth century. Most were arrangements of popular songs drawn from the province's vibrant popular music industry but there were also a number inspired by the French-Canadian folksong repertory. Copyright Gilles Vigneault, used by permission.

Figure 22.6. First page to the conductor's score of *Sunset Point Celebration* by Scott Rogal, published by Apro Music in 1989. Apro is the collaboration of two Edmonton based music educators who were guided by the philosophy of providing teachers with "music for educators, by educators." By the late 1990s the company had released at least twenty-nine titles focused on beginner to Grade 2 level ensembles. Source: Copyright ApRo Music. Used by permission.

Miser's March

Figure 22.7. Flute part to *Miser's March* by Larry Dureski, published by Upstage Innovations in 1998. Source: Upstage Innovations. Used with permission.

Figure 22.8. First trumpet part to *Jim* by Ron MacKay, published by *ronmacmusic* in 2014. Ron MacKay was a prolific writer and arranger both during and after his teaching years in Truro, Nova Scotia. The *ronmacmusic* catalogue currently contains listings for 58 arrangements and 32 original compositions for wind band ranging from beginner level titles to those for advanced ensembles. The title, *Jim,* refers to Jim Hargreaves, music professor for many years at St. Francis Xavier University in Antigonish, N.S.. Source: Example courtesy Karen MacKay. Used with permission.

Figure 22.9. Solo alto saxophone part to *Daydreams* by André Jutras, published by C.L. Barnhouse in 1988. Copyright Chesford Music Publications; used with permission.

Figure 22.10. First page of the 1st Bb cornet part to Arnold MacLaughlan's *A French-Canadian Suite*, published by Bourne Co. in 1987. This work has been favourably reviewed in both Canadian and American educational publications and is still available from the publisher. Source: A FRENCH-CANADIAN SUITE by Arnold MacLaughlan © 1987 Bourne Co. All Rights Reserved. International Copyright Secured ASCAP.

CHAPTER TWENTY-THREE

BLOW THE WIND SOUTHERLY

Just as Canada's landscapes, peoples and institutions have long inspired European and American artists, so too our folksong repertory has appealed to foreign composers of band music. The first decades of the twentieth century saw the use of Canadian melodies in descriptive pieces, known as "patrols" and marches by British composers including Albert Williams' *Canadian Patrol* (Boosey & Co., 1911) [see Fig.18.2] and T. Bennett's march, *O! Canada* (Hawkes & Son, 1911) [Fig. 23.1].[1] Oddly enough, the primary thematic materials used in both weren't folksongs at all but patriotic songs of the period including "O Canada" (Lavallée, 1880), "Le Drapeau de Carillon" (Sabatier, 1858) and "The Maple Leaf Forever" (Muir, 1867). Initially it appears as if "O Canada" was associated with French Canada and "The Maple Leaf Forever" with English Canada along with a number of English, Irish and Scottish folksongs representing a shared English-speaking ancestry. By the interwar period however, French Canada is increasingly portrayed musically with more popular and genuine folksongs, "Vive la Canadienne" and "Alouette." This was the case with Mackenzie Rogan's depiction of Canada in his *Festival of Empire* (Boosey & Co., 1929). In the case of Edwin Franko Goldman's *Alouette March* (Carl Fischer, 1938), English Canada is once again represented by a collage of English, Celtic and Gaelic themes while French Canada dominates the trio section with "Alouette." One of the most effective marches written by a non-Canadian is C.H. Jaeger's *Canada on the March* (Boosey & Hawkes, 1955). Jaeger was Director of Music of the Band of the Irish Guards during its visit to Canada in 1954 and that may have been the inspiration for the march's composition.[2] It is his skillful use of fragments of "Alouette," "The Maple Leaf Forever" and "O Canada" as countermelodies in the low brass, seamlessly interwoven with brilliant fanfare like figures and a lyrical second theme that make the work an ideal concert march for advanced level groups.

Place names also provided inspiration, especially for Belgian composers Paul Gilson and Alfred Mahy in the early twentieth century whose *Montréal, Allegro de Concert* (L'Echo, 1923) [Fig. 23.2] and *Montréal, Pas Rédoublé* (Sarly, nd.) respectively paid tribute to that city's large Belgian musical community. The last decades of the twentieth

---

[1] Copies of both works from the author's collection.
[2] Gordon and Alwyn Turner, *The History of British Military Bands, Volume Two: Guards and Infantry* (Staplehurst, Kent: Spellmount Limited, 1996) 37.

century also saw a surge in place name dedications by American composers including James Ployhar's *Lethbridge Overture* (Belwin-Mills, 1973), O'Reilly and Feldstein's *Canadian Shield March* (Alfred, 1981) and *Manitoba March* (Alfred, 1986) as well as Akey's *Norquay* (Queenwood, 1995) [named after Mount Norquay near Banff in the Canadian Rockies]. The Rockies were also the inspiration for *Canadian Sunset* (Meridian, 1956) by Eddie Heywood, one of the most enduring musical tributes to have ever been written. This light jazz classic appeared in both concert and marching band arrangements and has been covered by no fewer than fourteen jazz performers, both instrumental and vocal between 1960 and 2009.[3]

If the Rocky Mountains are one of our most recognizable geographical features, then the Royal Canadian Mounted Police are an institution equally synonymous with Canada. They certainly didn't escape the attention of operetta composers Rudolph Friml and Herbert Stothart who included a song entitled "The Mounties" into the list of musical numbers for their operetta *Rose-Marie* which premiered in New York in 1924. A band arrangement of the song was released in 1942 following the success of the 1936 film version starring Nelson Eddy and Jeanette MacDonald.

The Canadian National Exhibition, first established in 1879, began to welcome foreign bands in 1904 and by the 1920s, the fair's "Music Days" were attracting some of the finest wind bands in the world. These included Creatore's Band from New York, J.J. Gagnier's Canadian Grenadier Guards Band of Montréal, Herbert L. Clarke's Anglo-Canadian Leather Company Band and in 1929, the Edwin Franko Goldman Band of New York City.[4] In appreciation, Goldman wrote the *Canadian National Exhibition March* (Fischer, 1931). Like so many of its predecessors, it is a mosaic of Canadian melodies, including a rather dubious attempt to depict the musical voices of First Nations peoples as well as references to "Marianne s'en va-t-au Moulin" [representing French Canada], "God Save the King" and "The Maple Leaf Forever." Goldman also includes several themes of his own, especially in the Trio section. Thirty years later, the CNE's little sister, the Central Canada Exhibition, held annually in Ottawa, was presented with its own *Exhibition March* (Ludwig, 1961), written by Colonel George S. Howard, Chief, Bands and Music, United States Air Force Band. It is a concert march that in many ways represents the past; an advanced level work written by a conductor of professional adult wind bands.

The remaining years of the twentieth century witnessed a dramatic shift in emphasis as a growing number of American band composers focused their creative efforts on school-

---

[3] "Canadian Sunset," *Wikipedia* at www.en.wikipedia.org accessed 23 February 2021.
[4] Ed. Terziano, ed. *The Little Town Band That Grew and Grew: A Mini-History the Anglo Canadian Leather Co. Concert Band* (Huntsville, ON: Forester Press, 1986) 31.

based ensembles. One example of this trend towards new school focused repertoire was Paul W. Whear's *Canada A Folksong Set for Band* (Ludwig, 1976). Originally commissioned by the Vancouver School Music Teachers Association, the score incorporates several well-known Canadian folksongs, "Brave Wolfe," "Vive la Canadienne," "Huron Carol" and "She's Like the Swallow" in a variety of *solo*, *soli* and *tutti* settings. It also includes two rarely heard melodies from Western Canada, "Klondike" and "Far from Home" [B.C.]. Arranged for an intermediate level [Grade 3-4] ensemble, it is a work easily accessible to most high school bands.

Beginning level ensembles were not ignored. Perhaps one of the most successful American arrangements of Canadian folk music for band was Anne McGinty's *Two Canadian Folk Songs* (Queenwood, 1987). Her treatment of "Eskimo Lullaby" and "Donkey Riding," arranged for Grade 1 level ensembles was a staple of Canadian festivals for years. Not only were the melodies faithfully presented but care was taken to use *soli* passages to vary the presentation giving the work a remarkable degree of musical sensitivity [Fig. 23.3]. McGinty returned once again to the Canadian folksong repertory in 1991 with *Canadian Folk Fantasy* (Queenwood, 1991). This time she raised the technical level to Grade 1.5 – 2 and expanded her range to include "Land of the Silver Birch," "Brave Wolfe," "The Jones Boys" and "Alouette."

In 1996 Curnow Music Press released *Canadian Sketches*, also a Grade 1.5 level work arranged by the company's founder James Curnow. Three Canadian folksongs, the ever popular "Si mon moine voulait danser," as well as "Ojibway Lullaby" and "Johnny Doyle [Ontario]" were gathered in a musically coherent treatment that fully exploited the expressive potential in each source. Two more recent examples of Canadian folksongs being borrowed by American composers for American bands are Patrick Burns' *Overture on Canadian Folk Songs* (Daehn, 2005) [Fig. 23.4] and Robert Sheldon's *A Canadian Ballad (She's Like a Swallow)* (Alfred, 2010). Burns' *Overture* was commissioned for a middle school band in New Jersey. The two melodies used, "The Banks of Newfoundland" and "Who is at my Window Weeping" are subjected to a variety of *tutti*, *soli* and *solo* treatments that, as with previous selections included in this study, provide performers and audiences alike with a richly textured introduction to the Canadian folksong tradition.

In addition to turning to the folksongs as a source of thematic materials, American arrangers also used several Canadian popular music successes. Haygood Hardy's *The Homecoming*, cited in Chapter Twenty-Two, was also released by Warner Brothers Publications in 1976 in an arrangement for young band by Andrew Balent. Frank Mills' *Music Box Dancer*, originally written in 1974, reached number three on the *Billboard* Hot

100 in May of 1979. It was subsequently arranged for band by Robert Lowden and published by Theodore Presser that same year. Jazz flautist Moe Koffman's *The Swingin' Shepherd Blues* was arranged for band by Paul Halliday and released by Warner Brothers in 1994. In 1978, "Place St. Henri", a movement from internationally renowned jazz pianist and Montréal legend Oscar Peterson's *Canadiana Suite* was published in an arrangement for band by Robert O'Brien.

The Influence of the MEAE Philosophy

The shift in focus away from earlier compositions directed at adult performers for entertainment purposes was part of a complete rethink of the role of the wind band that began in the United States in the 1950s. Military bands were supported in order to provide appropriate music for parades, dinners, memorial services and public concerts. Community bands existed "...to entertain, although many of them contain[ed] amateur players who simply play[ed] for enjoyment."[5] Even the original community-based youth bands had a very clear purpose; to keep young people "out of mischief." Each of these groups required no further justification for its existence. The school band however, especially as the financial commitments in support of band programs grew, faced a philosophical dilemma. Whereas it was sufficient for a military or community band to simply entertain, the role of the school was to educate. How could an idiom that had evolved as a form of entertainment be directed toward education?

The question had been at the centre of several attempts to provide educators with a firm basis for the inclusion of instrumental music into the curriculum. Both the Yale Seminar of 1963 and the Tanglewood Symposium of 1967 focused their efforts on the exposure of students to "good" music.[6] The culmination of this focus was the publication in 1970 of Bennett Reimer's *A Philosophy of Music Education* (Englewood Cliffs, New Jersey: Prentice-Hall Inc., 1970). Central to Reimer's position was the contention that music was a collection of "art works" and that the "...artist captures his emotions in the art work."[7] Reimer went on to suggest that the expressive or aesthetic elements of music, those qualities that capture the artist's expressive intent, were "...melody, harmony, rhythm, tone

---

[5] Richard Franko Goldman, *The Wind Band: Its Literature and Technique* (Boston: Allyn and Bacon, Inc., 1961) 14.

[6] For an overview of the movement, see: Harold F. Abeles, Charles R. Hoffer and Robert Klofman, *Foundations of Music Education*, 2nd ed., (New York: Simon and Schuster, MacMillan, 1995)

[7] Bennett Reimer, *A Philosophy of Music Education* (Englewood Cliffs, New Jersey: Prentice-Hall Inc., 1970) 28.

colour, texture [and] form…"[8] It followed that any value or meaning was strictly internal, based entirely on how these elements were organised. Ultimately, the goal of music education was the study of these elements "…teaching and learning must be arranged so that aesthetic experiencing is central and all other matters play a supporting role."[9] The Music Education as Aesthetic Education philosophy [MEAE], as it came to be known, provided a desperately needed validation for music programs across North America and rapidly assumed a pre-eminent position in undergraduate music education programs.[10] The MEAE philosophy, with its emphasis on the art-work, also gave an enormous boost to composers and publishers of music for school band programs.

The last three decades of the twentieth century saw American band music publishers release ever growing numbers of compositions intended to satisfy the need for music "worthy of study." As these new publications swamped North American shelves, music educators found it difficult to keep up with the exponentially expanding repertory. Several publishers responded to this need with the publication of a series of guides to band literature suitable for school use. Each was a reflection of the MEAE philosophy and laid out in concrete form those criteria necessary for a work to be considered "quality literature." Perhaps the best presentation of these criteria was to be found in *Best Music for High School Band: A Selective Repertoire Guide for High School Bands and Wind Ensembles* by Thomas L. Dvorak, Robert Greschesky and Gary M. Ciepluch, edited by Bob Margolis. The authors selected three conditions, which they felt were critical to make any work worthy of study:

Compositions must exhibit a high degree of compositional craft.

Compositions must contain important musical constructs necessary for the development of musicianship. Among these…are: a variety of keys, major, minor, modal; a variety of meters, duple, triple, combinations…a variety of harmonic styles, ranging from traditional to contemporary to avant garde; a variety of articulation styles – smooth, light, heavy, detached, legato and so on.

---

[8] Ibid., 86.
[9] Ibid., 86.
[10] When the author was an undergraduate at the University of Western Ontario (1969-1973), Reimer's book was the basis for a compulsory third year music education seminar.

Compositions must exhibit an orchestration that, within the restrictions associated with a particular grade level, encourage musical independence both of individuals and sections.[11]

With clearly defined parameters in place, American publishers embarked on a quest to capture the largest possible share of the enormous school band market. They engaged composers, often music educators with little experience beyond the classroom, to supply the voracious demand for new "quality literature" aided by state contest lists that were being constantly up-graded to include the latest releases. During the entire period, it appears that few publishers, if any, bothered to ask whether this new music was in fact an improvement over what it had been designed to replace; just because it was new was it necessarily better? This was a question that had already been asked many years before by Harry Pleasants, a former Philadelphia newspaper music critic turned postwar CIA station chief.

Harry Pleasants had studied voice, piano and composition at both the Philadelphia Conservatory and the Curtis Institute of Music as well as trumpet with Harold Rehrig, third trumpet of the Philadelphia Orchestra.[12] For many years he was the new music critic of the Philadelphia *Evening Bulletin* until he joined the U.S. Army in 1942.[13] His *The Agony of Modern Music* (New York: Simon and Schuster, 1955) was a scathing indictment of the "serious" musical establishment of the day and at its core was a simple question: what is it that constitutes quality in a musical work, the intent of the composer or the skill and invention of the composer? Pleasants clearly demonstrated through rigorous analysis and historical study that skill and invention were the determining factors. He went on to suggest that serious contemporary [1955] composers, Piston, Harris, Thomson, Schumann and their more experimental colleagues, Boulez, Stockhausen and Cage no longer represented any type of legitimate musical expression. The real American music he argued was going on in the Jazz clubs, the movies and on Broadway. He was subsequently

---

[11] Thomas L. Dvorak, Robert Grechesky and Gary M. Ciepluch, edited by Bob Margolis, *Best Music for High School Bands and Wind Ensembles* (Brooklyn, N.Y.: Manhattan Beach Music, 1993) 10. Earlier titles included David Wallace and Eugene Corporon, *Wind Ensemble/Band Repertoire* (Greeley, Colorado: University of Northern Colorado School of Music, 1984) and Joseph Kreines *Music for Concert Band* (Tampa, Fl.: Florida Music Service, 1989)

[12] William Rehrig, son of Harold Rehrig and author of the *Heritage Encyclopedia of Band Music*, letter to Carl Ehrke, 21 June 1999, courtesy Carl Ehrke.

[13] Pleasants was not only a passionate advocate of Jazz and its place in modern music. From 1950 until 1964 he was a Foreign Service Officer, member of the CIA involved in Cold War espionage activities and a CIA station chief.

pilloried by the musical establishment but sixty-five years later, his observations proved to be remarkably prophetic.

By the late 1990s, Pleasants' observations could be easily applied to modern American music for school band. It was becoming increasingly clear to many that much of the "quality literature" being churned out by the publishing mills was anything but:

> … music composed specifically for school band is formulaic, emotionally superficial, monotonously alike, dull and didactic; …it fails to inspire students; and that by being removed from any genuine musical tradition, classical or popular, it fails to provide students with a true musical education or the basis for further independent exploration of music, either as a performer or as a listener.[14]

In 2005, proud band parent and columnist for the *Washington Post* Stephen Budiansky wrote an opinion piece entitled "The Kids Play Great, But That Music…"[15] It was one of those "the emperor isn't wearing any clothes" moments that forced a complete re-examination of much of the wind band repertoire that had dominated North American school band programs for years. The irony is that domination by American publishers proved to be a two-fold blessing for Canadian band music.

The first of these blessings was that Canada's publishers released few works for school band during the 1970s, 1980s and 1990s. With only a fraction of the U.S. market, it was impossible for Canadian publishers to compete with the musical winds blowing from the south. One measure of the enormous disparity between the amount of band music published by American and Canadian publishers in the late twentieth century can be found in the *Band Music Guides* prepared by the *Instrumentalist* Magazine. These were lists of commercially available music for band in print and there were ten editions in total, the last of which appeared in 1996.[16] The ninth edition of the *Band Music Guide* (Northfield, Illinois: The Instrumentalist Publishing Company, 1989) contained over 12,300 titles, in all genres, for both concert and marching bands. Not included in this number were solo and small ensemble compositions with band accompaniment.[17] The listing represented the works of over 2000 composers and arrangers from around the world published by 210 different firms. The 1989 edition of the *Band Music Guide* included sixty-seven Canadian

---

[14] Stephen Budiansky and Timothy W. Foley, "The Quality of Repertoire in School Music Programs: Literature Review, Analysis and Discussion," *Journal of the World Association for Symphonic Bands and Ensembles* 12 (2005) 2.
[15] Stephen Budiansky, "The Kids Play Great, But That Music…," *The Washington Post* (30 January 2005)
[16] Editor, *The Instrumentalist*, e-mail correspondence with the author, 01 June 2021.
[17] *Band Music Guide*. 1989 Edition (Northfield, Ill.: The Instrumentalist Publishing Company, 1989.)

compositions by twenty-five Canadian composers, representing less than one half of one percent of the total. Canadian publishers fared somewhat better: there were two, Toronto's E.C. Kerby and the Waterloo Music Company (one percent). The vast majority of the titles listed were American.

Because Canadian publishers couldn't compete, they didn't really try. What was left was the small but worthy body of literature already discussed; a literature that was equally at home with university ensembles, community bands as well as those in the schools. Add to that body of literature the contribution of the Canadian Music Centre associate composers, most of whom, unlike many of their American counterparts, were well rounded creative artists, limited not just to educational environments but fluent in many musical genres. Even the American composers who were drawn to our folksong tradition could rely on the intrinsic value of the original melodies to provide meaningful musical experiences. Taken together, Canadian band music in the closing decades of the twentieth century, although modest in number by U.S. standards was of a consistently higher quality.

The second blessing had far reaching effects. The preponderance of American educational scores, intended for use in school band programs, was entirely ill suited to the needs of Canadian military and community bands. Since the gradual demise of the British Military Band Journals (Boosey & Hawkes, Chappell) in the 1950s and 1960s, Canadian military bands had little new popular music to perform for the many school concerts, mess dinners and public concerts that were an integral part of their military duties. It was necessary to find a fresh source of music and ironically it was by looking to the past that they found the way forward.

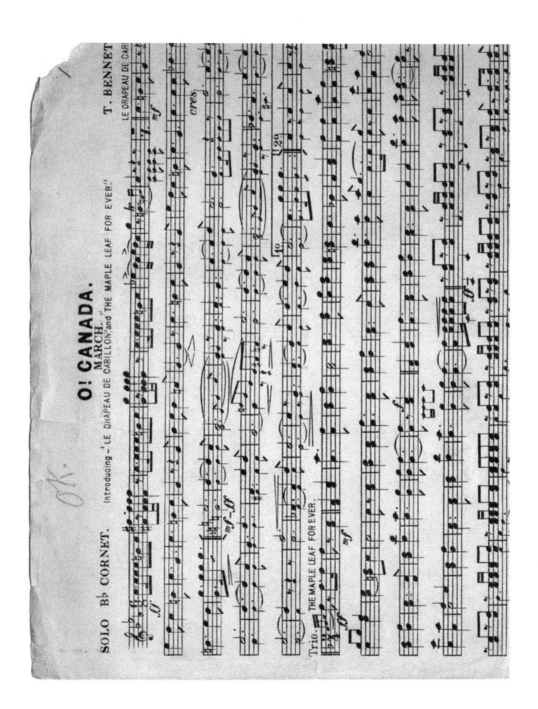

Figure 23.1. Solo cornet part to *O! Canada* by T. Bennett, published by Hawkes & Son in 1911. Introducing "Le Drapeau de Carillon" and "The Maple Leaf Forever"; the two melodies were intended to represent French and English Canada respectively. Source: author's collection.

Figure 23.2.   First page to the score of *Montreal (Allegro de Concert)* by the highly respected Belgian composer Paul Gilson (1865-1942).   Gilson wrote over thirty works for wind band as well as music for orchestra and the stage.   Source: author's collection.

Figure 23.3. First clarinet part to *Two Canadian Folksongs* by Anne McGinty, published by Queenwood Publications in 1987. McGinty's treatment of the "Eskimo Lullaby," originally collected from songs of the Cape Dorset Inuit and "Donkey Riding" for Grade 1 level band was on Canadian festival lists for years. Source: from "Two Canadian Folk Songs," arr. Anne McGinty. © 1987 Queenwood/Kjos. Reprinted with permission 2023 – www.kjos.com

Figure 23.4. First page to the flute part of *Overture on Canadian Folk Songs* by Patrick J. Burns, published by Daehn Publications in 2005. Score and parts are available from the C.L. Barnhouse Co.. Copyright Chesford Music Publications, used with permission.

CHAPTER TWENTY-FOUR

THE SPECIALS

As previously noted, British military bands in the late eighteenth century had relied on hand written manuscript parts to provide musical entertainment of a popular nature. From the mid-nineteenth century and for almost a hundred years thereafter, British and then later American military band journals focused largely on transcriptions of popular songs, operatic and symphonic selections and occasionally original works for wind band. In Canada, it was the army bands primarily that embraced this literature and a concert given by the First Canadian Infantry Battalion Band in 1953 under the direction of Captain James Gayfer is a representative sample:

BAND CONCERT

Quick March	Dunedin	Kenneth J. Alford
Overture	Die Meistersinger	Richard Wagner
Two Chorales	Sebastien/Passion	J.S. Bach
Second Suite for Military Band		Gustav Holst
Concert Piece	Praeludium	Armas Jarnefelt
Intermezzo	Tunbridge Fair	Walter Piston
Valse	Valse Triste	Jean Sibelius
Secular Motet	Ah, Dear Heart	Orlando Gibbons
Opera Selection	La Traviata	Guiseppe Verdi
Quick March	Holyrood	Kenneth J. Alford
Fantasia	Sussex Psalm	Russell Howland
Tone Poem	Mannin Veen	Haydn Wood

God Save the Queen[1]

During the Second World War, the Royal Canadian Air Force gained a reputation for being more lax and less disciplined than the army. Pilots were the "glory boys" of the war and anyone associated with the service took great pride in their rebellious "devil may care" attitude. Air Force bands were no exception and their approach to programming,

---

[1] Program courtesy of Mr. Ed Barlow

especially in the immediate postwar period was diametrically opposed to the use of the traditional military band repertoire favoured by the army. By the early 1950s, the RCAF Central Band in Ottawa prided itself on *not* playing marches but including "…lots of symphonic arrangements of Broadway show music, dance music, classical selections, but only those that could sound good when played by a top flight band…Kachaturian, Milhaud, some Tschaikovsky…."[2] The drive towards the performance of more popular American material, especially with the influence of newer technologies such as television in the early 1950s, required a literature that was not yet available from commercial sources. The RCAF Central Band was in the forefront of this movement away from what was considered both "British" and "Army." As a result, it was the first Canadian regular force band to engage staff arrangers to provide "new" music for its audiences. Back then, in the pre-music notation software age, the only way was with hand written manuscript scores and parts.

The RCAF Central Band Arrangers

In the late 1990s, the Canadian Forces Central Band library, formerly the RCAF Central Band library, contained 4,456 band scores. Of these, 844 were identified either as "specials" or "special arrangements"; a number representing over 20% of the total. Not included were manuscript works categorized as "Solos," "Miscellaneous" or "Christmas." These were unpublished arrangements created especially for the band, often by members of the band.[3] The 1960s were a golden age as the Central Band engaged three talented airmen as writers, Eric Ford, Gerry Hoelke and Ken Campbell. Most arrangements were of popular songs of the period as well as some classical transcriptions, jazz staples, solos with band and Latin numbers. Eric Ford's name appears on over forty-seven arrangements including a number of classical transcriptions of opera favourites by Verdi (*La Donna e Mobile*) and Donizetti (*Una Furtiva*) [After retiring from the military, Eric Ford assumed the position of Director of Music of the Burlington Teen Tour Band from 1968 to 1977]. Bassist Gerry Hoelke contributed another twenty-six with a fondness for Latin and jazz melodies (*Autumn Leaves, Flying Down to Rio, Siboney* and *Tico Tico* for accordian solo and band).

---

[2] Guy Fortier, *I Mean…Is That All You Do…Play in the Band?* (Ottawa: Privately Published Memoir, 1997) 42. Guy Fortier spent twenty years in the RCAF Central Band retiring in 1972.
[3] The author was presented with a Central Band library catalogue in the late 1990s which provided the information cited.

The combined total of both Ford and Hoelke however pales in comparison to the work of Kenneth Campbell, who for over twenty years provided the Central Band with more than 120 hand written scores. Campbell was the composer of two previously cited commercial band releases, *Capital City Suite* (Gordon V. Thompson, 1962) and *Puppet Parade* (Gordon V. Thompson, 1963). These were original compositions, but based on the number of his arrangements in the Central Band library, it is obvious that his greatest strengths lay in his talent as an arranger. Campbell had a gift "…for knowing the limits of everyone in the band so whatever he wrote was comfortable to play…[that] gave our band a sound that was the envy of all band musicians who heard us."[4] Initially the arrangements were restricted to the use of RCAF bands only, but with the introduction of photocopiers in the early 1970s, those that were particularly effective were distributed across the country's military band network. One of these, the *World War II Song Medley* has since become a staple in almost every regular/reserve/militia band library in the country. It is a collection of some of the most beloved melodies of the conflict, including "Don't Sit Under the Apple Tree," "We'll Meet Again," "White Cliffs of Dover" and "Wish Me Luck." Campbell's mastery of the band idiom, not just in his scoring but in the effortless grace of his bridge passages have made this score a perennial favourite at Remembrance Day gatherings across Canada for almost half a century. One genre that also appealed to all three RCAF arrangers was the music of Latin America. Campbell's version of the Ary Barroso classic *Brazil* enjoyed enormous popularity across the country (a popularity that was given new life with the release in 1985 of Terry Gilliam's film of the same name). In this particular work, the arranger's use of flutter tonguing in the solo flute passage, accompanied only by timbale, creates an atmospheric effect evocative of hot jungle nights which is made all the more intense by intermittent repeated statements of the "samba" motif in the low brass [Fig. 24.1].

In June of 2017, there was performance of the RCMP Musical Ride at "N" Division Headquarters in Ottawa. The opening act was a half hour concert performed by the Central Band of the Canadian Forces. It was a traditional program with marches as well as two movements from Holst's *Second Suite in F* and a complete performance of Vaughan Williams' *Folk Song Suite*. The concert also included another Kenneth Campbell classic, *Can Can for Trumpets*. This was a light hearted re-imaging of Offenbach's "Can Can" scored for trumpet trio and band [Fig. 24.2]. While the band was playing, a mini chorus line of several ladies in the audience spontaneously started to dance in the stands surrounding the equestrian ring to music that is both timeless and universally loved. This

---

[4] Guy Fortier, *I Mean….* 42.

was Campbell's greatest contribution: his arrangements take on a life of their own and continue to engage audiences long after their composition.

The last Canadian Army personnel to graduate from Britain's Kneller Hall Bandmaster's course did so in 1965. From that point on, all future candidates for the position of Director of Music in Canada's regular force bands underwent training at what was to become the Canadian Forces School of Music (CFSMUS). The intensive year long course, known as the TQ7s included studies in orchestration and one of the requirements for successful completion was that trainees compose a march and complete a workable arrangement for band. It was inevitable that not only would some of these future leaders show promise in the creative aspects of arranging, they would positively thrive. Although some of the pre-unification music officers completed arrangements in the Central Band library including Ron Milne [Fig. 24.3] and Bernard Bogisch [both of whom had published commercially], it was the post-unification cohort that really opened the floodgates. Several CFSMUS graduates in the 1970s and 1980s would contribute significantly: Jack Kopstein wrote twenty-seven arrangements for band, Terry O'Connor and Con Furey each added forty-two. Other arrangers included the Central Band's long-time Director of Music Derek Stannard as well as the country's first female regular force Director of Music, Heather Davis. Davis was a gifted and versatile musician capable of performing on oboe, trombone, keyboards and as a vocalist as well as being an arranger and conductor. During her twenty-seven year military career she arranged for dance bands, small ensembles, full band, marching band and vocal numbers. Since her retirement from the Canadian Forces in 2003 she has continued to arrange for regular force bands including a custom arrangement of Kathleen Johnson's *New Blue Suit* for the Central Band, *Kaleidoscope* for Québec's La Musique du Royal 22e Régiment and two medleys for Edmonton's Royal Canadian Artillery Band.[5]

Until its demise in 1979, the NORAD Band in Colorado Springs was also a posting for up to ten RCAF musicians. As with the Central Band, this international group was heavily reliant on "specials" with two of its civilian arrangers in the 1960s being Canada's Howard Cable and the American Warren Barker. Up to thirty-eight of their special arrangements also found their way into the Central Band library. In addition to scores from its own arrangers and the NORAD Band, the Central Band drew on the combined efforts of arrangers from the country's eight other regular force bands, who although lacking the depth of talent available to the Ottawa band, all produced capable arrangers including navy musicians Earl Fralick [arranger of Godfrey Ridout's *Fall Fair*] and Ken Garland.

---

[5] Heather Davis, e-mail correspondence with the author 09 March 2021.

The RCMP Band Arrangers

Extensive as the use of "specials" was in Canada's regular force bands, it still didn't even come close to the extent to which they were used in the country's only other professional brass-reed band: the RCMP Band. By 1974, the RCMP Band had three full time staff arrangers, Sgt. Blennis Pennell and Constables Gary Morton and Jim Seaman. Toni Chappell, Howard Cable and Boss Brass founder Rob McConnell were also associate arrangers. With that many arrangers it is not surprising that the band also had a full-time copyist, Sgt. Bernie Eberley. As noted in the first section of this study, the RCMP Band enjoyed enormous popularity not just through its annual Winter Season Concerts at Ottawa's National Arts Centre but also through its many nationwide trips held until its termination in 1993. A concert program from 22 February 1976 clearly illustrates the reliance on special arrangements; of thirteen numbers, ten are arrangements by the band's "inhouse" staff [Fig. 24.4]. A survey of eight other RCMP Band concert programs from 1974 to 1985 reveals a similar pattern: 75% or more of each consists of "specials" by the band's arrangers.[6]

The numbers are impressive. At dissolution, the RCMP Band library contained 2,167 listings, of which 840 were identified as "specials," representing over 40% of the total. The clear leader in terms of numbers were those by Gary Morton with 209 arrangements, followed by Jim Seaman, at 175, Blennis Pennell at 57 and Toni Chappell, who only appears in program notices until 1975, at 30. Sgt. Blennis Pennell was replaced in 1980 by Noel Casey who is credited with a further 36 special arrangements. There were other contributors; they included not just the band's own staff arrangers, but several military ones like Ken Garland, Eric Ford and "Jigger" Lee as well as the band's copyist, Bernie Eberley and its last Director of Music, Charlie Hendricks.[7]

The music arranged was drawn mostly from the "pop" literature of the day and was generally given an upbeat treatment reflected in the band's instrumentation, which was increasingly evolving towards that of a very large stage band. Movies, Broadway, T.V., Radio and Music Videos all had a place along with solos, vocals and some classical transcriptions. These were chosen for their audience appeal and although some became dated very quickly, there was always newer material to prepare. The RCMP Band was also a public face of the force. It toured nationally and visited smaller communities that

---

[6] Programs presented to the author by Dana Kaukinen, former member [trombone] of the RCMP Band.
[7] RCMP Band Library list is contained in Darrin Oehlerking "The History of Instrumental Wind Music Within the Royal Canadian Mounted Police Band" (D.M.A. thesis, University of Iowa, 2008) Appendix B, 120-176.

were rarely visited by larger performing ensembles whose stops were restricted to urban centres with lucrative box-office potential. The band's staff arrangers sometimes contributed to the group's success in these regional and smaller concert venues by writing music focused on them. Whether it was selections of songs from Québec, *Chansons du Québec* (arr. Seaman), *C'Est Moi* (arr. Morton), *J'Aurais Voulu Te Dire* (arr. Seaman) or music from the Maritimes, *Down East Medley* (arr. Wilkins) and *Let Me Fish Off Cape Saint Mary* (arr. Seaman), local audiences were engaged in a profoundly personal way. Some titles were even more specific: *Is There Anybody Here in Moose Jaw?* (unknown arranger).[8] The RCMP Band library catalogue offers a tantalizing glimpse of the group's travels during the last decades of the twentieth century through the titles of its "special arrangements" and many would be worthy of further study. Unfortunately, we will never get the chance.

At the end of 1993, the decision was made to terminate the operations of the RCMP Band. If its demise was a tragedy for the story of wind bands in Canada, what happened to its library was nothing short of **catastrophic!** As part of the final closure, it was decided to archive the Band library. Unfortunately, instead of keeping a copy of 1st, 2nd and 3rd instrumental parts, for each instrument, the individual [or individuals] tasked with the job only kept one copy of each instrumental part, trumpet, clarinet, etc., the rest were discarded. The result was that the library was functionally useless. In the end, it was all destroyed.[9]

The Community and School Band Arrangers

The use of "specials" wasn't just restricted to the professional military bands. From its inception in 1931, the Canadian Bandmasters Association strongly encouraged its members to compose for their own ensembles. In 1945, Lt. Reg Hinchey, founder of the Canadian Composers Guild stated "…All bandmasters should have a working knowledge of composition and arranging. That is part of their job…"[10] The tradition continued on into the remainder of the century. Band directors from across the country wrote or arranged music to accompany local, regional or provincial festivals with which their community bands were often associated. Examples include Howard Neill's *St. Mary's Band March* for the St. Mary's Band of St. John, New Brunswick [Fig. 24.5], the anonymous *Land of New Brunswick* or Bobby Gimby's *The Toronto Song.* The Nanaimo

---

[8] Ibid.

[9] Darrin Oehlerking, e-mail correspondence with the author, 04 March 2021.

[10] Frank McKinnon, "History of Canadian Band Association" *Canadian Band Journal* 16, no. 3 (Spring 1992) 21.

Concert Band library contains listings for two marches entitled *Bathtubs Away No. 1* and *Bathtubs Away No. 2*, both arranged by John Lewis.[11]   These were written for and performed at the city's annual Nanaimo Bathtub Races. For readers not familiar with this event, imagine old fashioned clawfoot bathtubs fitted with flotation devices and an outboard motor. The goal of the exercise is to see who can get across the Salish Sea from Vancouver to Nanaimo in the shortest time possible. Lunacy perhaps but very entertaining and a perfect excuse for the local community band to be part of a midsummer day's civic celebration.

Just as community band leaders across the country wrote or arranged for their own ensembles when commercial literature was either unavailable, unsuitable or just too expensive, so too did the nation's band teachers. The practical problem is that because the music they produced was either done by hand, or more recently, prepared using music notation software, there are limited copies available and, in most instances, these are restricted to one library only. Compounding the problem was the tendency of those that replaced these educators/arrangers, when they retired or moved on, to discard the arrangements. Such was the case with Ottawa's Henry Bonnenberg at Laurentian High School (1958-1979). While visiting the school in the early 1990s, the author was offered two boxes of manuscript arrangements by Bonnenberg that the current band teacher was planning to discard.   One contained an arrangement of the Mozart Bassoon Concerto (1774) [Fig. 24.6].   The extent of this "underground" literature elsewhere in the country however, is largely a matter of conjecture for the reasons listed above. There is however, another reason why it is best left undisturbed, copyright.

With the exception of Canada's professional wind bands, those in the Canadian Forces and the RCMP, it is unlikely that most community and school band arrangers of copyrighted materials sought permission to do so. For them, the obscurity brought on by having single copies only of their arrangements was perhaps a good thing; prosecution on such a small scale would be prohibitively expensive and largely ineffective. The problem with our military bands was solved legally by means of a long-standing policy involving negotiated settlements with Canada's performing rights societies. The Department of National Defence, through its Directorate of History and Heritage, makes an annual lump sum payment to SOCAN [Society of Composers, Authors and Music Publishers of Canada] in order to obtain blanket permission for the use of copyrighted materials.[12]

---

[11] Nanaimo Concert band library catalogue courtesy Mr. Gerry Klassen.
[12] Canada, Department of National Defence, Directorate of History and Heritage, e-mail correspondence with the author, 29 March 2021.

The "specials" are included in this study because they, as much as any other musical form, attest to the extraordinary vitality and relevance of the wind band in contemporary musical life. It is hard to imagine any other large instrumental performance ensemble in Canada that continues to inspire such an enormous amount of creative energy towards the production of "not-for-profit" music. Even though many of these scores, both documented and as yet undiscovered, are largely utilitarian in nature and may not achieve the same level artistically as much of the music discussed in previous chapters, their performance engages band musicians and audiences in a direct way that commercial materials often do not.

Figure 24.1.   First page of the solo clarinet part to Ary Barroso's *Brazil*, arranged for the RCAF Central Band by Kenneth Campbell, undated.   Source: © All rights reserved, this arrangement of "Brazil" reproduced with permission of DND/CAF (2022).

Figure 24.2. First Solo Trumpet part to *Can Can for Trumpets* by Kenneth Campbell, arranged for the RCAF Central Band, undated. Offenbach's famous "Can Can" from *Orpheus in the Underworld* has been re-imagined as a trumpet trio with band. The military arrangers were writing for professional ensembles and were not limited by technical considerations as the above example shows [trumpet high "C"]. The classical repertory, both symphonic and operatic was a rich source of material that was often updated for postwar audiences. Source: © All rights reserved, "Can Can for Trumpets" reproduced with permission of DND/CAF.

Figure 24.3.   First page of the conductor's score to *Auprès de ma Blonde* by Ron Milne, manuscript arrangement, 1965.   Source: author's collection.

PROGRAMME

Sunday February 22. 1976 / Dimanche le 22 février 1976

CHARADE — *Mancini — arr. Morton*

JUBILANT OVERTURE — *Reed*

PIECES OF DREAMS — *Legrand — arr. Morton*
Sid Arnold — Flugel Horn/Bugle

CHANSONS DU QUÉBEC — *arr. Seaman*

GEORGE WASHINGTON BI-CENTENNIAL MARCH — *Sousa*

CHATTANOOGA CHOO-CHOO — *Gordon/Warren — arr. Seaman*
Dean Tronsgard — Trombone

ROCKFORD FILES — *Post/Carpenter — arr. Pennell*

JONATHAN LIVINGSTON SEAGULL — *Diamond — arr. Morton*

INTERMISSION/ENTRACTE

SHOW BIZ — *arr. Seaman*

CONCERTINO — *Chaminade — arr. Wilson*
Guest Soloist Miss/soliste invitée Mlle Carmilia MacWilliam — Flute/flûte

ALL IN THE FAMILY — *arr. McConnell*

OVER THE RAINBOW — *Arlen/Harburg — arr. Seaman*
Garth Hampson — Vocal/solo vocal

HERE'S TO MANCINI — *Mancini — arr. Pennell*
HOMMAGE À MANCINI

O'CANADA / *Ô CANADA*

Figure 24.4.   Programme from the Sunday, February 22 Concert given by the R.C.M.P. Band at Ottawa's National Arts Centre as part of the 1976 "Winter Concert Series."   Of the thirteen numbers on the programme, nine were arranged by the band's staff arrangers, Constables Gary Morton, Jim Seaman and Blennis Pennell.   A tenth selection, *All in the Family*, was arranged by Rob McConnell, director of the internationally renowned Boss Brass.   Source: author's collection.

Figure 24.5. First page of the conductor's score to the *St. Mary's Band March* by Howard Neill, undated. Neill was conductor of the St. Mary's Band of St. John, N.B., from 1962 to 1982. This hand written manuscript, in pencil, was typical of many by local community band bandmasters composed for their own ensembles. Source: Doug Reece.

Figure 24.6. First clarinet part to the Mozart *Bassoon Concerto,* arranged for band and soloist by Henry Bonnenberg, undated. Bonnenberg taught at Ottawa's Laurentian High School from 1958 until 1979; a prolific arranger he was always encouraging his students to improve their skills through the performance of literature that was rarely available commercially. Source: author's collection.

CHAPTER TWENTY-FIVE

WORDS AND MUSIC

The preceding chapters in this section have introduced the reader to Canadian band music composed since the late eighteenth century. The present chapter will attempt to answer two questions that may be facing modern day band directors: how to identify and evaluate literature suitable for their own ensembles and where to get it.

In 2015, Dr. Mark Hopkins of Acadia University gathered in Toronto with university wind band directors from across the country to prepare a list of Canadian wind band repertoire worthy of study. Attendees included some of the most respected names in the Canadian wind band movement including Jason Caslor, Wayne Jeffrey, Keith Kinder, Fraser Linklater, Gillian MacKay, Wendy McCallum, Darrin Oehlerking, Angela Schroeder and others.[1] The nineteen participants assembled prospective titles from a variety of sources including published articles and citations from the CBA's *Canadian Winds* magazine, lists of representative Canadian works contained in Dr. S. Timothy Maloney's "Canadian Wind Ensemble Literature" (D.M.A. thesis: Eastman School of Music at the University of Rochester, 1986), entries in Michael Burch-Pesses' *Canadian Band Music* (Galesville, MD: Meredith Music Publications, 2008), selections from the "North Winds" recording project and the website of the Canadian Music Centre (CMC). Also added were submissions from individual band directors at the conference.

The final list included 800 titles dating from Antoine Dessane's *Pas Rédoublé sur les Airs "Vive la Canadienne" et "God save the Queen"* (1865) [Fig. 17.3] to John Palmer's *Odyssey for Concert Band* (2013). Over 500 of the works that made the final list were written by associate composers of the CMC with many others coming from successful writers including Brian Appleby, Scott Rogal, Robert Buckley, Vince Gassi, David Marlatt, Jeff Smallman, Douglas Court, Lindsey Stetner and Fred Stride. The music selected ranged from beginning level works intended primarily for audience appeal to difficult repertoire focused on serious artistic expression. The document, as yet unpublished, is an invaluable resource. It is a summation of a number of critical analyses of Canadian band music stretching back to the late 1980s. One of the most far reaching and helpful of these was written not by a Canadian, but an American.

Michael Burch-Pesses is one of those fortunate individuals whose formative musical experiences included military service as a musician and bandmaster (United States Navy).

---

[1] Dr. Mark Hopkins, e-mail correspondence with the author, 24 March 2020.

In that capacity he would have been exposed to the utilitarian function of the wind band, a function that was foundational to the ensemble's existence since its creation over two centuries ago. After leaving military service and completing post graduate study he found himself adjudicating a Band Festival in Red Deer, Alberta, and it was there that he was exposed for the first time to "Canadian Content", often in the form of band arrangements of Canada's folksong repertory. He was enchanted and his book, *Canadian Band Music* was the final result.[2] Following extensive research, he selected a total of 136 titles by 63 different composers at all skill levels. Of the composers selected, forty-three (over two thirds), were associates of the CMC. In his book, each composer is given a brief biography and then their composition(s) is (are) given a difficulty rating, duration and information is provided about availability. Explanatory notes about the work(s) are also included along with a brief stylistic analysis and historical context if necessary.[3] *Canadian Band Music* is an essential document for any modern Canadian band director seeking a broadly based, impartial assessment of quality Canadian literature but it is certainly not the only one.

The first issue of *Canadian Winds* appeared in 2002 and it was a frequent and vocal supporter of Canadian music for band with articles appearing regularly. It started right away with the inaugural issue which included Timothy Maloney's "20th Century Canadian Concert Music for Bands and Wind Ensembles: An Introduction."[4] From 2003 to 2009, articles were often focused on one work by a Canadian composer, ranging from those by established CMC associates including Oscar Morawetz, Harry Somers, Jack Sirulnikoff, Colin McPhee, Morley Calvert, Donald Coakley, Pierre Mercure, Maurice Blackburn, Elizabeth Raum, François Morel and Allan Gilliland to more commercially oriented titles by André Jutras, Ron MacKay and Jonathan Dagenais. There were also collaborative efforts on a wider range of titles including Denise Grant, Keith Kinder and Jeff Reynold's "Canadian Wind Band Repertoire" (Fall 2004), which contained references to the works of Douglas Court, Ron MacKay, Gary Kulesha, Donald Coakley, James Gayfer, Morley Calvert, John Herberman, John Weinzweig, Michael Colgrass and Harry Freedman. This particular article set in motion a series of sequels that would run for years. The second was authored by Michael Purves-Smith in the Fall 2005 issue and reviewed music by Louis Applebaum, Malcolm Forsyth, Derek Healey, Howard Cable, Peter Hatch, Alan Bell and David Marlatt. Starting with the Fall 2006 issue, the series was written by Fraser Linklater and would continue through to the Fall of 2016, a combined total of thirteen articles

[2] Michael Burch-Pesses, *Canadian Band Music* (Galesville, MD: Meredith Music Publications, 2008) ix.
[3] Burch-Pesses, *Canadian Band Music*.
[4] Timothy Maloney, "20th Century Concert Music for Bands and Wind Ensembles: An Introduction" *Canadian Winds* 1, no. 1 (Autumn 2002) 32-37.

spanning an enormous range of Canadian composers, CMC associates and commercially successful writers, providing readers with in depth analysis including references to form and structure, musical elements, technical considerations and stylistic influences.[5]

The *Canadian Band Journal* was the predecessor of the CBA's *Canadian Winds* journal and it too had a long history of promoting the use of Canadian band literature. These included articles on the music of Malcolm Forsyth (Robert George, Winter 1989), André Jutras (Sharon Fitzsimmons, Fall 1992), Jim Duff (Cathy Lynn Yorke-Slader, Summer 1993), Jack Freeman (Mary Thomas, Fall 1994), Eddie Graf (Mary Thomas, Spring 1996), Donald Coakley (Mary Thomas, Summer 1997) and Harry Freedman (Mary Thomas, Spring 1998). More comprehensive reviews included Jeremy Brown's "A Short List of Canadian Wind Band Literature," (Spring 1997) and Stephen Chenette, Patricia Shand and Cameron Walter's "Canadian Repertoire for Concert Band" (Spring 1998).

Two earlier reference sources, already cited in previous chapters were Patricia Martin Shand's *Guidelist of Unpublished Canadian Band Music Suitable for Student Performers* (Toronto: Canadian Music Centre, 1987) and *Canadian Music: A Selective Guidelist for Teachers* (Toronto: Canadian Music Centre, 1978). These, along with the periodical articles and Michael Burch-Pesses *Canadian Band Music* cited above provide reviews of hundreds of Canadian works for band; music for all tastes, from silly to sublime at all levels of difficulty. The analyses confirm that Canadian band music is not only worthy of study but that it should also be considered worthy of study. It hasn't always been the case. A broader compilation edited by Lynne Jarman entitled *Canadian Music: A Selected Checklist 1950-1973* (Toronto: University of Toronto Press, 1976) contained 300 titles, of which only five were for band: Applebaum's *Suite of Miniature Dances*, Cable's *Newfoundland Rhapsody*, Mercure's *Pantomime*, Morawetz's *Sinfonietta* and Willan's *Elegie Heroique*. A later text was even more restrictive; George A. Proctor's *Canadian Music of the Twentieth Century* (Toronto: University of Toronto Press, 1980) acknowledged only four works for band, Mercure's *Pantomime,* Willan's *Royce Hall Suite* and *Elegie Heroique* and Somers *Symphony for Winds, Brass and Percussion.* In retrospect, the limited number of works for band in these two compilations isn't surprising. The 1960s were a period of transition as the growing school band movement was just beginning to influence music publishers who had up to that time viewed band music only as a source of entertainment.

That's not to say earlier generations of band composers were inferior; Howard Cable's trinity of *Newfoundland Rhapsody, Quebec Folk Fantasy* and *Snake Fence Country* were

---

[5] Fraser Linklater, Canadian Wind Band Repertoire (5) *Canadian Winds* 7 no. 1 (Fall 2008) 34-40.

all composed in the 1950s as part of the Chappell Army Band Journal series and were primarily intended to serve that market. In 1952, the Canadian Broadcasting Corporation published a *Catalogue of Canadian Composers*, an enlarged and revised edition of J.J. Gagnier's ground breaking catalogue of the same name released in 1947.[6] The newer edition contained the names of 347 composers, living and deceased, dating back to Glackmeyer in the early nineteenth century, as well as brief biographical notes and listings of each composer's work in all genres. Thirty-six of these composers, many of whom have been discussed earlier in this study, had written a total of 312 titles, mostly marches, for band, both published and in manuscript. Although the numbers alone are significant, it is the brief biographies that are worthy of note. Those that chose to write for band often possessed the same academic and professional qualifications as their peers and in the case of some, exceeded them. Two of the most prolific interwar bandmasters, J.J. Gagnier and Charles O'Neill held doctoral degrees from L'Université de Montréal and McGill respectively while R.B. Hayward was Director of Wind Instrument instruction at the Toronto Conservatory [now the RCMT]. Equally important, many of those who wrote for band also composed in other forms; their passion for composition was not just restricted to the wind band. With their professional lives often closely associated with some of the finest performance ensembles in their respective communities, military or community bands, the pre 1950 cohort of Canadian band composers stood out as some of the most creative minds of their generation.

From the associate composers of the Canadian Music Centre today to the prewar bandmasters, there is a century long tradition of composition for wind band that has left this country with well over a thousand Canadian works waiting to be discovered. In conjunction with this study and the sources cited therein, there also exists ample resources for any band director in Canada to identify a range of possible programming choices for their own ensembles. These compositions are stylistically varied and have the potential to appeal to military, university, community and school bands of every skill level and new technologies are now making it increasingly easy to obtain them with just the click of a mouse.

The Canadian Music Centre [CMC] rental holdings surpass any other single source of Canadian band music. The CMC can be reached through its website at www.cmccanada.org or by phone at (1) 416 961 6601 [Toronto Office]. Most scores can be viewed online and many have accompanying recordings. If the reader has a particular

---

[6] Helmut Kallmann, ed. *Catalogue of Canadian Composers* (Toronto: Canadian Broadcasting Corporation, 1952)

composer in mind, go to the "Composer Showcase" and follow the links which will include a complete list of that individual's works held by the CMC.

The largest commercial publisher of band music in Canada is Eighth Note Publications; they can be reached online at www.enpmusic.com. Their concert band catalogue includes 405 titles for concert band at every skill level from Grades 0.5 [beginner] to Grade 5+. In addition to works by its own fine writers including David Marlatt, Jeff Smallman and Ryan Meeboer, the company also holds the rights to many compositions by CMC associates Donald Coakley, Stephen Chatman, Morley Calvert and Howard Cable. Also included are recent releases by commercially successful writers Vince Gassi, Jonathan Dagenais and John Herberman as well as arrangements of a large number of Canadian folksongs and well-known classics by composers from Tilman Susato to Claude Debussy.[7] Toronto's Northdale Music Press Limited, established in 1986, continues to publish works by Canadian composers including Howard Cable's *Ontario Pictures* and John Herberman's *The Fisher Who Died in His Bed*. The Northdale Press can contacted at www.northdalemusic.com .

There are also the smaller regional publishers: Halifax's ronmacmusic publishes over thirty-two original compositions and fifty-eight arrangements by the late Ron MacKay (d. 2008).[8] His music is written for all skill levels and much is inspired by the people and landscapes of his Nova Scotia home. All scores are available for viewing online and can be purchased and downloaded on PDF file. The company's website is www.ronmacmusic.com. In Edmonton, music educators Brian Appleby and Scott Rogal continue to operate ApRo Music, a small company specializing in music for young bands, Grades 0.5 to 2. With over 40 titles in their online catalogue, music can also be viewed and heard prior to purchase. In business since the late 1980s, ApRo is a prairie success story. They can be reached at www.apromusic.com.[9] Further west, tucked away in the shadow of the eastern Rockies lies Cranbrook B.C., home to Upstage Innovations, the small beginning band publisher created by Larry Dureski. Although the website only lists six titles for very young band [Larry has been a grade six band teacher for over thirty years], he has completed over twenty-five since the late 1990s. These are available by contacting him at www.upstageinnovations.com.

American publishers continue to recognize and support Canadian composers. André Jutras, whose *C'Est Noel* was first published in 1985, is still listed on the C.L.Barnhouse website at www.barnhouse.com with all nine of his scores available, ranging in difficulty

---

[7] Eighth Note Publications Concert Band catalogue at www.enpmusic.com accessed 16 February 2021.
[8] ronmacmusic catalogue at www.ronmasmusic.com accessed 15 February 2021.
[9] Apro Music catalogue at www.apromusic.com accessed 16 February 2021.

from *Daydreams* [Grade 2] to *Moventa* [Grade 4]. Fellow Canadian David Eastmond is also a Barnhouse contributor with a total of five compositions, all for intermediate band, listed in their catalogue. California based Alfred Music at www.alfred.com is home to four scores by Newfoundlander Jim Duff as well as the creative output of Toronto's Vince Gassi, a writer for Alfred since 2006, whose name is to be found on fifty-seven works for band, both arrangements and original compositions. Vancouver's Robert Buckley is even more prolific; his music is distributed by the Hal Leonard Corporation of Wisconsin at www.leonardmusic.com and to date includes seventy-two original compositions and arrangements. Hal Leonard now also holds the distribution rights for Curnow Music Press, home of the band works of Toronto's Douglas Court. One small American publisher, Bourne at www.bournemusic.com, deserves inclusion because it continues to publish Arnold MacLaughlan's *A French Canadian Suite*.[10] One non-American foreign publisher still distributing the work of Canadian composers is the Dutch publisher Molenaars Music at www.molenaar.com. They are distributors of six works each by Bernhard Bogisch [Dutch spelling] and Thomas Legrady. As with most websites, these compositions are available for viewing and listening online, with one particularly worthy of close examination, Bogisch's five movement *Suite Acadienne* (1997).

Several Canadian publishers cited earlier in this section are now defunct, but their music is still available. The Waterloo Music Company catalogue, active since the 1930s is now controlled by Mayfair Music, at www.mayfairmusic.com.[11] Of particular interest to readers are Robert McMullin's *Prairie Sketches* and David Roe's *Three Canadian Folk Songs* published in the 1970s and 1980s. The Gordon V. Thompson catalogue was acquired by Counterpoint Music Library at www.cpmusiclibrary.ca and lists works by a range of Canadian composers including Kenneth Campbell, *Capital City Suite*; Dolores Claman, *A Place to Stand*; Howard Cable, *McIntyre Ranch Country*; Pierre Mercure, *Pantomime* and Morley Calvert, *Romantic Variations*. Like the CMC, the Counterpoint Music Library rents titles from its catalogue as well as selling them.

Many of the early works of both Howard Cable and Robert Farnon were published as part of the Chappell Army Journal series including *Newfoundland Rhapsody*, *Quebec Folk Fantasy*, *Snake Fence Country*, *Derby Day*, *Dominion Day*, *Seashore* and *Toronto City*. These are still available through the Chappell Army Journal Archive Service of the U.K. based Studio Music. A complete listing is available online at https://studio-music.co.uk .

---

[10] Bourne also holds the rights to the compositions of Frank Erickson, one of the greatest of America's postwar band composers.

[11] Carol Simpanen, Mayfair Music, telephone conversation with the author 11 March 2021.

It is also possible to obtain revised editions of selected nineteenth century Canadian works by composers cited in previous chapters including Dessane, Lavallée, Vézina, H.L.Clarke and A.W. Hughes. Compositions by these and others were assembled in the Canadian Musical Heritage Society's *Music for Winds I: Bands*, edited by Timothy Maloney and published in 1998; they are now available through the CMC.

As part of the early research for this project, the author prepared a number of revised band editions of seminal Canadian scores, many of which have been cited in this volume. These arrangements are in both manuscript and notation software formats and can be purchased directly from the author. Available titles include d'Argenson's *Royal Fusiliers Arrival at Québec, 1791* and *Marche de Normandie* (1791); Henry Prince's *Mermaid Polka* (1856); Antoine Dessane's *Pas Rédoublé* (1865); Joseph Vézina's *Canadian Rifles Waltzes* (1871), *De Calgarry à MacLeod, Marche* (1886), *Prière* (1888) and *Première Neige, Polka* (1888); L.P. Laurendeau's *Twilight Whispers, Intermezzo* (1895), *Stampede Galop* (1896), *Danse des Ecureuils* (1902), *Laurentian Echoes* (1908) and *Long, Long Ago, Fantaisie for Clarinet* (1912); Job Nelson's *Imperial Native March* (1907); John Slatter's *Canadian Patrol* (1911); William Delaney's *In Canada: Hudson's Bay Patrol* (1929); A.W. Hughes' *Specialty Overture* (1931) and W.R. Spence's *Moonlight on the Rideau, Waltz* (1936).

There is one other alternative for obtaining Canadian band music from the late nineteenth and early twentieth centuries; if it is in the public domain all you have to do is copy it. First of all, it will be necessary to define what constitutes "public domain" and for that we need to review Canada's existing copyright laws. **The author is not a lawyer and the information presented below is an overview only of existing legislation. It is not intended as legal advice nor should it be relied upon as such.** Canada's most recent copyright legislation is the Copyright Modernization Act, Bill C-11 of 2012, an amendment to the Copyright Act (R.S.C. (Revised Statutes of Canada) of 1985, known as bill C-42.[12] Musical works, defined as follows "…any work of music or musical composition, with or without words and including any compilation thereof…" are protected under the terms of the Act.[13] Section 6 of the Act refers to the term of copyright and states: "The term for which copyright shall subsist, except as otherwise expressly provided by this Act, be the life of the author [composer], the remainder of the calendar year in which the author dies, and a period of fifty years following the end of that calendar

---

[12] "An Act to Amend the Copyright Act," *Copyright Modernization Act (S.C. 2012, c.20)* at www.laws-lois.justice.gc.ca accessed 30 September 2021.

[13] "Interpretation-definitions," *Copyright Act (R.S.C. (Revised Statutes of Canada), 1985, C-42* at www.laws-lois.justice.gc.ca/eng/acts/C-42/ accessed 13 March 2021.

year."[14]   **This has since changed**.   Under the terms of the Canada United States Mexico Agreement [CUSMA] which was ratified by Canada on July 1st, 2020, the term of copyright protection has been extended to seventy (70) years.   **Effective 30 December 2022, copyright protection now subsists for a period of seventy years following the calendar year of the death of the composer.**   This extension however does not apply to works that have already passed into the public domain under the provisions of the previously existing legislation.   Once the term of copyright has expired, a work then passes into the public domain.   In the case of musical compositions, those whose composers died on or before 31 December 1972 are now said to be in the public domain and are free of any restrictions.   One recent case would be the band music of Healey Willan, composer of the *Royce Hall Suite* (Associated, 1952) and *Elegie Heroique* (B & H, 1971); Willan passed away in 1968 and consequently both works are now in the public domain even though their copyright notices were published in countries whose terms of protection are longer.

This last point is the source of some confusion.   The copyright law that is in effect is **the law of the country in which the activity takes place**.   If Canadians were required to obey U.S. copyright law in the performance of their duties in Canada, then that would be a case of extra-territoriality, applying one country's laws in another's jurisdictions.   It is a situation no sovereign nation could tolerate [imagine going to the U.S. and trying to apply Canadian legislation there!].   Nations around the world have solved the problem by means of the Berne Convention.   Originally established in 1886, signatories agreed to enforce copyright laws within their borders on behalf of all participating members and as of 2021, there were at least 179 state signatories to the convention. Regardless of where any musical work is originally copyrighted, if the copying activity takes place in Canada, Canadian law applies and it is Canadian law that applies with respect to the duration of copyright protection: seventy years after the calendar year of the death of the composer.   Of course, if a public domain work is revised and the revision published, then copyright is reassigned on the reworked version.

The practical advantage is that if a modern band director can obtain a score or set of parts of a work composed by any composer who died prior to 01 January 1972, then they are free to make copies as necessary.   But there is a catch.   Over the past hundred years, the instrumentation of the wind band has evolved and in the case of conductors' scores and two instruments in particular, horns and flutes, modifications may have to be made.   A century ago, band music was popular music, it was intended for popular audiences and publishers considered full scores an unnecessary editorial luxury.   For much of the prewar

---

[14] "Term of Copyright," *Copyright Act. Section 6.* accessed 13 March 2021.

literature for band published by both Waterloo and Whaley, Royce and Co., as well as most American publishers, a score was little more that a Solo Cornet part with cues. On occasion a two-line piano score would be provided, especially if the work in question was a transcription of a "serious" classical composition. Flute/piccolo parts were often written for D flat flute, an instrument that was popular in British military bands until well into the twentieth century although most U.S. publishers provided C flute parts from about 1920 on. Horn parts were almost always written for E flat alto horns, sometimes written simply as "Eb Altos". In both cases transpositions are necessary to make the parts work: the Db flute/piccolo sounds a semitone higher than written, and modern horns in F require Eb Alto parts to be read a whole tone lower. Wherever possible, if a revised edition is available, such as Darrin Oehlerking's revision of Charles O'Neill's *Souvenir de Quebec* (Eighth Note Publications, 2020), it is the preferable option as a full score is provided and horn parts are all in F requiring no extra effort on the part of the band director. If the reader is still interested in obtaining copies of public domain scores for their own ensembles, there is a commercial source. The picturesque town of Chatfield, Minnesota, is home to the Chatfield Music Lending Library, one of the largest collections of concert band music in the world. Included in its catalogue are the works of many Canadian composers, cited in this study, whose works are now in the public domain. The music lending library can be contacted at www.Musicrequests@chatfieldband.lib.mn.us.

The above information has been supplied to give band directors from across Canada the opportunity to explore over a century of literature for band by composers who were and continue to be musical leaders in their communities. It is a richly varied resource, ranging from music appropriate to beginner bands to works requiring the skills and discipline of our finest adult wind ensembles. As with our wind bands, which have shown the world that they are amongst the world's finest, so too our Canadian music for band, in all its forms, need not be ignored because of any preconceived notion that "Canadian" means second best.

EPILOGUE

This book is a love letter to a musical formation and its hundreds of thousands of practitioners who for almost 250 years have been present at almost every significant event in Canadian history. In times of peace and war, depression and prosperity, wind bands and wind band musicians in every province and territory, of all ages and all skill levels, have shared their talents and enthusiasm with audiences from communities both large and small. Of equal importance, these groups attracted musicians from all segments of Canadian society: foundry workers to businesspeople, First Nations youth to Family Court judges, prairie housewives to medical doctors and common soldiers to post graduate students in our finest universities. Of the over 350 online sources surveyed for the chapter on contemporary community bands, not one restricted admission to potential members for any reason other than technical skill for advanced level ensembles. Many of these same community bands are also models of multigenerational inclusion. Hundreds of online images reveal memberships that range in age from high school students to octogenarians. With the exception of our nation's choirs, what other type of social organization unites participants, sometimes separated in age by half a century or more, as equals, in the pursuit of a common artistic goal?

Perhaps more than any other large instrumental performing group, Canadian wind bands at all levels have the advantage of containing within their membership both performers and audience. As we have seen throughout this study, most community, school and cadet bands exist largely because those that perform in them do so for the joy of performing. They (or their parents) are also prepared to pay for that privilege either through annual dues, registration fees or fund-raising activities. Community bands especially are self-sustaining and require little external funding to maintain their operations. The same cannot be said for many of the country's pre-eminent professional musical arts organizations, especially in the field of "serious" music: the symphony orchestras, ballet schools and operatic societies. These rely on paying audiences, government grants and private sector philanthropy to ensure their continued viability.

Canadian wind bands are uniquely placed to demonstrate the power of music to engage us in a socially interactive creative endeavour that makes us fully human. One of the defining characteristics of that humanity is the capacity to love and to direct one's energies on its behalf. That is the only way to explain the epic story of wind bands in Canada: for the love of music.

BIBLIOGRAPHY

Antmann, Willy. *Music in Canada 1600-1800*. Montréal: Habitex Books, 1975.

ApRo Music. "Concert Band." Accessed 16 February 2021.
https://apromusic.com/cb-alphabetically.html

Atkins, H.E. *Treatise on the Military Band*. 2nd ed. Boosey & Co., 1958.

Barnard, W.T. *The Queen's Own Rifles of Canada 1860-1960: One Hundred Years of Canada*. Don Mills, Ont.: The Ontario Publishing Co., Ltd., 1960.

Barrie Historical Archives. "Barrie Central Collegiate Band." Accessed June 2019.
https://www.barriearchive.ca/source/barrie-central-band/

Battisti, Frank. *The Twentieth Century American Wind Band/Ensemble: History, Development and Literature*. Fort Lauderdale, Fla.: Meredith Music Publications, 1995.

Beal, George W. *Family of Volunteers: An Illustrated History of the 48th Highlanders of Canada*. Toronto: Robin Brass Studio, 2001.

Binns, P.L. *A Hundred Years of Military Music: being the story of the Royal Military School of Music Kneller Hall*. Gillingham, Dorset: The Blackmoor Press, 1959.

Bird, Will R. *North Shore (New Brunswick) Regiment*. Fredericton, N.B.: Brunswick Press, 1963.

Black, Conrad. *Rise to Greatness: The History of Canada from the Vikings to the Present*. Toronto: McClelland and Stewart, 2014.

Bowman, Durrell and Stanley L. Osborne. "Thomas Legrady." In *The Canadian Encyclopedia*. Historica Canada. Article published 07 February 2006; last edited 10 December 2013.
https://www.thecanadianencyclopedia.ca/en/article/thomas-legrady-emc

Bourassa, Dominique. "La Contribution des bandes militaires britanniques au développement de la musique au Québec de la conquête à 1836." Master's thesis, Université Laval, 1993.

_____. "Regards sur la formation et la composition de la bande des Fusiliers Royaux en garnison à Québec de 1791-1794." *Cahiers de la société québecoise de recherche en musique*. 2/2 (1998) : 73-78.

Bourbonnais, Gabrielle. *Inventaire Sommaire du Fonds J.J. Gagnier*. Montréal: Bibliothèque Nationale du Québec, 1989.

British Columbia Beefeater Band. "About." Accessed 03 December 2019.
https://beefeaterband.wordpress.com/about/

British Regiments in Canada: Infantry I: Regiments of Foot 1st through 50th. Accessed 17 December 2020. https://freepages.rrotsweb.com/-crossroads/genealogy/regiments/regiments-infantry.html

Brown, Jeremy S. "The Wind Conducting Diploma Program of Calgary 1984-1996: A Touchstone of the Core Repertoire for the Wind Band." *Canadian Band Journal* 22/2 (Winter 1997): 8, 23-25.

_____ . "A Short List of Canadian Wind Band Literature." *Canadian Band Journal* 21/3 (Spring 1997): 5-6.

Brown, Keaton. "The North Battleford City Kinsmen Band to celebrate 70th anniversary." *Battlefords NOW* (Aug 30, 2019). Accessed 01 March 2020. https://battlefordsnow.com/2019/08/30/the-north-battleford-city-kinsmen-band-to-celebrate-70th-anniversary

Brown, Kingsley Sr., Kingsley Brown Jr. and Brereton Greenhouse. *The History of the Royal Hamilton Light Infantry (Wentworth Regiment) 1862-1977.* Hamilton, Ont.: The RHLI Historical Association, 1977.

Bukofzer, Manfred. *Music in the Baroque.* New York: W.W Norton, 1947.

Burlington Teen Tour Band, The. "History." Accessed 01 December 2019. https://www.teentourband.org/history

_____ . "Honours and Awards." Accessed 10 November 2020. https://www.teentourband.org/about

_____ . "TV and Silver Screen." Accessed 01 December 2019. https://www.teentourband.org/tv--silver-screen

Calderisi, Maria. *Music Publishing in the Canadas 1800-1867.* Ottawa: National Library of Canada, 1981.

Calgary Stampede Showband, The. "Programs." Accessed 10 November 2020. https://foundation.calgarystampede.com/youth-programs/the-calgary-stampede-showband/

Camp Musical d'Asbestos, Le. "Le Camp." Accessed 05 November 2019. https://www.centreo3.com/fr/le-camp

Camus, Raoul F. *Military Music of the American Revolution.* Westerville, Ohio: Integrity Press, 1975.

Canada, Department of National Defence. *Report No. 47, The History of Bands in the Canadian Army.* Ottawa: National Defence Headquarters, 1952.

Canada, Department of National Defence. *Traditions and Customs of the Canadian Forces Part 3 – Bands and Music.* Ottawa: National Defence Headquarters, 1990.

Canada, Department of National Defence. "Canadian Forces Bands." Last modified 24 August 2021. https://www.canada.ca/en/services/defence/caf/showcasing/music/bands

Canada, Justice Laws Website. "Copyright Act (R.S.C., 1985, c. C-42)." Last modified 29 September 2021. https://laws-lois.justice.gc.ca/eng/acts/C-42/Index.html

Canada, Justice Laws Website. "Copyright Modernization Act (S.C. 2012, c.20)." Last modified 29 September 2021. https://laws-lois.justice.gc.ca/eng/annualstatutes/2012_20/fulltext.html

Canada-United States-Mexico Agreement (CUSMA). "Canada-United States-Mexico Agreement (CUSMA) – Chapter 20 – Intellectual Property Rights." Last modified 23 July 2020. https://www.international.gc.ca/trade-commerce/trade-agreements

Canadian Cadet Organizations. "About Cadets." Last modified 21 December 2020. http://www.cadets.ca/en/about/cadets-faq.page

Canadian Cadet Organizations. "Cadet Corps and Squadron Directory." Last modified 01 October 2020. https://app.cadets.gc.ca/directory-repertoirev2/en/cadet-directory.html

Canadian Music Centre. *Catalogue of Works for Wind Band in the Library of the Canadian Music Centre.* Toronto: Canadian Music Centre, 1999.

Canadian Music Centre. "Composer Showcase." Accessed January-May 2021. https://collections.cmccanada.org/final/Portal/Composers-Showcase.aspx?lang=en-CA

Carl Fischer. "Marche Slave." Accessed 11 September 2021. https://www.carlfischer.com/j157.marche-slave.html

Cassin-Scott, Jack and John Fabb. *Military Bands and Their Uniforms*. Poole, Dorset: Blanford Press, 1978.

Castonguay, Jacques. *Les Voltigeurs de Québec : premier régiment canadien-français.* Québc : Les Voltigeurs de Québec, 1987.

Caswell, Mark. "The Toronto Youth Wind Orchestra." *Canadian Winds* 6/1 (Fall 2007): 5-8.

"CBA News: National Youth Band of Canada's 25th Anniversary." *Canadian Winds* 15/2 (Fall 2016)

Cercle Philharmonique de St. Jean sur Richelieu, Le. "Histoire." Accessed 16 July 2018. www.cercle-philharmonique-de-st-jean.org/histoire.html

Chadwick, Dianne. "George McRae's 90th Birthday." *Malvern Musings* (Spring 2016). Accessed 20 November 2019. https://malverncollegiate.com/mandm/musings-spring-2016

Charles, Charles E. "The Music of John Slatter and Charles F. Thiele." *Canadian Winds* 5/2 (Spring 2007): 75-78.

_____. "The Band Music of Quebec (1) / La Musique d'harmonie au Québec (1)." *Canadian Winds* 6/1 (Fall 2007): 17-23.

_____. "The Band Music of Quebec (2) / La Musique d'harmonie au Québec (2)." *Canadian Winds* 6/2 (Spring 2008): 76-82.

_____. "The Band Music of Quebec (3) / La Musique d'harmonie au Québec (3)." *Canadian Winds* 7/1 (Fall 2008): 24-29.

Charles E. Charles. "'O Canada' in Popular Band Literature." *Canadian Band Journal* 19/2 (Winter 1994): 25.

_____. "The Military Band Journals (1)." *CBA (Ont) Fanfare* (Summer 2000):12.

_____. "The Military Band Journals (2)." *CBA (Ont) Fanfare* (Winter 2001): 12.

_____. "The Military Band Journals (3)." *CBA (Ont) Fanfare* (Summer 2001): 12-15.

Chenette, Stephen. "Northdale Concert Band," *Canadian Winds* (Spring 2010). Accessed 28 September 2020. www.northdaleconcertband.ca/history.html

Chenette, Stephen, Patricia Shand and Cameron Walter. "Canadian Repertoire for Concert Band." *Canadian Band Journal* 22/3 (Spring 1998): 21-22.

C.L. Barnhouse Company. "Our Composers-Andre Jutras." Accessed 17 February 2020. https://barnhouse.com/composer/andre-jutras

Concert Band of Cobourg, The. "History." Accessed 24 February 2020. https://www.theconcertbandofcobourg.com

Côté-Angers, Jean Philippe. "Joseph Vézina et l'orchestre à vent: l'expression d'un nationalisme musical canadien." M.Mus thesis, Université Laval, 2010.

_____. "La Musique des Voltigeurs de Québec." *Canadian Winds* 7/1 (Automne 2008): 9-13.

Crawford, Sybil Carol. "George Henry Ziegler 1889-1981)." *Waterloo Historical Society Journal* 76 (1988): 54-77.

Dawe, Michael. Red Deer Community Bands. "History." Accessed 02 March 2020. https://www.reddeerroyals.com/about/history

Deaville, Bernard and Betty Nygaard King. "Robert McMullin." In *The Canadian Encyclopedia*. Historica Canada. Article published 22 November 2007; last edited 15 December 2013. https://www.thecanadianencyclopedia.ca/en/article/robert-mcmullin-emc

Diamond, Beverly. *Native American Music in Eastern North America*. New York; Oxford University Press, 2008.

Dougherty, Michael. "The Coaticook Band: 140 Years of History." *Canadian Winds* 9/2 (Spring 2011): 88-91.

Draper, Norman. *Bands by the Bow: A History of Band Music in Calgary*. Calgary: Century Calgary Publications, 1975.

Dust, Tom and George Buck. "Dunbow School Brass Band and William Scollen: Two Alberta 'Firsts'." *Canadian Winds* 7/1 (Fall 2008): 3-6.

Duchesne, Laurier. *Le Régiment du Saguenay : 1900-2000*. Lac St. Jean, QC: Les Éditions Felix, 2000.

Dvorak, Thomas L., Robert Grechesky and Gary M. Ciepluch. *Best Music for High School Band*. Brooklyn: Manhattan Beach Music, 1993.

East York Concert Band. "About." Accessed 30 August 2020.
www.eastyorkconcertband.ca/about-the-band/band-history

Eighth Note Publications. "All Concert Band." Accessed 16 February 2021.
www.enpmusic.com/catalog.php?Prefix=CB

Elliott, David. *Music Matters: A New Philosophy of Music Education*. New York: Oxford University Press, 1995.

Etobicoke Youth Band. "About." Accessed 23 October 2020.
www.eyb.com/background

Falardeau, Victor and Jean Parent. *La Musique du Royal 22e Régiment : 50 Ans d'Histoire*. Québec: Éditions Garneau, 1976.

"Farewell to the Kilties." *The Daily Intelligencer* [Belleville]. 10 September 1904.

Farmer, Henry George. *History of the Royal Artillery Band*. London: Royal Artillery Institution, 1958.

_____. *Military Music*. London: Max Parrish & Co., 1950.

_____. *The Rise and Development of Military Music*. London: William Reeves, 1912.

Farwell, Byron. *Mr. Kipling's Army: All the Queen's Men*. New York: W.W. Norton & Company, 1987.

Fedération des Harmonies et Orchestres Symphoniques du Québec. "Historique." Last modified October 2012. https://fhosq.org/a-propos/historique

_____. "ressources." Accessed December 2019. https://fhosq.org/ressources/harmonies-et-orchestres-seniors-municipales/

Fennell, Frederick. *Time and the Winds*. Kenosha, Wisc.: Leblanc Publications, 1954.

Field, Keith. "The Lakeshore Concert Band Celebrates 50 Years." *Canadian Winds* 16/2 (Spring 2018): 3-5.

Finch, Kevin. "The Nova Scotia Youth Wind Ensemble." *Canadian Winds* 15/2 (Fall 2016): 7-10.

Fisher, Mark. *Notes in Time: A History of W.A. Fisher and the Barrie Collegiate Band*. Barrie, Ont.: Private digital publication, 2021.

Fort William Girls Military Band. Accessed 12 August 2021.
https://fortwilliamgirlsmilitaryband.ca

Fortier, Guy. *I Mean – Is That All You Do – Play in the Band? Or 20 Years in the RCAF*. Ottawa: Private Memoir, 1997.

Foss, Michael. *The Royal Fusiliers (The 7th Regiment of Foot)*. London: Hamish Hamilton, 1967.

Gaudry, Danielle. "Pork, Beans and Hard Tack: The Regimental Band of the Royal Winnipeg Rifles." *Canadian Winds* 6/2 (Spring 2008): 58-61.

Gillis, Glen. "Bands at the University of Saskatchewan: A Brief History." *Canadian Winds* 4/2 (Spring 2006): 97-100.

Gilpin, Wayne. *Sunset on the St. Lawrence: A History of the Frederick Harris Music Company.* Oakville, Ont.: The Frederick Harris Music Co., Limited, 1984.

Goldman, Richard Franko. "Fifty Years of Band Programs and Audiences." *Instrumentalist* 22 (1968): 42-43.

Goodspeed, D.J. *A History of the Royal Regiment of Canada: 1862-1979.* 2nd ed. Toronto: Royal Regiment of Canada Association, 1979.

Grand Prairie Marching Band Association. "About Us." Accessed 13 November 2020. https://www.gpmarchingband.ca/about_us

Gravel, Jean-Yves. *L'Armée au Québec : un portrait social 1868-1900.* Montréal: Boreal Express, 1974.

Green, J. Paul and Nancy Vogan. *Music Education in Canada: A Historical Account.* Toronto: University of Toronto Press, 1991.

Green, R.E. and A. Okazaki. "ZEEP: The Little Reactor that Could." *CNS Bulletin* 16/3 (Autumn 1995). Accessed 03 July 2016. https://www.cns-snc.ca/media/history/ZEEP/ZEEP_CNS Bulletin_Fall1995.html

Greene, Kay. "Bridgewater Fire Department Band." *Canadian Winds* 10/2 (Spring 2012): 31-34.

Guidone, Steve. *Trail Maple Leaf Band 90th Anniversary Photo Album 1917-2007.* Salmon Arm, B.C.: Steve Guidone, 2007.

Gwyn, Richard. *John A. The Man Who Made Us; the life and times of John A. MacDonald,* Volume One: 1815-1867. Random House Canada, 2007.

Halifax Concert Band. "HCB History." Accessed 31 August 2020. www.halifaxconcertband.ca/hcb-history

Hamilton Concert Band, The. "Bobby Herriot." Accessed 19 June 2019. https://hamiltonconcertband.com/bobby-herriot

Hamilton, Robert F. *Guelph's Bands and Musicians.* Guelph, Ont.: Hamilton Art Studio, 1996.

Hal Leonard. "Douglas Court." Accessed 18 February 2021. https://www.halleonard.com/search.action?keywords=Douglas+Court

Hannotte, Katelyn. "North Battleford City Kinsmen Band at 65." *Canadian Winds* 13/2 (Spring 2015): 29-31.

Henderson, Ken. "Truro District Schools Band Program." *Canadian Winds* 5/2 (Spring 2007): 62-65.

Herbert, Trevor and Helen Barlow. *Music and the British Military in the Long Nineteenth Century.* Oxford: Oxford University Press, 2013.

Herman, Arthur. *How the Scots Invented the Modern World.* New York: Broadway Books, 2001.

Historicalstatistics.org. "Historical currency converter." Last modified 10 January 2016.

Holgate, Tina. "Westwinds Music Society: 30 Years of Learning, Playing and Having Fun." *Canadian Winds* 17/2 (Spring 2019): 3-4.

Hollick, Alexander, Bandmaster. *RCASC Band War Diary: April 1944 to October 1945.* Unpublished document, 1945.

Hopkins, Mark. "In Memoriam: Ronald MacKay 1928-2008." *Canadian Winds* 7/1 (Fall 2008):53.

_____. "The National Concert Band/Denis Wick Canadian Wind Orchestra." *Canadian Winds* 11/1 (Fall 2012) 25-26.

Hunt, Bill. "The Best Band in the World." *The Belleville Intelligencer*. 31 December 1999:17.

Instrumentalist, The. *Band Music Guide 1975*. Evanston, Ill.: The Instrumentalist Publishing Company, 1975.

_____. *Band Music Guide 1982*. Evanston, Ill.: The Instrumentalist Publishing Company, 1982.

_____. *Band Music Guide 1989.* Northfield, Ill.: The Instrumentalist Publishing Company, 1989.

International Music Camp 1956 – 2005: Celebrating 50 Years of Service to Youth Souvenir Booklet. Minot, N.D.: International Music camp, 2005.

International Music Camp. "Location." Accessed 27 October 2019. https://internationalmusiccamp.com/about/location/

Jarman, Lynne, ed. *Canadian Music: A Selected Checklist 1950-73*. Toronto: University of Toronto Press, 1976.

Jenson, Paul. "History." Sackville [N.B.] Citizens Band. Accessed 19 February 2019. https://sackvillecitizensband.wordpress.com/history/

Kappey, Jacob. *A Short History of Military Music*. London: Boosey & Co., 1896.

Kallman, Helmut, Gilles Potvin and Kenneth Winters, eds. *Encyclopedia of Music in Canada.* Toronto: University of Toronto Press, 1981.

Kallman, Helmut, ed. *Catalogue of Canadian Composers*. Toronto: Canadian Broadcasting Corporation, 1952.

Kallman, Helmut. *A History of Music in Canada 1534 – 1914.* Toronto: University of Toronto Press, 1960.

Kastner, Georges. *Manuel Genéral De Musique Militaire: À L'Usage des Armées Françaises 1848*. Genève: Minkoff Reprint, 1973.

Keillor, Elaine. *Music in Canada: Capturing Landscape and Diversity*. Montréal and Kingston: McGill-Queen's University Press, 2006.

_____. "Musical Activity in Canada's New Capital City in the 1870s." in *Musical Canada: Words and Music Honouring Helmut Kallman*, edited by John Beckwith and Frederick A. Hall. Toronto: University of Toronto Press, 1988.

"Keith Mann Outstanding Band Director Award – In Honorarium." MusicFest Canada. Accessed 19 November 2019. https://musicfest.ca/awards-scholarships/i-keith-mann/

Kelly, Nora and William. *The Royal Canadian Mounted Police: A Century of History 1873-1973.* Edmonton, Alberta: Hurtig Publishers, 1973.

Kendrick, Ian. *Music in the Air: The Story of Music in the Royal Air Force.* Baldock, Herts.: Egon Publishers Ltd., 1986.

Ketchum, W.O. "Faces of Ottawa: Henry Bonnenberg." *Ottawa Journal* (21 June 1969) 2. Accessed 10 June 2019. https://www.newspapers.com/clip/2763982/faces-of-ottawa-henry-bonnenberg/

Kinder, Keith. "Winds of the North II: Canadian Wind Band Works on Folk Music Themes." *WASBE Journal* 10 (2003), 66-78. Accessed 16 August 2022. https://wasbe.org/wp-content/uploads/2018/02/WASBE_10_2003

King, Betty Nygaard and Barry J. Edwards. "Robert Farnon." In *The Canadian Encyclopedia.* Historica Canada. Article published 20 February 2007; last edited 04 March 2015. https://www.thecanadianencyclopedia.ca/en/article/robert-farnon-emc.

King, Gerald. "David Dunnet: One of Canada's Finest Band Directors, pt.1." *Canadian Band Journal* 20/1 (Fall 1995): 23,25,30.

_____. "David Dunnet: One of Canada's Finest Band Directors, pt. 2." *Canadian Band Journal* 20/2 (Winter 1995): 19,21.

"King was Delighted with Belleville Kilties." *The Daily Intelligencer* [Belleville], 28 September 1904, 7.

Kitchener Waterloo Youth Concert Band. "About the Band." Accessed 23 October 2020. www.kw-ycb.ca/about

Kopstein, Jack. *When the Band Begins to Play: A History of Military Music in Canada.* Kingston, Ont.: Applejack Publishers, 1992.

Kopstein, Jack and Ian Pearson. *The Heritage of Canadian Military Music.* St. Catharines, Ont.: Vanwell Publishing Limited, 2002.

Kreines, Joseph. *Music for Concert Band: A Selective Annotated Guide to Band Literature.* Tampa, Fla.: Florida Music Service, 1989.

Kritzweiser, Kay. "These are airmen who fly on wings of song." *The Globe Magazine* (Toronto) 22 November 1958: 13-14.

Kurath, Gertrude Prokosch. *Bulletin 220: Dance and Song Rituals of Six Nations Reserve, Ontario.* Ottawa: National Museums of Canada, 1968.

Label, Marc, Pierre Savard et Raymond Vézina. *Aspects de l'enseignement au Petit Séminaire de Québec (1765 – 1945).* Cahiers d'Histoire No 20, La Société Historique de Québec, Québec, 1968.

Laird, Gordon. "The Kitsilano Boys Band." *Canadian Winds* 5/1 (Fall 2006): 10-13.

Lamonde, Yvan et Raymond Monpetit. *Le Parc Sohmer de Montréal 1889-1919.* Québec : Institut québécois de recherche sur la culture, 1986.

Larkin, Irfona et al. "Summer camps and schools." In *The Canadian Encyclopedia.* Historica Canada. Article published 03 April 2008; last edited 16 December 2013. https://www.thecanadianencyclopedia.ca/en/article/summer-camps-and-schools-emc

Laughton, Wallace, and Betty Nygaard King, "Kenneth Bray." In *The Canadian Encyclopedia.* Historica Canada. Article published 09 May 2011; last edited 13 December 2013. https://www.thecanadianencyclopedia.ca/en/article/kenneth-bray-emc

Library and Archives Canada. "Collection Search." Last modified 09 August 2021. https://www.bac-lac.gc.ca/eng/collectionsearch/Pages/collectionsearch.aspx

_____. "Collection Development Framework." Approved 30 March 2005. https://www.collectionscanada.gc.ca/obj/003024/f2/003024-e.pdf.

"Liner Notes." *Catholic Central Band Presents*. Sound Recording. London, Ont.: Academy Records International 8041, 1969.

Linsley, Kerry. "Yorkton and District Band Programme." *Canadian Winds* 4/1 (Fall 2005): 6-7.

Locat, Raymond. *La Tradition Musicale à Joliette : 150 ans d'histoire*. Joliette, QC: Librairie Martin, 1993.

Lorenz, Tanya. "The First Wind Bands in Edmonton (1)." *Canadian Winds* 15/2 (Fall 2016): 42.

_____. "The First Wind Bands in Edmonton (2)." *Canadian Winds* 16/1 (Spring 2017): 39-41.

MacKinnon, Frank. "History of CBA." *Canadian Band Journal* 14/2 (Winter 1989): 21-22.

_____. "History of CBA." *Canadian Band Journal* 14/4 (Summer 1990): 26-27.

MacMillan, Ernest, ed. *Music in Canada*. Toronto: University of Toronto Press, 1955.

MacMillan, Keith and John Beckwith, eds. *Contemporary Canadian Composers*. Toronto: Oxford University Press, 1975.

MacPherson, Roger. "Women We Won't Forget-Remembering Great Saskatchewan Women: Marion Mossing (1885-1975)." *Pink Magazine* (Regina, Sask.): December 2016.

Maloney, S. Timothy. "Canadian Wind Ensemble Literature." D.M.A. thesis, Eastman School of Music, University of Rochester, 1986.

_____. "A History of the Wind Band in Canada." *Journal of Band Research* 23/2 (Spring 1988) 10-29.

Maloney, S. Timothy, ed. *Music for Winds I: Bands*. Ottawa: The Canadian Musical Heritage Society, 1998.

Manitoba Band Association. "Honour Concert Bands." Accessed 25 October 2020.
    https://www.mbband.org/honour-concert-bands

Mann, Keith, ed. "Edmonton Schoolboys Band Holds 60th Reunion." *Canadian Band*
    Journal 21/2 (Winter 1996): 25.

Mantie, Roger. "A Preliminary Study of Community Bands in Ontario." *Canadian Winds*
    7/2 (Spring 2009): 59-62.

McGee, Timothy J. *The Music of Canada*. New York: W.W. Norton, 1985.

McIntosh, Dale. *History of Music in British Columbia 1850 – 1950*. Victoria, B.C.:
    Sono Nis Press, 1989.

Mellor, John. *Music in the Park: C.F. Thiele Father of Canadian Band Music*. Waterloo,
    Ont.: Melco History Series, 1988.

Memory BC. "North Vancouver Youth Band." Accessed 21 October 2020.
    https://www.memorybc.ca/north-vancouver-youth-band-2

"Militia General Orders." *Canada Gazette*. Ottawa: 02 June 1883.

Milne, James. *A History of the Governor General's Foot Guards Band*. Ottawa:
    unpublished history, 1988.

Mirtle, Jack. *The Naden Band: A History*. Victoria, B.C.: Jackstays Publishing, 1990.

Mochnacz, Shawna L. "The Royal Canadian Artillery Band." *Canadian*
    Winds 3/1 (Fall 2004): 7-8.

Molenaar Music. "Bernhard Bogisch." Accessed 13 February 2021.
    https://www.molenaar.com/home
    _____. "Thomas Legrady." Accessed 13 February 2021.
    https://www.molenaar.com/home

Morey, Carl. *Music in Canada: A Research and Information Guide*. New York: Garland
    Publishing, 1997.

Morton, W. L. *The Kingdom of Canada: A General History from Earliest Times*, 2nd ed.
    Toronto: McClelland and Stewart Limited, 1969.

MusicFest Canada. "The Denis Wick Canadian Wind Orchestra." Accessed 09
    September 2021.
    https://musicfest.ca/national-honour-ensembles/dens-wick-canadian-wind-
    orchestra/

Nasby, Graham. "Community Band and Orchestra Resources." Last edited 25 July 2021.
    www.grahamnasby.com/misc/music_local-resources.shtml

New Horizons International Music Association. "Dr. Roy Ernst." Accessed 04 September
    2020. https://newhorizonsmusic.org/Dr._Roy_Ernst
    _____. "What is NHIMA." Accessed 04
    September 2020. https://newhorizonsmusic.org/about

Noel, Wanda. *Copyright: Guide for Canadian Libraries*. Ottawa: Canadian Library
    Association, 1999.

Norcross, Brian H. *One Band That Took a Chance: The Ithaca High School Band from 1955 to 1967 Directed by Frank Battisti*. Ft. Lauderdale, Fla.: Meredith Music Publications, 1993.

Northdale Music Press Limited. "Compositions." Accessed 17 November 2020. www.northdalemusicpress.com

Oehlerking, Darren Wayne. "The History of Instrumental Wind Music within the Royal Canadian Mounted Police Band." D.M.A. thesis, University of Iowa, 2008.

Ontario Band Association. "Honour Bands." Accessed 25 October 2020. https://www.onband.ca/honour-bands

Orchestre à Vents du Suroît, L'. "Nouvelles." Accessed 23 October 2020. www.ovs.ca/wp/nouvelles

Orchestre Philharmonique de Saint-Hyacinthe, L'. "Historique." Accessed 02 April 2020. https://spsh.wordpress.com/historique/

Ostry, Bernard. *The Cultural Connection: An Essay on Culture and Government Policy In Canada.* Toronto: McClelland and Stewart, 1978.

Overhill, Daphne. *Sound the Trumpet: The Story of the Bands of Perth 1852 – 2002.* Perth, Ont.: A. Rosenthal, 2002.

Pacific Symphonic Wind Ensemble. "About Us." Accessed 25 September 2020. https://www.pacificsymphonicwindensemble.com/about-us

Pinchen, Arthur Henry. *Count Every Star: The Memoirs of Arthur Henry Pinchen.* Edmonton: privately published, 2017.

Proctor, George A. *Canadian Music of the Twentieth Century*. Toronto: University of Toronto Press, 1980.

Purves-Smith, Michael and Jacqueline Dawson. "An Interview with Howard Cable." *Canadian Winds* 4/2 (Spring 2006): 72-77.

Queen's University: Queen's Encyclopedia. "Queen's Bands." Accessed 01 December 2019. https://www.queensu.ca/encyclopedia/q/queens-bands

"R.C.H.A. Band 1905 – 1968." *The Canadian Gunner*. Shilo, Man.: The Royal Canadian School of Artillery (1968): 44-47.

Rehrig, William H. *The Heritage Encyclopedia of Band Music*, 3 vols. Westerville, Ohio: Integrity Press, 1991.

Reid, John, ed. by Barb Hunter. "The Life and Music of Howard Cable." *Association of Concert Bands Journal* (June 2014): 19-22.

Reimer, Bennett. *A Philosophy of Music Education*, 2nd ed. Upper Saddle River, N.J.: Prentice-Hall, 1989.

Resendes, Joseph. "Herbert L. Clarke and the Anglo-Canadian Leather Company Band." *Canadian Winds* 16/2 (Fall 2017): 37-40.

Reynish, Timothy. "Retrospective: a brief history of wind music seen through British eyes." *Winds Magazine: Journal of the British Association of Symphonic Bands and Wind Ensembles* (1999): 3-23.

Ronmacmusic. "Catalogue-Concert Band." Accessed 15 February 2021.
www.ronmacmusic.com/catalog-concert.html

Rosenfield, L., 2002. "A History of the Northdale Concert Band." Northdale Concert Band. Accessed 28 September 2020.
www.northdaleconcertband.ca/history.html

Rowell, Payson. "Codiac Concert Band: A Young Band with a Rich History." *Canadian Winds* 12/1 (Fall 2013): 32-33.

Royal Canadian Sea Cadet Corps John Travers Cornwell VC Alumni, "Winnipeg Sea Cadet Band." Accessed 02 April 2022.
www.jtcvcalumni/stories1_1927_htm

Royal Military College of Canada. "The Band of the Royal Military College of Canada." Accessed 21 May 2022.
https://www.rmc-cmr.ca/en/training-wing/band-royal-military-college-canada

Sangma, Benzie. "A Music Legacy Which Continues Today." *The Belleville Intelligencer* 28 May 2007.

Saskatoon Lions Band, The. "History." Accessed 01 March 2020.
https://www.saskatoonlionsband.org/history/

Scott, Jennifer. "History." American Bandmasters Association. 1995, last edited 2006.
www.americanbandmasters.org/history/

Scholfield, Michael. *OHMS: On Her Majesty's Service*. Victoria, B.C.: Freisen Press, 2015.

Senior, Elinor Kyte. *British Regulars in Montreal: An Imperial Garrison, 1832-1854*. Montréal: McGill-Queen's University Press, 1981.

Shand, Patricia Martin. *Canadian Music: A Selected Guidelist for Teachers*. Toronto: Canadian Music Centre, 1978.

_____. *Guidelist of Unpublished Canadian Band Music Suitable for Student Performers*. Toronto: Canadian Music Centre, 1987.

Shonn, Audrey. "Edmonton's Cosmopolitan Music Society – 40 years old and still blowing strong." *Canadian Winds* 2/1. (Fall 2003): 11-12.

Simcoe, Mrs. John Graves. *The Diary of Mrs. John Graves Simcoe: Wife of the First Lieutenant Governor of the Province of Upper Canada 1792 – 1796*. Compiled with notes and a biography by J. Robertson Ross, 1911. Reprint, Toronto: Prospero Books, 2001.

Smith, Norman. *March Music Notes*. Lake Charles, La.: Program Note Press, 1986.

Spitzer, Michael. *The Musical Human. A History of Life on Earth*. NewYork, NY: Bloomsbury Publishing, 2021.

Stevens, W. Ray. *The Harps of War*. Oakville, Ont.: The Frederick Harris Music Co. Limited, 1985.

Stock, Patricia Gail. "Richard Franko Goldman and the Goldman Band." M.Mus. thesis, University of Oregon, 1982.

Stotter, Douglas. "The Repertoire and Programs of Edwin Franko Goldman and the Goldman Band." *Journal of Band Research* 36/2 (2001): 1-2.

Terziano, Ed, ed. *The Little Town Band that Grew and Grew*. Huntsville, Ont.: Forester Press Limited, 1986.

Thorold Citizens Centennial Committee. *Thorold, Its Past and Present*. Thorold, Ont.: Thorold Citizens Centennial Committee, 1968.

Trendell, John. *A Life on the Ocean Wave: The Royal Marines Band Story*. Dover, Kent, U.K.: The Blue magazine, 1990.

_____. *Colonel Bogey to the Fore: A Biography of Kenneth J. Alford*. Dover, Kent, U.K.: The Blue Magazine, 1991.

Turner, Gordon and Alwyn Turner. *The History of British Military Bands*, 3 Vols. Staplehurst, Kent, U.K.: Spellmount Limited, 1994.

Turner, Kerry and John White. "New Westminster and District Concert Band." *Canadian Winds* 12/1 (Fall 2011): 32-33.

Valois, Gilles. "Harmonie Calixa-Lavallée de Sorel, Québec: 90 ans d'histoire." *Canadian Winds* 7/4 (Printemps 2006): 64-66.

VanBuskirk, Kelly. "St. Mary's Band: Going Strong after 115 Years." *Canadian Winds* 17/2 (Fall 2018): 32-33.

Wakeling, Melissa. "Belleville Kilties Souvenir Album." Glanmore House National Historic Site. Accessed 19 January 2019. https://www.glanmore.ca/en/artifact-collections/online-collections-database.aspx

"Walter Eiger." In *The Canadian Encyclopedia*. Historica Canada. Article published 19 March 2007; last edited 16 December 2016. https://www.thecanadianencyclopedia.ca/en/article/walter-eiger-emc.

Wasiak, Ed. "Saskatchewan's First Bands, Pt. 1." *Canadian Band Journal* 22/1 (Fall 1997): 20-23.

Wasiak, Ed. "Saskatchewan's First Bands, Pt. 2." *Canadian Band Journal* 22/2 (Winter 1997): 10-12.

West Vancouver Youth Band. "History WVYB." Accessed 22 October 2020. https://www.wvyb.ca/copy-of-our-history

Wehrle, Marlene. "E.C. Kerby Ltd." In *The Canadian Encyclopedia*. Historica Canada. Article published 07 February 2007; last edited 13 December 2013. https://www.thecanadianencyclopedia.ca/en/article/ec-kerby-ltd-emc

White, William Carter. *A History of Military Music in America*. New York: The Exposition Press, 1944.

Wikipedia. "Canadian Sunset." Last edited 20 July 2021. https://www.wikipedia.org/wiki/Canadian_Sunset

Wikipedia. "Lady Godiva Memorial Bnad[sic]." Last edited 10 May 2021.
    https://en.wikipedia.org/wiki/Lady_Godiva_Memorial_Bnad

_____. "Papal Zouaves." Last modified 21 June 2021.
    https://en.wikipedia.org/wiki/Papal_Zouaves

_____. "Rose-Marie." Last edited 17 August 20212.
    https://www.wikipedia.org/wiki/Rose-Marie

_____. "Royal Canadian Air Cadets-Summer Training." Last edited 19 August
    2021. https://en.wikipedia.org/wiki/Royal_Canadian_Air_Cadets

_____. "Royal Canadian Army Cadets-Summer Training." Last edited 27 June
    2021.
    https://en.wikipedia.org/wiki/Royal_Canadian_Army_Cadets

_____. "Royal Canadian Sea Cadets-Summer Training." Last edited 17 August
    2021. https://en.wikipedia.org/wiki/Royal_Canadian_Sea_Cadets

_____. "Western Mustang Band." Last edited 11 March 2021.
    https://en.wikipedia.org/wiki/Western_Mustang_Band

Williamson, Patricia Bernard. "William Ramsey Spence: a case study." M.A. thesis,
    Carleton University, 1993.   Accessed 10 December 2020.
    https://curve.carleton.ca/cc868258-9362-4e33-b833-95fbfb

Wilson Keith Allan. *The Making of a Tattoo: Canadian Armed Forces Tattoo 1967*.
    Victoria, B.C: Freisen Press, 2017.

Wilson-Smith, Anthony. "Canada's Century: Sir Wilfred Laurier's Bold Prediction." In
    The Canadian Encyclopedia. Historica Canada. Article published 11
    November 2016; last edited 15 November 2016.
    https://thecanadianencyclopedia.ca/en/article/canadas-century-sir-wilfred-
    lauriers-bold-prediction

Windsor Optimist Youth Band. "About Us." Accessed 14 November 2020.
    https://woyb.ca/about-us

Winnipeg Wind Ensemble. "About." Accessed 28 September 2020.
    www.winnipegwindensemble.ca/?page_id=164

Winnipeg Youth Wind Ensemble. "About." Accessed 23 October 2020.
    https://www.winnipegyouthwinds.com

World Association for Symphonic Bands and Ensembles. "Past Conferences." Accessed
    05 November 2020. https://wasbe.org/past-conferences

Wults, Philip M., Jean Crittal and Glen B. Carruthers. "Music in Thunder Bay." In *The
    Canadian Encyclopedia*. Historica Canada. Article published 07 February
    2006; last edited 16 December 2016.
    https://www.thecanadianencyclopedia.ca/en/article/thunder-bay-ont-emc

Zealley, Alfred Edward and J. Ord Hume. *Famous Bands of the British Empire*. London:
    J.P. Hull, 1926.

Zealley, Alfred Edward. *Music Ashore and Afloat: Famous Bands of the RCN*.
    Unpublished Copy, n.d. (c. 1945)

COMPOSER – TITLE INDEX

Page references in **boldface** indicate musical examples or illustrations.

SUBJECT INDEX

Page references in *italics* indicate an illustration, photograph or musical example.

Printed in the USA
CPSIA information can be obtained
at www.ICGtesting.com
JSHW050827120224
57159JS00002B/9